CROSSING BORDERS

ARP Books (Arbeiter Ring Publishing)
205-70 Arthur Street
Winnipeg, Manitoba
Treaty 1 Territory and Historic Métis Nation Homeland Canada R3B 1G7
arpbooks.org

Design and layout by Relish New Brand Experience
Cover image: Ian Wallace, *Abstract Painting (Blue on White)* (2011)
Printed and bound in Canada by Imprimerie Gauvin on paper made from 100% recycled post-consumer waste.

Canada Council for the Arts Conseil des arts du Canada
MANITOBA ARTS COUNCIL CONSEIL DES ARTS DU MANITOBA

Canada Manitoba

ARP Books acknowledges the generous support of the Manitoba Arts Council and the Canada Council for the Arts for our publishing program. We acknowledge the financial support of the Government of Canada and the Province of Manitoba through the Book Publishing Tax Credit and the Book Publisher Marketing Assistance Program of Manitoba Culture, Heritage, and Tourism.

LIBRARY AND ARCHIVES CANADA CATALOGUING IN PUBLICATION

Title: Crossing borders : essays in honour of Ian H. Angus / edited by Samir Gandesha & Peyman Vahabzadeh.
Names: Gandesha, Samir (Samir Suresh), 1965- editor. | Vahabzadeh, Peyman, editor. | Angus, Ian H., honouree.
Identifiers: Canadiana (print) 20200185551 | Canadiana (ebook) 20200185586 | ISBN 9781927886335 (softcover) | ISBN 9781927886342 (ebook)
Subjects: LCSH: Philosophy, Modern. | LCSH: Philosophers—Canada. | LCSH: Canada—Study and teaching. | LCSH: Phenomenology. | LCSH: Critical theory. | LCSH: Communication. | LCGFT: Festschriften.
Classification: LCC B995.A544 C76 2020 | DDC 190.9/05—dc23

FSC www.fsc.org MIX Paper from responsible sources FSC® C100212

CROSSING BORDERS

Essays in Honour of Ian H. Angus

Edited by Samir Gandesha
& Peyman Vahabzadeh

ARP Books
Winnipeg, MB

Table of Contents

Viviana and Ian Angus at the protest against Kinder Morgan pipeline. Vancouver, 2018. PHOTO CREDIT: GEORGE RAMMELL.

Acknowledgements

This book is the fruit of profound friendships resulting in a truly collaborative project. The editors would like to thank the contributors of this Festschrift who made it possible and the process of its publication a smooth, timely, and rewarding one. In particular, we thank George Rammell and Ian Wallace for their original artworks. A special debt of gratitude is owed to Maxwell Kristen for his careful copy-editing and project management of this book. We would also like to thank Huyen Pham for various forms of logistical, administrative, and moral support. The editors would like to thank the Institute for the Humanities and Jennifer Simons of the Simons Foundation for providing vital financial support for this project, which included hosting the public event "In Conversation with Ian Angus," held on the Simon Fraser University Harbour Centre Campus in Vancouver on 6 April 2019. Special thanks, as well, to Professor Stephen Collis for chairing that event. Last but not least, many thanks to Todd Besant, Irene Bindi, and Patricia Sanders at ARP Books for their professionalism and attention to detail through an expedited publication process.

On the personal level, Samir Gandesha thanks his family: Rachia, Ruby and Milan, for their love and support over the years for this and many other projects that have occupied so much of his time. Peyman Vahabzadeh thanks Giti and Emile for their unending encouragement, love, and understanding.

Introduction

Samir Gandesha and Peyman Vahabzadeh

For over 40 years, Professor Ian Angus has been teaching communications, philosophy, Canadian Studies, theory, and humanities in the United States and Canada. His intellectual legacy includes a wide range of scholarly books, several edited volumes, numerous journal articles and book chapters, and multiple invited lectures or public talks. He has taught generations of students, at both undergraduate and graduate levels. He has trained and supervised many graduate students and his intellectual presence has touched the research of many more. At least a dozen of his graduate students are now professors in Canada, the United States, and the United Kingdom. His works and myriad intellectual interventions have had a vivid, powerful, and enduring impact on the philosophical and political debates of our time.

In his most important contributions, he specifically addresses the significance of marginalized or peripheral places through what he calls "locative thought," the relation between social movements and democratic processes, and the role of the university, whose genuine vocation, in contrast to its current neo-liberal incarnation, according to Angus, is to foster the "eroticization of the question." If his prodigious and important contributions can be summed up in a few words, then they would be a sophisticated and sustained critical engagement—or what is called in German an *Auseinandersetzung* with "Platonism."

"Platonism" itself can, of course, be defined in many ways, but perhaps the most influential understanding of it is established in a line running from Friedrich Nietzsche through Martin Heidegger and Hannah Arendt to Jacques Derrida. Platonism thus understood is a metaphysical account of Being understood as "presence" or a "metaphysics of presence." On the basis of such a metaphysics, paradigmatically established in Book VII of the *Politeia* or *Republic*, is an account of the unchanging, eternal *eidos* (εἶδος) or forms. Plato establishes a series of hierarchies including the priority of the practice of philosophy over rhetoric or sophistry, essence over appearance, and aristocracy or the "rule of the best" over democracy. The "best," for Plato, were not simply those high of birth but those in whom reason, allied with spirit or *thymos* (θυμός), governs insatiable bodily appetites or drives. Plato argues that the philosopher or well-ordered individual stands the best chance of establishing a just order in the political community. The philosopher is therefore both literally and figuratively an architect of both soul and the city. It is on this basis of a kind of ethereal architectural imagination, though paradoxically beyond space itself, that Plato empties particular places—signified by the famous allegory of the cave—of meaning or substance. Such places are simply understood to be realms of shadowy illusion and untruth that require the enlightenment of those who, in the very process of journeying arduously away from them, upward beyond the cave towards the sunlight—allegorizing the difficult process of dialectic itself—become philosophers. Philosophy, in other words, is understood to be precisely antithetical to locative thinking.

Angus takes Platonism to task in each of the following aspects: in his deconstruction of the opposition between philosophy and rhetoric and defending the "discursive" or rhetorical turn in social theory;

in defending the phenomenological valence of the lived experience of *place* and emphasizing transversal relations between places as opposed to the vertical relation of periphery and centre, particular and universal; and, perhaps most importantly, in his robust defence of democracy as an always incomplete or indeed incompletable process of universalization of the particular or the claims of difference. Yet, one may notice, there remains a felicitous trace of Platonism in Angus's defence of the university (literally the "Academy," which was the name Plato gave to his own school; Aristotle's was called the "Lyceum") as the space of the "eroticization of the question."

However, being an anti-Platonist defender of democracy is not an unambivalent position for a Critical Theorist such as Angus to take up. This isn't simply due to the fact that the most influential critic of Platonism was anything but a democrat who, paradoxically, theatrically played the role of the philosopher-king.[1] It has also got to do with the fact that it is possible to read Plato's writings as a product of *trauma*. Indeed, it may be possible to formulate the hypothesis that all great philosophical texts are less constructive exercises in designing the good or just city than they are, in a sense, works of mourning that respond to historical ruptures and wounds or what the young G.W. F. Hegel, referring to the French Revolution and its aftermath, termed *Zerissenheit* (literally: tornness or diremption).[2] Think, for example, of the way in which St. Augustine's *City of God* addresses the fall of Rome; or the manner in which Thomas Hobbes's defence of Absolutism in *Leviathan* responds to the English Civil War; or the way Theodor W. Adorno opens *Negative Dialectics* with an invocation of the moment to realize philosophy that was missed. Perhaps any political philosophy worthy of its name, then, is less a response to *thaumazein* (θαυμάζειν) or "wonder" at Being,[3] of why there is *something* rather than *nothing*, than it is to a profound rent or tear in the fabric of Being itself. Plato's originary trauma explored in *Apology*, *Crito*, and *Phaedo*, of course, was democratic Athens' trial and execution of his friend and teacher Socrates for "corrupting the minds of the young, and of believing in deities of his own invention instead of the gods recognized by the state."[4]

As a result of this trauma, Plato sought to make the world safe for philosophers (his thinking would perform a similar function later for popes, bishops, and cardinals as well as for mullahs) by providing a powerfully influential justification for the rule of philosophy or ontotheology (a metaphysical account of the Being-as-God) against *democracy*.[5] The rule of philosophy, in Plato's view, stood the best chance of breaking democracy's compulsion to put philosophy itself to death. Socrates's position is, ultimately, that of the intellectual or social critic who speaks truths that polities—including democratic ones—are often reluctant to hear. Paradoxically, Socrates establishes a line running from Nietzsche through Sigmund Freud and Karl Marx to Frankfurt School Critical Theory, placing him deeply at odds with his most influential student in much the same way that Christ, as Fyodor Dostoevsky pointed out, was deeply at odds with the institution founded in his name.[6]

There is, then, a moment of truth in Plato's siding with philosophy against democracy per se. As is well known, the word "democracy" is formed out of the Greek words *demos* (people) and *kratia* (rule). It means, of course, that the people govern themselves. Yet, this is not possible without rational critique grounded in historical self-knowledge. Reflecting on the trauma of the trial and death of Socrates, Plato reasons that democracy—which for him was the rule of those governed not by reason but by their desire for things—is always in danger of producing demagogues. It is an excessive desire for liberty "and the neglect of all other things that revolutionizes th[e] [democratic] constitution and prepares the way for the necessity of dictatorship."[7]

"Democracy" understood simply as the self-governance of the "people" is, therefore, fraught—as we see today with the dramatic rise of authoritarian populists challenging the power of "elites" precisely in the name of the people—if it is not limited by constitutionalism, checks and balances on executive authority, an independent judiciary, and a free press. Indeed, democracy must be limited by the scrutiny and critique secured by the freedom of the university, which means the freedom of the university from the ever-more stringent, disciplinary measures of quantification. That freedom plays an irreducible role in contributing to the formation and maintenance of a critical public sphere within which political power can be held to account by political subjects, both citizens and what Jacques Rancière calls "the part that have no part." This is why Angus's particular defences of the academy and democracy are of such vital importance. He argues that liberal democracy in its current form is less comprised of elections and majoritarian rule tempered by constitutionality, a broader rule of law and institutions, than of processes of struggles and contestation or agonism among those historically excluded from its ambit. It is precisely these struggles that provide the basis for a rational contestation of the universal and for deepened, more adequate, forms of self-rule. This is a vitally important lesson today when the rationality of contemporary democracy—itself, of course, a product of the historical struggles of workers, suffragettes and feminists, anti-colonial movements, and the "wretched of the earth," as well as First Nations—is being squeezed by both the far right and certain segments of an increasingly authoritarian left.

Outline of the book

As an amplification of this introduction, the editors of this volume, Samir Gandesha and Peyman Vahabzadeh, engage in a public conversation with Ian Angus (hosted by the Institute for the Humanities and held in April 2019 at Simon Fraser Vancouver University campus) on the various aspects of his contributions to Canadian Studies, communications and cultural studies, and philosophy. The conversation is much enriched by questions and interventions from the attendees.

Next, George Rammell provides some concrete and existential reflections on Angus, his family, and their friends in his narrative;

and Stephen Collis offers the sketch of a poem for Angus. Susan Pell focuses on Angus's contribution to Canadian Studies through his concept of "emergent publics" and approach to social movements, which, according to Pell, decentres the existing conventional approaches in Canadian Studies that primarily concentrate on the state and its institutions. She argues that Angus's inversion of the relationship between universality and particularity allows for a new project centred on self-determination.

Robert Schwartzwald then critically revisits arguably the most influential book on Canadian Studies by Angus, *A Border Within*, in particular his decentring English Canada as representing Canada as such in this book. Schwartzwald shows the potential of Angus's critique while demonstrating how the location of Quebec within Canada also challenges such a critique.

Similarly, in his chapter on empire and justice, Claude Couture observes that in cases of the language rights of francophone minorities in other provinces, Quebec has sided with the provinces and not its fellow French speakers. In an interesting use of "English-speaking philosophy," Couture employs Angus's vocabulary of terms such as "locative thought," "dispossession," and a "people who have not yet found a place" to illuminate the plight of such a minority.

Also drawing on his engagement with English Canada, in particular on Angus's book *Identity and Justice*, Leonard Findlay problematizes the limitations of such philosophical locating. Pointing out English Canada's connection to the "Empire," Findlay opts for a decentring of Angus's position in light of Indigenous thought and for a new form of what Findlay provocatively calls "feral federalism."

At the centre of Johannes Maerk's contribution is the comparative study of political thought in Canada and Mexico—two countries separated by their powerful neighbour, the United States. Offering readings of George Grant and Leopoldo Zea, he probes the models of dependency in these countries and points out the similarities—namely, the marginalization of Indigenous peoples.

The next two chapters register the debate between Indigenous scholar Leroy Little Bear and Ian Angus. Little Bear submits that the universalizing tendency in Western thought has consistently ignored the Aboriginal mode of knowledge, which is noun-oriented and relational. While recognizing the similarities between Indigenous world views and European ecological thought, Angus acknowledges the limitation in European knowledge in grounding value in the Being of beings.

Shifting the focus to communications studies, Lenore Langsdorf draws on phenomenology and pragmatism—that is, Edmund Husserl and John Dewey—to invite shifting our attention to the processes by which interest in an object is constructed through constitutive intentions of the individuals. She concludes that communication contains horizonal possibilities. In his contribution, Daniel Adleman presents a reading of Angus's work in the field of communications that places it in dialogue with the "New Rhetoric," which emphasizes the way in which media environments are at their core suasive or influencing.

Jerry Zaslove's epistolary contribution begins with a personal connection with Angus, and offers an "open letter" to German thinker Siegfried Kracauer (1889–1966), through which he reflects on memory, extraterritoriality, and exile as a "zone of experience." Exile, he submits, is constituted by posthumous time. Kevin DeLuca, by reflecting on his experience of skiing at the Jackson Hole Mountain Resort and building on the writings of Angus, Harold Innis, and Marshall McLuhan, offers theoretical propositions regarding media and communication as modes of experiencing nature. Since experience of the earth is not possible without mediation, it arises from the assemblages that make it possible.

Linking the momentous year of 1968, the year of global revolution, to psychoanalysis, in her contribution, Hilda Fernandez-Alvarez discusses the *marxisant* psychoanalytical approach of La Borde Clinic in France as a springboard for a critical engagement with the concept of desire in Gilles Deleuze and Félix Guattari, which leads her to a new approach in psychotherapy grounded in the critique of institutions. Drawing on Angus and Marx, Jaden Adams develops concepts of association, community, and belonging that lead to a "higher communism." This results in a re-envisioned left populism based on the universal principle of particularity of needs.

Graeme Nicholson problematizes the Enlightenment concepts of Truth and Reason. He launches critical engagements that point out the limitations of the contemporary defences of Reason in the work of Joseph Heath and Steven Pinker. In a play on Angus's 2008 book *Identity and Justice*, in which Angus seeks to show that Canadian philosophy is characterized by opposition to Empire, past and present, and the desire for self-rule, Samir Gandesha argues that Angus ought to be more attentive to the way in which identity, rather than necessarily grounding a process of universalization in the particularism of place (locative thinking), can ultimately undermine the aspiration to universalism tout court.

Through critical topology, Peyman Vahabzadeh reflects on the modes of defiant acting against technological "busy-ness" in our age of global neo-liberal capitalism. Drawing on Angus's concept of "locative thought," Vahabzadeh proposes the concept of "locative acting," which refers to the action arising from a particular place but not bound to normative expectations. Last but not least is Ian Angus's own important "Statement to the Court before Sentencing" (May 2018). Here, he addresses the court about the significance of civil disobedience and why it was important for him as an informed citizen to join the pipeline protest in Burnaby, British Columbia, and challenge the court injunction.

The cover is based on an original work titled *Abstract Painting (Blue on White)* (2011) by influential Vancouver artist Ian Wallace, who has been a friend of Angus's and ours and a habitué of the Institute for the Humanities for many years. A timeline of Angus's past and present life pursuits wraps up the book.

Notes to Introduction

1 This critic, of course, was Martin Heidegger and his infamous *Rekoratsrede* or inaugural speech as the Nazi-appointed rector of Freiburg University in May 1933, entitled "The Self-Assertion of the German University."

2 See Rebecca Comay, *Mourning Sickness: Hegel and the French Revolution* (Stanford: Stanford University Press, 2010).

3 Plato, *Theatetus* 155d, in *The Collected Dialogues of Plato Including the Letters*, ed. Edith Hamilton and Huntington Cairns (Princeton, NJ: Princeton University Press, 1989).

4 Plato, *Apology*, 24b, in *The Collected Dialogues of Plato Including the Letters*, ed. Edith Hamilton and Huntington Cairns (Princeton, NJ: Princeton University Press, 1989).

5 Hannah Arendt, "Philosophy and Politics," *Social Research* 57, no. 1 (Spring 1990): 78. See also Alan Ryan's interpretation in his *On Politics*, vol. I: *A History of Political Thought: Herodotus to Machiavelli* (New York: Liveright Publishing Corporation, 2012), 31–70.

6 See Friedrich Nietzsche, *Anti-Christ*, in *Twilight of the Idols and the Anti-Christ*, trans. R. J. Hollingdale (London: Penguin Books, 2003).

7 Plato, *Republic*, 562c, in *The Collected Dialogues of Plato Including the Letters*, ed. Edith Hamilton and Huntington Cairns (Princeton, NJ: Princeton University Press, 1989).

Part I
In Conversation

Chapter 1

Ian Angus in Conversation
Beyond Phenomenology and Critique

Ian Angus, Samir Gandesha, Peyman Vahabzadeh

The following conversation with Ian Angus was held as a public event and hosted by the Institute for the Humanities at Simon Fraser University (SFU) at the SFU Harbour Centre Campus in Vancouver on Saturday, April 6, 2019.

The participants were Stephen Collis; Samir Gandesha, associate professor in the Department of Humanities and the director of the Institute for the Humanities at Simon Fraser University; Peyman Vahabzadeh, professor of sociology at the University of Victoria; and Ian Angus.

Collis opened the event by acknowledging that the SFU Harbour Centre Campus is on the unceded territories of the Musqueam, Skxwú7mesh (Squamish), and Tsleil-Waututh (Slay-wa-tooth) peoples.

STEPHEN COLLIS: Good afternoon, welcome to the Institute for the Humanities at Simon Fraser University. My name is Stephen Collis. I've been on the steering committee of the institute for quite a few years now, having had the pleasure of working with Ian Angus and

Samir Gandesha for some time. So it's really wonderful to be here today to celebrate Ian's work and career with this—discussion, interview, intervention, interrogation?

SAMIR GANDESHA: All of the above!

COLLIS: All of the above. But it's more—definitely more—in the celebration realm, celebrating by engaging with the ideas that Ian has brought into the world and discussed with so many of us in this room, over so many years.

Samir Gandesha and Peyman Vahabzadeh are long-time associates, colleagues, and friends of Ian Angus. For over 40 years Ian Angus has been teaching cultural studies, communications, philosophy, Canadian Studies, and humanities in the United States and Canada. His intellectual legacy includes a wide range of monographs, several edited volumes, numerous journal articles and book chapters, and multiple invited lectures and public talks. He has taught generations of students, both undergraduate and graduate. I believe about a dozen of Ian's graduate students are now professors in Canada, the United States, and the UK. He has taught modern European thought and Canadian intellectual history at SFU. His teaching has been in both these areas in the Department of Humanities.

In 2007 and 2008 he was director of the Prague Field School, which is based in the Department of Humanities. His intellectual formation began with the twentieth-century European philosophies of phenomenology and the Frankfurt School of Critical Theory. His first book, *Technique and Enlightenment* (1984), probed the historical sources of the instrumental reason that legitimates the modern advance of technology and argued for a form of technology assessment that is not only ethical but pertains also to the construction of human identity. A significant turn in Angus's work occurred when he began a critical engagement with the history of English-Canadian social and political thought, which resulted in *A Border*

Within: National Identity, Cultural Plurality, and Wilderness, widely reviewed in both the academic and popular press. It was followed up by the later book *Identity and Justice.* Other works—*(Dis)figurations: Discourse/Critique/Ethics; Primal Scenes of Communication: Communication, Consumerism, and Social Movements;* and *Emergent Publics: An Essay on Social Movements and Democracy*—have presented his positions on contemporary political philosophy and communication theory. *Love the Questions* was an investigation into the possibilities for enlightenment in the current university. Just that range of titles gives you a sense of the kinds of issues that Ian has engaged with over many years.

And now, please welcome our panel.

SAMIR GANDESHA: Thank you very much, Steve. I'm going to be chairing the session. I really would like to get into the conversation, into the questions that Peyman and I have prepared for Ian. But before I do I have a few things to say to set up our evening. This is a celebration of the life and work of our good friend and colleague Ian Angus. The larger context is that Peyman and I are preparing a *Festschrift* for Ian. This is just a fancy word for a celebratory volume of writings that pay tribute to somebody who is in retirement but who—and I want to be clear—isn't at the end of their career. Far from it! Ian is constantly working, constantly producing, and will continue to do so, I'm sure, for several decades to come. It is a nice way to mark a certain body of work, a certain kind of intervention into a series of intellectual debates, academic debates, and also the public sphere—and the public sphere, for Ian, is really very crucial.

I've known Ian since I came to SFU in 2003. I've known him as an esteemed colleague in the Department of Humanities, a very important and influential member of the steering committee at the Institute for the Humanities, and, beyond the academy, as a really good friend. His role at the institute, it cannot be overemphasized, has been really crucial. Ian has said to me over and over again, "The institute can't simply lag behind events; it can't simply respond to events; it must try to, as much as it can, set an agenda." Ian remains on the steering committee and is very, very active. Ian is also a public intellectual. For those of you who don't know his statement on civil disobedience, which he made upon being arrested in the attempt with many others to forestall construction of the Kinder Morgan pipeline, I would highly recommend it as an example of Ian's intervention in the public sphere, of taking what we try to teach in the classroom and putting it into practice in the world. It is a wonderful and remarkable exemplification of an intellectually engaged academic, and it's very inspiring. You'll find that on the *Ricochet* website [also reproduced as chapter 20 of the current volume]. Another thing about Ian that's really crucial is his attention or attentiveness to the role of *place* in thought. There are many academics all over the world, but especially in Vancouver, who really wish they were somewhere else, somewhere where the pulse of history beats loudly: New York, London, Berlin, Paris, other parts of the world where things seem to be really happening, unlike Vancouver. I think that what Ian has taken to heart—and I think this has really influenced the institute—is that we need to make interventions *here*. We need to figure out what's going on here, *in this place*, and try to address those things. The university is unavoidably situated in a particular, lived, historical reality. So, while academics working in the university, I think by definition, try to address the "universal" as it is established by their specific disciplines, they also cannot escape the fact that they live somewhere particular, they live in a particular location, a particular place. And it behooves them, sometimes, to take notice of this fact, as much as they may resist it and as much as they dream about being elsewhere, somewhere glamorous. This is something that comes through in Ian's whole approach. This is what we try to do in the institute, and I think it's important. Another thing about Ian that's really, really important is how influential he has been for his students. He has been an amazing teacher. A number of his students, or graduate students, have ended up as professors in universities throughout North America, and perhaps beyond. So impactful has Ian's teaching, supervision, and mentoring been that we have three students who have come from abroad to be here tonight, specifically for this celebration. This is probably the best testimony that one could have as a teacher. I would like to extend a special welcome to Jaden Adams, Poonam Pillai, and Shakuntala Rao: welcome, and thanks for being here. I think Ian really appreciates it, and so do we.

So, Ian, just to get the ball rolling: Could you please tell us a bit about your intellectual and political formation?

IAN ANGUS: My intellectual formation: I finished high school in Ontario after grade 13 in 1967. I was 18 years old. I went to university and studied mathematics for one year and was bored with it. And, then, it was 1968. Without going into detail, a lot of other things were happening. Like a lot of people my age, I felt the necessity to come down on one or another side of a number of public issues—the Vietnam War being a very important one, which was later mutated into struggle against Canadian complicity in the Vietnam War. I became, to some extent, politically active. I wouldn't want to overestate that, but it was something that was important to me. It affected who I met, what I thought about, what I did, and so on. At approximately the same time, in 1968, I took a course in philosophy and, two months after that, dropped out of mathematics in the middle of a statistics class. With everything that was going on, I just couldn't do that kind of thing anymore. It didn't seem to matter. I started to study philosophy and developed a passion for philosophy. About two years after that, I met somebody who became my teacher in philosophy, José Huertas-Jourda, who taught at the University of Waterloo. Those have, essentially, been the two passions that have driven my intellectual life: philosophy and politics. They sometimes coincide but, unfortunately, only very rarely. Usually one feels oneself pulled in one way or another, doing something primarily for political reasons and compromising philosophically; and occasionally saying "to hell with whether anybody understands this, I want to work out this problem." That's more or less what I've been doing since then.

GANDESHA: In some ways it's possible to describe you as quintessentially Canadian in the way you philosophize and the way you think because Canadian philosophy, and Canadian thought more generally, has been associated with an attempt to think through technology. One thinks of figures such as Harold Innis, Marshall McLuhan, George Grant—who was very important for you—also you could say Crawford B. Macpherson as well. That's just one way of characterizing what a Canadian philosopher is and does: thinks about technology. The second way, I think even more so, is your emphasis on what you call "locative thought," and that puts you into an interesting kind of dialogue with post-colonial thinkers such as Dipesh Chakrabarty, who thinks about provincializing Europe, but then also decolonial thinkers such as Glen Coulthard, who talks about "grounded normativity." So the question is: Can a shared sense of place be the basis of a reinvented form of Canadian identity, or the basis of a decolonial post-Canadian identity?

ANGUS: From the beginning, I understood the vocation of philosophy from my teacher José not to be about universities primarily, not to be primarily about books or scholarship but to be, in the Greek sense, a way of life. For whatever reason, I, as somebody who was about 22 years old and was full of a lot of enthusiasm and not that much understanding, took this very seriously. So as I started to study philosophy, I obviously needed to know a lot more, but I was also thinking about what this meant for how my life was going to unfold. Then I read *Technology and Empire* by George Grant, which I thought was a wonderful book. It was about Canada, and Canada was important to me because I'm an immigrant. I came here with my parents in 1958 from Britain. So the questions became: What is Canada? Do we belong here? How do we fit in? Should I have stayed in England? Such questions were always with me until much later, and, to some extent, still. But Grant's book was not only about Canada; it was a philosophical account of Canada and a radical critique of contemporary society. I wrote him a letter. He was very kind to a young enthusiast telling him how great his book was, which he may have suspected already. He very kindly wrote me back and invited me to come to McMaster University to meet him. I did that and then attended his course on technology, which has become a bit of a myth in Canadian intellectual history because all sorts of people were in that course. It was a graduate course. There were maybe about 10 people actually registered in it and there were about 50 people in the room. He was very generous with young people and taught me a lot about the way one takes young people's concerns seriously. Looking back, I see that he must have realized that I was operating with very naïve formulations of problems. Occasionally, he would point to me in the class and say, "If you were a Marxist, like Angus here, you might think like this." I wasn't sure whether I was a Marxist or not. I knew I was interested in Karl Marx and I had my suspicions about capitalism. But I was young; I hadn't thought things through very much. But the way he put one on the spot and made one take a position addressed me as a person already involved in the debate in a lovely way. It was through George Grant that I understood that one of the tasks for a philosopher who was, in some sense, Canadian—even though it had to be figured out exactly in what sense—had to be working through what the country was about and, from my own take on it, find what could be said and done about the large problems of social inequality and injustice. So that's how I got involved with thinking about Canada.

GANDESHA: Could you talk a little more about this idea of "locative thought"? What does it mean and how could it contribute to a reimagining of Canada in terms of the specificity of place, because place, the land in particular, is such an important dimension of Indigenous thinking? Is this kind of a bridge, then?

ANGUS: One of the very interesting things about George Grant's work on Canada is that he associated modernity with a kind of universality and the leading edge of that modernity with the United States. "Modernity"—one can use the word "modernity" or the word "capitalism" or "technology"—means the development of an abstract intellectual scheme that treats any place as arbitrary and then restructures places as dependencies of that scheme. It is, in principle, universal, so that any specific place is arbitrary, or merely particular. Grant saw that this posed a problem for Canada, being subordinate to the United States as the engine of technological modernity. What justification was there, then, for any independent existence of Canada? How can any justification not fall into mere particularity? That was Grant's formulation, and that's where I started with this questioning. I have probably meditated on that question ever since.

Gradually, Grant's formulations have been replaced by my own. The concept of "locative thought" that you pick up from a much later book, *Identity and Justice* (2008), is a following through of an itinerary that began there and changed in a number of important ways but always had to do with the relationship between a particular standpoint from which one thinks and the universalizing claims characteristic of philosophy. I mean claims that are universalizing in the sense that they appeal to others for agreement but are not simply given as universal. They appeal to others to create some kind of common discourse. This is not to take a common discourse as given, because the problem with what's given is that it has been formed by exclusions—which, in the history of our country, go back to the British Empire, the empire and colonialism, systematic inequalities. Thus, one has to be very careful to distinguish universalizing from that which has been taken as universal, though has not been established theoretically or intellectually but by power and history.

I should also add that the problem of empire was, for me, always connected to Marx's analysis of the exploitation of labour. They are connected by the modern abstract conceptual system that dominates living, concrete activity. I thought about that in various different ways over the years.

Your question was about locative thought and about Indigenous thinking, such as Glen Coulthard's. I consider myself, above all, a philosopher, a phenomenologist, which means to me that one thinks in the first person. One thinks as someone who is in the middle of the world already. One doesn't start at the beginning and never gets to see the end. One is in the middle. One takes up certain questions because they are questions experienced in the first person with a certain exigency. Therefore, one cannot help but assume some things, take some things as granted at a certain time in one's world and accept them, even though later one might think: "Hmm, I should think again about that. I should go back and not assume that." One of the things that I took for granted was the existence of the Canadian so-called nation and then nations-state, in the plural. The more I thought about the imperial thread in all this—which is something I did really think about for a long time—the more it seemed to me that the Canadian nations-state is simply a continuation of the British Empire, and that, therefore, one has to be open to different forms of political association that are non-imperial, more transversal between groups. By the time of *Identity and Justice,* I had become very interested in the concept of a treaty: What is a treaty?

And, in particular, what is the difference between the broadly Aboriginal understanding of "treaty" as setting up a relationship between two different peoples and the broadly Anglo-imperial conception of "treaty," which is making an agreement so we can move on with the exigencies of modernity and capitalism.

I found also an analogue of this in nineteenth-century European thought in the thought of Joseph Proudhon, a French anarchist thinker, whose concept of political association is very much like that of a treaty, a treaty between groups. At that point, I finally said goodbye to any conception of political organization that is legitimated or oriented to the nation-state as an ideal. To that extent, I became very positively disposed toward other forms of political association that are non-imperial and decolonizing.

Nevertheless, I would never, because of what I said about being a first-person thinker, try to speak from the viewpoint of Aboriginal peoples or Québecois people. That's why I always wrote about English Canada—"English" referring not to background and genetics but to the language of common interaction. I tried to think about English Canada in terms of its identity in a manner that could recall, articulate, and justify motives for a kind of a decolonizing understanding. Of course, these have never been the predominant motives because of how things have turned out—well, I can't say that we know how things have turned out, of course, because we never know how things have finally turned out because it's not yet the end of the story. But the predominant historical force has been to squash these localizing tendencies. So I've recalled Louis Riel and some interesting statements from the North-West Rebellion about what constitutes legitimate political association. They are articulate and logical and have the status of constitutional claims. My final thinking about English Canada is a very long way from my starting point in George Grant's thought. It is concerned with a localizing tendency that has coexisted with empire but has never predominated, a localizing tendency that would have a different relationship to Indigenous forms of association and which I have tried to think about philosophically, that is to say, in a universalizing manner.

GANDESHA: I think that's one of the most powerful aspects of your 2008 book, *Identity and Justice*; really, really quite fascinating. So let's take up this idea of transversal relations as opposed to vertical and centre/periphery kinds of relations. I think this ties in very nicely with your attempt in many writings to develop a kind of communications theory of society, which is quite different from that elaborated by Jürgen Habermas. For you, it's very much—and unlike Habermas—tied to the post-structural discursive turn; but I don't think you are happy with that term because it's misleading in a way. It doesn't understand language as a kind of metaphor for other kinds of practices that are language-like but are not language, and it's often a misstep there. Could you explain more about this communication theory of society, and then elaborate on how it could help us understand our digital present? It seems as if our world is ever-more digitally mediated and such a theory of society is ever-more relevant today. We have AI, robotics, various forms of virtuality within which we seem to be caught.

ANGUS: I fell into thinking about communications entirely by accident. My dissertation advisor, Bill Leiss, was chair of the School of Communication here at SFU in the late 1970s and early 1980s. He hired me into my first job and I remember saying to him over the phone, "I don't know anything about communications," and he replied, "You do, you do, you just don't know that you do." I said, "Really?" and he said, "Just come, you'll find out." So I came. I had studied European philosophy exclusively, but I had also been reading various important works from Canadian intellectual history simply because it interested me. So I knew Harold Innis. I knew a little bit about McLuhan. I knew George Grant quite well, and I came in and just started teaching that material in relationship to communications. Then, as it turned out, life being unpredictable, I ended up teaching communications for quite a few years and went to the United States to the University of Massachusetts Amherst, from which two of my students from that period have graciously come today. So I have ended up with a relatively developed notion of what communication is and why it's interesting.

I don't see any connection to Habermas in what I have to say about communication. However, there is a very interesting book edited by Richard Rorty called *The Linguistic Turn*, which argues that twentieth-century philosophy thinks about language as the fundamental problem from which other problems could, perhaps, be solved—theories of science, politics, et cetera. So after reading that book, I thought, "Why isn't language just one form of communication?" Very few of us can actually talk, and therefore think, while holding our hands still. Movement, gesture, standing, sitting, shouting, grunting, singing—all those other aspects of communication are just as much a part of meaning as "language" in the sense of "words"—especially if one means by "words" the internal sense or definitional meaning rather than what they *do* by being uttered. What does this mean for the idea of a linguistic turn? Language functions after the linguistic turn as a metaphor, a metaphor that suggests that all problems can be helpfully addressed as forms of language. But this is not to say that other forms of perception, action, and thought are exactly forms of language. This building, for example: In what sense is it a form of language? It has communicative aspects and so forth, but also it has to do with the fact that certain pieces are heavy and others are not. How would one grasp that in language? One could say that it's heavy, of course, but one can also say that *this* is heavy and it's not. In this way, the possible limitation of a linguistic model was always on my mind. Nevertheless, over time I developed an approach to communication that is a version of what is now called "media ecology."

Later, while I was in the United States, I encountered the tradition of rhetorical analysis and was able to connect that to my philosophical studies of the ancient Greek controversy between philosophy and rhetoric, and, even further, to deepen that understanding into a conception of rhetoric as the figuration of forms of knowledge and action. The book *Dis-figurations* came out of this development. The apex of that argument was that the construction of silence in a media-saturated society could reconstitute the project of philosophy. In that way, my understanding of communication as a constitutive phenomenon of social life developed considerably.

GANDESHA: Language functions metaphorically all the time; for example, we also talk about "architectural vernaculars."

ANGUS: Yes, indeed. I was not interested in just the metaphorical aspect of this, but with taking language in an expanded sense to refer to all forms of communication, and then to make it a metaphor for all social life. What happens then? That was really just a hypothesis. It's not something I ever felt entirely committed to, but it was something that emerged from my working through the intellectual milieu of the time, especially in the 1980s. A lot of people in social and human sciences were reading literary and cultural theory. I was caught up in that too, and I think to some extent, as a non-solitary intellectual, one has to take up things from the prevailing milieu and address them, even if one would never have framed the issue that way oneself. That was essentially what I was doing: picking up the communication problem from there.

Does it help us to deal with more contemporary problems like algorithms, the Internet, and such?

Well, that's a big question that can be answered only by performing those analyses themselves. It is another one of those questions that are much easier to ask than to answer. Probably, yes. Except, one of the things that I wanted to say as part of a communication theory of language—and this was specifically to try to get it away from language theory itself, or discursive theory—I later called the "materiality of communication." That idea was taken directly from Harold Innis and his notion that a medium of communication has certain physical characteristics: for example, paper is light, it can be moved around, you can write on it, you can rub things out, you can write on it again. These characteristics make it a certain kind of communication. The telephone is different because it has wires—or used to have wires—and so forth. All of these are material characteristics of different media of communication. In some sense, through their complex interaction, the plurality of media constitutes all the ways in which we can communicate with each other and therefore make up a form of society. That's the basic idea. That approach is part of a Canadian contribution to studies of communication, which is based in the history of the country due to extractive industries and the need to get the furs from Manitoba to Paris for the fashionable hats, which drove the Canadian economy for a while. Paris fashion drove the fur economy. That deep disparity linking two very different forms across space was something that I thought was very useful to bring to the study of communication and, therefore, into the discursive turn: to actually make the whole idea of a linguistic or communicative approach much more "material," for lack of a better word. We can talk about that word if you like. I mean it in the sense of an embodied, sensual, practical activity based in the social human body to which Marx refers in the *1844 Manuscripts* and to which Edmund Husserl refers as the "kinaesthetic unity of bodily activity." Thus, I always saw my work on communication to be a form of phenomenological Marxism even though that might have been less evident to the reader.

So, finally, to the Internet. Yes, it should, in theory, be possible to apply such an approach to the Internet and to electronic communication in general. Thus far, I have found it necessary to develop such a material communicative approach in order to understand the changes that the Internet and network society are making in the university. In this, I used a communicative analysis of the production, storing, and passing on of knowledge through seminars, lectures, publications, and the library as a model for the traditional university. On this basis, I could begin to establish what is changing. Notice that seminars have become moribund, when they are actually the live centre of university education; lectures have begun to imitate written material; reading is restricted; and the library has become a portal to electronically available material on the Internet. At the same time, transversal communication of contemporary "information" is much more fluid and available, so knowledge tends to take on a similar form. Indeed, I have spent some time working through what the concept of "information" itself means. All of these phenomena have to be thought through thoroughly. My book *Love the Questions: University Education and Enlightenment* (2009) does some of that, but there remains a lot more to be done.

In a manuscript on which I am currently working, I address whether digital and electronic communication alters significantly the conceptions of crisis developed by Marx and Husserl. To what extent does digital communication undermine the generation of meaning? To what extent does digital labour alter the relation between labour and capital and thus the form of capitalism?

GANDESHA: So some of your current research is going in this direction?

ANGUS: Some of it, yes. I don't know if it would be good idea to try to further summarize it now.

PEYMAN VEHABZADEH: Let me first begin by again acknowledging the Musqueam, Skxwú7mesh, and Tsleil-Waututh, the Coast Salish peoples on whose unceded territories we stand. This is important to acknowledge precisely because of the colonial history that we have inherited—unwillingly inherited, to some extent—but we have a responsibility to rectify. This pertains to your work to some extent, Ian. You spoke about it; I wanted to ask questions about that, and in this relationship. Before we proceed with my question, I have to say that I have known Ian since 1993 as an undergrad, and then a graduate student. I came here after some interesting saga as an exile from Iran and, like a totally displaced person, was thrown here because I was a refugee; I didn't choose to be here and yet somehow ended up here. And then I met Ian Angus and found out that Ian was not quite in place either, especially because he was teaching in the Department of Sociology and Anthropology, which didn't quite fit for the kind of work that you did, Ian. That's a really interesting notion that as a displaced person, you actually come from another place, expecting other people to be in their place, and, yet, they are not in their place. Not being entirely in place, of course, makes Ian's work so much relevant and fascinating. It gives his work a certain unique critical stance.

I have two questions with respect to the university. The first question is with regards to your book—your *Love the Questions* about university and education and so on. You criticize, quite rightly, the corporatization of the university, and I noticed that in that work you have something like "faith" in the foundation of public university that somehow can challenge this process. And, to quote you on page 91 of that book, you say, "Even under the corporate agenda, one can argue that there is a need for publicly oriented, university-based research because it has a greater purchase on the public trust due to its presumed independence." I wonder if you agree that this public-private distinction, which you still hold in your book, is actually diminished by this time, or it's being almost diminished? Your kind of "faith," or your hope, that the public will actually be able to challenge this—it may just be a hope.

ANGUS: Yes, it may well be, that is certainly the main tendency of neo-liberal politics, which is undermining central presuppositions of earlier liberal society. In my defense, it was more of a political statement that you have quoted, and political statements have to be revised as times change. Ideally, philosophical statements should hang around a bit longer. I didn't want to work myself into the position that I see as characteristic of a certain kind of defeatist Marxism—which I find *completely* unhelpful—which is the notion that everything is messed up because of capitalism and everything will remain messed up as long as there is capitalism. The conclusion that we have to get rid of capitalism may well be true, but this formulation leaves one with absolutely nothing to do. Everything we do to change the system is going to be entirely within the capitalist system, so one has to find little breaks, refuges, tensions, that one might mine to head in the direction of change. Change is always partial and embedded in the prevailing system in that sense.

Consider the fact that I taught for seven years in the United States. I would say that the public university system in Canada is something that we should defend even though we all know it has been degraded and very little of its original purpose remains. This situation was a problem for that book. I know the public university is being degraded in Canada and elsewhere. I know that tuition is going up. It's getting a lot worse for students than it was when I went to university. But, if we just say, "It's all gone, it's no good," where are people going to learn? Where are they going to go? How could we reform it with such a closed pessimism? I had to leave open the possibility that some kinds of reforms are possible, and I think that they are. I do think that one such possibility is expressed in the quotation that you chose. Now, whether people will pick up on it is not clear. But one of the things that happened during the Stephen Harper government—and it's absolutely characteristic of neo-liberalism in general—is that all the regulatory commissions of the government and so on were turned over to the people they're supposed to regulate! The oil industry is supposed to regulate the oil industry. The pharmaceutical industry is supposed to regulate itself. Property realtors, too. We can see how this tends toward a totally unregulated neo-liberal capitalism with very dangerous and cruel consequences. I would think that most average Canadians have an interest in there being some kind of public overseeing of what pharmaceuticals are available, how they're regulated, where they're made, et cetera. A reform such as this wouldn't be the end of capitalism, but it might be an argument why people would be willing to put money into public institutions to regulate systems that affect them. That's what I was thinking of when I was writing that. Moreover, reforms of that type would build upon persisting solidarities and construct new ones—which I take to be a fundamental aspect of the *ongoing process* of change. Does it commit me to some kind of hard distinction between public and private? I don't really think so, and I think I can agree with you that neo-liberalism does, has been, and will continue to erode that distinction. But if you pose the question from the other side of what can we do to make society a little fairer, regulate the cruel uses of certain products and services and so on, then we're going to need public institutions, even if we haven't found a way beyond capitalism.

Public opinion, whatever that is really, doesn't follow right behind economics. It is often several steps behind or several steps ahead. There is still, among many people in this country, the sense that public institutions like universities, hospitals, law, et cetera, should work for them. It should work for Joe and Jane Average. Now, I know that many, many times it doesn't. In fact, even maybe a majority of times it doesn't, but that idea is still a productive idea. If we were to junk it, where would we go?

VAHABZADEH: My second question is also about the university: this time, about academic freedom, and, once again, your book *Love the Questions*. You talked about the administrative assault on procedures that actually remove the academic input into the overseeing and overall workings of the university, and I totally agree with that. You mentioned somewhere that the chairs of the departments used to represent the department to the administration; now they represent the administration to the department. That stood out for me as being very significant. This is a change that happens in such a fashion that we cannot understand that this process is taking place until it has already taken place. I considered that this phenomenon imposes a push or limitation on academic freedom, but I want to look at it from the other side of it, and from the classroom side of it, since you talk about it in your book. You, yourself, by virtue of your standing for the pipeline issue, having engaged in other public issues on the side of the progressive movements, have a clear standing in regards to the critical problems in our time. However, we are witnessing at times in the academy this environment being built by a certain understanding of identity politics, moral panics, political correctness that imposes limitations on critical discussion, whose place is absolutely in the classroom. And some students expect the classroom to be basically an affirmation of their belief rather than a critical engagement with everything that we do. Every criticism, I was raised to believe, must be also, at the same time, a self-criticism. And this kind of identity politics is catered to by the neo-liberal push on the university, because the university administration does build on these gestures towards being progressive, while taking the university on the neo-liberal path. Nancy Fraser called this process "progressive neoliberalism." So, my question, or my concern, here is: How do you think we can deal with this situation, this double assault on academic freedom? On one side, there's the administration with its cryptic proceduralisms that impose limitations on academic freedom, and, on the other side, there's this expectation that progressivism means certain things, which means this kind of political correctness doesn't involve the kind of very radical critical thinking about what we actually do to change the world.

ANGUS: You're right about that, and I will take it as a valid critique of my book. I was a little bit aware at the time that I was writing it (about 10 years ago) of the problem you're talking about, of the comforting idea that one's prejudices and assumptions shouldn't be unsettled by university education in the name of a "safe place," but I didn't deal with this issue in the book at all. The book is dominated by the figure of intervention into academic affairs by university administrators and corporate forces outside the university, none of which is finished or over with, of course. It was dominated by that because of the recent experience of administrative interference in our attempted hiring of David Noble in the Department of Humanities at SFU and of similar issues elsewhere. I was very conscious of the role of the administration in that and the way in which they work, and I was attempting to try to parse that out and say, "Why does that work the way it works and what can we do about that?" Alongside that, I wanted to explain the role of financial restraint and control by government bodies in restructuring the university. So I really didn't deal with the question you're talking about. I would agree that it's an equally important issue today and must be addressed in any contemporary critique of the university. The threat to critical education comes not only from corporate and state powers but also from the self-satisfied power of popular prejudice. How can we reconcile respect for traditionally denigrated minorities with the necessity to question accepted assumptions? Can we mandate respect or at least respectful discourse, and is there a price to be paid, or resisted, for this? These important issues aren't addressed in my book.

VAHABZADEH: Could you offer some reflections on how to deal with this? As an instructor, you're under moral pressure, supposedly because you're being critical as part of the movement, or the global movement, that actually tries to counteract this neo-liberalism that's everywhere now. But then you're impeded because you're not following those politics to the letter.

ANGUS: Yes. We're in a time, strange as it may seem, of terrible conformism. Perhaps it is not an overall social conformism, but there seem to be these pockets that are determined by incredible conformism within them. So it's very hard to be a thinker without aligning oneself with some set of rigid assumptions that ties one to the interests of a social group. An independent, critical thinker just cannot do that. One has to hold many things that people will find sacred, even things that one personally finds sacred, up to criticism. A critic may in one sense be part of, and an advocate for, a group, but it is no less important that a critic, to be a critic, must be critical also of that group itself, its activities and its assumptions. If not, one is just simply not up to the job. That's one of the hard parts of it.

GANDESHA: I think it's here that Marx's slogan "for a ruthless criticism of everything existing" really springs to mind.

ANGUS: Not only did Marx not get tenure, he didn't even get a job! More seriously, that slogan is a good expression of the teleological idea of criticism. It is the same idea as Husserl's "critique of the life-world as a whole." But it does not adequately address the embodied existential situation of an actual critic—who can never in a single moment criticize everything and therefore leaves some assumptions in place, at least temporarily. The existential itinerary of an actual critic—such as that which you are tracing in my work—is always based on decisions rooted in the critic's life. In that sense, the critic is stretched between the universal teleological demand and the particular unquestioned assumptions that cement a group. One's existential itinerary is woven from the decisions through which one navigates this tensional space.

GANDESHA: The cantankerous Marx did get lots of carbunkles, though! I think that this is an interesting question of how one can respond, and I agree with you wholeheartedly in terms of the importance of finding a kind of shelter from which to do work. I think the material conditions for the possibility of such shelters are really a crucial question. The institute has been able to do a lot of work that's been very critical and it has generated criticism precisely because it has an independent endowment for which we're infinitely grateful. And, just to make the point about neo-liberalism, progressive and otherwise, we've been attacked by different kinds of groups that reveal their identity at the end of the day. We've been attacked by mining companies, we've been attacked by Zionist groups, and we've also been attacked by identity groups. And all of these groups have an understanding that the university is there to serve its customers. Research will serve industry, teaching will serve students; but they're customers. But, surely, that's not the only thing the university is for. As you put it, it's to create a condition in which there is a love for the questions. Or, as you put it elsewhere, in a kind of eroticization—that's a provocative word these days, I know—of the question, the question is loved for itself, not for something else beyond it. And this is such a valuable contribution that you make, Ian.

ANGUS: I would like to say that this is part of my eternal debt to Jerry Zaslove for bringing me into the Institute for the Humanities in the mid-1990s and allowing me to participate—which is now about 25 years of activity. The institute has been enormously important for social and intellectual criticism precisely because it has a certain kind of independence. It doesn't have a lot of money, but it has always been the money that's used very, very carefully to do a lot. It has been very important to me to participate in the institute's activities.

GANDESHA: I think the principle is: you've got to piss people off; but you have to make sure that, more or less, it's the right people. This brings me to my question about democracy. You've provided a convincing account of democracy in your book *Emergent Publics*. It's one that reminds us that a democracy is neither about participating in elections every now and then nor is it exclusively about the institutions of liberal democracy. Rather, it's based on a kind of memory of social struggles, the struggles of social movements to create what we have, and then, also, the struggles of social movements in the present to deepen democracy. So, it's a social movement account of the labour movement, the suffragettes, and civil rights movements, and then today you'd say Idle No More or Black Lives Matter. These movements push for a process of universalization. So, expanding the ambit of who's included because every universal excludes, as you put it—and I think there's a really nice connection with Hannah

Arendt's emphasis on reflective judgment, which we won't go into—this is a really nice dimension where you start with the particular, and then you generate a universal out of the particular, as opposed to taking some abstract notion and then subsuming particulars beneath it. So it's much more dynamic, it's historical, it's engaged. I think, though, we might be at the end of a certain kind of understanding, self-understanding of social movements, insofar as there's a disavowal now of not just the existing form of universalism, not just the universal with its myriad forms of violence and exclusions, but skepticism even about the very process of universalization itself. I think identity politics is about creating boundaries. It's about fixing and, in a very static way, what a particular group is, what its identity is, what its borders are and so on. Therefore, it foregoes this process or this claim to universalization. You see this on both left and right: you see this in terms of identitarianism on the right, and you see this in terms of identity politics on the left. It leads to a kind of disavowal of criticism and disavowal of politics and to a kind of glorification/celebration of identity. Really, it's a celebration of identity by particular self-appointed representatives of groups. There's a lack of democracy in the group itself; it turns very authoritarian. Meanwhile, the space has really taken up by the far right. Matteo Salvini in Italy has just called, today, for a kind of universal solidarity amongst far-right organizations in the run-up to the European elections. This doesn't seem to really register on the left, which is just in a process of implosion amongst those identity groups. There's a certain fluorescence of democratic socialism in the United States. I've yet to see it in this country for some reason, and it would be very interesting to hear what you say about that. But I'm wondering if this social movement theory of democracy needs some rethinking.

ANGUS: You started off by asking me about my political and intellectual formation. It's obviously better to live for a reasonably long time than it is to check out early, but there are disadvantages as well.

One of the things one finds out is that the way in which one started to formulate questions begins to fall apart after a certain point in time. One has to begin again to make sense out of things. Those of us who were alive and active in the 1960s had to live through the 1980s: Ronald Reagan, Margaret Thatcher. And then, in Canada—this is relevant to the last part of your question—these things seem to delay a bit, to lag behind. I'm not sure exactly why, but Harper lagged behind Reagan and Thatcher, even though it was essentially the same phenomenon. I think Frank Cunningham could relate this to his work in the 1980s, trying to look around and find some useful progressive forces to think about and promote. That's where a lot of new social movement theory comes from. It had at least one good effect, I would say. It took away the notion that social change was oriented primarily to the state. It took the state out of being the centre, away from the question of who is going to capture electoral politics. That was, I think, a really positive thing that came out of it—though that does not mean that the state can be ignored as such. But the question in social movement theory in the 1980s and 1990s was: What puts all these movements together? Can they be put together through class analysis or some equivalent? Later, the notion that it could be a grand alliance of social movements arose; perhaps an alliance could be understood as a transversal form of treaty or Proudhonian federalism (as I formulate it) as opposed to an underlying commonality such as class. It occurred to me to point out at the time, and it was not very popular, that feminism, for example, has been most successful where it hasn't aligned itself with other movements but precisely where it has aligned itself with bourgeois individualism and such questions as how many women are there on boards of directors. If you wanted to ask that question, I would say, "Sure! I think there should be just as many women on boards of directors." Does it make any difference? Well, no, I don't really think it does. So, in fact, in this bubbling cauldron of social movements, quite often one of them succeeds to the disadvantage of another. That's when this one-upmanship that you're talking about arises and the self-appointed speakers for movements conceived as closed start to take over, where identities are taken as if they're *something*: it's *something* to be a feminist and it's *something* to be an environmentalist. These are substantializations. The movement is made into a noun, and when movements are made into nouns, they become *things*. As things, the question is: Who owns that thing? So we've now got people who think they're in charge of these things and they battle it out over resources and allocations. But the real questions about social movements are: How do they get going? Why did they get started? Where did they start? Why is the movement a movement? Why isn't it a thing but a movement—a verb, something that's in process, is *happening*? From that point of view, when something's in process and happening, it's very hard for somebody to be in charge. All of the moments at which social movements were really interesting were precisely these moments of happening. The beginning of the environmental movement when one didn't know if it was an environmental movement or a wilderness movement or an ecological movement: then it was interesting. Now, it's all divided out amongst certain people who are speaking in the name of these things.

Your question had to do with democracy. The situation has changed after 1999, and I would probably, like other people, date it from the Battle in Seattle—which Jaden Adams, a student of mine, was involved in organizing. I think the change was that then it became a question of what does hold these movements together into a critique of society, of something that is capable of proposing an alternative system, ultimately. Once that question comes back on the agenda, the social movements, and the questions about social movements, shift, because they will divide. There is what we used to call "bourgeois feminism," and then there's a feminism that is much more radical and more interested in really confronting powers. It is the same with environmentalism, the same with all the ethnic and racial politics.

There is a divide between those who want to hold onto and speak for a movement as a substantive noun and those who explore the movement as a verb in its interaction with other movements and the possibility of alliance. A lot of future politics will occur in and through that divide.

GANDESHA: One could say that the key determining factor in the way in which the politics of these social moments play out is a principle of articulation. And this is something that is a continuity from the mid-1980s.

Hegemony and Socialist Strategy by Ernesto Laclau and Chantal Mouffe, published in 1985, about the defeat of the miners' strike and the rise of new social movements that needed a kind of stitching together and a principle of unity, is an example. And this is what they've thought. It has had a kind of political dimension insofar as the Spanish movement that came out of Indignados; Podemos was very influenced by them. SYRIZA, I don't want to say so much about SYRIZA, but they were influenced by Laclau and Mouffe, and other movements as well. There is, now, a kind of left populism on the table. It would seem to me that there is a real tension between a new identity politics that have emerged and then this very possibility of articulation. You have to be able to engage in give-and-take in order to enter into some kind of hegemonic or post-hegemonic alliance with other groups, which is forestalled or foreclosed by identity politics.

VAHABZADEH: In relation to that idea, you said, "When we begin to think about what is the alternative, then that's where the dividing line will form," I think that dividing line is absolutely necessary for the ideal formation of the specific groups involved in radical politics. Then that polarization will be able to actually implement, in due process and with all the challenges involved, a new alternative order.

ANGUS: Yes, exactly. That's what Laclau and Mouffe call the "enemy," defining the enemy. I was thinking about these matters when I read *Hegemony and Socialist Strategy* in the 1980s. I wrote a piece about it and corresponded with Ernesto. Then in the late 1990s, Ernesto and Chantal were here for a few days.

I did an interview with them for the Knowledge Network. It was called "Conflicting Publics." In that work I was very influenced by Ernesto—and more Ernesto than Chantal, really, if you get into the details of their thinking. I have one big disagreement with Ernesto Laclau and that is around his Lacanian conception of universality. According to him, Jacques Lacan had three theories and this is the last one because of problems with previous ones. The Lacanian notion of universality, according to Ernesto Laclau, is that there is no universality, and that any universality is just a particular of some sort claiming the universal space to speak for everyone. I think that's wrong. In theory I think it's wrong and I think in practice it's problematic because it does tend to rule out precisely the kind of hegemonic alliance that you would think their theory actually points towards. There can be universalizing claims that can be accepted from other standpoints and, thereby, there is something not entirely arbitrary about the universalizing claims. For Ernesto, there is something in principle always arbitrary about a universal claim or any claim to a universal position. I'm not sure about Lacan, but it seems to me to be a Nietzschean position. From my perspective, that does not allow us to get beyond the kind of dead ends of identity politics to which you were pointing. It seems to me still possible to seek a rational basis for an alliance based upon the needs and demands of the present situation. The alliance that has emerged in British Columbia and elsewhere around opposition to the Trans Mountain Pipeline is an example of this. Indigenous sovereignty, climate change activism, and local resident mobilization all converge in a politics that is internally differentiated but united against a common antagonist, which is in this case the nexus of the federal government, extractivist corporations, and probably banks as well. It is a new antagonism that targets the system as a whole.

GANDESHA: Would it be correct to characterize your intellectual project as a whole in terms of a critique of "Platonism"? Platonism, according to Martin Heidegger, is a metaphysical account of Being understood as "enduring presence." As such, it founds a series of oppositions such as philosophy and rhetoric, concepts and metaphors, abstract universals and sensuous particulars, the rule of the philosopher and the rule of the people or *demos*. At the same time, though, in your book on the university, you pay a kind of tribute to Plato in your view of philosophy and perhaps the vocation of the university as such as an "eroticization of the question."

ANGUS: Heidegger's thesis that philosophy has since Plato been plagued with a "metaphysics of presence" functions as a kind of myth or rhetorical flourish. Such myths have an intriguing function in the history of philosophy. They are a necessary recourse of the philosopher in expressing a philosophical truth in language dominated by common sense. Plato was self-conscious about his use of myth, which is one of the things that made him a great, perhaps the greatest, philosopher. Heidegger's myth allowed him to characterize the whole history of philosophy from Plato to G.W.F. Hegel in a way that opened up a new direction for him by replacing presence with the triad presence, presencing, and the opening. Marx's conception developed in 1843 to 1847, of the "upshot of philosophy," functioned in much the same way. So I don't think the right question to ask about such sweeping characterizations is whether they are right or wrong. It would be easy to show that Plato's conception of the "good beyond being" in no way participates in a fixation on presence. Neither does Hegel's conception of "dialectic" in which negation always haunts any given state of being. It was a way for Heidegger of breaking into thinking of being as openness, as coming and going, and the real question is whether his formulation of negation is to be preferred to those of Plato, Hegel, or others. Philosophy necessarily breaks away from what is given as it is given and thinks of the coming-and-going of beings and, further, the space in which coming-and-going becomes open to the thought and experience of humans.

I have never been committed to Heidegger's rhetorical myth as such and I have always had a similar skepticism regarding Hegel's conception of dialectic. I don't think that I began to think philosophically at this level until I began to develop a conception of privative negation some 15 years ago. At this point I understood that it is a fundamental question why humans live in a world of appearance. In Parmenidean terms, if there is a way of truth, why do we begin from appearance, and how do we exit from appearance to truth? What is such an exit? Where is the going-away of appearance and the coming-closer of truth? In this question, which is what drove Heidegger to his myth, Plato to the good that trumps the good of being, and Hegel to a dialectic of appearance and truth, I am closer to Parmenides, Heraclitus, and privative negation. I hope to be able to think of this clearly in the coming years.

It is true that a series of oppositions comes out of a clarifying sweeping gesture of this sort—precisely because it clears a path to an articulation of what goes beyond common sense and participates not only in being but coming-and-going. The way in which one of these oppositions has plagued the history of philosophy has concerned me a great deal: the connection between the distinction between knowledge and opinion and the social distinction of classes. It is true that the history of philosophy has contained an aristocratic political component based upon the necessary distinction between appearance and truth. The epistemological distinction has been written onto the social order in a manner that makes the philosopher either the king or the king's advisor. In my last few years of teaching, I confronted this question in a number of ways and through a number of different texts, both ancient and contemporary. This connection does indeed begin with Plato and persists until Hegel. Marx's concept of "the upshot of philosophy" throws this whole tradition into question. The upshot of philosophy is the idea that the philosophical tradition developed the conception of the sensuous, social human being developing itself historically through interaction with nature—that is to say, philosophy has guarded the notion of human fulfillment, although in an idealistic form. For me, it was essential to distinguish clearly between Socrates and Plato in order to show that Plato's continuation of Socrates was only one possibility of several. I consider my work another continuation of Socrates that maintains his democratic, topic-bound inquiry in determinate circumstances. I am now trying to write down such a Socratic phenomenology in the contemporary context of a critique of scientism, a critique of the binding of sensuous social individuality to determining form (the regime of value), and an intercultural dialogue about the sources of reason and value.

Thus, I distinguish between Plato and the Platonic tradition even though I agree that some aspects of the Platonic tradition were indeed established by Plato. I am indeed a critic of the Platonic tradition, especially its aristocratic component and its writing of the hierarchy of opinion-knowledge onto the structure of being. Nevertheless, there are aspects of Plato, especially those that pertain to the essence of philosophy, which seem to me to be simply true. That philosophy is the construction of a community of friends united by the goodness of being is one of these. That philosophy is an erotic activity is another. It certainly poses problems for the contemporary university, but, one must recall, philosophy is not primarily an institutionalized activity or limited to the university, even though in some respects it inhabits the history of this conflicted institution. One cannot abandon institutions because they are the given places where certain human activities are encouraged, but neither can one suppose that such activities are limited and defined by such institutions. There always remains the negation, the withdrawal, the manifestation that can found another possibility.

VAHABZADEH: The next question is about one of my favourite concepts in your work—"constitutive paradox"—which comes out in *(Dis)figurations*, published in 2000. Can "constitutive paradox" be applied to universal-particular relations?

ANGUS: It is indeed an attempt to theorize the relation between particular and universal, which is probably the red thread through most of what I've done. Why? I don't know exactly, but I think it is.

In the 1980s, Habermas proposed the very influential idea of a "performative contradiction" in order to criticize those whom he called postmodernists, who in his view were all relativists, and he opposed them fundamentally. This was in a book called *The Philosophical Discourse of Modernity*. He charged them with committing a performative contradiction—that they actually assumed in speaking that other people could understand them and assumed that they could be criticized with regards to criteria of truth and so forth. And yet, what they were saying, according to Habermas, denied that other people could understand them and denied that there were conditions of truth. It was a pretty sophisticated move but really failed to deal entirely with what was going on intellectually at the time. He tried to build a wall and say that nobody was allowed over that side of it, much in the way that Bertrand Russell and Alfred Whitehead attempted to ban self-referential statements with their theory of types. Habermas similarly tried to ban self-reference from social critique and its philosophical justification, even though the self-referential character of critique was, and is, an essential aspect of immanent (or internal) critique that aims at the total system of which it is a part.

I tried to think about it differently and came up with the notion of "constitutive paradox." It seems to me that every philosophical, that is to say universalizing, claim is made from some standpoint, and that standpoint is not irrelevant to the statement—neither its meaning nor its truth conditions. The standpoint of enunciation can be treated as if it might be irrelevant in certain limiting cases, such as "two plus two equals four" because it doesn't seem to matter whether I say it or whether you say it—there has been a social stabilization such that the standpoint of enunciation is equal, as it were, from most standpoints.

Logic, ideally science, perhaps theology, will try to be included in that category where it doesn't matter who is speaking. In other words, their contents are always spoken about already in a universal voice. Let me not deal with those cases because I think that it can be shown that even in mathematics some form of subjectivity is involved in the judgment. I would rely on Husserl here. That's a little esoteric, but the point is that in any field that has to do with social and political matters, the standpoint of enunciation always matters. Then, there seems to be this problem, which is what Habermas was trying to deal with: if we know that you're saying it, then the so-called postmodernists—a somewhat mythical group, as it turns out—are going to say, "It's not true then! It's just something you are saying." In other words, the fact that you're saying it is reduced to its being legitimate only for you. And the corresponding other side, which was Habermas's side, is that a statement is simply universal if it is meaningful and true, which means it doesn't matter who says it. It's just universal. Now, to me, this dilemma is a false dilemma, but it's also a very deeply entrenched one in the way people bounce back and forth between a kind of relativism and a kind of false universalism.

So, to arrive at the concept of constitutive paradox: I first brought up that idea in trying to think about the subject of the social critic. The social critic is immersed in what they are criticizing and yet, at the same time, are, in some sense, outside it, insofar as they were able to criticize it. "Inside-outside" is again a very broad, simplifying distinction that one shouldn't get stuck in too much. One needs to express a situation in which one does speak from a certain place and that place is relevant to both meaning and truth, but one speaks to a *world* that is beyond that place of articulation and that therefore makes a claim on other people. That claim is universalizing, though, not simply universal. Behind the distinction between universal and universalizing is a theoretical history from Immanuel Kant's *Critique of Judgment* through Hegel's conception of history to Hannah Arendt's concept of political judgment. I have drawn from and learned from this theoretical history, but my own conception is not quite the same. I have attempted to clarify this in some writings that are more philosophically esoteric, but the basis of that work, and of the concept of "constitutive paradox," is that the standpoint of enunciation is not itself external to that which is enunciated. Thus, there is a necessary reflexive moment that must be theorized and not exorcized.

VAHABZADEH: You were speaking of the universal-particular relation in the context of constitutive paradox.

ANGUS: Oh, yes. Since the initial idea of constitutive paradox as an expression of the self-reflexive character of critical discourse that constitutes the subject to which it also refers, a lot more has come out of continued reflection on what prompted that concept. The idea of "locative thought" in *Identity and Justice* comes out of that concept. The relation between concrete and transcendental ego in my current manuscript also struggles with it. The reason why there's a constitutive paradox for the social critic who is criticizing a society of which they are a part is because the subject is not static. It's not a substance. As I was saying before with regard to movements, it is not a thing. What that means is that the process of criticism is self-constituting of the subjectivity of the critic. The activity of criticizing changes the subject, and in so doing opens up other possibilities. It's very important—it comes back to the same thing you were saying here a moment ago, Samir—not to see the subject as a fixed entity, to see the subject as something that is temporal and overlaps with different definitions. One can have a distinct identity, but also another and another and another. And, as far as I know, there's no limit to how many one can have or be.

GANDESHA: I would like to suggest that, in addition to the idea of the constitutive paradox, there's also the possibility of imminent critique because that's where you bring in the object. Just as a subject is non-identical to itself—it's constantly dynamic and in motion—the object is non-identical to itself. The object—meaning society, its normative structures—makes a certain claim to justice, equality, and fairness, but it constitutively fails to live up to its *own* normativity. And that's a space for criticism, isn't it? Theodor W. Adorno says somewhere that we must think about a possibility of a society in which the principle of free exchange comes into its own, as opposed to the notion of exchange value, which is an unfree exchange. There's the possibility still of immanent critique. So, constitutive paradox of the subject is related to the constitutive paradox of the object.

ANGUS: Yes, that's right. And that is the issue with universals. If we take a universal like "One Man, One Vote," which is one of the basic principles of the democratic revolution, it stays the way it is for a while and then somebody comes along and says—in fact, it was four people who came along in Canada and said—this "man" here, is that a man-man or is that a human-man or person? And we have the famous "Person's Case" in Canada, which has decided that the meaning of "One *Man*, One Vote" is "One *Person*, One Vote." This is linguistically a small thing but politically a very, very big thing. I won't take the time now to drag this out with other examples. Any universal is always concretized in something that is not thoroughly universal. Whereas Laclau would insist that the universal claim is "really" an imposition by the particular, gendered "man," my point is that the necessary universalization by the particular contains the possibility for critique and expansion of the referent. So that "man" worked for a while as a critique of the aristocratic running of society without input from the bourgeoisie. They expanded the concept of "man" to refer to any male who owned property. Later, the working class expanded the concrete referent of "man" to apply to any sane adult male. At some point, the limits of the referent were reached and breached by becoming applied, through political struggle, to an expanded referent. There are also other examples—concerning race, for example—that similarly show that the referents of concepts, which are treated as if they were simply universal and true, instead are quite dynamic. I agree completely with you that it is in that dynamism that politics happens.

VAHABZADEH: I understand you are writing a book on Husserl. Why is it important to return to Husserl? What does he have to offer us today after Heidegger, Maurice Merleau-Ponty, Jacques Derrida, and others?

ANGUS: There are biographical reasons and there are philosophical-historical reasons. For me personally, there are two books that have loomed over all my thinking and writing even though I have mentioned them only occasionally: Husserl's *Crisis of the European Sciences* and Marx's *Capital*, volume 1. I never studied either of these books in a class. I studied them on my own and they both influenced me fundamentally. My first encounter with them was when I was an MA student and I studied them carefully in order to prepare for my first academic publication: a review of the English-language translation of Enzo Paci's *The Function of the Sciences and the Meaning of Man*. So I would say that in a personal sense it is less a return than a making explicit of what has been implicit throughout much of my work. I came out of the milieu of phenomenological Marxism in the 1960s, and my current manuscript is a return to those sources and an attempt to present a version that is both more contemporary and more philosophically viable.

The philosophical-historical reasons are more difficult to state, and an adequate answer can be provided only by the manuscript as a whole. In broad outline: the critique of one-sided rationalism in favour of a deeper concept of reason that prevailed in the 1960s gave way to critiques of reason that either rejected or were agnostic to such a deeper conception of reason. I have never been satisfied with that and have attempted to take on board the valid contributions of post-structuralism, et cetera, without ceding that reason is simply a confirmation of social power. In this respect, Husserl's rational critique of reason has no peer. By returning to it but also working through and beyond it, one can address more deeply the solidarity of human thought and reason with human and extra-human life. For philosophy, it must be a main goal to re-establish this solidarity. This can be genuinely accomplished only through a form of thought that is rooted in first-person experience and existential commitment. In contrast to many superficial attempts to step beyond the philosophical tradition as a whole, Husserl's work takes us to the centre of the idea of philosophy itself and the relation of philosophical thought to the history of philosophy. For me, the role of philosophy in the conduct of human life is a matter of supreme importance. Through this connection, in which Husserl's work plays an important mediation, I hope to develop a Socratic conception of phenomenology that would loosen its ties to an encyclopediac conception of knowledge and root it in embodied self-reflection. This would, I hope, be my philosophical legacy.

GANDESHA: As they say on the London Underground, "Mind the gap." I think it is probably time now. I'm being told here that we need to move on. I'm sure there are a few people out there who would like to say a few things. I'm sure a lot of people would like to speak. Please keep your comments and your questions concise.

Q&A Period:

HILDA FERNANDEZ-ALVAREZ: I have three little things to address to Ian. One, because this is the recognition for your work and often academia just takes the influences at the level of the ideas, but also it's important to recognize the influence at the level of community building, I just want to say that you allowed the Lacan Salon (based in Vancouver) to connect to the institute at the very first time, and I want to thank you for that. That's one. The second one, it's a personal question: Who are your theoretical guys or gals? Name three. I'm very curious about that. And the third point is, with all of the discussion about universality, I think Laclau got Lacan wrong, evidently, because universality is not about a positive quality, which the identitarian claims; it's more. One interprets Lacan in terms of the universal-singular: That is, the thing that it is, like the identity in every man or every woman, but in the sense that we don't have, which is a little bit like the proletariat for Marx. These qualities of the negative and how much that should be the universal as the negative as the one that we aspire for it. That's it.

ANGUS: You want three people who are most important to me? Edmund Husserl and Karl Marx; I don't know who the third is. I can mention others, but right now I can't think of anyone else I would put alongside them.

I am not the guy to say what Lacan did or did not mean, assuming he meant something! Ernesto claimed that Lacan's position was that the universal position is empty. It's always in principle empty, meaning that we put something in that place, but what we put in that place is a function of our desire. It has no more belonging or location there than anything else. I can't really talk about the validity of Alain Badiou's and Laclau's reading of Lacan, because I'm not a strong reader of Lacan and I would defer to you at this point, Hilda. You refer to the proletariat in Marx's sense here as the particular that is also a universal. I agree that Marx's formulation of that problem—which, of course, goes back to Hegel and has a long philosophical pedigree—is the origin of this problematic of the universal and particular or concrete universal. It is the problem of our age even though, in my view, one cannot assert the solution in Hegelian terms. Once it gets substantialized and it becomes the proletariat, then there are all of the problems that follow from substantialization.

Once it is substantialized, it's not a negative and loses its critical status. Jacques Rancière addresses this point by saying the proletariat is always that which is left out. Politics is always about that which is left out, in any system—the place that has no place. That is one way of addressing this issue, which is to make the negative space—and every system has at least one negative space—its unconscious, one can say, which it can't fully incorporate. One can speak about that without substantializing it and making it a thing. If one is a Marxist in the predominant sense, one has to believe in the proletariat because it is the substance, the defined vehicle. It is no longer a negative. This forces us to the question of what is a negative. If one considers the negative as just a zero, as a nothing, it is not really meaningful. It is only a meaningful negative if it is not something. This is not strictly just negative; it is what is called a "privative." The space of universality is defined through a privative. Peyman has written brilliantly about this recently in *Violence and Nonviolence*. How do we even get an intimation of what justice is except when we come across something in the world and we say, "That's not just, that's not right"? How do we know that? This is a big, long question, obviously, but it starts with a "no, no." The space of the universal, it would seem to me, is a privative negation. The two who have best thought about that to my knowledge are Hermann Cohen (the nineteenth-century neo-Kantian) and Moses Maimonides (the mediaeval Jewish theologian).

Thus, one can accept neither the notion of a given universal, which would become a still point, thus a foundation in the bad sense from which "reality" could be deduced as in an argument, nor as an empty space in Laclau's sense—that is to say, there never is anything other than particulars so a supposed universal is really just a peasant who has stolen the king's clothes and walks around in front of others in them. Hegemony, for him, is this kind of a particular assuming itself to be the universal and rhetorically convincing others to go along with it. He doesn't seem like much of a reference point for Ernesto, but this is, in my view, a Nietzschean reversal of the first "metaphysical" position. With "universalization" I am after something different that has to do with claiming a universal, and thus transforming the "mere" particularity of the particular without becoming any sort of still point.

In conclusion, the contribution that psychoanalysis can make at this point, and I would accept this as a valid criticism of the implicit rationalism of some of my previous formulations, is that of the desire that operates in the universalization. Here, one must understand desire in a way that doesn't simply individualize it and therefore collapse back into Ernesto's position. One must count this desire in a way that allows for its universalizing as a project or a utopia or something that inherently escapes substantialization. This is where I am currently working it out through privative negation—which would be compatible with a certain reading of desire as psychoanalytically understood.

BOB HACKETT: *(Inaudible question.)*

ANGUS: Bob Hackett is asking about whether there is a narrative outside BC that could challenge extractivist politics without marginalizing Indigenous narratives. I don't really know. I will say that we are lucky, even possibly blessed, in BC to have such active and articulate Indigenous people capable of leading important struggles and capable of articulating a direction. And—this is maybe going beyond what I really know—I suspect that that's not as strong elsewhere in the country, and so it's not such an alternative. But there are very many places where it is there. You may be asking me to estimate something that I don't really know how to estimate. Can it work? Well, one of the big tasks for us now, politically speaking (and I think your question embodies this as you do, too, from being at the pipeline blockade along with many others who were there: there were 200 people a year ago and 130 or 140 the year that Steve Collis and Lynne Quarmby got arrested up there and were deeply threatened by Trans Mountain in a legal suit; it will take many more to stand up and be counted, and in this, I'm one amongst many people), is we desperately need a narrative that will work for people who are committed to being Canadians and for Indigenous people who, for colonial reasons, don't identify with being Canadian. How to do that is a real political task without a certain conclusion, but, as I indicated before, it does seem to me to be a flashpoint for a new alliance. And it has been put on the national agenda by the Truth and Reconciliation Commission. We all know that there are many ways in which the potential for truth and reconciliation is being pushed aside and trivialized. There are also many voices that are pointing that out and suggesting other more meaningful ways. The Trans Mountain struggle and similar struggles against extractivist capital are, or may be, a turning point in national and international politics. So I am hopeful. In part this is happening because the country is unravelling and indeed most nation-states are unravelling. What that means is that there is an opportunity to put something together, a different kind of a narrative that takes a kind of poetic genius that I don't think I have. There's room for work here, right? But that is exactly what is needed.

GERARDO OTERO: I would like Ian to address whether he acknowledges any influence from Antonio Gramsci and, in particular, his concept of "national popular" in regard to what he just said. I mean, if there's something to rebuild; the word "nationalism" seems like a dirty word for the most part, because it's usually associated with nationalism of the right. But can there be a nationalism of the left, a national popular democratic?

ANGUS: Well, the short answer is yes, there is an influence from Gramsci in my thought. It is not a philosophical influence but came in when I was thinking about politics over a long historical perspective. When I was writing *A Border Within* in the 1990s, I reread Gramsci, and the "national popular" was the exact concept that seemed to me most important. It did seem to me that in Canada the idea of national or nationalism means, above all, *not being Americans*. It may mean other things, too, but first and foremost it means not being Americans. I used it there as a possibility of opening up to a kind of a national popular alliance that would begin from wanting a different sort of society from that in the United States and which the US imperial agenda pushed on other countries. To the second part of the question, yes also. I, and others, too, didn't at that time have to spend a lot of ink trying to explain why nationalism isn't always a kind of aggressive right-wing nationalism that leads to oppression of other peoples, war, et cetera. Such nuances are hard to get into political discussions these days. I think people who come from Mexico or South America or so on realize that if they're going to have a different kind of society, they will end up confronting the power of the United States. In that sense, the national popular is always part of the picture these days.

GANDESHA: I think that's especially important right now in Québec. The future of that society really hinges upon how that national popular will is going to be articulated. It's very much in question right now.

OLIVER HOCKENHULL: Isn't this dependency, or poaching nationalism, whether it be left or right? I mean, because it's a brand! Nationalism, these days, is more a brand than anything else. I think that we need to break open the idea of a brand and abolish it, because it's almost as if we are at the point, with our technology, to be very much a global society. The point of the brand of Canada, I think, is that it's not only not American, but post-nationalism.

ANGUS: Could be, Oliver. The thing that concerns me in that, and we'd have to talk more to see if I agree with you or not, is that it seems to me that we live in a society that is constitutively for economic neo-liberal reasons radically individualist and radically looking to the self only, vis-à-vis others. That is the basic problem that I see with any kind of social change: Where are the sources of solidarity? And so that's the spirit in which I answer about the national popular: whether it may be the source of a certain kind of solidarity. However, I'm not actually attached to its being national in the sense of the nation-state. I do think increasingly, as I've lived in British Columbia, that I live on "The Coast," that that's a place with which I identify much more than I identify with Canada per se. I'm sure a lot of you could relate to this. I'm not trying to locate it at a definite place, but what I am looking for in the idea of the national popular is: What is the source of a sense of common place, a common place that we're not willing to sacrifice, a compelling universalization? It would hurt me in my gut if there was oil in the inlet. I don't know how I would get through it. All of us who feel that way, and I'm sure there are a lot of us, have some basis for a "national popular." That's what I'm trying to talk about with that term. The nation-state could go tomorrow; that wouldn't bother me nearly as much as the fate of the inlet.

COLLIS: I don't know if adding "left internationalism" adds anything to the conversation.

ANGUS: Yes, it does.

COLLIS: And whether that can do anything about right nationalism. A relatively recent historical example that's always really struck me goes back to 2013, when the protests were happening in Turkey, especially in Istanbul—there was a moment where, at the same time, there were massive demonstrations in Brazil. I'm trying to remember which order it happened in, but when it started happening in the other place, in solidarity, the actors suddenly had, say, Brazilian flags, they were carrying in protests in Istanbul. And same thing in protests in Brazil: they were carrying Turkish flags as a sign of solidarity. And now, interestingly enough, both those countries, subsequently, have essentially fallen to neo-fascist regimes. Not that that tells us anything, but, with such a wonderful history, the left had to be international at one time.

ANGUS: This is something in discussing nationalism, a point that always has to be made: there is no formal left-wing nationalism that isn't internationalist as well. This is something that's been very deeply entrenched in Scottish nationalism and Irish nationalism, for example. Given the issue of being under the thumb of another country, to want out from it usually requires some form of nationalism, in the sense of "We here, in this group, have got something against what you've been doing to us." But it doesn't mean that we want to be isolated, that we really think we're radically distinct from or better than everybody else, that we don't want anybody here from Turkey immigrating, or an enclosed mentality like that. It doesn't mean that at all. The press has a lot to answer for here, always phrasing the issue in these terms: "Oh, you're a backward-looking nationalist." Well, you might be, because there are people like that, but the notion that every form of nationalism is self-enclosed and aggressive is just completely wrong. Left-wing nationalism, generally speaking, contains a universalizing element because of its critique of structural inequality that points it toward internationalism—not in opposition to nationalism but as its necessary complement. Decolonization has always contained that dynamic.

Aron Vidaver has a question about settler people acknowledging themselves as settler identities, and what might be accomplished by that. I would agree that when the issue of settler identity came up, I found it difficult. I found it difficult to think about what it would mean to call myself a "settler." But I thought about it for a while and now have written something in which I do use that term. The difficulty with it is that it seems almost entirely negative in content. It seems as if one might be associating oneself with the colonial project when at the same time what one is trying to do is dissociate oneself from it in a meaningful and not just rhetorical way. One can't associate oneself with colonization but neither can one entirely dissociate oneself from it. This difficulty is very interesting, and I would say that it is helpful to the decolonization project to work it through. It is helpful to use the term "settler," but I would think that it's not good enough, that one has to put also some positive content into it that makes one an actor, so that it is not just a statement of guilt. And statements of guilt are paralyzing because they leave out those things that are much more positive and active. I would say that, as a piece of a self-description, it can be helpful. It can be decolonizing, but one then has to put some further, active content into it as well. As several people have asked: How do we find language and narrative for a common project without thinking in a way that will homogenize people? As settlers, we are not going to become the same people as Indigenous people, obviously. They've got their different history, their different customs, et cetera. We need something common but retaining difference. "Treaty" is a wonderful metaphor for that. Two boats sailing down the same river. So I think I'm giving you a cautious yes in answer to that question.

GANDESHA: There is something jarring about it, isn't there? I think your third favourite philosopher was Adorno, and he said, "Wrong life cannot be lived rightly." It might take a bit of agency away, but it's meant to be jarring. We're complicit; we are living on stolen land. So what are we going to do about it? Is an acknowledgement going to be enough? Well, maybe not. I think that it should be that kind of provocation.

ANGUS: Jerry Zaslove, I think you're asking me about the ethical element in thinking and how it relates specifically to displaced and dispossessed people. First, I should say that you are right. Jan Patočka is indeed the third major influence on my work. I don't know why I forgot him earlier. For some reason, I was dismayed by being asked to name three. Perhaps it seemed too Christian and I couldn't do it. Not only Patočka's philosophical writing was influential but also his placing in Czechoslovakia and his dissidence during the period of the Communist dark night after 1968. He always impressed me very deeply from the time I read little pieces of his work as it came into English in the early 1970s through *Telos* magazine. It seems to me that he took up the task of phenomenology in an existential sense much more deeply than Husserl himself, who was quite frankly just an old-style intellectual in which everything really came down to getting the ideas right. In that sense, Patočka is a much more serious philosopher. It was Patočka who said that when you decide to do something, that can be very important, but those things that choose you are much more important. There is a deep understanding of history in that statement. He was called to stand for Charta 77 for human rights in Czechoslovakia. He refused because he said he could not take the honour from two or three other people who, in his estimation, deserved it more. When they went to these people, for various reasons, they said, "No, Patočka should have this." So he took up the position of being spokesperson for Charta 77 and had the honour of being imprisoned and questioned at great length. He was over 84 or 85 years of age, something like that, and he died of a heart attack very shortly afterward. There's something very deep about Patočka and his sense of having accepted this, and I think he genuinely saw it as an honour. He is perhaps the only genuinely Socratic figure of the twentieth century. He saw it as an honour to be able to do this, and it has to do with what is one's historical situation: the fence you can't jump over; the thing that holds one so that one's experience of life is what it is. I was saying before that to some extent one must take on formulations of ideas because they are around and one has to address them in some way. One can't just ignore them—or if one does, one becomes a kind of specialist thinker. But Patočka is a step above that: he not only accepted his situation and its demands intellectually, but he put his life into it, his death into it. There's nothing more serious. How do you know when you've come to that point? Where is that point? Where is that fence that you can't jump over? I don't know. I think one just probably knows it when one sees it.

IRWIN OOSTINDIE: Everyone knows Cindy, a Dutch settler, waiting for the Coast Salish Federated Government to accept applications for naturalized citizens. At risk of coming back to the previous question from Aron, your thoughts on the use of spectacle? The Jody Wilson-Raybould thing is a great example of crystallizing the hypocrisy of the Canadian prime minister's feminism and his commitment to reconciliation. Your thoughts on that? It's very common; it's very popular right now, but it's a great opportunity for people to kind of deepen their analysis of the failure of spectacle being deployed by the state.

ANGUS: I do agree. I can't help but take a certain degree of pleasure in seeing Justin Trudeau revealed for what he is. It didn't come as news to me that he is all flash and no substance, and I'm sure many other people knew also, but it's certainly great to see it as public news. The danger is all too clear, which is that the right will seize this opportunity. We've got this pipsqueak who's the head of the Conservative Party now being promoted as a leader who is attempting to take advantage of the crisis in the Liberal Party. That's the start of it, isn't it? This is the thing: you never know how it's going to go or what the long-term consequences are going to be, or even the short-term consequences, really. There are a lot of things one could say about Jody Wilson-Raybould's position in this because one could ask what she was doing hanging around with these people in the first place. Did she not understand that there would be a price? And if she didn't understand that, what was she thinking? How does she think that politics works in Ottawa? Nevertheless, I tend to be a little ...

"forgiving" might be the word, insofar as I think people have different and quite often contradictory commitments in their lives. I don't have any inside information, but the way I read it is that, as a lawyer, Jody Wilson-Raybould thought she could be a Liberal and still uphold the law. Eventually, it came to a point at which it didn't seem like that was possible from her reading of the situation. Not from somebody else's, but from *her* reading of the situation. So it seems to me she did what she felt she had to do. A genuine existential decision about who she is and will be. That's always admirable, isn't it?

GANDESHA: It's just unfortunate that this is where she chose to draw the line as opposed to when the RCMP entered Wet'suwet'en territory to do the dirty work of a natural gas company. This is unconscionable. Why not? Why not there?

ANGUS: Well, because it wasn't about the law. I do think that was where her commitment was, the law.

COLLIS: Please join me in thanking Ian, Peyman, and Samir for this discussion.

Chapter 2

Ian and Viviana, Kids, Dogs, and Other Parents

George Rammell

It's amazing who you meet through your kids.

When our daughter, Nicola, was in grade three, our son, Coulter, was in grade one at Hastings Elementary School. He had a circle of new playmates. One was Cassandra, a little ball of energy who was usually bouncing on her backyard trampoline when she wasn't at school. Her mom, Viviana, and my wife, Nancy, became friends and active school volunteers. They spelled each other off with play-dates as we lived three blocks apart.

I was pleased Nancy invited Viviana and Ian over for a back-yard barbeque; any excuse for a barbeque is fine with me, especially when our kids were playing above us in their new tree fort. Our dogs, Mika and Golda, became instant buddies. I discovered Ian shared three of my great passions: good beer, barbequed meat, and a good debate about the first two topics. Ian was one of the few people to ever show interest in stories of my bow-hunting trips and the care that went into butchering venison. It's been 20 years now and we're still negotiating those topics as their tentacles branch into every human endeavour on the planet. Due to my interests, I'm used to being considered an eccentric around parents, or anyone else for that matter, but Ian turned out to be equally eccentric and a raving, ranting academic, too, but unlike almost all ranters, he published. I sculpted. He had his words; I had my clay. Nancy and Viviana's discussions took a different tack, but they sounded equally engaging.

Viviana taught Nancy to speak Spanish; Ian informed me about faculty rights and academic freedom through his new book *Love the Questions: University Education and Enlightenment*. Among other things, he described Machiavellian tactics administrators use to re-engineer university programming outside of academic plans and collective agreements. Ian invited me to his book launch, where a panel of writers weighed in from across the country. The next day I went to the Simon Fraser University (SFU) bookstore, bought six copies, and hand-delivered them to the reigning administrators at Capilano University in a last-gasp attempt to educate them on the basics of ethical governance. The interim American president, Dr. Kris Bulcroft, was cutting our Studio Art and Textiles programs. She was on a campaign to prune back the humanities and replace it with job-ready courses for film and business programs. Once Bulcroft's unilateral cuts were announced, I responded by making a large ventriloquist dummy entitled *Blathering On in Krisendom*. It was a satirical portrait of her and her large poodle wrapped in an American flag. (She was the only person on campus who was allowed to bring her dog to work.) I then played the David Letterman role at a faculty assembly, giving my newly sculpted "her" my copy of Ian's book on stage during a mock interview. Not everyone was amused: half the audience looked like they caught a bad case of automatonophobia. They were terrified their programs would be next on Bulcroft's chopping block. My sculpture was ordered confiscated and destroyed by the board chair. When I eventually received the pieces back following a 53-day hostage taking, I resculpted them into a new work entitled *Margaux and the Monarch*, which included my version of the university mace, a symbol of trust invested in the university president. The piece is still officially banned from the university, but it was part of the "City on Edge" exhibition at the Museum of Vancouver and is now part of their permanent collection.

At another barbeque I was still blathering on about administrative abuses when Ian reciprocated with stories about his Centre for Canadian Studies at SFU being axed by administrators who clearly didn't support it. Programs we nurtured suffered horrible deaths, defending them took its toll on us and our families, then new projects emerged and life eventually went on as usual.

Many events have transpired since we met through our kids. Ian and Viviana have been active participants in my studio openings and sculptural actions, such as my archery paintings or carrying *Notley* (my pipeline with a knot in it) at various anti-Kinder Morgan rallies. But the best is yet to come. This Saturday Ian, Viviana, and I are planning to protest within Kinder Morgan's injunction zone at its oil-tank farm on Burnaby Mountain. By the time you're reading this story, we'll have been arrested at the hands of the RCMP and we'll wear the prosecutions like a badge of honour. We live near Burrard Inlet so the issue called for our response. We'll be meeting again at the Supreme Court to explain to Judge Affleck why we broke his injunction that defends this company to go on logging, drilling, and excavating without permits for a project that will put our waterways at risk and expand the Alberta tar sands for decades. There's always something exciting to look forward to. I can't afford to pay big fines so I keep telling myself the worst-case scenario is the luxury of a few weeks in jail to get some reading done. Ian doesn't appear stressed about going to court. The only time I have ever seen him panic was when he arrived at a neighbourhood party where a group of guys were jamming on their guitars in the living room. He just stared with a guitarless look on his face, then he bolted out the back door and ran up the lane for it.

I need to back up here to share two decades of observations regarding the dual phenomenon that is Ian Angus, a man who appears to live in two worlds. He loves Viviana, he loves Cassandra and his elderly dad downstairs. He loves his barbeque, his culinary skills, his back deck, kitchen, house, dog, and his neighbourhood where all his domestics take place within his "Republic of East Vancouver." He squeezes in chats with his neighbours between lawn cutting and hedge trimming, but when I'm cycling past his house on the way to my studio, I can't help but notice the other Ian silhouetted through the window of his refuge, sitting behind his touch-screen or playing a few rifts on his guitar in his backyard studio. It was a garage he renovated himself. I saw him in carpentry mode, stuffing bundles and bundles of insulation into the walls, floor, and ceiling for the noise and climate outside. No one can interrupt his thoughts when he's in there because no one can find him there. It doesn't look as iconic as Malcolm Lowry's squatter's shack, but it's a very clever disguise camouflaged into his perfectly domestic neighbourhood. It's Ian's command central where he warriors-up to take on his topics of empire, nationhood, the Métis, cultural homogenization, consumerism, technological change, the commoditization of education, Hegel's influence in Canada, and countless other topics.

One summer evening we were sitting with Ian and Viviana on their deck, surrounded by big cherry trees. We'd finished dinner and I indulged in a small glass of liqueur and a cookie whose ingredients included bits of green foliage. Nothing happened for the longest time, then, much to my amazement, I saw a massive tree emerging out of Ian's head: there was a script of his subjects written all over the insides of its branches like a mediaeval illumination of the tree of life.

My perspective of Ian may have been surrealistically altered, but it was a subconscious vision connecting the breadth of his topics with the beautiful trees that surround him.

Occasionally I've read books that I've found truly life changing. I'll offer them to Ian when we get together. He holds unfamiliar books like they might hold water. He looks like he's squeezing out the words, scanning the contents, perusing a few paragraphs, then he'll push them aside to assess later or sometimes react to the authors with complete contempt. One evening I made the serious mistake of offering him Michael Ignatieff's *The Rights Revolution*. Surprisingly, that went over like a hailstorm on a family picnic. It's an unpredictable game, like sliding food towards a suspicious animal, then standing well back to watch what happens.

It's all worth the risk, though; occasionally my offers are rewarded with genuine appreciation for a book that informed his current line of thinking, such as Joanne Drake-Terry's book *The Same as Yesterday*, a chronicle of genocide perpetrated against the Interior Salish people of Lillooet. I'm a friend of the author and her husband, Grand-Chief and sculptor Saul Terry.

Unlike most people I've lent books to, Ian always returns them, regardless of whether they're good or bad.

Throughout my teaching years I'd hold year-end critiques during our annual "Graduation Exhibition" at the university. In the interest of exposing students to informed and objective opinions, I've always invited a guest artist, except for the year I invited Ian. I thought a philosopher would shed an interesting interdisciplinary perspective on their work. Ian was reticent at first, but with a few stouts and some well-timed prying, I got him to commit. The resulting dialogue with my students reassured my suspicions that Ian's shift from the philosophy classroom to the sculpture studio would be seamless. The ideas students were negotiating through their work were related; it was just the means of communication through materiality that was different.

Another reason I thought Ian would be a good analyst for studio art is that he's intrigued by the intense degree of technique involved in the execution of a sculptural idea. As a writer he understands that concept and skill are more than casually related: their influence on each other is what makes things work. Anyone who gets that also sees the arrogance of class distinctions between art and craft, conceptualizing and the physical act of making. I also thought he'd be unbiased as he's free of prejudice and loyalties to art genres and immune to art politics.

One of my students, a former social worker, was exhibiting an installation of life-sized homeless people she cast in shredded paper and stuffed in garbage cans. Ian recognized that her piece was very literal, but rather than exposing that shortcoming, he nurtured her forward, suggesting she should never give up her pursuit of humanist content. He didn't want her to be discouraged, because it wasn't her empathy for the subject that fell short. To Ian, there's no reason why social and political content can't be integral to a well-resolved concept, especially when you bury your metaphors deep within the work.

I remember showing Ian an essay I wrote for the *Vancouver Sun* to defend the sculptural legacy of the late Haida artist Bill Reid. I took on the role of criticizing a foundation that was established in Reid's name. In their early stages they were planning dubious, digitally resized bronze editions of his monumental bronzes. The situation was complicated by an earlier dirty-laundry-style article about the artist, written by Jane O'Hara, in *Maclean's* magazine. Ian said he thought there were some really good ideas in my article because I was at the centre of it, having worked as Reid's studio sculptor throughout the 1980s. Ian said the ideas we choose can be important, but it is the ideas that choose us that are really important. He thought I should rewrite my piece by starting from where it ended. To him, the half- posthumous conversation I was having with this complicated mentor, who died in possession of his defences, is an excellent place to relaunch my story. This tactic appears to be Ian's device to dig deeper as a philosopher, writer, and educator. He sees plateaus as places to launch from, to delve much further into the subject.

I beat Ian to retirement as I was fired from Capilano University along with 35 of my colleagues. I thought life would slow down, but things seem to be speeding up with more studio time, activism, and house repairs. Our kids are grown up now; they're all doing fascinating things we never could. Golda and Mika are chasing cats together in the sky, and now Stella and Lupin are the new four-legged family members.

Ian has always spoken of his solo hikes in the woods, those sacred places of rejuvenation where ideas wander down unknown paths and real thinking takes place. The best thing I can say to Ian in his new role is, *take a hike*. We'll fire up the barbeque at sundown.

October 7, 2018

Ian Angus, by George Rammell

DRAWING ON PAPER, 30 X 65 CM, JULY 2018

Chapter 3

Sketch of a Poem for Ian Angus

Stephen Collis

I

It's not a matter of what we think
so much as it's what *thinks us*

Great blue heron / monkey tree
coastal junk and westerly wind

Slide of the author in
a forest on the screen

Who sees all beings in her own self
and herself in all beings loses fear

No arrows are seen in time's flight
but birds fall to the earth just the same

Years ago I read Neruda's *Memoirs*
on a fishing boat at dusk by the pier

Simply wanting to make the invisible visible—
structures / ideologies / drives and drivers

2

Like willows drying up
this is boundless

Trees tapping at windows
trying to get in

I could give you words
but then what would I have?

The bath running all night
the soaked carpet and sagging drapes

Waves lapping at the insides
and the growing things left out

In a dry wind on an odd night
ripples running through words as they turn

Send me no flowers of evil
send me no hourglass of hate

3

Desire to tenderly map all our failures
for which Emily sends her love

Russians in red October
send their love

Ancient Greeks alone on sad islands longing
send their love

Our theme is building and has vista:
time not an arrow but a recurring spiral

I see the past just ahead
the future was fine

Shots at the clocks in their towers
marked the beginning of the uprising

Then we can parse the new identities
howling in the bones of an electric face

4

Doesn't it honestly come to / love?
the chemical seas stars and cells

That all springs up as
writing not thinking

Is what love is / is energy
is profound instabilities

Of the project / life / doubt
recurs so / as dead bees do

The book is what we make—
the inside

Remains hidden inside
as springs in the language do

What one reads is still unwritten
a tower of unsung song

5

What one knows is
the utter fallibility of one's self

And beauty is what continues
by folding back into itself

Magnets / a lantern moon / sound
crumpled buildings climbing into trees

Leaps up ladders and opens
onto fields and scrubland and streams

This fact that time is
a continuum

Which the poet alone
practises the bending of

So a spiral starts out again
from the key in the lock in the wind

Part II
Canadian Studies

Chapter 4

Rethinking Canadian Studies through Emergent Publics

Susan Pell

Introduction

This paper considers Ian Angus's contribution to the field of Canadian Studies, particularly the English-Canadian intellectual tradition, and how his concept of "emergent publics" contributes to a rethinking of Canadian political culture. For Angus, emergent publics arise within social movements and point to people seeking inclusion of new issues and identities within the political processes that have the potential to create and renew democratic institutions. The concept of emergent publics not only changes the relationship between social movements and institutions, it also emphasizes democracy as an ongoing practice that requires participation and engagement with a plurality of others with different traditions and varying responses to questions of the "good life." I suggest that understanding Angus's concept of emergent publics can shed light on his approach to Canadian Studies. By placing emergent publics and social movements at the centre of political life, Angus inverts the more conventional approach in Canadian Studies that focuses on state institutions. More specifically, Angus approaches the English-Canadian intellectual tradition through a thinking from the periphery. It is a political and philosophical intervention that seeks to open a discursive space that privileges a plurality of traditions. Politically, his turn to social movements decentres the state within political culture and aligns the agenda of Canadian Studies with those on the margins. Philosophically, Angus utilizes Canada, which he sees as uniquely placed because of its history of dependency and the ongoing necessity to negotiate identity and difference within its political culture, to reconceive the relationship between the particular and universal through a critique of empire. His post-imperial rethinking of English Canada is not just academic, however.[1] I argue that across his work in Canadian Studies, Angus approaches philosophy as a task, adding his voice to public discourses and political projects.

Emergent Publics: A Radical Approach to Canadian Democracy

Democracy is a process, not a result. To confuse democracy with institutional arrangements is not only to put the cart before the horse, it is to miss the essence of the process altogether—which is movement and creativity, the desire for change, for inclusion.[2]

Emergent Publics: Social Movements and Democracy is an extended essay published in 2001 in which Angus brings his philosophical thinking to the question of democracy. Democracy, for Angus, is a way of life as self-government, where those who are affected by a decision should be part of the decision-making process. Publics are intrinsic to this view of democracy. Through publics, groups of citizens identify and define the common problems; introduce new actors and issues into public discussions; and evaluate, transform, or potentially create public institutions. For Angus, social movements are critical to the formation of publics as they are the means through which citizens voice their concerns.[3] Through the internal deliberative processes and practices of social movements, publics clarify for themselves what the problems are and how these might be solved; with these critical discourses, publics then participate within larger public spheres.[4] Social movements thus perform two public functions: they are spaces in which issues and identities are constructed, and they are sites from where the publicity of issues is disseminated to the broader political culture. In principle, interactions between multiple publics create communities that address questions of what kind of world we want to live in and how to act to make that world possible; and ideally, as a result, a common language and civic identity emerge within the political culture that is rooted in a diversity of experiences and traditions.[5]

By addressing debates about democracy through the perspective of social movements, Angus argues against institutional and procedural understandings of politics, seeing instead that democracy is dynamic and an ongoing process driven by the collective actions of citizens. In the place of institutional democracy, he advocates for an active notion of "radical democracy" that is generated and expanded through the activities of social movements in the public sphere. He explains: "When understood radically, democracy is about the processes of public decision-making to which economic, social and cultural institutions must be subjected in order to be legitimate and binding upon citizens. Such a radical concept of democracy is concerned to *judge* social, economic and political institutions, not presuppose their legitimacy."[6]

Radical democracy shifts the centre of power from institutions to citizens: the state is beholden to citizens, and it is citizens who set the political agenda and evaluate the legitimacy of public institutions. Moreover, social movements are positioned as the innovative force of democracy, being sources of newness in terms of contemporary political issues, practices, and institutions. By moving private experiences into public discourse, they motivate (and demand) institutions to change, helping to keep them responsive to citizens and to extend democratic participation.[7] Angus explains: "We might say that they express the failures of the institutional structure. In this way, social movements criticize the forms of exclusion that the public sphere used to accept, and propose more inclusive practices and ideas. For this reason, social movements are important to genuine participation in democratic institutions."[8]

To this end, social movements perform a diagnostic function in contemporary society.[9] As Angus states, "Social movements embody the lively and creative responses of the public to problems that movements define and to which they propose solutions."[10] Angus's approach to democracy challenges the conventional approach to political culture by decentring the state as the site and authorizer of politics. Social movements are, instead, privileged as the creative and emergent side of democracy and the guarantor of participatory decision making in democratic institutions.[11] As such, democracy is not fixed within institutional arrangements but is a movement towards greater inclusion.

Placing social movements at the centre of understanding democracy, Angus provides both a methodology for studying political culture and a task for civically minded intellectuals. As a methodology, *Emergent Publics* encourages a perspective of politics from the margins, the outside, the periphery, as it is from here that one can see the current failures in democracy and possible alternatives. A view from the periphery renders power at the centre visible (particularly the trick of making the status quo seem natural and inevitable) and reminds one that difference, experimentation, and change are possible, and often necessary. Starting from movements on the periphery thus questions the assumed legitimacy of public institutions and decentres the privilege of dominant groups. Such an approach is particularly important for Canadian Studies, an academic field that takes the country (nation-state) as its site of inquiry and which can easily default to a focus on the state and public institutions, forgetting that these (for example, libraries and health care) are oftentimes legacies of past social movements. Moreover, approaching Canadian Studies from the periphery lays the foundation for Angus's rethinking of identity and difference—a project that focuses much of his work on English Canada, and which he believes can help to place plurality and mutual respect at the heart of public life. He thus sets himself the task of contributing to a reimagination of the political culture and articulating a discourse to ground a more democratic and just future for Canada.

Canadian Studies: Institutional and Movement Approaches

"The point is to turn the tradition. If one attempts to escape it, one is more likely simply to repeat it."[12]

Angus's work is deeply committed to engaging with English-Canadian social and political thought in order to rethink discursive traditions particular to Canada in such a way as to open space for new forms of cultural and political relations. It is a philosophical and political project. He sees English Canada uniquely positioned to reimagine, and possibly enact differently, the relationship between identity and difference, which, in privileging the dominant, has too long caused violence and suffering in Canada and elsewhere. Borders, peripheries, and locative thinking are some of the analytic devices Angus uses to critique empire, to which Canada has been subjected and which it has perpetuated and maintained.[13] Angus is not alone in this interrogation: these are the axes around which much of Canadian Studies rotates. As Sourayan Mookerjea, Imre Szeman, and Gail Faurschou, in their collection of essays of Canadian cultural studies, explain, "cultural studies in Canada [is] an exploration of the multiple passages *between empires*—an exploration that turns critically on the contradictions of national identity, difference and belonging, opportunity, and oppression."[14] Borders, space, and movement are key concepts with which to analyze Canada, and debates about sovereignty, multiculturalism, and globalization have been of central concern. Angus has both contributed to, and provoked, these debates.[15] Perhaps more significantly, he has also been critical in shifting the ground on which to understand Canada from institutions to social movements.[16]

Institutional Approaches: Canadian Deference and the Absent Nation

Central to many studies of Canadian political culture has been grappling with the lasting effects of (British, French, American) empires on the formation of the country and its people and, increasingly more so, Canada's own settler colonialism. One such tradition that began in the 1960s coalesced around a "tory" theme as scholars attempted to understand Canadian political culture, particularly relative to the liberalism of the United States. "Toryism," here, indicates a more communitarian form of politics that is also marked by conservatism and deference to authority. Pivotal in this account, Gad Horowitz argued that Canada's uniqueness in North America was defined by a liberalism with a significant "tory touch."[17] He lists the characteristics of toryism as corporate, organic, and collectivist, as opposed to liberalism's rationalism and egalitarianism. As he states, "It is not simply their emphasis on loyalty to the crown and to the British connection but also a touch of the authentic tory aura—traditionalism, elitism, the strong state, and so on."[18] In not having a single ideology, as in US liberalism, the Canadian political party system, as has been argued by Horowitz, was seen to be more diverse and tolerant of multiple ideologies, and allowed for the development of socialism within political institutions.[19] Others have suggested that toryism has left Canadian political culture with a lingering elitism and rigid social stratification,[20] self- imposed censorship and deference to authority,[21] and complicity between the state and corporate elites.[22] The "tory touch," much debated in the mid-twentieth century and beyond, thus points not only to the communitarian aspects of Canadian political culture but also to its underbelly, that of an authoritarian and elitist state that limits critical public debate. Currents of this discourse continue within critiques of the Canadian policy of multiculturalism, which are described as marginalizing and silencing the public and shoring up the power of the already privileged.[23]

A parallel discourse, equally interested in the mutedness of Canadian political culture, describes Canada as an "absent nation," lacking an organic civil society. Conceptualized in "Technological Nationalism," Maurice Charland argues that the dominant anglophone discourse has been a product of the Canadian state. This official rhetoric sought to create commonality through public institutions (for example, Canadian Pacific Railway and the Canadian Broadcasting Corporation) as a means to constitute a nation that would legitimate its own extension of power.[24] This national identity was created without participation of the people, hence Canada is an "absent nation."[25] Charland explains: "Canada is a country whose *national* experience follows its state experience. Consequently, a Canadian identity and culture would be rooted in the state itself, for it is through the state that Canada's populace is constituted as a people."[26] Seen through the directives of the state, there is no self-constituted "people," and the state itself contains the political.

This thesis about the centralizing power of the state and the weakness of the Canadian people extends to Michael Dorland and Charland's *Law, Rhetoric, and Irony in the Formation of Canadian Civil Culture*.[27] They describe five performative modes within Canadian civil culture, as expressed within the realm of law, forming the country's constitutional history. All emphasize the authoritarian image of the state. Of the performative mode in the nineteenth and twentieth centuries, they write, "This legal-administrative style attempted to constitute from above a Canadian civil society in the image of the central state, in a forcing of cultural nationalism."[28] Further,

> One might also say that in such endeavours as the attempt to micromanage into being a form of civil society that was really a political creation of the centralizing state of law, the weight of history was more favourable to arbitrariness and undemocratic methods than the contrary. The apolitical public sphere inherited from the French regime, the British mode of rule by parliamentary oligarchy, the fractured legal culture, part-French, part-English, that was never permitted to form a new whole—all of these institutional antecedents helped constitute a civil culture that would seem to be at best one of public antagonism, and at worst one of resentful withdrawal in the private realm, with an endless nursing of particularistic wounds and grievances.[29]

As the most recent performative mode, the legal-administrative style is described by Dorland and Charland as the official, and dominant, rhetorical style and one that prevents public culture and criticism. In this analysis, Canada has a weak participatory civic culture, and one that is turned away from the public. The only alternative to this state-controlled rhetoric, they locate in Canadian irony. Irony, a concurrent performative mode to legal-administrative, was a means to challenge and subvert the tradition of deference to authority. Dorland and Charland explain that "irony can become a lever *into* civil discourse, allowing those who have been excluded from the public sphere (e.g. women, First Peoples, and so on) to ironize official discourse and by mocking its civility (i.e., both nonviolently and playfully) forcing it to live up to its manifest content."[30] Dorland and Charland thus recognize the voice of the marginalized and highlight Canadians' frustration with the dominant state of affairs. Irony was used to expose inconsistency between principles and practices within official political culture; however, it needs to be emphasized that irony is not the same as demanding change. Irony's reactive and referential nature keeps the focus of analysis within the domain of official discourse.

Dorland and Charland's contribution to the understanding of Canadian civil culture is substantial, yet it reiterates a dominant thesis in studies of Canadian political culture: the strength of the state and the weakness of the Canadian public. Their work on Canadian civil culture repeats and perpetuates an analysis of political culture that takes the state, and public institutions (in this case, law), as the starting point to understand publics within Canada. In doing so, they view political and civil culture through the state's gaze. This in effect blinds Dorland and Charland to sites of discourse not bound to the official culture of the nation-state, and to factors outside of the state that agitate for change. Analyzing the state as the de facto site of political culture is thus not benign, neither epistemologically nor politically. It limits the ability to view and understand emergent publics in Canada and obscures the existence of political cultures beyond the state and public institutions.

While it is understandable that much of Canadian Studies has focused on the state and public institutions, analytically it risks reducing Canadian publics to institutions, and, furthermore, politically it risks naturalizing the centrality and legitimacy of the state-centric status quo. Angus's focus on social movements as a means to understand political culture is thus significant within Canadian Studies, and necessary to decentre the state's privileged position. Using a social movement perspective does not ignore the state or contradict studies that find deference within Canadian political culture. However, it pivots to look at action at the periphery; and, in not seeing the centre as fixed, it is interested in movement at the borders and agents of change.

Angus thus reads Dorland and Charland's account of the various performative modes not as those of civil culture but of empire.[31] Specifically, Angus criticizes the lack of attention to what is outside of official discourse and draws out its effect. He explains, "When it is not investigated how the limit that defines official civil discourse is drawn, both the outside motive for 'progress' and the 'official-ness' of official culture become invisible."[32] He further argues, "Canadian culture extends beyond official civil culture characterized by tradition and continuity to the experiences on the land which motivated a break with tradition. History represents the official and conservative component of Canadian culture, while geography, traversal and inhabitation of the land, is the place of its disruptive, radical component."[33]

Angus calls attention to radical practices in Canadian political culture that are obscured when discussions remain centred on state-based politics, and emphasizes a tradition of political and social struggles located in particular places that inspire resistance and revolution against official civil culture. Moreover, he criticizes analyses of official culture that treat it as equivalent to Canadian civil cultures, arguing instead that studies need to account for impetuses of institutional change and to recognize the relationship between the inside and outside of political cultural, both of which demand going beyond the state to the political activities and social identities practised on the margins by emergent publics.

Movement Approach: Locative Thinking

Angus's work in English-Canadian social and political thought aims to reorient the tradition, and the public discourses rooted in it, toward greater possibilities of social justice in Canada. To do so, he looks within the "tory" thesis for alternative motivations and conclusions. Starting from foundational texts in Canadian Studies, Angus turns the "tory" tradition emanating from Harold Innis and George Grant in a different direction: not as suggestive of public deference but as essentially a critique of empire.

Emphasizing their *red* toryism, Angus links their thinking to left nationalism—a movement to protect Canada from the "destructive individualistic and polarizing effects of capitalism."[34] During the postwar era up until the signing of the North American Free Trade Agreement, discourses of English-Canadian left nationalism revolved around critiques of economic dependency (drawing from Innis's staple theory) and demands for cultural autonomy (drawing from Grant's emphasis on the "love of one's own"),[35] and served to mobilize groups on the left to see the potential of the Canadian state to restrict the power of transnational corporations. Angus reads the red tory tendency towards conservatism as a demand to preserve Canada's particularity and autonomy, locating within it a more radical discourse of conservationism. He explains, "If we think of the well-documented conservative component of Canadian culture, a tendency toward deference to authority, [my] argument may be thought of as an attempt to shift the focus of deference in the national tradition from political authority to a natural sublime and a plurality of cultures with internal integrity."[36]

Angus highlights shared themes of conservatism in English-Canadian thought and preservation in social movements (for example, ecological, feminist, Indigenous), and, in connecting the two, emphasizes the latter's defence of the alterity and a maintenance of difference and plurality.[37] This interpretation brings together dominant discourses in Canadian Studies with the thinking of social movements, allowing Angus to make space for "the prospects [of] tying Canadian Studies to an emergent radical democratic and ecological politics of social movements."[38] Such a reorientation of the discourse also extends to the possibility of an alternative, more radical and democratic, formation for English-Canadian identity.

Angus's reworking of English-Canadian social and political thought within Canadian Studies thus goes even further away from affirming the importance of the Canadian state or traditional forms of authority. He takes the broader tendency to think about conservation and particularity of place in Canadian discourses as an opportunity to decentre the importance of the state, and to even call its very legitimacy into question. In a "turn of the tradition," he explains, "if an argument for the continued existence of Canada must appeal to the rights of particularity, why cannot the rights of particularity, as instantiated in the cities, regions or elsewhere, be appealed to against the Canadian nation-state? Why, indeed, is the Canadian nation-state any better an example of particularity than the many and diverse local attachment within it, or the other 'localities' that have been articulated by social movements?"[39]

Angus takes the tendency in Canada of claiming rights of particularity against external forces as precedence for groups within Canada to demand rights against impositions by the state: in effect, legitimating their claims to autonomy. This questions the conventional location of rights. The Canadian nation-state may be one site in which to seek defence of particularity (against transnational corporations, the US, et cetera); however, it is not inherently the privileged site of collective national identity within the body politics and it is not only rights as sanctioned by the state that one might want to claim or seek recourse to. Rather, Angus repositions the nation-state as one among a plurality of identities, whose legitimacy as a common foundation must be established rather than assumed.

Towards a Canadian Public Philosophy: Particularity, Universality, and Peace

There is continuity across Angus's work in Canadian Studies that brings into question assumed forms of privilege to disrupt binaries and sees power from the perspective of the marginalized in order to move towards greater possibilities of respect for difference and plurality of traditions in Canada. It is an approach that ties public philosophy to social movements.[40] He explains in "Identity and Deference":

> My formulation of identity-difference was to undermine the supposed independence and centrality of the first term [in the metaphors: self-Other, human-nature, language-silence]—identity, self, human, language—in favour of an argument that these terms were dependent on the second,

> supposed derived and inferior terms—difference, Other, nature, and silence.... Analysis begins from the traditionally denigrated side to show both the constitution of the supposedly independent centre and also the possibility of a more respectful relation between them. It is this political and philosophical possibility that *A Border Within* attempted to sustain.[41]

Like the inversion of the relationship between institutions and movements articulated in *Emergent Publics* that privileged citizens over institutions, Angus unsettles fundamental Western binaries that maintain inequality, legitimate injustices, and perpetuate violence. While the political project is radical democracy and greater equality and justice, the crux of Angus's intervention in Canadian Studies is a post-imperial philosophical rethinking of the universal through the particular grounded in a critique of empire, or, as he describes it, "trying to *think* here." For Angus, Canada is uniquely positioned for this task because of its continuing history of dependency and plurality of traditions. Located as it is on the global periphery, it offers a critical view of the centre.

A critique of empire, Angus argues, is necessarily a critique of centrism that can best be formulated from the periphery. Centrism involves the tendency to subsume diverse experiences within an explanatory scheme of the universal, where there is a slide from "imperial instance to theoretical universality,"[42] missing much that is different in the process. In contrast to the self-referentiality of imperial thinking, universality grounded in justice and democracy (and not in domination and violence) must begin from the periphery and the experience of dependency and inhabitation of place. As Angus explains, "a return to concrete and particular experiences does not negate universality, but opens the possibility that a genuine universality might emerge through the displacement of centrisms."[43] A critique of centrism cannot happen in the abstract. It requires thinking from a place. "A border within" is one means by which Angus thinks from a place and sees the possibility of repositioning the centre-periphery relationship to maintain internal plurality and the equality and integrity of the Other. A border operates as a relationship between places, or more specifically between "localities." "Locative thinking" from the periphery, as a challenge to abstract thinking from the centre, offers an alternative route to universality through the concrete that is based on maintaining particularity and creating dialogue between traditions.

As Angus describes it:

"Location requires a placing *in relation to* other places. Thus, it is not only a matter of connection, but *the connection as it emerges from and defines a specific place....* Locative thinking dwells in the moment in which connection is made to other places beginning from here. It thinks through Canadian problems as a practice that forges non-administrative relations to other places. These relations define our location in a larger world.... [It] can be described as *the thinking of the particular as it leads outwards to other particulars*."[44]

The universal is reached through movements between, and beyond, these particulars, from the specific to the common, as established in dialogue and negotiation. Such locative thinking contextualizes Angus's mode of public philosophy that begins in engagement with the dominant discourses of Canadian political culture and social and political thought in English Canada (that is, what is particular to here), and from there articulates ethical propositions for a more just, equal, and democratic society. It is only through an immersion in the thinking of here, of understanding the particular and concrete experiences of English Canada, of being a global periphery and of peripheries internal to it, that one can both critique the centrism of empire and locate universality in renewed critical discourse.

Angus thus offers a "post-imperial" English-Canadian philosophy that is also a political project of self-rule.[45] He writes in *Identity and Justice*,

> My unfolding argument in this text is that the secret of English Canada is the unofficial dream of self-rule at the periphery that unfolds in tandem with the critique of empire. It is kept secret through the perpetuation of the lie that the empire, then the nations-state, sets the neutral rules whereby its parts interact. The tendency of official culture is to cover up its opposite in a land-based ethic, to substitute historical continuity for the break represented through inhabitation of the land. The task for critical interpretation of English-Canadian culture is the development of a philosophy of independent parts through a conception of universality that does not subsume parts by giving them the rule, but subordinates the rule itself to a negotiation between the parts.[46]

This is universality as articulated from the Canadian periphery that favours specificity over abstraction and the recognition of interdependency. It is an ongoing dialogue between identity and difference (self and Other) that is not determined by the centre/state (or by oneself). Rather, it is founded upon and practised as connections between localities (particularities) that seek forms of association based on principles of mutual respect and radical democracy, where no one group sets the rules or controls the game. Angus states that a dream of self-rule thus requires "de-centred, political discourse and a plurality of interacting public spheres."[47] And, of course, self-rule depends on emergent publics, working to keep institutions responsive to the needs of citizens and reflective of a continuously negotiated civic identity.

Conclusion

I have suggested in this chapter that Angus's concept of "emergent public" can be read as a concept, methodology, and task, helping to explain his intervention into Canadian Studies and Canadian political culture. As a concept, "emergent publics" emphasizes the participatory side of democracy, where social movements are valued over institutions, as it is in the collective actions of citizens that institutions are imagined, created, criticized, and transformed. In this sense, emergent publics evaluate the legitimacy of public institutions and are responsible for their renewal, in effect, making social movements the drivers of democracy. Emanating from this concept of emergent publics comes a methodology that is cognizant of the political effect of knowledge-making practices, and, in the study of political culture, seeks to decentre the state in order to render visible its subordination on the outside, and also its dependency on it. As a methodology, then, it begins analysis from social movements, borders, and peripheries as a means to understand relations of privilege and power, and to challenge it. Emergent publics illuminates Angus's approach to English-Canadian social and political thought as a philosophical and political task to take seriously philosophy as a way of life. This task demands one actively engage with one's traditions, that one risks contributing their understandings to public discourses, and, for Angus, one seeks to bring into the world greater justice and equality. Taking up this task brings together philosophy and politics, and can be seen in Angus's work to critically rethink central tenants of Western philosophy (for example, universality, identity, difference) from the Canadian periphery, and to offer a post-imperial critique of empire that replaces domination, oppression, and exploitation of people and the environment with self-rule in the context of mutual respect, open-ended and meaningful dialogue, and non-violence.

The influence of emergent publics on Angus's approach to Canadian Studies does not only go in one direction, however. Within Angus's approach to Canadian Studies, one finds the motivations for action, for being a public intellectual: attachment to place and love of one's own. Seeking the good, seeking equality and justice, requires speaking from a specific place and moving from its traditions to engage with the specificity of other traditions. Through valuing the particularity and plurality of different ways of life, we can work together to better our world. Angus's lasting legacy, then, has been one of encouraging others to follow a path that starts thinking from where one is, to (first and foremost) be reflective of our own traditions and assumptions, to always look for what is excluded and on the outside, and to consider how this has been used to justify the power of the privileged at the expense of the marginalized. In place of this, he asks that we think instead from the periphery, we interrogate borders, and we challenge forms of centrism. Angus thus finds in the study of Canadian political culture a hopefulness in an ever-present possibility of peace.

Notes to Chapter 4:

1 Angus's work in Canadian Studies has predominantly focused on "English Canada," because, as he explains, it is the group that he belongs to, and discussions of identity require a reflexive element, so speaking about and from the group to which one belongs. He states, "The practice of critique implies an involvement in that which is criticized. I cannot investigate other identities in the Canadian nation-state—or embroiled with it but perhaps not *in* it, like the First Nations—with the same understanding of lived history and emotional attachment as that of English Canada, and, indeed, this is the only identity of the Canadian nations-state from which I can write as a participant, one for whom its destiny is also my own. This does not mean that one should never speak of others—as one must, of course—or that external perspectives are never relevant, but rather that genuine critique is, in the first place, self-critique. Self-critique presupposes a particular identity and a participation in that identity from which one begins to reflect. I admit to a suspicion of any discussion of identity that is not reflexive in this sense, that is not about one's own identity, since it would seem to slide into a classification, and perhaps even demonization, of others which is eminently to be avoided." See: Ian Angus, *Identity and Justice* (Toronto: University of Toronto Press, 2008), 10.

2 Ian Angus, *Emergent Publics: An Essay on Social Movements and Democracy* (Winnipeg: Arbeiter Ring Publishing, 2001), 48.

3 Ibid., 59.

4 Angus draws here from the work of Nancy Fraser's discussion of subaltern counter-publics. See: Nancy Fraser, "Rethinking the Public Sphere: A Contribution to the Critique of Actually Existing Democracy," *Social Text* 25, no. 26 (1990): 56–80.

5 Angus, *Emergent Publics*, 35. Angus develops ideas of creating a common civic identity in Canada regarding difference and a plurality of traditions across a number of works. See, for example: Angus, *Identity and Justice*; Ian Angus, "Identity and Deference: A Border Within 15 Years On," *International Journal of Canadian Studies* 50 (2014): 325–46. In the former, he calls for "associated federations," which would be based on treaties that embrace difference and respect and preserve particularity.

6 Angus, *Emergent Publics*, 10.

7 Ibid., 46–49.

8 Ibid., 49.

9 Ibid., 58.

10 Ibid., 48.

11 Ibid., 72.

12 Angus, "Identity and Deference," 339.

13 See, respectively: Ian Angus, *A Border Within: National Identity, Cultural Plurality, and Wilderness* (Montreal and Kingston: McGill-Queen's University Press, 1997); Angus, *Identity and Justice*; Ian Angus, "Locality and Universalization: Where Is Canadian Studies?" *Journal of Canadian Studies* 35, no. 2 (Fall 2000): 15–32.

14 Sourayan Mookerjea, Imre Szeman, and Gail Faurschou, "Between Empires: On Cultural Studies in Canada," in *Canadian Cultural Studies: A Reader*, eds. Sourayan Mookerjea, Imre Szeman, and Gail Faurschou (Durham: Duke University Press, 2009), 15.

15 See, for example: Richard Day, "Can There Be a Postcolonial Multiculturalism? A Response to Ian Angus," *International Journal of Canadian Studies* 26 (2002): 127–32.

16 Others in the mid-1990s, such as Bill Carroll, also shifted focus onto social movements within Canada. See: William Carroll, ed., *Organizing Dissent: Contemporary Social Movements in Theory and Practice, Studies in the Politics of Counter-Hegemony* (Aurora, ON: Garamond Press, 1992). A social movement perspective in Canadian Studies has become much more common since. See, for example: Richard Day, *Gramsci Is Dead: Anarchist Currents in the Newest Social Movements* (Toronto: Between the Lines, 2005); Susan Pell, "Mobilizing Urban Publics, Imagining Democratic Possibilities: Reading the Politics of Urban Redevelopment in Discourses of Gentrification and Revitalization," *Cultural Studies* 28, no. 1 (2014): 29–48; Catriona Sandilands, "Domestic

Politics: Multiculturalism, Wilderness, and the Desire for Canada," *Space and Culture* 4, no. 5 (2001): 169–85.

17 Gad Horowitz, *Canadian Labour in Politics* (Toronto: University of Toronto Press, 1968), 7.

18 Ibid., 20.

19 Ibid., 6, 16–17.

20 Seymour Martin Lipset, *The First New Nation: The United States in Historical and Comparative Perspective* (New York: Basic Books Inc., 1963), 87, 199, 270.

21 Edgar Friedenberg, *Deference to Authority: The Case of Canada* (White Plains, NY: M. E. Sharpe Inc., 1980), 21, 131.

22 Leo Panitch, "The Role and Nature of the Canadian State," in *The Canadian State: Political Economy and Political Power*, ed. Leo Panitch (Toronto: University of Toronto Press, 1977), 3–27.

23 See, for example: Himani Bannerji, *The Dark Side of the Nation: Essays on Multiculturalism, Nationalism, and Gender* (Toronto: University of Toronto Press, 2000).

24 Maurice Charland, "Technological Nationalism," *Canadian Journal of Political and Social Theory* 10, nos. 1–2 (1986): 203.

25 Ibid., 198.

26 Ibid., 217; emphasis in the original.

27 Michael Dorland and Maurice Charland, *Law, Rhetoric, and Irony in the Formation of Canadian Civil Culture* (Toronto: University of Toronto Press, 2002).

28 Ibid., 309.

29 Ibid., 309–10.

30 Ibid., 313.

31 Ian Angus, "Louis Riel and English Canadian Political Thought," Simon Fraser University, accessed February 27, 2019, http://www.sfu.ca/personal/iangus/riel.pdf.

32 Ibid., 3.

33 Ibid., 5.

34 Angus, "Locality and Universalization," 17.

35 Angus, *A Border Within*, 27–28.

36 Angus, "Identity and Deference," 338.

37 Angus, *A Border Within*, 8.

38 Angus, "Locality and Universalization," 16.

39 Ibid., 19.

40 Ibid., 16. Elsewhere, Angus describes this task in the context of national philosophy. He explains that to "address in a public voice issues of widespread concern ... one must address it [the national style of philosophy] and root one's divergences and critiques in the same soil.... To the extent that philosophy is not a formal-logical matrix but an articulation of human experience, it engages with such historical materials and speaks to the common life of a people." See: Angus, "Identity and Deference," 329. This suggests there is a critical link for Angus among his work in Canadian Studies, his training as a philosopher, and his activism as a public intellectual.

41 Angus, "Identity and Deference," 329–30.

42 Angus, *Identity and Justice*, 9.

43 Ibid.

44 Angus, "Locality and Universalization," 24; italics in the original.

45 Angus, *Identity and Justice*, 8.

46 Ibid., 12.

47 Ibid., 65.

Chapter 5

Ian Angus's *A Border Within*, a Generation Later

Robert Schwartzwald

Ian Angus and I were young professors together in the 1980s at the University of Massachusetts Amherst, he in the department of Communication and I as the newly hired specialist of Québec literature and culture in the department of French and Italian Studies. Both of us participated in the Canadian Studies program of the Five Colleges consortium that, in addition to UMass, includes three of the United States's most venerated four-year liberal arts colleges—Amherst, Mount Holyoke, and Smith—and the relatively new, experimental Hampshire College. Surprisingly—at least to me—there was an established interest in Canada in the Five Colleges. I discovered a professor of theatre at Smith who adored Michel Tremblay; a historian of colonial and nineteenth-century New England and Québec at Mount Holyoke; and another historian, John Conway, who directed the Five Colleges Canadian Studies program in the genteel manner of an Ivy League college don—a manner entirely foreign to me and epitomized in his deliberately provocative way of referring to the city on the Bosporus as Constantinople!

Unlike me, Ian had not come to the Five Colleges to teach primarily about Canada, but he did arrive with a strong formation in English-Canadian political philosophy, communications, and dependency theory. In 1990, he published "Crossing the Border" in *an/other Canada*, a special issue of *The Massachusetts Review* guest edited by me. The essay set out to explore "the ground from which Canadian philosophy begins."[1] Seven years later, the essay appeared in revised form as "Maintaining the Border," chapter 5 of Ian's *A Border Within: National Identity, Cultural Plurality, and Wilderness* (1997).

Through the Canadian Studies program, Ian and I were engaging Americans in the aftermath of the 1980 Québec referendum on independence, or "sovereignty-association," as the question would have it.[2] Looking back, the result was not even close—a 60/40 split in favour of the "No" side—but the election of the first Parti Québécois government in 1976 had made Québec, and by extension Canada, *interesting* to its southern neighbour, not to mention the rest of the world. I recall attending, as an observer, the Parti Québécois convention that set the stage for the referendum campaign and meeting prominent journalists from France and *la francophonie*, but also from Britain, the United States, and Latin America. There was a widespread fascination with a nationalist government in North America with a broadly social-democratic program, with leaders who understood independence as completing work in the Americas begun by Simón Bolívar, José de San Martin, George Washington, and Thomas Jefferson, but whose militants were often fonder of citing Frantz Fanon, Che Guevara, and other twentieth-century proponents of decolonization. There were Germans, too, accustomed to thinking of Pierre Trudeau as a champion against resurgent forms of nationalism and, despite their misgivings about Canadian multiculturalism, a cherished ally of what the Germans call "constitutional patriotism."

For them, events in Québec were above all disruptive of the postwar European dreams they had projected upon Canadian federalism.

But the 1980 referendum was mainly disruptive for Canadians. Inside Québec, pro-independence forces greeted the campaign as a celebratory occasion; but for the most part, those on the "No" side saw it as an unnecessary and particularly harmful interruption of their daily lives (in truth, throughout the 1970s they had grown used to living with such "interruptions": the October Crisis, the militant Common Front labour struggles, the campaign for a "McGill français," et cetera). Outside Québec, there was a climate approaching panic as it dawned on political actors and observers alike that the future of the country was at stake. Various commentators in the United States invoked the delusional fear of a second Marxist state on America's doorstep; in 1980, "national independence" still resonated predominantly with "national liberation"—in other words, with Algeria, Cuba, and Vietnam—or at the very least with what was known as the "non-aligned" world. With their feet planted more firmly on the ground, their Canadian counterparts acknowledged the relative vulnerability of the pan-Canadian state to the forceful claims made by Québec independentists. They recognized in terms of both coercion and consent, as Antonio Gramsci would have it, that "Canada" was not in a particularly strong position. As a relatively young country, its sense of self, as distinct from its French and British colonial origins, was only beginning to emerge.

Significant symbolic moves in this direction had been enacted by the federal Liberal government—the "logo-style" maple leaf of the new Canadian flag (1965), which became the country's brand in signage and advertising, the festivities surrounding the Centennial of Confederation in 1967, and a multicultural policy (1971) that "wrote over," or occluded, the restrictive histories of immigration in Canada to reconfigure the nation as the all-welcoming, first post-national nation.

As it turned out, they need not have worried quite so much. In 1980, Trudeau *père* resumed his role as prime minister, adding crucial rhetorical heft to the "No" forces in Québec. The feeling in English Canada was that he owed at least this much. Initially, Trudeau's suspension of civil liberties and his use of the military in the 1970 October Crisis had been greeted with broad approval—only the NDP and its leader Tommy Douglas distinguished themselves by denouncing the War Measures Act as an egregious, opportunistic *coup de théâtre*—but soon enough, the savoured victory against "separatism" turned to ashes. After all, what had the election of the Parti Québécois government in 1976 confirmed, if not that the desire for independence in Québec had only grown?

Beyond the threatening and fatuous discourses of federalist leaders—"You will lose the Rockies!," "No country will trade with you!," "You will never eat an orange again!" (I heard this last canard pitched by a Liberal politician to a group of senior citizens)—Canadians were enlisted to dissuade Québecois from voting "Yes" in efforts that were mainly sentimental in nature, with wounded self-pride at their heart. Conjugal metaphors abounded: "Have I been such a bad spouse? Can we not save this marriage?" The "love rally" held in Montréal just days before the referendum, with Air Canada flying in thousands of supplicants from all over the country, was the most extreme—and, for many in Québec, the most ridiculous—manifestation of this tendency. I recall being struck at the time by the overwhelming, solipsistic refusal to *listen*. Instead, Canadians came to Montréal to *declare* their "love." In retrospect, however, these histrionics revealed how very much Québec still mattered to the ways that English Canadians imagined their nation-state.

The rise of the Parti Québécois, and especially of social militancy in Québec in the 1970s, had led to an acknowledgement of historical grievances among most liberal and progressive Canadians and the need, if not always the actual desire, to address them. Essentially, many on the left in English Canada proposed what Marxists call "economistic measures" to palliate the aggravated forms of capitalist exploitation in Québec—the legacy of lower wages, higher rates of infant mortality and work-related deaths, lower life expectancy, et cetera—as confirmed by the Laurendeau-Dunton "Bi & Bi" (Bilingualism and Biculturalism) Report (1967–1970). Some proposed "alliances" between dependent Canada and super-exploited Québec against US imperialism. What they could not hear was the critique of Canada as itself an imperialist power, as a "Great Nation" with its own forms of chauvinism—Canada as a "prison house of nations," as many on the far left claimed.[3] This was not only because the charge might have seemed offensive, given the self-image that even most progressives had of Canada as an honest broker on the international stage, but inconceivable: How could such a reserved group of people, reluctant to wave the flag and engage in patriotic display, *oppress* anyone, least of all their "own"?

And that's where Ian Angus comes in. While many Canadians who came as visitors to the Five Colleges issued confident pronouncements about Québec's place within Canada, Ian forthrightly acknowledged that his reflections on the state of his country and the challenges it posed to a philosopher interested in having a public impact did not, and could not—yet—account for Québec. In *A Border Within*, Ian specifies that the "ground" for philosophy with which he is concerned was, for the time being, strictly speaking *English* Canadian. In other words, he understood that his project was grounded in, and addressed, the tradition of *English*-Canadian social and political thought but that for it to proceed, it would have to become unfamiliar to itself, that is, to disentangle the philosophical task from a metaphysical being-at-homeness borne by a Canadian mythology at once monadic and cosmic.[4] It would involve rejecting foundational myths even if, paradoxically, these were relatively recent. Defined by Ian as "the holding together of a culture with its origin in unreflective narrative unity," such mythmaking would need to be adjourned in order to make room for a philosophical approach that "begins with homelessness."[5] Canada, Angus recognized, was working hard to construct its "home," but this risked becoming a too-hurried and insufficiently (self-)critical venture: "In calling itself as Canada, [English Canada] has elided the key question of its relations to the others and especially the history of violence whereby the Canadian state, as all other states, was constructed."[6] Here, Angus was explicitly referring to the distinct subaltern positions of First Nations and Québec. In his terms, each was a "content" that could not simply be subsumed as a particularism into a larger, universal entity. Neither was he willing to participate in a growing refrain that, over the decades of the two referendums and the repatriation of the constitution engineered without Québec's signature, regarded Québec as an incorrigible irritant or impediment toward the Rest of Canada's (a term I prefer to "English Canada")[7] *enjoyment* of its newly emerging self-regard as a post-national nation. Angus was skeptical of such claims and took his distance from the way they were weaponized ideologically against Québec: "the temptation—introduced mainly by the postmodern turn in the human sciences—to regard all references to national identity as necessarily repressively homogenizing."[8]

Today, these terms—"First Nations" and "Québec"—sound incommensurate when spoken in the same breath. The colonial violence of the Canadian state and its predecessors toward Canada's Indigenous peoples—First Nations, Métis, and Inuit—is at the urgent heart of much new knowledge production by academics, but "Québec" has shifted as a signifier to occupy a synecdochally singular position in relation to this violence: for many progressive intellectuals in English Canada, the failure of their counterparts in Québec to sufficiently acknowledge their status as inheritors of European settler colonialism means they have also surrendered the right to legitimately defend a Québec national specificity in relation to Canada.

This shift was already part of the background to the inter-referendum conversations Ian and I were having in the 1980s and 1990s. In 1990, two events became emblematic of the new framework for "imagining" Québec in Canada: the Oka Crisis and the rejection of the Meech Lake Accord. The former provided the perfect scenario for those seeking to ascribe a unique racism to Québec: the sorry spectacle of a *de souche* (the semi-ironic term used in Québec to describe native-born Québecers of French- Canadian ancestry) francophone municipality determined to expand its golf course by destroying a pine forest sacred to Indigenous residents; in other words, a distinctly petit-bourgeois, trivial, and "white" use of the land. But the confrontation was especially spectacularized through famous images of Canadian soldiers going toe to toe with Mohawk warriors and the burning in effigy of Indigenous leaders by South Shore suburbanites enraged by delays to their commutes into Montréal because Kahnawake Mohawks were blocking access to bridges in solidarity with the Kanesàtake resistors at Oka. As for the Meech Lake Accord, its takedown is symbolically associated with Elijah Harper, the recently deceased Indigenous member of the Manitoba Legislative Assembly who effectively vetoed its adoption because he did not see why Indigenous people, after hundreds of years of waiting, should see Québec recognized and constitutionally protected as a distinct society while federal policy toward First Nations stubbornly remained a toxic brew of assimilationism and negationism.

Much had changed internationally, too: in the 1960s and 1970s, a generation of modern independentist thinkers in Québec had motivated their political option by invoking the urgent need to move *outward*, not inward; to abandon constraining, ossified versions of identity so as to become an interlocutor among, and within, the community of nations. This was still the age of heroic independences, with the United Nations adding members and flags in front of its New York headquarters at a dizzying speed. In the 1990s, the collapse of the Soviet Union and the struggles that followed during the breakup of Yugoslavia shattered the festive discourse of national liberation. In Bosnia-Hercegovina, imagined as a haven of tolerance—as a model of what in Québec is called *vivre-ensemble*—the library of Sarajevo was deliberately bombed and set ablaze in an attempt to erase the evidence that such forms of coexistence were even possible. Then there was the siege of Sarajevo and its Sniper's Alley, and the mass murder of Muslim boys and men at Srebrenica. Like many others who were unwilling to pronounce nationalism reactionary in its very nature, Angus found himself forthrightly acknowledging that nationalism "is a form of social identity in which violence towards the other seems a permanent possibility. Ethnic identity contains the same threat, and when the two are combined in ethnic nationalism, there seems to be no limits to the terror that can erupt."[9] No wonder, he conceded, that "many thinkers (today) are in retreat from the politics of (national) identity for this reason."[10] In the new millennium, most new flags were raising doubts, not hopes, but Canada presented itself, and indeed thought of itself, as an alternative model to "Balkanization," which, shaken from its decades-long position as a historical metaphor, had taken on a very contemporary, literal, and sinister meaning.

The "Yes" campaign in the second Québec referendum on independence in 1995 was anything but oblivious to these ominous shifts and attempted to develop a better-case scenario that took them into account. Posters for the "Yes" side, some of which still cling to balconies in the Plateau neighbourhood of Montréal where I live, featured peace symbols and images of the earth seen from space, linking the élan for Québec sovereignty with anti-militarism, nuclear-free campaigns, and environmentalism. In other words, campaign strategists determined that the large numbers of francophones whose votes would be needed for the referendum to succeed had to be reassured that national independence would mean acceding to a global community as a sovereign nation in ways other than acquiescing to the hegemony of capitalist globalization. But if this was the case, how to explain the relative indifference in Québec toward the Canada-US Free Trade Agreement or FTA (and, later, North American Free Trade Agreement or NAFTA), at least compared with the vociferous opposition it provoked among academics and left nationalists in English Canada? There, many feared the agreements would threaten the living conditions of Canadian workers and the role of the state in the areas of health care, social benefits, and culture. Of course, there *was* opposition to NAFTA in Québec from trade unions, social movements, and community groups—especially on the first two points—but among artists and intellectuals in particular, it was hard to escape the feeling that the *cultural* fear that was animating the English-Canadian side was largely absent. It was not so much the sentiment that French-language culture, conveyed through film, television, popular music, theatre, and publishing, would resist the worst forms of American interference; there was also the curiously smug notion—curious, because regarding cultural anxiety in English Canada as a singular opportunity for *schadenfreude* involved setting aside the axiomatic position that Québec is in a permanent state of cultural vulnerability on a continent where English enjoys undisputed hegemony—that the reason their English-Canadian counterparts so greatly feared the destruction of their cultural sovereignty was, in reality, because there *was* no English-Canadian culture, or at least none that could resist or hold its own against the American onslaught. For once, let English Canadians stew in *their* cultural insecurity, seemed to be the attitude! Many in the cultural sphere, in a counterintuitive alliance with Québec businesses, bought into the argument that free trade would allow Québec to diversify markets, an advantage imagined as an emancipation of sorts from an abusive and restrictive pan-Canadian relationship.

In the heat of the free trade debate, then, there was considerable light between Québec and English-Canadian nationalisms. According to Angus, the latter drew upon the notion of Canada as a "political continuity articulated through the public intervention of the federal state and a sense of break, or difference [from the USA], elucidated through relationship to the land, nature, environment."[11] As he points out, "public-enterprise culture is a *mitigating* reaction to the capitalist worldview, not a tendency of equal strength. However, it is a mitigating formation that has become an important part of identification for English-Canadians."[12] Arguably, intellectuals and artists in Québec had, for several decades, an even higher attachment to public-enterprise culture than the Rest of Canada, thanks to the reforms of the Quiet Revolution, but in the "Québec Inc." atmosphere of the late 1980s and 1990s, it was the celebration of private entrepreneurship that bore the symbolic weight of showing Québec to be a viable nation. As Angus reminds us, "identification with a nation—or any other social identity, for that matter—is an *active process* of selection of salient contents and their articulation by an actor."[13] At the juncture of the free trade debates, the "salient contents" of national identifications in English Canada and Québec lay at a significant distance from each other. The response to Québec's perceived lukewarm opposition to the (NA)FTA in English Canada was to cry betrayal: Québec was now cast as Canada's worst cheerleader for US-led globalization and as the valet of Prime Minister Brian Mulroney, whose Progressive Conservatives were elected in 63 out of 75 Québec ridings in the 1988 "Free Trade elections." And so, at the beginning of the 1990s, post-Meech Lake and post-(NA)FTA, progressives in English Canada were already turning away from "the Québec question."

The defeat of the 1995 referendum by a razor-thin margin marked another watershed for relations between English Canada and Québec. In the federalist camp, once the exhilaration of victory, heightened by the earlier panic of near defeat, had passed, it became clear that by saying no twice, Québec had ceded a real advantage to the adversaries of independence. Hence the Clarity Act (2000), adopted unilaterally by the Canadian parliament, which was designed to legitimate a determining role for Canada in any future plebiscite on Québec sovereignty. This was definitely *not* the mutually determined "rules of the game" agreed to by the UK and Scotland before the holding of the 2014 referendum on Scottish independence; but neither was it the violent intervention of the Spanish state into the 2017 Catalan referendum, where police sent from other parts of Spain ransacked ballot boxes and shut down polling stations, occasionally injuring voters along the way. But it would be fair to say that for the first time, more than a reactionary fringe in English Canada could begin contemplating the legitimacy of a forceful, coercive intervention by the Canadian state should there ever be an attempt to hold a third referendum without the blessing of the Canadian parliament.

A generation later, the project of finding a ground for Canadian *philosophy* that fulfills Angus's preconditions seems even more elusive than in the period from which he was writing. No such project is now able to present itself, let alone convince, without responding to the demand that Canada assume responsibility for the actuality, and not merely the historicity, of its colonial relations with Indigenous peoples. The terms have been set forth in numerous ways over the past several years: the demand for progress on land claims that continue to be met with delay and obfuscation; struggles for healthy water and decent housing, on the one hand, and opposition to environmentally destructive projects and pipelines, on the other; the reframing and valorization of Indigenous forms of organizing and an emerging young leadership, particularly through movements like Idle No More, the Calls to Action of the Truth and Reconciliation Commission into Indian residential schools, and the controversies surrounding the federal inquiry into Missing and Murdered Indigenous Women. All have been accompanied by, and refracted through, a burgeoning Indigenous cultural scene in the visual arts, literature, music, theatre, and cinema. This has been broadly referred to as "Indigenous Resurgence."

Today, "bringing [Canadian] identity to philosophical articulation"[14] would be a differently triangulated relationship among technology, modernity, and "wilderness" that must emerge from an unprecedented dialogical engagement with Indigenous peoples. This may be the prerequisite for meeting the standard that, as Angus said, "'one's own', as [George] Grant called it, be regarded as sufficiently significant to motivate and sustain philosophical inquiry [and] is not really marginal to understanding the human condition."[15] Today, rendering such a "wager" credible involves radically rearticulating "Canadian experience" by acknowledging the colonial basis of the Canadian project, from its inception to the current period. In other words, reconciliation is a process that demands recognizing a settler colonial responsibility that does not end in "history" but extends wholly into the present. As Matthew Dorrell (among others) has pointed out, First Nations do not want to *be* reconciled, or enfranchised unilaterally, by the Canadian state: "In the call for a 'new relationship between aboriginal peoples and *other* Canadians,' it appears that Aboriginal people have been enfranchised on the sly. For members of sovereign First Nations in particular, reconciliation by enfranchisement is wholly contrary to their longstanding demands for state recognition of the unceded sovereignty of First Nations."[16]

In other words, the happy inclusion of First Nations into a multicultural model is a too-easy, and completely inadequate, response to a decolonizing imperative in which even new Canadians, both immigrants and refugees, are implicated. This means moving beyond a tendency to present the overcoming of discriminatory and racist practices toward Indigenous peoples as a matter of recognizing their human rights—as in the series of vignettes in the CMHR (Canada Hall of the Canadian Museum for Human Rights) in Winnipeg, where individual exhibits focus on the suppression of Indigenous languages, abuses in residential schools, and the repressive measures against Indigenous spirituality within the broader context of human rights violations against African Canadians, Québécois (the War Measures Act), Jews, LGBTQ persons, and so on.[17] The debates among curators and academics over whether to label the historical record of Canada toward First Nations as "cultural genocide," or even genocide *tout court*—the TRC settled on the former, the CMHR refuses both—reflect paradigm shifts that are being demanded … and resisted.[18]

One consequence of these epistemic shifts—of what we (now) know Canada to be—is that Québec has lost its urgent status in English-Canadian political thought—except, perhaps, as an expedient foil. In other words, it is largely figured as outside, and even hostile, to these reframing efforts. In part, this is because with Québec increasingly cast as uniquely intolerant of immigrants and out of sync with the identity that the Rest of Canada has been forging around a particular construction—and critique—of multiculturalism and pluralism, there is no longer a general acknowledgement of the need to include it as a "salient content."[19] Worse, to engage—or "indulge"—Québec, it is often implied, would be to divert precious time and resources away from this other, primordial task. In this way, progressives in English Canada participate in a more general discourse that casts Québec as the *enfant gâté*—the spoiled, attention-seeking child—by identifying reactionary attitudes about "illegal immigration," the "threat" of Islam, and other such hot-button issues with an already depreciated object.[20] When a blatantly reactionary provincial government is elected in Ontario, progressives may well be "ashamed" of their fellow citizens, but they nevertheless regard it as an aberration to be analyzed and explained; the election of a centre-right government in Québec determined to ban the wearing of so-called conspicuous religious symbols by public sector workers, however, is seen as revealing something essential about Québec bigotry and small- mindedness and in need of no further explanation. Such attitudes are in themselves enactments of concrete, material relations of domination and marginalization, performances of privilege and power, and they remain manifold in English Canada's relations with Québec.

There *is* a tendency among those whom Guillaume Lamy (2015) calls "civic republicans" in Québec to frame the right to cover one's head if one is a Muslim woman, for example, as the absolute privileging of certain individual rights over the will of "the majority," as reflected in the mature institutions of representative democracy, especially the Assemblée nationale. Behind such claims, there is often the fantasy of attaining a conflict-free society, to be brought about by the successful "integration" of those who are positioned as outsiders.[21] This can sometimes assume sadly farcical forms, as when former Premier Pauline Marois insisted that a transitional period of five years would be adequate for weaning veil-wearing Muslim women away from the practice through a second-wave feminist program of consciousness raising.[22]

Yet, the question of majority/minority status, simplified so deceptively by the stark slash that separates the two terms, yields to significant complexities in Québec, where it is quite possible to be both at the same time. For example, even francophone immigrants leave Québec in search of work elsewhere in Canada because they find the densely woven networks of personal, professional, and corporate relations among *Québécois de souche* difficult to penetrate (although recent figures show this phenomenon to be diminishing). More generally, for francophone Québécois to be a national or linguistic minority in Canada and to object to being treated as one can at the same time provide cover for refusing to think through the implications of being an ethnic or cultural majority in Québec, or a settler colonial majority in the Americas, for that matter.

If surveys are to be believed, in Québec both "independence"—which, since the defeat of the 1995 referendum, the Parti Québécois has formulated increasingly as the project of an ethnically defined "nous," or "us" (as well as the more conservative variant, *sans* independence, embodied by the current Coalition Avenir Québec, or CAQ, government)—*and* Canada as a "homeland" have become less relevant, especially among the young.[23] But this, too, is the stuff of fantasy: there come moments when the imaginary refusal to acknowledge Canada collides with reality, whether it be through a Supreme Court decision or the imposition of a constitutionally mandated exercise of federal authority that has a direct and tangible impact, for better or worse, on the lives of Quebecers.

But if the fantasy in Québec is a narcissistic "integration" of "others," I would venture to say that today Canada fantasizes about the successful "disappearance" of Québec. There is something uncanny in these parallel structures of wish fulfillment, but it could also be said that facts on the ground give a certain comfort to Canada's fantasy: Québec's demographic weight in Canada is constantly declining, which has a direct impact on its share of seats in parliament, for example. When it comes to enacting policy, Québec "matters" less and less—except, perhaps, at election time, when, through block (detractors would say "tribal") voting, it may still be capable of denying English Canada the government it seeks.

Ian Angus provides us with a number of concepts that could support an argument that engaging with Québec, rather than projecting onto it, remains an indispensable task in English Canada.[24] Perhaps the most important of these is "the patterning of contents," in which "what is inside is separated from the outside, not by a unique content, but by a distinctive *relation* between contents."[25] As we saw earlier, Angus introduced this concept to support a claim that distinguishes Canada from the United States, not on the absolute basis of the former's preference for state involvement versus free market dominance but a relative one that signifies a productive difference. It would be a "grave error," he reminds us, "to dismiss such historically based sources of identification on merely empirical grounds of the comparison of isolated contents."[26]

Seeking to include this difference, rather than abjecting it, might well still be crucial to articulating the ground for the project of "undoing dependency," requiring as it does "shifting significance from origin to the new context of application, from provenance to destination."[27] In other words, a more informed consideration of how certain topoï, including secularism (*laïcité*), "cultural appropriation," and "republican" critiques of individual rights-based liberalism, intersect differently in Québec might support Angus's hope that "in place of the paradox between local parochiality and foreign universality,[28] we may then discover an interest in the distinctiveness of our arrangement of contents."[29] Such a "patterning of contents" is also infinitely expandable and unconstrained by the zero-sum forms of logic that predominate today.

In *A Border Within*, Ian Angus's situational declaration of English-Canadian not-knowing—about Indigenous views and views from Québec—placed him as far away as one can be from a disingenuous power play; instead, *listening* was the necessary threshold and precondition for moving forward. Similarly, what if we proceeded *not* by seeking reliable and consistent form but by allowing for unevenness instead? What if fantasies of an at-home *jouissance* were set aside in favour of a commitment to working through the unsettling anxieties of a complicated Canadian "homelessness"? To put it in Angus's terms, could the patterning of contents that might result render Canada a truly salient example for a world that, in myriad forms, is in the throes of a democratic crisis?

Notes to Chapter 5:

1 Ian Angus, "Crossing the Border," *The Massachusetts Review* XXXI, nos. 1 & 2 (Spring–Summer 1990): 33.

2 For Ian's recollections of our time together in the Five Colleges, see "Interview with Ian Angus on Nationalism by Jean-Philippe Warren," available on Ian's website and at Academia.edu/980647. The interview was subsequently translated into French and published as Jean-Phillipe Warren, "Le nationalisme canadien: la multiplication des nations est-elle la solution? Entretien avec Ian Angus," trans. Martine Béland and Jean-Phillipe Warren, *Argument: Politique, société et histoire* 9, no. 2 (Printemps–Été 2007), 94.

3 The term has a long history. Famously, it was used by Lenin to describe the Tsarist Empire, and in turn was used by others to describe the Soviet Union. It was also invoked by various national movements within the Austro-Hungarian Empire.

4 For the latter, I am thinking, for example, of Lawren Harris's paintings of Lake Superior: "Harris's vision was distinctly modern and idealized; his landscapes offered a bold 'idea of north' (to borrow a phrase from the Canadian pianist, composer, and broadcaster Glenn Gould). A founding member of the Group of Seven, Harris progressed from a defiantly nationalistic

interpretation of the northern landscape towards a universal vision of nature's spiritual power. This evolution would ultimately lead him to a clinical and analytic approach to abstraction, informed by theosophy and transcendentalism." From the website of the exhibition "The Idea of the North: The Paintings of Lawren Harris," https://hammer.ucla.edu/exhibitions/2015/the-idea-of-north-the-paintings-of-lawren-harris/.

5 Ian Angus, *A Border Within: National Identity, Cultural Plurality, and Wilderness* (Montreal and Kingston: McGill-Queen's University Press, 1997), 123.

6 Ibid., 112.

7 Since it is Ian's work with which I am primarily in dialogue, I will continue to refer to English Canada—not the Rest of Canada—in this essay.

8 Angus, *A Border Within*, 9.

9 Ibid., 9.

10 Ibid., 4.

11 Ibid., 114.

12 Ibid., 118.

13 Ibid., 117.

14 Ibid., 105.

15 Ibid.

16 Matthew Dorrell, "From Reconciliation to Reconciling: Reading 'What We Now Recognize' in the Government of Canada's 2008 Residential Schools Apology," *English Studies in Canada* 35, no. 1 (March 2009): 36; emphasis added. Dorrell's article appears in "Aboriginal Redress," a special issue of *English Studies in Canada*, edited by Jennifer Henderson and Pauline Wakeham, which includes several illuminating contributions to the debates over reconciliation, redress, and recognition.

17 For a more detailed description, see Robert Schwartzwald, "Responses to Indigenous Trauma in Canada: The Truth and Reconciliation Commission on Indian Residential Schools and the Canadian Museum for Human Rights," in *Wor(l)ds of Trauma: Canadian and German Perspectives*, ed. Wolfgang Klooss (Münster: Waxmann, 2017), 231–47.

18 A thorough discussion of the issues may be found in Karen Busby, Adam Muller, and Andrew Woodford, eds., *The Idea of a Human Rights Museum* (Winnipeg: University of Manitoba Press, 2015), published to celebrate the opening of the Canadian Museum for Human Rights in Winnipeg.

19 A recent EKOS pan-Canadian poll suggests that Quebecers are hardly uniquely hostile, or even exceptionally so, to non-white immigrants. While some 42 per cent of all respondents agreed that Canada has been admitting

too many immigrants from "visible minorities," 74 per cent answered "too many" in Saskatchewan, 56 per cent in Alberta, 46 per cent in Ontario, 43 per cent in Manitoba, 31 per cent in British Columbia, and 30 per cent in Québec. In Atlantic Canada only 21 per cent agreed. EKOS Politics, "Increased Polarization on Attitudes to Immigration Reshaping the Political Landscape of Canada," April 2019, http://www.ekospolitics.com/index.php/2019/04/increased-polarization-on-attitudes-to-immigration- reshaping-the-political-landscape-in-canada/.

20 Anecdotally, one could point out that Maxime Bernier's new People's Party received significant support—over 10 per cent of the vote—in the BC riding of Burnaby in the February 25, 2019, federal by-elections, not in Outremont.

21 Lamy addresses this issue in his study of the controversy over secularism (*laïcité*) in Québec from the "reasonable accommodation" debate of 2006 to the Parti Québécois government's attempt to legislate a Charter of Values in 2014. By way of contrast, he refers back to the sociology of Max Weber and Georg Simmel, who see conflict not as an anomaly but as "*le germe d'une future communauté*"—the seed of the future community (Guillaume Lamy, *Laïcité et valeurs québécoises; les sources d'une controverse*. Montréal: Québec-Amérique, 2015, 20–21).

22 In fact, feminists have been bitterly divided over legislative attempts in Québec to ban the wearing of "conspicuous" religious symbols by public sector workers. Feminists who support the new Québec government's Bill 21 tend to regard the veil as unambiguously and exclusively a sign of women's oppression and submission.

Some of the most vocal supporters of Bill 21 come from countries where the reintroduction of the veil has been associated with the curtailment of women's rights in the public sphere. They insist that the proposed law would provide needed state protection to Muslim women who are pressured by male family members into wearing head-coverings. Opponents of Bill 21 (and of similar proposed legislation by previous Parti Québécois and Liberal governments) assert that the law further complicates the struggles of women to assert their autonomy by banning them from an enormously important swath of Québec's economic and social life. They point to the paradox that in the name of emancipating women, pro-Bill 21 feminists are contributing to keeping them in the home. The motives of pro-Bill 21 forces range from the socially ameliorative to the punitive, but if there is one thing that has indisputably emerged from this rancorous debate, it is the stigmatization of Muslim women who wear "the veil." It is they who now primarily bear the burden of this larger social debate. That burden is literally upon their heads.

23 I need to moderate this claim somewhat in view of the recent Québec election results, where the pro- independence, leftist Québec Solidaire won 10 seats in the National Assembly, one seat more than the Parti Québécois, given the

decision of one PQ deputy to sit as an independent. Unlike in previous elections, this time QS won seats outside Montreal, especially in ridings with large student and young professional populations. QS has also come out strongly in opposition to the CAQ government's Bill 21 that prohibits the wearing of religious symbols in the public sector.

24 In 1997, Ian remained cautiously optimistic that English Canada could do better than "discovering ourselves mainly on the rebound with our encounters with others" and thus "at last begin to appreciate the claims and desires of the other two main groups," adding nevertheless, "But is it too late for this option?" Angus, *A Border Within*, 27.

25 Angus, *A Border Within*, 107.

26 Ibid., 117.

27 Ibid., 108.

28 For a broad sample of brief but concise contributions in this regard, see Jonathan Livernois and Yvon Rivard's anthology, *L'urgence de penser: 27 questions à la Charte* (Montréal: Leméac, 2014).

29 Angus, *A Border Within*, 108.

Chapter 6

Empire, History, and Justice in an Undiscovered Country

Claude Couture

When I was invited to participate in this *Festschrift* in honour of Ian Angus, I was reading the book *The Debate on Postcolonial Theory and the Specter of Capital*,[1] more precisely Vivek Chibber's criticism of post-colonialism from the point of view of Marxism and universality. Since the publication of Chibber's first book in 2013, *Postcolonial Theory and the Specter of Capital*,[2] I have been amazed by the convergence of this debate among the international left with the debate launched during the previous decade in Canada by Ian McKay and his thesis about Canada being a project of liberal hegemony.[3]

Both contributions, Chibber and McKay, were articulated from the perspective of Marxism. Both contributions implied a discussion of the influence of Antonio Gramsci and his concept of hegemony, something that is also present in Ian Angus's work.[4] Chibber pleaded for a recognition of eighteenth- and nineteenth-centuries' universalism, and McKay for a recognition of liberalism as an ideology shaped by capitalism. Both defined capitalism as a universal system with its own logic and laws. For both authors, in the last instance, what is relevant is the globality of the capitalism system. For me, the work of these two authors, however fascinating, is in slight contrast with Ian Angus's more subtle analysis of national specificities and/or local cultures and various forms of resistance in the global context of both the capitalist system and the "Empire."[5]

This contribution to the *Festschrift*, inspired by these debates, is more specifically about the discussion of liberalism as a dominating political philosophy, its place in the history of capitalism and what it could mean for Canada, more specifically British Canada, in the sense of its English and British roots, 150 years or so after the British North America (BNA) Act. Several political philosophers, among them John Rawls, Will Kymlicka, and Amartya Sen, have argued that utilitarianism was a more dominant political philosophy in the English-speaking world at the peak of the colonial period between 1850 and the 1930s.[6] They defined "utilitarianism" as a political philosophy based on the rejection of the abstract principles of the Enlightenment and the opposite principle of defining humans strictly by their quest for pleasure and their concrete situation. While liberalism is associated with concepts like the social contract and universal rights, utilitarianism measures the ethical value of a political action by the greater pleasures it creates for a greater number of people. The implication is that utilitarianism produced a political culture hostile to the notion of universal rights.

Nevertheless, too often, utilitarianism had been erroneously confused with liberalism or overlooked. I make a case here that Canada, instead of being a strict project of liberal hegemony created by capitalism, as argued by Ian McKay, was also, and still is to a certain extent, a project of utilitarianism and colonial hegemony. British-Canadian elites operating in the global context of the British Empire might have been caught by the competition between liberalism, as defined by Rawls-Kymlicka-Sen, and utilitarianism. These two political philosophies were clashing at the time of the colonial period, and that clash still resonates today. In other words, I do think, inspired by the writings of Rawls-Kymlicka-Sen, that liberalism and utilitarianism are antithetical. I believe this is important from the perspective of the "location" of culture and, more specifically, the location of the political culture of British Canada. It is too often assumed that British Canada has been fashioned by a culture of rights. Digging out the influence of utilitarianism could help to understand why today, with the rise of right-wing populism, there is so much hostility to the notion of rights. But first, let's go back to the debate among the left about the importance of culture.

International Left, Marxism, and Canada

In a text exploring "English Canada," published in French in a collection of essays assembled in honour of Québec historian and sociologist Gérard Bouchard,[7] Ian Angus described, as he did in other texts, three main characteristics or "prongs" of the "official discourse" about "English Canada": "If one were to use Bouchard's six strategies to characterize English Canadian culture, I think that one could identify an official culture with three main prongs: one which aims at values regarded as universal, especially democracy and human rights and which therefore doesn't significantly distinguish itself from other polities; another which embraces ethnic diversity as multiculturalism, and a third which focuses on geography or nature."[8]

He goes on to write:

> In calling it "the official discourse," however, I am implying that something is being left out which is significant for a popular, non-elite, non-hegemonic cultural formation and which may even be key for such a new politics. Critical social theory requires a concept through which it can express the limitations of the official discourse and the possibility

> that popular culture may be more significant in a future formation—that is to say, to express the current political restriction and future creative possibility, or, to say it a bit differently again, to understand the present not as simply given in the present but temporally as coming-into-presence and passing-away. I have suggested in my own work that the concept of empire can play this role.[9]

The concept of "empire" is crucial and that is one among many reasons why I believe that the international debate on post-colonialism and Marxism is so important. Those who follow the debates among the international left in magazines like *Jacobin* or the *International Socialist Review* or publications by *Verso* have been fascinated in the last five or six years by what is now referred to as "the Vivek Chibber debate." In 2013, Chibber published *Postcolonial Theory and the Specter of Capital*, followed in 2017 by the publication of *The Debate on Postcolonial Theory and the Specter of Capital*.[10]

According to Chibber, the key concept at the heart of post-colonial theory is the concept of "difference." By post-colonial theory, in his 2013 book, Chibber refers mainly to the first series of the *Subaltern Studies* from 1982 to 1985 and historians such as Ranajit Guha, Dipesh Chakrabarty, and Partha Chatterjee. He does not pay much attention to other schools of thought in the post-colonial sphere and authors such as Edward Said, Gayatri Chakravorty Spivak, and Homi Bhabha.

Post-colonial theory, at least from the authors Chibber singled out in his first book, challenged the notion inherited from the liberal Enlightenment that both East and West are subject to historical laws and principles. Post-colonial theorists concluded that the theoretical frameworks of the West cannot be applied to the East. They, according to Chibber, insisted that capitalism has globalized the world but not universalized it; consequently, different cultures had shaped different patterns of capitalism. Capitalism in the East being different from capitalism in the West, resistance, according to post-colonial theorists, must be organized differently depending on the importance of cultural factors. This is exactly the idea that Chibber is criticizing by pleading for a return to eighteenth-century Western universalism and the nineteenth-century Marxist approach to understand the universality of capitalism.

One of the authors criticized by Chibber, Dipesh Chakrabarty, in *Provincializing Europe*,[11] interrogated the way social sciences had been constructed around the fictitious role of Europe as the sole carrier of modernity around the world. He pleads for a provincializing of Europe defined as one element among others and connected, through colonialism, to many key elements around the world. It is the simultaneity of the processes made possible by these connections that created modernity, not the superior culture of Europe, a *nuance* that seems to escape Chibber. For Robert Young,[12] "subaltern studies, therefore, was not so much a critique of colonialism as a critique of the writing of history itself, a question that has always been at the heart of postcolonial studies, which has sought to develop ways in which the world's history might be written outside the traditional perspective and framework of the expansion of Europe."[13]

The notion of "traditional perspective" is in reference to a typical narrative about the exportation of a Western superior culture through colonialism, while critics of colonialism have been insisting on the fact that Western hegemony was less an exportation of a superior culture and more, if not uniquely, an exportation of coercion, both moral and physical. Thus, the concept of provincializing Canada, if used in the sense given by Chakrabarty, would mean the questioning of the notion, in the Canadian context, of a superior liberal culture as the essence of an almost natural evolution resulting in today's Canada. Even when the analysis is critical of that political culture, for example in the case of defining Canada as "a project of liberal hegemony,"[14] it seems to assume that liberalism, being connected to capitalism, was the main if not the only ideological form of the period serving, and still serving, the interests of capitalism. The rediscovery of utilitarianism as an important ideological vision linked not just to the capitalist system but also to imperialism is a way to recall that the colonial dimension of the nineteenth century and first half of the twentieth is as important as the capitalist dimension and not just a consequence of it. Despite its many flaws, the great contribution of post-colonial theory has been to constantly remind us of the importance of the cultural aspects of both Western capitalism and colonialism.

Canada as a Project of Liberal Hegemony?

Ian McKay wrote in 2000: "The core argument is succinct: the category 'Canada' should henceforth denote a historically specific project of rule, rather than either an essence we must defend or an empty homogeneous space we must possess. Canada-as-project can be analyzed through the study of the implantation and expansion over a heterogeneous terrain of a certain politico-economic logic—to wit, liberalism."[15] And again: "A liberal order is one that encourages and seeks to extend across time and space belief in the epistemological and ontological primacy of the category individual."[16] He continues: "Canada as a liberal project of rule was shaped not only by its founding values but by the necessary and often difficult compromises that were required if such values were to be hegemonic—, that is, durably install themselves in law, daily experience, personal conduct, and intellectual life."[17] Finally: "In the mid-century making of Canada, the signs of bargaining with hegemony were everywhere: a language of politics in which civic humanism, contractualism, and utilitarianism were woven together."[18]

Although it would be interesting to explore the connection between civic humanism and various forms of liberalism and its opposition to classical liberalism, the focus here is strictly on the relationship between liberalism and utilitarianism.[19] It is often assumed that British political and intellectual culture had been greatly influenced by what Louis

Hartz had described as the Lockean ideological fragment, meaning a certain form of liberalism where property and individualism are the key elements.[20] Hartz's thesis was that in Europe in general, including the British Isles, the liberal or Lockean fragment was attached to another and contradictory fragment, the "feudal" fragment, where community and security were more important than property and individualism. Although critical of Hartz, McKay's intent of understanding Canada as a project of liberal hegemony is not without resemblance to Hartz's thesis. The difference, it seems to me, is that where Hartz saw liberal hegemony and domination as the pillar of American exceptionalism, McKay claimed also for Canada a liberal hegemony in the Gramscian sense of a subtle ideological and cultural domination by the Canadian elite to the point of an acceptation of its vision and values by other classes of the Canadian society.

The Forgotten Link?

In reference to the centrality of the notion of "empire," Ian Angus recalls that the "dominant figure of Canadian Hegelianism, John Watson," defended the British Empire

> because of its success in "combining the freedom of the separate organs with the unity of the whole" (Watson, 1919: 272). He also claimed that "the only justification for the rule of a superior over an inferior people is that the former should regard as its special task the elevation of the latter to its own level," even though "a whole foreign civilization cannot be imposed upon a people" (Watson, 1919: 274, 275). These assertions, made in 1919, contain the whole ambiguity of English Canadian official discourse. On the one hand, it claims that the association of parts into a whole is based upon freedom and equality whereas, on the other hand, it makes provision for those parts that can be ceded neither freedom nor equality.[21]

I believe that the influence of utilitarianism played a crucial part in the "provision for those parts that can be ceded neither freedom nor equality." Utilitarianism was not really a coherent political philosophy in the Western world until the end of the eighteenth century when it constituted one of the contradictory legacies of the Enlightenment. As Amartya Sen observed, the Enlightenment had not one but several legacies and they were not coherent.[22] On the one hand, the theories of the social contract in which the various versions of liberalism could be traced implied an "abstract" definition of rights. On the other hand, as a fundamental opposition to this approach based on "abstract" rights, other philosophers insisted on founding a theory of justice that would be based on the actual situation of the members of society, their concrete experience. The founder of this philosophy was Jeremy Bentham (1748–1832). The hedonistic utilitarian philosophy as formulated by Bentham was based in the idea that the moral value of any action should be measured by its consequences in the sense of procuring material happiness to the majority. It was the foundational principle of the many versions of utilitarianism that developed in the subsequent centuries until today.

According to John Rawls and Will Kymlicka, contradicting the Hartzian theory of the fragment, utilitarianism had been, throughout the nineteenth century and probably the first half of the twentieth, the major political philosophy of the English-speaking world, even in the United States.[23] At the beginning, it was an historical and progressive break against any conservative essentialist approach, as well as an opposition to "abstract" liberal theories based on the notions of a social contract resulting from the definition of a state of nature as a prerequisite for protecting "rights," particularly property rights linked to individual freedom.

Throughout the nineteenth century, because of the influence of intellectuals like James Mill (1773–1836) and his son, John Stuart Mill (1806–1873), utilitarianism became an elaborate philosophy capable of addressing in detail questions related to policy, legislation, justice, and economics. Both worked as bureaucrats of the East India Company, and the philosophy of utilitarianism became, it seems, the paradigm of British bureaucracy at the time of the second empire.[24] Following J. S. Mill, Henry Sidgwick (1833–1900), as a professor at Cambridge, had a great influence in the propagation of utilitarianism among the British elites. Subsequently, many philosophers, bureaucrats, or political leaders in the English-speaking world, including the United States, applied the principles of utilitarianism.

Thus, it seems to be a mistake to associate utilitarianism with liberalism or to reduce it as a branch of liberalism when, in strict terms of principles in political philosophy, these were opposed political philosophies. Utilitarianism, at the peak of British colonialism, was arguably the most influential political philosophy among the British elites.[25] Canada, consequently, was more of a project of a colonial and utilitarian order. Even today, in Canada, despite the self-proclaimed human rights revolution of the 1960s described recently by many authors,[26] I believe that the colonial utilitarian culture is still influential, perhaps even dominant, hegemonic, to the point that we do not see it, hiding behind this narrative of a "natural" liberal evolution linked to capitalism. In order to see more clearly this influence, as pointed out by Angus, the study of Canada should never be dissociated from the history of the British Empire and its relevance even today. To illustrate that point, I would like here to provide as an example one of the 30 court cases that have gone to the Supreme Court of Canada since 1982 regarding the rights of French-speaking minorities outside of Québec.

The Caron Case in Short

In 2015–16, four legal cases in Alberta and British Columbia, including three decisions by the Supreme Court of Canada, revealed how widespread the resistance is in English Canada to the notion of linguistic minority rights. These cases were: *Caron* case in Alberta

(Supreme Court of Canada, 2015); *Commission scolaire francophone v. Yukon* (Supreme Court of Canada, 2015); the *Rose des Vents school against British Columbia* (Supreme Court of Canada, 2015); and the case of the *Commission scolaire francophone against British Columbia* (Supreme Court of British Columbia, 2016).[27]

In the Caron case, the three members of the Supreme Court who voted in favour of the "historical" thesis in support of the constitutional obligation of bilingualism for Alberta and Saskatchewan clearly reiterated the "historical" argument based on the point of view of French Canadians and Métis in particular.[28] On the contrary, the six judges who opposed the "historical" thesis nevertheless developed themselves another "historical" thesis but clearly from the dominant British point of view.[29] These six judges insisted that the "Canadian legislators" between 1867 and 1914 "knew" how to protect language rights.[30] It is this notion of "knowing" how to protect the rights associated with British colonial administrators that I see as odd, considering the perspective of the global imperial culture of the time. But first let us remember the main dimensions of this complex case.

In December 2003, Gilles Caron received a ticket for speeding in Edmonton.[31] As Ed Aunger explains, it took almost three years for Gilles Caron, who immediately challenged the constitutionality of this contravention because it was written in English only, to have his trial in French.[32] Judge Léo Wenden was assigned to this case and the proceedings began on March 1, 2006. On July 2, 2008, Wenden acquitted Caron and Pierre Boutet, who added to the complaint, and concluded that the Traffic Safety Act, being written in English only, was unconstitutional.[33]

The Alberta government retorted by filing an appeal in the Alberta Court of Queen's Bench with respect to the decision of Justice Wenden of the Provincial Court of Alberta. Subsequently, the decision of Judge Kristine Eidsvik on behalf of the Alberta Court of Queen's Bench was rendered in 2009 and was against Caron.[34] The Alberta Court of Queen's Bench had to decide whether the trial judge erred in concluding that the province of Alberta had a constitutional obligation to publish its legislation in both French and English. The Court of Queen's Bench decided that indeed Judge Wenden erred and that Alberta and Saskatchewan had no constitutional obligation with respect to bilingualism.[35] This decision was confirmed by two ulterior decisions of the Alberta Court of Appeal, the first in 2010 on the right to appeal the decision by Mr. Caron and his lawyers and the second in 2014 on the content of the case.[36] Finally, as previously mentioned, the Supreme Court decided in 2015 to uphold the thesis of provincial autonomy in linguistic matters and the absence for Alberta and Saskatchewan of a constitutional obligation to apply bilingualism.

In each proceeding, the courts were to determine whether this constitutional right existed in the history of Rupert's Land and the North-Western Territory prior to their annexation to Canada and whether that right had been included in the Royal Proclamation of December 6, 1869, or in the Decree in Council on Rupert's Land and the North-West Territory, dated June 23, 1870 (referred to as the "1870 Order"), which included the 1867 and 1869 Addresses, two very important documents issued respectively in December 1867 and May 1869 by the House of Commons of Canada and the Senate and sent to her Majesty Queen Victoria concerning Rupert's Land and the North-Western Territory.

In her judgment, Justice Eidsvik of the Court of Queen's Bench took great care to recall the facts that had been presented to the Provincial Court regarding the history of the annexation of Rupert's Land and the North-Western Territory and later the creation of the province of Alberta. She rightly recalled that discussions on the annexation of Rupert's Land and the North-Western Territory to Canada had first taken place among Great Britain, the Government of Canada, and the Hudson's Bay Company (HBC), which governed these territories at the time. An interesting detail, revealing the colonial context, the HBC had first to cede these territories to Great

Britain before the transfer for annexation to Canada. The HBC's deed of transfer to the United Kingdom was finally accepted on November 19, 1869, and sanctioned by the Queen on June 22, 1870. The transfer of territories to Canada was made by the Decree of July 15, 1870.[37]

Judge Kristine Eidsvik, whose judgment on behalf of the Court of Queen's Bench greatly influenced, I believe, the reasoning of the six majority judges of the Supreme Court in the decision in this case, continued her historical reminder by referring to the fact that at the time of the cession of the territories by the HBC to the United Kingdom, the inhabitants of the territories, the Red River Métis for example, had been neither consulted nor informed of the details of all the discussions. Also, in order to appease the climate of tension that prevailed, the British Crown issued, as mentioned before, a Royal Proclamation, December 6, 1869, printed in English, French, and Cree, which promised to respect "civil and religious rights and privileges," after the transfer of territories.[38] Previously, section 5 of the Temporary Government of Rupert's Land and North-Western Territory Act of June 1869 provided that "laws in force in Rupert's Land and the North-Western Territory would be maintained."[39]

At the same time, negotiations were undertaken with the inhabitants, which led to the holding of two conventions, the first of which, held on December 1, 1869, included language claims, such as the publication of laws in French and in English.[40] The second agreement, from January 25, 1870, to February 10, 1870, is described by Judge Edsvik at paragraph 75 of her judgment:

> A second agreement was held at Fort Garry from January 25 to February 10, 1870. For this "grand convention" 40 delegates were present, 6 of whom came from outside the Assiniboia district: 20 from French-speaking parishes and 20 from English-speaking parishes. A second list of rights emerged from the grand convention: Exhibit 84046. This

second list was for the North West and, like the first list, contained independent claims on language rights: trial judgment, at para. 83, 206, 210, 212. Articles 12 and 13 of this second list are as follows:

12. That the English and French languages be in the Legislature and Courts, and that all the public documents and Acts of the Legislature be published in both languages.

13. That the Judge of the Supreme Court speak the French and English languages.[41]

Subsequently, in her judgment, Judge Eidsvik described the circumstances of the 1870 Order of July 15, 1870, and, the same day, the passing of the Manitoba Act, 1870. After having carefully described the historical context, Judge Eidsvik repeated one by one the main points of each of the contradictory narrations, in one instance taking the point of view of the inhabitants of the Red River, or on the contrary taking the point of view of the members of the Canadian and British colonial apparatus. Her conclusions finally appeared in paragraphs 282–83 which I quote:

> [282] In my opinion, there is no doubt that the inhabitants of Rupert's Land and the North-Western Territory enjoyed the protection of certain linguistic rights before the annexation of territories. Indeed, all their local laws were published in French and English. There is no doubt that these language rights were of fundamental importance to the population of the day, which was divided equally between francophones and anglophones.
>
> [283] Most of the initial annexation negotiations took place between Great Britain, Canada and the Company. Later, residents also participated in the negotiations, and changes took place because of their demands. These changes have led

> to the creation of the province of Manitoba where language rights are constitutionally protected, but I do not believe they have led to the same constitutional protection in the rest of the new territories. Neither the Royal Proclamation of 1869 nor the Decree of 1870 had the effect of constitutionalizing linguistic rights for the rest of the territories. The result of the annexation is that the Parliament of Canada was granted full power in the area of language rights in these territories, subject to section 133 of the Constitution Act, 1867. Thus, when the Parliament of Canada created the province of Alberta and established its constitution in 1905, there was no constitutional requirement to subject that province to the constitutional obligation to publish provincial legislation in both English and French.[42]

The British Empire and Us

Following the judgment of the Court of Queen's Bench, in a judgment of the Court of Appeal in 2014, Judge Frans Slatter wrote that the documents presented in this complex case should be interpreted considering what the "Victorian decision makers who drafted the relevant documents would have assumed and had in mind." In a way, this is what Judge Kristine Eidsvik did, recognizing at first that linguistic "rights" had been practised before the surrender of the territories in Canada, but that these rights had been constitutionalized only for the territory of Manitoba, a very Victorian way of limiting "rights" language.[43] Moreover, as noted above, at the beginning of the Supreme Court's decision in the Caron case, the six majority judges, strongly inspired by the judgment of the Court of Queen's Bench, made it clear that "the Canadian Parliament **knew** how to entrench language rights and did so in the *Constitution Act, 1867* and the *Manitoba Act, 1870* in very similar and very clear terms. The total absence of similar wording in the contemporary *1867 Address* or the *1870 Order* counts heavily against that and the contention that the words 'legal rights' should be understood to include language rights."[44]

When I read this passage, I spontaneously thought about the results of a poll published in December 2016 indicating that Canadians, for the most part, believe that Canada became an independent nation in 1867.[45] Canada, in 1867, was a grouping of colonies that united in a federal system but remained subject to the British Empire. We still have in 2019 this unchanged passage of the Constitutional Act of 1867 to remind us of it: "And such as a Union would lead to the welfare of the provinces and promote the interests of the British Empire."[46] To "know" how to enshrine language rights as early as 1867, or in 1870, as the six majority judges of the decision against Caron believed, there should have been, I think, a specific and hegemonic political culture of recognition of rights in Canada as well as in the empire in general. But it was not the case. There were countless episodes in other parts of the empire at the time of the Métis rebellion of complete disregard for universal "rights": for example, a few years before the Métis rebellion the violent repression of a similar rebellion in Jamaica conducted by Governor Eyre.

In this context of a very conservative colonial culture, I think that when there was a recognition of rights, including the recognition of linguistic rights as in the BNA Act of 1867 or the Manitoba Act of 1870, it did not mean that the majority of Canadian/British legislators "knew" how to protect these rights, in the sense that we understand the concept of "rights" today. These rights were recognized because of the actions of groups resisting British hegemony, especially in the Canadian context of 1870, French Canadians and Métis. This universal view of rights did not come from a superior culture, as John Watson would have stated, but from the point of view of those who were supposedly from an inferior culture but were nevertheless fighting for these rights.

In other words, the reasoning of Justice Eidsvick, as well as the reasoning of the six members of the Supreme Court who voted against Caron, illustrated today, in the twenty-first century, is one of the great paradoxes of the imperial era. It seems, basically, that nothing had really changed: the constant friction, in a very dialectical way, in the imperial culture, of a rhetoric of rights in full opposition of a political culture strictly based on the superior importance of the utility, meaning the material well-being, of the political majority of the colonial power, the white, Protestant, and English-speaking middle classes and elites of the empire.

Conclusion

I have suggested that Canada, as a product of the British Empire, had been, in terms of its political culture, inevitably shaped by the influence of major networks of the empire, one of them being the influence of the political philosophy of utilitarianism. Remembering the importance of utilitarianism in the British Empire and its possible influence in Canada is provincializing Canada. It is a way of recognizing the fact that Canada had been the product not necessarily of a liberal order but of a colonial order in which the political philosophy of utilitarianism, based on an opposition to the principle of "abstract" rights, was influential in the imperial web. Thus, we need to further investigate the influence of utilitarianism in Canada. Today, if there is a culture of rights in Canada, it is less as the result of the evolution of a liberal culture and more as the result of the opposition to the colonial order and resistance of several groups, among them Indigenous nations, women, African Canadians, descendants of Black Loyalists, working-class people, immigrants, and French Canadians or Métis in Manitoba in 1870, as bearers of linguistic diversity and resistance to anglo conformity.

Contrary to the great narrative about the role of Western culture, particularly the role played by the Anglo-Protestant world, in the march to "progress," and the assumed link between liberalism and capitalism, protection of rights and "free enterprise," it is fascinating to observe that perhaps there was an extraordinary gap between that narrative and reality: for almost two centuries from the end of the eighteenth to the mid-twentieth century, a political philosophy designed to oppose liberalism was dominant, or at least very influential, among elites of the British Empire. Again, in this scenario, if we have "rights" in Canada, it has been *de facto* the result of the battle of groups who were and are still in constant opposition to a culture where "rights" came and still come second to utility. One has simply to observe the actual assault in Ontario, conducted by the Doug Ford government, in the name of utility, on basically all institutions based on the general principle of rights. Every time I read or listen about Doug Ford, I say to myself that definitively the empire still resonates; James and John Stuart Mill, who, by the way, never repudiated utilitarianism, are still among us. I will be always grateful to Ian Angus for pointing out a long time ago the still very active importance of the empire.

Notes to Chapter 6:

1 Vivek Chibber, *The Debate on Postcolonial Theory and the Specter of Capital* (London: Verso, 2017).

2 Vivek Chibber, *Postcolonial Theory and the Specter of Capital* (London: Verso, 2013).

3 Ian McKay, "The Liberal Order Framework: A Prospectus for a Reconnaissance of Canadian History," *Canadian Historical Review* 81 (2000): 617–45, reproduced in *Liberalism and Hegemony: Debating the Canadian Liberal Revolution*, ed. Jean-François Constant and Michel Ducharme (Toronto: University of Toronto Press, 2009), 35–63.

4 Ian Angus, *The Undiscovered Country: Essays in Canadian Intellectual Culture* (Athabasca: Athabasca University Press, 2013).

5 Ian Angus, *A Border Within: National Identity, Cultural Plurality, and Wilderness* (Montreal and Kingston: McGill-Queen's University Press, 1997); Ian Angus, *Identity and Justice* (Toronto: University of Toronto Press, 2008).

6 John Rawls, *Lectures on the History of Political Philosophy* (Cambridge, MA: Harvard University Press, 2007), 251–316; Will Kymlicka, *Les théories de la justice* (Montréal: Boréal, 1999); Amartya Sen, *L'idée de Justice* (Paris: Flammarion, 2010).

7 I will be quoting here the initial version in English, before translation, of a text published in French by Ian Angus: "Le concept d'Empire dans la théorie sociale critique," in *Autour de l'œuvre de Gérard Bouchard: Histoire sociale, sociologie historique, imaginaires collectifs et politiques publiques*, ed. Srilata Ravi and Claude Couture (Québec: Presses de l'université Laval, 2015), 39–52.

8 Ibid., 41.

9 Ibid., 43.

10 Chibber, *Postcolonial Theory*; Chibber, *Debate on Postcolonial Theory*.

11 Dipesh Chakrabarty, *Provincializing Europe: Postcolonial Thought and Historical Difference* (Princeton: Princeton University Press, 2000).

12 Robert J. C. Young, *Empire, Colony, Postcolony* (Oxford: Wiley Blackwell, 2015).

13 Ibid., 165.

14 McKay, "Liberal Order Framework," 623.

15 Ibid., 621.

16 Ibid., 623.

17 Ibid., 640.

18 Ibid.

19 Benjamin T. Jones, *Republicanism and Responsible Government: The Shaping of Democracy in Australia and Canada* (Montreal and Kingston: McGill-Queen's University Press, 2014); Michel Ducharme, *Le concept de liberté au Canada à l'époque des révolutions atlantiques 1776–1838* (Montreal and Kingston: McGill-Queen's University Press, 2010).

20 Louis Hartz, *The Liberal Tradition in America: An Interpretation of American Political Thought in America* (New York: Harcourt, Brace, & Co., 1955).

21 Angus, "Le concept d'Empire," 47.

22 Sen, *L'idée de Justice*, 11–57.

23 Rawls, *Lectures on the History*, 269; Kymlicka, *Les théories de la justice*, 18.

24 Bart Schultz and Georgios Varouxakis, eds., *Utilitarianism and Empire* (Oxford: Lexington Books, 2005).

25 Ibid., 1–33.

26 Dominique Clement, *Canada's Rights Revolution: Social Movements and Social Change, 1937–1982* (Vancouver: University of British Columbia Press, 2008); Bryan D. Palmer, *Canada's 1960s: The Ironies of Identity in a Rebellious Era* (Toronto: University of Toronto Press, 2009); José Igartua, *The Other Quiet Revolution: National Identities in English Canada 1945–1971* (Vancouver: University of British Columbia Press, 2006).

27 *Caron c. Alberta, 2015 CSC 56, [2015] 3 R.C.S. 511; Commission scolaire francophone du Yukon, district scolaire #23 c. Yukon (Procureure générale), 2015 CSC 25, [2015]*

2 R.C.S. 282; Association des parents de l'école Rose-des-vents v.British Columbia (Education), 2015 SCC 21, [2015] 2 S.C.R. 139; Conseil-scolaire francophone de la Colombie-Britannique v. British Columbia (Education), 2016 BCSC 1764 (CanLII), retrieved Octover 13, 2017, <http://canlii.ca/t/gtvdv>.

28 *Caron c. Alberta, 2015 CSC 56, [2015] 3 R.C.S. 511,* 40–73. Rosalie Silberman Abella, Richard Wagner, Suzanne Côté.

29 *Caron c. Alberta, 2015 CSC 56, [2015] 3 R.C.S. 511,* 13–40. Beverley McLachlin, Marshall Rothstein, Thomas Albert Cromwell, Michael J. Moldaver, Andromache Karakatsanis, Clément Gascon.

30 *Caron c. Alberta, 2015 CSC 56, [2015] 3 R.C.S. 511,* 4.

31 Edmund A. Aunger, "L'anatomie d'un procès contre la langue française: *Sa Majesté la reine c. Gilles Caron,* 2003–2008," *Revue de droit linguistique* 1 (2014): 30–81.

32 Ibid., 32.

33 2008 *R. c. Caron, ABPC* 232.

34 2009 *R. c. Caron, ABQB* 745.

35 2009 *R. c. Caron, ABQB* 745.

36 2010 *ABCA* 343 and 2014 *ABCA* 71.

37 François Laroque, "The Royal Proclamation of December 6th, 1869," *Manitoba Law Journal* 33, no. 2 (2009): 299–327; Sophie Bouffard and Peter Dorrington, *Le statut du français dans l'Ouest canadien: la cause Caron* (Montréal: Éditions Yvon Blais, 2015).

38 2009 *ABQB* 745, 38.

39 2009 *ABQB* 745, 71.

40 2009 *ABQB* 745, 63.

41 2009 *ABQB* 745, 66.

42 2009 *ABQB* 745, 75.

43 2014 *ABCA 71,* 103.

44 *Caron c. Alberta, 2015, CSC 56, [2015] 3 R.C.S. 511,* 4.

45 "Most Canadians Think Canada Became Independent Nation in 1867, Poll Finds," *Ottawa Citizen,* December 30, 2016, https://ottawacitizen.com/news/local-news/most-canadians-think-canada-became-independent-nation-in-1867-poll-finds.

46 Constitution Act 1867, Justice Law Website, Canada, http://laws-lois.justice.gc.ca/eng/Const/page-1.html.

Chapter 7

After "English Canada"

The Indigenous Humanities and the Feral/Federal State

Leonard Findlay

In this essay I engage with Ian Angus's understanding of English Canada, and the hazards and enticements of that heavily overdetermined notion. In *Identity and Justice* (2008) Angus claims, "If one wants to understand a country like Canada, one has to begin from the centre-periphery relation intrinsic to an empire." He elaborates: "The secret of English Canada is the unofficial dream of self-rule at the periphery that unfolds in tandem with a critique of empire. It is kept secret through the perpetuation of the lie that the empire, then the nations-state, sets the neutral rules whereby its parts interact."[1] I agree in broad terms with these contentions and much of what Angus argues on this basis. However, his intellectual self-location in philosophy, combined with his allegiance to English Canada as a key philosopheme and social formation, hinders his and Canadian Studies' work with identity for justice. The Eurocentric Humanities and Canadian Studies need a more radical Indigenization in order to connect reconciliation with redistribution and enhanced ecological stewardship and sustainability. To that end, I offer an insurgent intellectual formation, the Indigenous Humanities, in dialectical tension with Indigenous, ecological, and aesthetic instanciations of the feral, in order to expose more fully the "lie" of the federal, and the fact that Canada 150 was an identity, justice, and culture bust because the state loves power even more than it fears imagination.

English Canada: From Imperialist to Post-Imperialist-Lite

The idea and actualities of English Canada are clearly derivatives of one empire (British) living on and living differently in relation to a European rival (French) conquered but accommodated post-conquest, and an imperious neighbour (the United States) threatening to acquire parts or the whole of Canada or at least to replace the United Kingdom as the English-speaking, ultra-capitalist overseer of what is understood and done in the name of English Canada. How can this complicated outcome survive today as an apparently commonplace fact or feature of any formal or informal description or discussion of Canadian confederation or nationhood, and how can that persistence be uncoupled more thoroughly from colonial moorings and put to work in new ways Angus would welcome as proudly local, confidently universalizing from that locality, and capable of association with other creative margins and locales in communities of concern for the well-being of their inhabitants and (therefore) the health of the planet?

Moreover, how can "immanent critique" model this phenomenology and politics of location so that philosophy in a recovered eighteenth-century sense functions as what Angus calls "an inquiry into the depths of a particular way of life"[2] that can be accessed and reactivated not by "political theory" but rather by "political philosophy" capable of offering a "theory of the absence of political theory, a guide to living in the community without true knowledge"?[3] These questions capture the magnitude of the challenge Angus poses to himself. In their acuity and developing interconnection, these questions also indicate the remarkable quality of the answers that ensue, even in a fairly short book.

Angus identifies English Canada as a product of empire but not an entirely compliant or enthusiastic one. He recognizes that English Canada is widely seen as the default version of the dominion and then the nation: Canada's centre and essence resented and resisted by French Canada, Indigenous Canada, ethnic Canada, and alienated individuals and enclaves within its own anglophone numbers.

Angus, in a typically bold move, deprivileges and then reanimates English Canada as a potential network of peripheral communities capable of decolonizing themselves beyond conditions, presumptions, and imaginings imperially determined and continuing in a sovereign state with the British monarch as its constitutional head, parliamentary democracy as its operating system, and a governor general and array of lieutenant-governors as the monarch's proxies. English Canada may no longer be identical with British Canada. It never was, despite Lord Durham's confident prediction of a comprehensive anglicization of Canada by virtue of accelerating British immigration and the two founding processes of assimilation and elimination that such immigration would assist or enforce.[4] But, diverse as it now is beyond anything that Durham could have imagined or feared, Canada remains, like a diverse Britain itself, subject still to the shell and shill of empire.

Ever alert to the imprecisions and lubricity of language, Angus notes a "double slippage" where many have recognized none or only one: "The discursive space of English-Canadian cultural identity came into existence through a double slippage: between English Canada and Canada and between distinctiveness and the good.... The two slides were as follows. It was unclear whether the object of analysis was Canada or English Canada, because English Canada was taken to stand for Canada outright. In addition, the argument for distinctiveness was taken as significant evidence that there was something here worth preserving."[5]

This pressing for clarity and rigour is helpful but inadequate. Some historical detail is necessary to bring out the imperio-emulative function of "England" and "English" in Janet Ajzenstat et al.'s *Canada's Founding Debates*.[6] Across this large collection of texts, even Scots, Irish, and French Canadians employ "England" as an unproblematic synecdoche for the recent (1801) and unstable United Kingdom and regularly endangered imperial state of Great Britain and Ireland, whose administration of its colonies to its own benefit was a focus of much lucrative, hypocritical effort. "England" was already a hegemonic centre with multiple domestic and colonial peripheries. But no one in that collection of founding debates uses the expression "English North America," only "British North America." The cachet and referential scope of the epithet "English" in the Canadian cultural context are underwritten and overlaid by British imperial military force, investment capital, and legislative power. The "hegemonic fixture of the nation-state"[7] (a wonderful expression capturing the state's desire for permanence, the uncertain outcome of a sporting encounter, and the reliable appeal of political plumbing) is, in the early nineteenth century, already in a regular fix as it attempts to control constitutive differences in the British homeland and its colonies while manipulating, as Angus says, "cultural identities to appear natural and therefore unproblematic."[8]

Angus, in my view, would have been well advised to connect the "double slippage" he identifies to the *double privation* enacted by Durham in his *Report* (1839) when he claims that French Canadians were "a people with no literature and no history."[9] This sweeping dismissal of the French fact comes from "Radical Jack" Lambton, a pioneering reformer as well as a peer of the realm and experienced diplomat. It reveals the underlying francophobia and contempt for the colonized to be found in ostensibly progressive English people.[10]

And it resulted in something very different from the assimilation of the *Canadiens et Canadiennes* it was designed to justify. Durham's *Report* accelerated the rise of that very literature and history Durham refused to the Québécois despite his own fluency in French (or perhaps because of its Eurocentric character). The form and force of Durham's declaration remind us that colonial speech acts preceded the post-colonial, multicultural speech acts Angus sees as key to the anti-imperial project.[11] Moreover, speech acts, whether imperiously monocultural or inclusively multicultural, come with no guarantees, except perhaps of resistance to what they aim to bring into being. Durham's is an expression of political desire as much as Angus's, and with arguably more to back it up at the moment of enunciation (in the form of the extraordinary discretionary powers accorded him by the British government). We therefore have to be careful not to overestimate the power of either repressive or emancipatory speech (and script; and the connection between the two is never innocent in colonial contexts where Indigenous orality and symbology are constantly threatened with subordination to imperial stenography and colonial settler print). Angus provides important tools for the retrospective and ongoing unmasking of imperial "neutrality." He does this recurrently and well, stressing the conditions and conventions ("the relations of ruling," as Dorothy Smith famously phrased it) of linguistic exchange and the imperial pseudo-universals such illusory neutrality is calculated to advance.[12] But more historical context and comparators would have strengthened his argument by chastening it. Detailed attention in particular, and in the interest of "particularities" as the source of resistance and reimagining,[13] would have helped his arguments significantly. As it is, their sparseness encourages the slack narrativity of (agentless, or at least faceless) framing sentences such as this: "If English Canada is *haunted* by its constitution by empire, its social and political thought is no less constituted by a critique of imperial assumptions."[14] As I have argued elsewhere,[15] any discussion of haunting in Canada needs to take seriously the witnessing of those assumed to be vanishing if not already ghosts, by which I mean the inhabitants of Indian country and the French Canadians who increasingly feared a similar fate for themselves during and immediately post- Durham.

In sum, the shift from a presumptuously imperialist to an openly and effectively anti-imperialist English Canada within a thoroughly post-colonial multinations-state is a shift I look forward to as eagerly as does Angus. However, empire and "old stock" Anglocentrism linger on and are serially reinscribed in Canada in ways that stretch from *Prince* Rupert on to *Lord* Durham and a succession of heavily titled governors general, via *Albertsland* and *Victorialand* as proposed names for the new *Dominion*, through *Sir* John A. Macdonald KCB, to *Viceroy* and The Right Honourable Vincent Massey, to The *Lord* Black of Crossharbour, to the Stephen Harper government's reinvigorated allegiance to "the" old country, its ancient (though selective) liberties, its ceremonies, religion, militarism, whiteness, and wealth.[16] Imperial majesty and its current vestiges and derivatives continue to claim sufficient interest and allegiance from English Canada as to require a more realistic and radicalizing version of it than Angus's "English Canada, by which I mean the multicultural polity whose public language is English."[17] Immigrants to Canada often come from the British Commonwealth's post-colonial global diaspora and bring with them distinct but analogous experiences and memories as imperial subjects, as do members of *La Francophonie*. Neither should we be surprised by the longevity and reach of the English connection, in light of the facts of British imperialism captured with lip-smacking causticity by Perry Anderson:

> The major impact of imperialism was almost certainly on the character and ethos of the *ruling bloc*. But its feedback was not limited to this. A general internalization of the prestations and motifs of Empire undoubtedly occurred. Its most prominent expression was, of course, *the religion of monarchy*

> which marked the late Victorian era—inaugurated, predictably, by the creation for the Queen of the title of Empress of India. The Durbar, and its domestic derivative the Jubilee, became the symbol of a whole society present to itself, celebrating its own *plenitude*.
>
> The 'manifest' function of the monarchy was (by assertion) to *unify* the nation; its 'latent' function was (by example) to *stratify* it. The two were equally important. Probably at no period in peacetime history was *English* society so suffused with chauvinism and so glutted with rank.[18]

The mother of all Family Compacts and Chateau Cliques accorded responsible government to Canada as a white-settler federation while refusing it to India and restricting it at home. The British Empire claimed and staged self-presence in the midst of self-dispersal for the settling and administration of empire, while in Canada the efforts at consolidation in dominion and then nationhood continued to produce only, in Smaro Kamboureli's astute phrase, "the *semblance of plenitude*."[19] Vimy Ridge did not free Canada instantly and forever from the thralls of empire, despite conforming to the pattern of a violent national birth,[20] but instead encouraged new initiatives in the name of a less abject loyalty and a Canadian sovereignty reassuringly coded for many as post-imperial-lite. What *would* we Canadians do, after all, without regular Royal visits, weddings, and babies?

Locating Indigenous Difference: Beyond Riel

Angus's chapter "Critique of Empire" is strewn with insights and salutary challenges to received wisdom, and (as he wrote in a private communication to me) he is rightly proud of his analysis of the Declaration of the People of Rupert's Land and the North-West, a single-page text published in late 1869. This document is key to Angus's affirmation of "the radical outside of empire"[21] as an achievable, desirable goal, and his interpretation of the Declaration in that light. The exuberant eclecticism of the Declaration causes Angus to exclaim: "This mixture of historical and original components is enough to confound the advocates of both ancient and modern constitutions!"[22] At the moment of transfer of authority from the Hudson's Bay Company (HBC) to "Canada," the newly minted "Provisional Government" proclaims its own existence and refuses to recognize the claims on its territories and rights to self-governance by "a foreign power." Angus is attentive to the explanatory force of "abandonment" and to the failure to consult the people of the territory about their transfer from the authority of HBC to the authority of "Canada, which pretends to have a right to coerce us, and to impose upon us a despotic form of government even more contrary to our rights and interests as British subjects." Unfortunately, just when he needs to dig in further to the formal, rhetorical, and referential features of his key text, Angus goes seeking in a later Riel text an enunciation of the right to self-rule as he wishes it to be. There, Riel claims, "The expulsion or annihilation of the invaders has rendered our land natal to its children."[23] From this Angus concludes that it is natal proof of "occupation" that justifies their right to self-rule, demonstrating "the claim of the periphery to become innovative and independent, to undermine the claim of the empire to provide the rules for negotiation."[24]

Angus proceeds to locate such insurgency outside the conservative, compliant peripheries of English Canada and the "history" that secures from them their loyalty to Britain. This new "civil culture" in the West is a product of "geography—traversal and inhabitation of the land—as the place of its disruptive, radical component."[25]

What Riel makes clear in the Declaration and the later communication to his people has a distinctively chthonic settler basis on which Angus seizes: "While this experience *leans* on various doctrines available at the time, such as *natural rights*, its *primal* character is not *dependant* on any such doctrine. It is *equally*, indeed more, *drawn* to the *pre-Enlightenment, ancient* doctrine by which the land belongs to those who work it and those who work it belong also to the land—an identity rooted in the inhabitation of a place which empire must necessarily repress. This *archaism* survives within Canadian political culture even though it is expelled from official culture."[26]

In this dense weave of key argumentative threads, too many opportunities for textual support and qualification go a-begging. For instance, the Declaration's third paragraph maintains that the transfer of these territories from HBC to Canada is "contrary to the law of nations." Angus ignores or merely hints at the fact that this is an unmarked allusion to a celebrated work by Emer de Vattel (1714–1767) and to doctrine that became part of the template of emancipation because of its use during and after the American Revolution.[27] This is not "archaic" but current, not irrelevant or subsidiary but substantive and powerful, indicating the productive entanglement of North American nation formation with its European antecedents. This appeal in the 1867 Declaration is of a piece with its generously genitive title ("of ... of ... Rupert's"), which combines a proto-imperial designation with a geographical one, neither one neutral. The first and second genitives announce and affirm the place-based, compound yet unitary identity and sovereign presence of a "People" expressed in an implicitly comprehensive, apparently unanimous voice. The second genitive seems to "govern" the North-West as well as Rupert's Land.

However, this confident identity claim is simultaneously unsettled by the referential residue of imperial geography and compass ("north-west" of what and whom?). This land never belonged to Prince Rupert of the Rhine but was assigned to him as a commercial responsibility appropriate to an aristocratic investor in, and the first governor of, the HBC by his cousin Charles the Second. He is charged with governing the lands covered by the HBC charter, a trading territory including unknown peripheries located at the sources of all the rivers that flowed into what had become known as Hudson Bay. The extent of that territory is now better known in the mid-nineteenth century than in the seventeenth. However, title to it is not clarified but dramatically complicated by the actions of a self-styled "Provisional Government."

Neither is this all that needs to be said about the contestable political grammar of the Declaration's title. The First Peoples of this territory will in the document's final paragraph be described as "the *neighbouring* tribes of Indians against whom *we* have defended our country in frequent *wars*" (emphasis added). If the Indians are neighbours within a territory that covers one-third of present-day Canada, then, according to the overarching land-based claim to peoplehood, they are members of "the People" with whom the settlers apparently now enjoy "friendly relations." If the Indians are neighbours "invading" from outside the now more known and knowable limits of Rupert's Land and the North-West, then why are they not recognized as peoples too, each "tribe" indeed a "foreign power" or "strange power" (an indication of Louis Riel's francophone understanding of étrange) whose lands have not been ceded to the British Crown or to the HBC and its merely commercial administration? If the use of the term "war" cunningly suggests pre-existing statehood for the people now arrogating to themselves that status in this Declaration, then wouldn't those with whom they have waged "war" surely deserve the same status as those would come to be known as First Nations? As with Jacques Derrida's reading of "the people" in the US Declaration of Independence,[28] in the brief text signed by John Bruce and Riel things get very murky very quickly. Can a written text available only in English but self-evidently representing Métis aspirations plausibly claim to speak for those who are non-literate or who know only French or Michif or the language of one of the "neighbouring tribes"?

Angus is rightly forgiving of the derivative elements in the Declaration, but if he had delved a little more deeply into their nature and implications he might have seen them as not only part of an act of "self-foundation" but as self-destabilizing and exclusionary. Moreover, this might have encouraged him to think more conjuncturally about

Riel's attempts to free his people from imperial framing and past and imminent rule and regulation, because this effort occurs at the same time as concerted attempts to remake First Peoples in the Dominion of Canada as massively regulated wards of the state. And such reflection might in turn have led Angus to consider alongside Riel's resistant recourse to print culture in English the distinctive if asymmetrical semiotics of treaty making in progress under the leadership of Alexander Morris,[29] and also the connections of this activity to treaty federalism and to *sui generis* citizenship rather than the abject, derivative sort of citizenship that Angus in his fourth chapter rightly rejects in favour of community membership and the radical potential of "association."

Just as the polity behind the Imperial Crown is rife with archaisms, most notably the institution of monarchy itself,[30] so the First Peoples of Canada exemplified modernity at its most radically imaginative in their notions of sharing and stewardship of the land. "Empire" is an archaic institution wrapped in the acquisitive garb of modernity and progress. "Indigeneity" is misidentifed by newcomers as backward and primitive when it is in fact a compelling incarnation of the locative, chthonic, anti-capitalist thinking and practice towards which Angus's book moves. In restricting his discussion of First Nations' resistance to English Canada's imperial and national impetus and pretensions to the example of the 1910 Declaration of the Lillooet Tribe,[31] Angus expunges from the moment of Bruce/Riel the mixed nature of both imperial and anti-imperial assertiveness, and the mixed temporalities and spatial understandings of both Dominion expansionists and the multi-nations, active, and self-reproducing occupants of Rupert's Land and the North-West. In too narrowly identifying history with empire and geography with resistance, Angus tends to disregard oral history, winter counts, and ceremonies of remembrance whereby Indigenous peoples on Turtle Island did and continue to locate and narrate their sustainable occupation and unrivalled natality in their traditional territory. The protocols of Clio and of modern cliometricians make Angus rightly wary of history and understandably eager to counter its hegemonic heft with the testimony of place expressed in the "locative case" and not in the discreetly or blatantly overbearing discourse of imperial acquisition and settlement. Angus holds that "we are now in a time in which the imperial legacy that was taken over into the nation-state, then nations-state, has begun to unravel such that the dream of self-rule can be dreamed again."[32] While Riel might have dreamed for the first time of self-rule, for First Nations it was not a dream but a living reality never ceded or abandoned, even and especially as they traversed distance or opened their territories for the making and "signing" of the Morris treaties. Indigenous law and diplomacy were very much in action in this process, notwithstanding the fact that they might not be recognized as such by the Colonial Office in London and its representatives in the Dominion. The man soon to become revered as the Old Chieftain, John A. Macdonald, is notorious today for supporting Canadian emulation of the American policy of "aggressive civilization" and the consequent necessity of "killing the Indian in the child." Far less known and considered is his suggestion (supported by his fellow "Fathers of Confederation") in the fourth draft of what became the British North American Act (BNA) that Canada be known therein and thereafter as "The Kingdom of Canada."[33] Compared with Macdonald's archaic and pathetic pseudo-modern mix of loyalist abjection and anglo-avaricious affirmation,[34] the sophistication and stamina of "Indigenous diplomacy"[35] suggests a worthier rival of Whitehall and the Quai D'Orsay! And that diplomacy turned then and turns still on relations and doctrine, inherent and treaty rights, articulated in parallel with the Crown, whose honour requires not the instruments of imperial dispossession, exploitation, and betrayal but the alignment of imperial and Indigenous identities with justice.[36]

After English Canada and into the Anthropocene: The Indigenous Humanities and the Feral/Federal State

Political philosophy in the Angus mode is an essential piece of a larger puzzle, which includes in the accelerating Anthropocene the co-optation of universities as social license providers for extractive and other corporate interests whose practices are tied to socially and ecologically unsustainable global flows of poisons and prosperity. The co-optation of the Canadian academy requires its urgent and thorough decolonization, so that empire's disciplinary accomplices, including humanists, can join with keepers of Indigenous Knowledge and defenders of Indigenous rights in the coarticulation and collaborative pursuit of a just and sustainable future. This process can happen in parallel Indigenous and settler trajectories as expressed in the Two Row Wampum, but also in convergent efforts when and where a justice portage requires hands of all sorts to the portage straps.

An example of what I think is required is the Indigenous Humanities project begun more than 20 years ago at the University of Saskatchewan by a group of five scholars: a Mi'kmaw authority on education, a Chickasaw authority on Native Law, an art historian, a scholar active in the area of Indigenous co-operatives (especially those run by Indigenous women), and a literary scholar (me). We were inspired by the *Report of the Royal Commission on Aboriginal Peoples* (1996), the United Nations Decade for Indigenous Peoples (1995 to 2004), and an international summer institute supported by the Social Sciences and Humanities Research Council on our campus in 1996, and resulting in the collection edited by Marie Battiste, *Reclaiming Indigenous Voice and Vision*. As we figured out what needed to be done, we turned our efforts ever more assuredly towards decolonizing our and other Canadian universities, working in a number of forms and fora (including the Royal Society of Canada, the annual Congress of Canadian Learned Societies, and the Canadian Association of University Teachers) to critique and replace narratives of deficiency and belatedness aimed at First Nations, Inuit, and Métis peoples and to hold the settler state to restoring the Honour of the Crown.[37] Key aspects of this endeavour included Indigenous leads on most research projects, with Eurocentric knowledge taxed mostly with exposing its own pretensions and complicities.

From this preliminary process emerged an anti-colonial shared agenda, and Indigenous internationalism drawing on networks established through two decades of organizing at the United Nations.

Indigenous knowledge, research, and pedagogy have guided much of what our group has since done, while respecting protocols and working strategically within imperio-colonial state frames and judicial discourses (regarding the Crown, citizenship, title, treaty, and [free, prior, and informed] consent). We have used academic platforms to pose the question of justice in the Anthropocene in deliberately stark terms: as the choice, for example, between Canada as a Transcanada Gulag or as a Justice Archipelago.

The unsettlement caused by such language usually produces conversation, concession, and rethinking, both because of and in spite of recent state discourses of apology and reconciliation. Moreover, blunt commentary, like Angus's, has enabled new alliances and associations with class-based organized labour and socially progressive groups in parallel and convergent efforts for mobilization and resistance. These anti-racist, anti-colonial, culturalist coalitions provide broadly feral constituents and agendas for a feral/federal interface, both employing state instruments against themselves and exposing, ignoring, and circumventing the state's appeasement of corporate capital and its insatiable shareholders.

In this way, the hitherto exoticized or demonized anti-imperialist peripheries develop a mutually radicalizing dialectic between the creative and the complicit, in which archaic and innovative elements can be found on both sides of feral/federal interaction while sustainable and self-transformative identities engage in the frame breaking and refusal that may lead to a polyglot, polycentric configuration of interests, outcomes, and desires. The shift from *terra nullius* to Terralingua and its magazine *Langscape* captures the essence of change from Canada as a commercial, primarily staples, Anglosphere appendage to Canada as a humanistic, multi-lingual, multi-nations state increasingly protective and promoting of biodiversity. The braid of the nation now goes far beyond Alexander Morris's "triple cord" of English, Scottish, and Irish settlers thought to bind English Canada together as core Canada.[38] The original sweetgrass braid of Indigenous filiations and the crops they favoured is no longer seen by many as John Locke-lite but rather as the foundational social and ecological sustainability adaptable to the exigencies and resistant to the idiocies of the Anthropocene. In helping to rehabilitate the feral, both culturally and materially, as so much more than inconvenience or embarrassment and décor, the Indigenous Humanities may continue to help us travel closer to a creative, much-delayed, ever-vulnerable rapprochement between identity and justice in territory, a rapprochement of a kind that might warrant even Ian Angus's wary, provisional support.

Since the appearance of Angus's book in 2008, we have witnessed the resurgence of ethnic nationalism, American isolationism, and angry white populism but also extraordinary resistance in global peripheries to climate change and environmental degradation. Meanwhile, the academic humanities navigate the contradiction of institutional beleaguerment and enhanced social and conceptual relevance in the refiguring of the nature and role of the human within the Anthropocene. Angus's example as an engaged, unflinching humanist intellectual needs to become the norm rather than the exception. And this can most effectively occur through building on and enriching from non-settler traditions of Angus's connections between association and treaty making for peace and sustainability across radical peripheries and into redeemable centres through universalizing from the margins. For too long, associative communities have been subordinated to commercial contracts and corporate "social" licence, and this within public discourse reducing economic possibilities to market fundamentalism, the liberal arts to the neo-liberal ones, and human imagination and accomplishment to lower taxes. However, the feral arts and humanities, post-colonial in their openness to association across difference in the multi-nations state, can occupy and communicate across peripheries while preserving much more than their own distinctiveness, and achieving and reconceiving subsidiarity as "doctrine, formula, and symbol" within the "urgency" of the Anthropocene.[39] The Angusian, the Indigenous, and the Environmental Humanities are aptly "wild" in their capacity for critique and in their allegiance to sustainability in face of the manic extractivism and subordination of production to consumption in the name of modern, civilized living. This feral antidote to post-Enlightenment commercial society cannot pre-empt "ecological imperialism," "eco-racism," and "mass extinction,"[40] but without it, identity will surely coagulate and then freeze in a deeply incriminating form, while justice abandons the planet to catastrophe.

Coda

I will remain in dialogue with *Identity and Justice* and its author for as long as for me the sun shines—and we can see and feel it while breathing clean air; and for as long as the rivers flow—along their ancient courses, sustaining as they go a rich diversity of riparian and aquatic life. I can offer no stronger commendation of the courage, intellect, and accomplishments of this Canadian political philosopher than this dialogic commitment.

Notes to Chapter 7:

1 Ian Angus, *Identity and Justice* (Toronto: University of Toronto Press, 2018), 5, 11.

2 Ibid., 11.

3 Ibid., 91.

4 E. D. Blodgett offers an excellent overview of "the Durham effect" on literary and intellectual culture in Québec in "Francophone Writing," in *The Cambridge Companion to Canadian Writing*, ed. Eva-Marie Kröller (Cambridge: Cambridge University Press, 2004), 49–69. For a more detailed analysis of rejoinders to Durham from a leading poet and historian of the period, see: L. M. Findlay, "Towards Canada as Aesthetic State: François-Xavier Garneau's *Canadien* Poetics," *Studies in Canadian Literature* 32 (2007): 28–42.

5 Angus, *Identity and Justice*, 18.

6 Janet Ajzenstat et al., eds., *Canada's Founding Debates* (Toronto: University of Toronto Press, 2003).

7 Angus, *Identity and Justice*, 40.

8 Ibid.

9 Lord Durham, *Lord Durham's Report: An Abridgement of* Report on the Affairs of British North America [1839], ed. G. M. Craig (Toronto: McClelland and Stewart, 1963), 150.

10 See: L. M. Findlay, "Memory's Hegelian Estate: Class, 'Race,' Treaty, and the Canadas of Alexander Morris (1826–89)," *Essays in Canadian Writing* 80 (2003): 656–58.

11 Angus, *Identity and Justice*, 80–82.

12 See: Dorothy E. Smith, *The Everyday World as Problematic: A Feminist Sociology* (Boston: Northeastern University Press, 1987).

13 Angus, *Identity and Justice*, 8.

14 Ibid., 13; emphasis added.

15 L. M. Findlay, "Spectres of Canada: Image, Text, Aura, Nation," *University of Toronto Quarterly* 75, no. 2 (2006): 656–72.

16 The Harper government's rewhitening and reanglicizing of Canada is especially evident in the changes of emphasis and detail in the materials it developed to educate and orient those seeking Canadian citizenship. See: L. M. Findlay, "'The Toil and Spoil of Translation': A Godardian Reading of the Study-Guide: Discover Canada/Guide d'étude "Découvrir le Canada," in *Trans/Acting Culture, Writing, and Memory: Essays in Honour of Barbara Godard*, ed. Eva C. Karpinski et al. (Waterloo: Wilfrid Laurier University Press, 2013), 149–66.

17 Angus, *Identity and Justice*, 72.

18 Perry Anderson, *English Questions* (London: Verso, 1992), 21; emphases added.

19 Smaro Kamboureli, "Preface," in *Trans.Can.Lit: Resituating the Study of Canadian Literature*, ed. Smaro Kamboureli and Roy Miki (Waterloo: Wilfrid Laurier University Press), ix; emphasis added.

20 See Robert Zacharias, "'Some Great Crisis': Vimy as Originary Violence," in *Shifting the Ground of Canadian Literary Studies*, ed. Smaro Kamboureli and Robert Zacharias (Waterloo: Wilfrid Laurier University Press, 2012), 109–28.

21 Angus, *Identity and Justice*, 44.

22 Ibid., 45.

23 Louis Riel, "To the Inhabitants of the North and the North-West," 70/04/07, Cited in Angus, *Identity and Justice*, 46.

24 Angus, *Identity and Justice*, 46.

25 Ibid., 47.

26 Ibid.; emphasis added.

27 Benjamin Franklin received the copies of the French original of Vattel's text from Franklin's Dutch-based friend and pro-American spy, Charles W. F. Dumas. This work was well known also to Hamilton, Washington, and their peers. See the summary in James Brown Scott, "Preface to the reproduction of Books 1 and 2 of the original edition of *Le droit des gens: ou, Principes de la loi naturelle, appliqués à la conduite et aux affaires des nations et des souverains* (Washington DC: Carnegie Institute, 1916).

28 Jacques Derrida, "Declarations of Independence," in *Negotiations: Interventions and Interviews 1971–2001*, ed. and trans. Elizabeth G. Rottenberg (Stanford: Stanford University Press, 2002).

29 See: Findlay, "Memory's Hegelian Estate," 2003.

30 See Tom Nairn's mordant and prescient analysis of the upper classes of "Ukania" in *The Enchanted Glass: Britain and its Monarchy* (London: Radius, 1988).

31 Angus, *Identity and Justice*, 47–48.

32 Ibid., 84.

33 The naming of the Dominion of Canada, like the great flag debate a century later, provides strong support for Angus's understanding of identity as processive, contingent, and a revealingly major national pastime. There were more than a dozen contenders by the mid-1860s for the new name—hare-brained acrostics, topgraphical clunkers, and ultra-traditionalist attempts to be inclusive of Canadian differences yet emphatically British as well (see Heritage Canada). But the British (like Heritage Canada today) were not willing to annoy or alarm the still volatile United States with a name like "the Kingdom of Canada." See: Eugene A. Forsey, rev. Richard Foot, "Dominion of Canada," in *The Canadian Encyclopaedia* (Toronto: Historica Canada, 2018).

34 For graphic examples of the abject-affirmative Macdonald, see: Ajzenstat, *Founding Debates*, 203–7.

35 See: James (Sákéj) Youngblood Henderson, *Indigenous Diplomacy and the Rights of Peoples: Achieving UN Recognition* (Saskatoon: Purich Publishing, 2008).

36 See: James (Sákéj) Youngblood Henderson, *Treaty Rights in the Constitution of Canada* (Toronto: Thomson Carswell, 2007). 37 For more details of this struggle, see: Marie Battiste, Lynne Bell, and L. M. Findlay, "Decolonizing Education in Canadian Universities: An Interdisciplinary, International, Indigenous Research Project," *Canadian Journal of Indigenous Education* 26 (2002): 820–45; Marie Battiste et al., "Thinking Place: Animating the Indigenous Humanities in Education," *Australian Journal of Indigenous Education* 34 (2005): 7–19; Daniel Coleman, "Different Knowings and the Indigenous Humanities," *English Studies in Canada* 38 (2012): 141–59.

38 See: Findlay, "Memory's Hegelian Estate," 2003.

39 See the discussion of subsidiarity in Amanda H. Lynch and Siri Veland, eds., *Urgency in the Anthropocene* (Cambridge, MA: MIT Press, 2018), 22–23.

40 See: Robert S. Emmett and David Nye, *The Environmental Humanities: A Critical Introduction* (Cambridge, MA: MIT Press, 2017), 15, 18, and 207, respectively.

Chapter 8

Dependency and Empire

*Comparative Political Thought in Canada and Mexico**

Johannes Maerk

> To break with the colonial *mentality* requires massive, intellectual effort and a risk of even further marginalisation.
>
> IAN ANGUS & BRIAN SHOESMITH, "DEPENDENCY/SPACE/POLICY" (1993)

Ian Angus has worked extensively on topics related to Canadian Studies and the identity of English Canada. He is one of the few philosophers who critically engaged in a dialogue with Latin American thought as a philosopher (and not as an area specialist of Latin America).

In this chapter, I compare some topics of socio-political thought in Mexico and Canada. In the case of Canada, I am referring to the Anglo-Saxon part, so-called English Canada.[1] I use this denomination in Angus's sense,[2] who defines "English Canada" mainly as that part of Canada that employs the English language as a means of communication for everyday use (in contrast to the old criterion of "ethnic origin," since many immigrants nowadays no longer come from the British Isles).[3] Angus argues that English Canada is one of the three nations of Canada (the others being the First Nations people and the Québécois) that has not referred (contrary to the others) to itself as a nation. In calling itself "Canada" (as the whole of the nation-state), "it has elided the key question of its relation to the others and especially the history of violence whereby the Canadian State, as all other states, was constructed."[4] I would like to shed a little light on specific questions and issues that were raised by writers both south and north of the border to the United States. These questions revolve around the quest for identity, the authenticity of (philosophical) thinking, the relationship with the United States, and multiculturalism.

Both in Mexico and Canada the intellectual construction of identity was forged, in large part, through so-called Area Studies—Latin American/Mexican Studies and Canadian Studies, respectively. And, in both cases, support for these studies came from the state and from public universities. Since 1982, Leopoldo Zea, as the director of the CCyDEL (Centro Coordinador y Difusor de Estudios Latinoamericanos), promoted research on the continent south of the Rio Grande. It was to become one of the most important centres in Latin America for Latin American studies due to its research, teaching, and publishing activities.[5] The activities at the CCyDEL were an important part of the "non-written" work of Zea, according to the Mexican-Argentinean philosopher Enrique Dussel.[6] This construction of knowledge was and is a kind of Latin American militancy linked to the political project of the continent's integration through the recovery and reconstruction of its own "history of ideas." The impulse for the systematic study of such a "history of ideas" was given by the philosopher José Gaos, a student of Ortega y Gasset, who emigrated to Mexico in 1938, fleeing Franco's dictatorship. An important disciple of Gaos, Zea became a key thinker of the History of Ideas school in Mexico. It is interesting to note that Leslie Armour also argues that, for most of the founding philosophers in Canada, they understood their disciple as thoroughly historical.[7] Thus, knowledge of the history of ideas seems to be the starting point of intellectual reflection in both countries.

Canadian Studies has one of its origins in the founding of the Institute of Canadian Studies at Carleton University in 1957 and in the creation of the *Journal of Canadian Studies* in 1966.[8] An important impulse for the emerging field of Canadian studies was Thomas H. B. Symons's report for the Commission on Canadian Studies, entitled *To Know Ourselves,*[9] which placed an emphasis on the growing recognition of the values of area studies and the importance of the "national interest," and maintained as the main thesis that "a citizen's primary duty is 'to try to know what should be changed in his society and what should be preserved'—a responsibility that we cannot begin to discharge until, as citizens, we know our country."[10] In the 1990s the Cameron report appeared. Entitled *Taking Stock: Canadian Studies in the Nineties,* it was commissioned to analyze the development of Canadian Studies since the Symons report.[11] Both documents can be seen, according to Greg Nielsen and John Jackson, as "political documents" concerning the institutionalization of Canadian Studies within the formal structures of education (universities and research centres), though losing strength as a field of understanding and as an intellectual enterprise.[12] Likewise, Angus argues that the practice and rationale for Canadian Studies have drastically lost their original legitimacy due to the fact that it has been separated from any discernible political project. He calls for a reconstruction of a national-popular collective will for Canadian Studies instead of its insertion into the mainstream structures of universities and the state as a whole.[13] The final blow to Angus's idea came with the government of Stephen Harper. Harper, as first prime minister of the new Conservative Party (from 2006 to 2015), cancelled the 35-year-old Understanding Canada Program, which had included scholarships for foreign researchers and financial resources for Canadian Studies programs in universities abroad.[14]

There is a long tradition in Latin American countries of importing ideas and concepts from Europe and the United States and applying them indiscriminately to the social reality of Latin America. In other words, social researchers "copy" foreign theories, concepts, and methods regardless of whether they are applicable to their object of study. Gaos called this epistemological situation the "imperialism of the categories": for example, categories originating from Europe travel to Latin America without receiving the necessary modifications and adaptations that the case requires.[15] In the same way, the Canadian philosophers Elizabeth Trott and Leslie Armour argue that not all the problems of Canadian philosophy can be solved by the use of imported ideas and theories.[16]

I have named this process of importation and imitation a "cover" science, and the task of the best philosophers in both countries has been to offer innovative and original responses to so-called universal inquiries from a Mexican or Canadian perspective.[17] In Latin America, this is the case with dependency theory, the sociology of exploitation—theories and concepts that were and are attempting a sort of "import-substitution" of knowledge.

George Grant also urged one's "own" approach to philosophical traditions. At a Canadian Studies meeting in Halifax in 1982, Grant discussed what it means for Canadian intellectuals to study Canada and reached the following conclusion: "My study of Rousseau is a Canadian study." Mentioning this anecdote, Angus argues that, for Grant, the task of philosophy in Canada was the creation of ideas through dialogue with the great "universal" philosophers: "Argue with Rousseau, argue with Plato, through this dialogue we make Canadian philosophy."[18]

In Canada and Mexico, the Indigenous are the most marginalized group in these respective societies. The social situation (in terms of suicide rate, levels of poverty, and health) of Canadian

First Nations differs greatly from the non-Indigenous population.[19] According to the *United Nations Human Development Index*, Canada has one of the highest levels in the world in terms of literacy rate, schooling, life expectancy, and per capita income. However, when Indigenous peoples are considered separately, their life expectancy is seven or eight years shorter. Karen Charleson—a writer and member of the Hesquiaht First Nation located near Vancouver—concludes that Indigenous peoples in Canada find themselves in a similar socio-economic situation to their peers in the Global South.[20] Whereas the status of the Indigenous population has many similarities, both in Canada and Mexico, the political and intellectual debate about their relationship with the majority population is different. In Canada, a great emphasis is placed on the debate about multiculturalism;[21] whereas, in Mexico, the debate focuses on the exclusion of Indigenous people from the *mestizo* national identity.

In the case of Canada, multicultural politics has, according to John W. Friesen, several important dimensions: the promotion of policies that guarantee equity and access to government services for people of different ethnic groups; and the support, promotion, and preservation of the linguistic and cultural particularities of the different ethnic groups in a country.[22] Multiculturalism as a federal policy was the result of a Royal Commission on Bilingualism and Biculturalism in the years 1962 to 1969. This commission recognized the British and the French as the two "founding races/Charter Nations" and gave their languages the status of official languages in the country. This policy implied the exclusion of Indigenous languages.[23] As Angus points out, the difference between the predominant founding group (that is, Anglo-Saxon Canada) and the rest of the two founding groups (French or Québécois Canada and First Nations) is the key point of the matter.[24] Therefore, both the representatives of the last founding groups reject their inclusion in Canada through multiculturalism. Above all, the intellectual representatives of the Canadian First Nations have made the critical claim that multiculturalism aims to equalize the rights of recent immigrants who arrived in Canada with their own. Thus, as Marianne Boelscher and Ronald E. Ignace say, multiculturalism "tends to acknowledge ethnic diversity as diversity without history, without inherent collective rights to political, economic and cultural self-expression, which, in turn, aboriginal peoples have historically maintained for themselves and continue to strive to have recognized."[25] As a possible solution for the Indigenous people of Canada, the university professor and member of the Mohawk tribe Taiaiake Alfred proposes a "native nationalism" that reconstructs the social and governmental institutions of indigenous culture.[26]

In Mexico, however, the central debate focuses on the relationship between the Indigenous population (minority) and the mestizo (majority) population. Luis Villoro points out that the cultural and legal situation of the Indigenous populations worsened after independence in comparison with their situation during colonial times when religious orders and the Crown managed to raise barriers against the oppression of conquerors.[27] Indigenous rights were recognized by specific laws (the so-called *Leyes de la Indias* or Laws of the Indies) that offered a space where parts of Indigenous cultures were preserved and their specificity recognized. Through the direct appointment of their own authorities, the Indigenous communities had some autonomy from the colonial authorities. In the case of Canada, the situation was very similar with the 1763 Royal Proclamation (declared by the British Crown) and its application, which, according to Boelscher and Ignace, "while turning the Crown into the sole agent to deal with Indian people's interests and lands, guaranteed a measure of protection of these interests, and recognition of aboriginal 'nations,' along with their rights and lands."[28]

After independence this situation changed in both countries. In the case of Mexico, after gaining independence in 1821, the sovereignty falls to the "people," understood as the community of individuals equal before the law. The aforementioned difference between subjects disappears within the newly founded Mexican state. In reality, the constitution of the new state is the work of a group of creoles and mestizos that imposes itself on the multiplicity of ethnic groups and regions of the country, without consulting them. The Indigenous peoples are not recognized by the political and legal structure of the new nation.[29]

This new relationship between the majority population and the Indigenous population was named by Mexican sociologist Pablo González Casanova "internal colonialism":

> The notion of "internal colonialism" has its roots in the great independence movement of the old colonies. The experience of independence has customarily stimulated new notions about independence and development. With the creation of the nation-state as a motor of development and the disappearance of the "imperialistic ogre," there appears a need for technicians and professionals, for contractors and capital. With the disappearance of the direct domination of foreigners over natives, the notion of domination and exploitation of natives by natives emerges. In the political and historical literature of the nineteenth and twentieth centuries it can be observed how the Latin American countries absorb these new experiences. The "pro-Indian" and liberal literature of the nineteenth century point to the substitution of the domination of Spaniards by that of the "creoles." Interestingly, the exploitation of the Indians continues, having the same characteristics it had before independence.[30]

Thus, colonialism cannot be seen only from an international perspective but also as an internal phenomenon that can be observed not only in Latin America but also in Canada or Australia.

The EZLN (Ejercito Zapatista de Liberación Nacional—Zapatista Army of National Liberation) uprising in the Mexican state of Chiapas in 1994 brought the debate on the status of the

Indigenous population to the forefront. For the Mexican writer Hector Diaz-Polanco, the greatest contribution of the EZLN was its linking the demands for autonomy of the Indigenous peoples of Chiapas with the national struggle for democracy and social justice.[31] Likewise, the Mexican Zapatista movement inspired constitutional changes in favour of the Indigenous peoples in the Andean region at the turn of the twentieth to the twenty-first century.[32]

George Grant and Leopoldo Zea can be considered as the most important and influential philosophers of the twentieth century in their respective countries.[33] Both authors dedicated a part of their vast work to the question of the "marginality" of their nations with respect to the United States, and both were deeply influenced by German historicism. One of the starting points of the thought of George Grant is his doctoral thesis written with reference to the work of the English theologian John Wood, who maintained the thesis that "the true integral fulfillment of religion" is done "in freedom and independent thought, to discover our true relationship with the past and with society."[34] The thinking of Zea received important impulse from his teacher, the Mexican-Spanish philosopher José Gaos, who takes up the basic axiological principle of the person who is the central axis in which a historical circumstance is judged. In almost all his writings, Zea establishes the mediation between philosophy and history with the aim of liberating the person from colonial rule. Thus, Grant and Zea have been, as Michael Weinstein says, "seeking universal significance through their specific historical circumstances, especially that of the dependence of their respective countries on the American empire."[35]

For both Grant and Zea, the United States is the supreme example of "modernity," which both link to a technological empire that tends to generate a universal and homogenizing condition.[36] According to Arthur Kroker, Canada's main contribution to North American thought consists of "a highly original, comprehensive, and eloquent discourse on technology."[37] For Grant, technology is universal in the sense that each person in the world's economic and political system is included and submitted to it. It tends to be homogenizing because it causes the standardization of life and culture in almost all parts of the world: technology breaks with and destroys particular traditions.[38] In a parallel way, Zea maintains the thesis that the predominance of the United States in matters of technology subordinates collective entities—forms of daily life that embody interests that transcend the individual—to a form of daily life defined by the interests of the individual. In a community, individuals are intertwined and live together by virtue of an end that transcends them; in a society, each individual seeks in daily life the elements that allow its improvement and ensure that their efforts towards social good result in the dessert for its own benefit.[39] Thus, both see the homogenization and the selfishness of the technological society as destroying communities. Canadian philosopher Leslie Armour argues that Canada constitutes (or at least constituted in the beginning) a counter-model against pragmatism and American individualism: Canada is an organic society in which there is room for a mutual interest, a mutual dependence, and for a common good that transcends.[40]

Both Grant and Zea overcame the limitations that academic life imposes on intellectuals. Grant participated in televised debates and declared himself to be a philosopher inspired by Christianity—a fact that alienated him from official philosophy in Canada.[41] Grant's marginalization became evident, for example, in University of Toronto philosopher David Gauthier's criticism of his failure to use methods of logical or linguistic analysis.[42] Likewise, Zea was a tireless promoter of Latin American Studies and academic and journalistic publications. Grant and Zea dedicated their life and work to aspiring, in the words of Ortega y Gasset, to "the height of the times."[43] That is, they tried to link their thinking to the historical circumstances in which they had to live. Both Canadian and Mexican thinkers provide elements to make clear that the thinking and intellectual discussion of their respective countries are profoundly different from that of their "big neighbour." As we have seen in the ideas presented here, there are many similarities and points of coincidence in the thinking in both countries. One of the central topics is the issue of marginality within an imperial history that, according to Angus, calls for an ethical critique of empire in dependent countries like Canada and Mexico, "whose articulation must pass through the structuring and publication centres of empire, are treated as 'cases,' whereas issues of human universality can be treated directly if one resides at the centre, that is to say, shares the assumptions that underpin empire."[44] By addressing and overcoming this dependency, Canada and Mexico could benefit mutually from their ambiguous relations with the United States.

Notes to Chapter 8:

* This essay is based on my article, "Dependencia e imperio: Algunos aspectos comparativos del pensamiento en Canadá y México," *Cuadernos Americanos* 5, no. 113 (2005): 91–106. The present text is an updated and revised version of the original text in Spanish. The elaboration of that text was possible thanks to a grant from the Canadian government (Faculty Research Grant) in 2004. The research stay was carried out at the Department of Humanities (Simon Fraser University). I especially appreciate my host, Ian Angus, for his great hospitality, generosity, and support to explore the similarities and differences of Canadian and Mexican thought. In the same way, I learned a lot from conversations with Andrew Feenberg, Arthur and Marielouise Kroker, Philip Resnick, and Samuel LaSelva. Of course, this essay is my own responsibility.

1 A very important aspect of Ian Angus's work is the reflection on the social identity of "English Canada." See, for example: Ian Angus, "The Paradox of Cultural Identity in English Canada," *Topia: A Canadian Journal of Cultural Studies* 10 (2003): 23–38.

2 Ian Angus, *A Border Within: National Identity, Cultural Plurality, and Wilderness* (Montreal and Kingston: McGill-Queen's University Press, 1997), 112.

3 The relations between French Canada (Québec) and Mexico (and Latin America in general) are not part of this essay.

4 Angus, *A Border Within*, 112.

5 The CCyDEL was renamed in 2016 to CIALC (Centro de Investigaciones sobre América Latina y el Caribe).

6 Enrique Dussel, "Philosophy in Latin America in the Twentieth Century: Problems and Currents," in *Latin American Philosophy: Currents, Issues, Debates*, ed. Eduardo Mendieta (Indianapolis: Indiana University Press, 2003), 26.

7 Leslie Armour, *The Idea of Canada and the Crisis of Community* (Ottawa: Steel Rail Publishing, 1981), 110–11.

8 Johan H. Wadland, "Voices in Search of a Conversation: An Unfinished Project," *Journal of Canadian Studies* 35, no. 1 (2000): 52–75.

9 Thomas H. B. Symons, *To Know Ourselves: The Report of the Commission on Canadian Studies* (Ottawa: Association of Universities and Colleges of Canada, 1975).

10 Ibid., 19–20.

11 David Cameron, *Taking Stock: Canadian Studies in the Nineties* (Montreal: Association for Canadian Studies, 1996).

12 Greg M. Nielsen and John D. Jackson, "Cultural Studies, a Sociological Poetics: Institutions of the Canadian Imaginary," *Canadian Review of Sociology & Anthropology* 28, no. 2 (1991): 279–98.

13 Angus, *A Border Within*, 37.

14 Brooke Jeffrey, *Dismantling Canada: Stephen Harper's New Conservative Agenda* (Montreal: McGill-Queen's University Press, 2015), 343.

15 José Gaos, *En torno a la filosofía mexicana* (Mexico City: Alianza Editorial Mexicana, 1980), 34.

16 Elizabeth Trott and Leslie Armour, "The Faces of Reason and Its Critics," *Dialogue* XXV, no. 1 (1986): 105–6.

17 Johannes Maerk, "Overcoming Cover-Science in Latin American Social Sciences and Humanities—An Intervention," in *Power and Justice in International Relations: Interdisciplinary Approaches to Global Challenges*, ed. Andreas Oberprantacher and Marie-Luisa Frick (Abingdon: Routledge, 2009), 185.

18 Angus, *A Border Within*, 232.

19 Philip Resnick, *Thinking English Canada* (Toronto: Stoddart, 1994), 61.

20 Karen Charleson, "Third World Canada," *Canadian Dimension* 32, no. 1 (1998): 12.

21 This has changed in recent years due to the establishment of the TRC (Truth and Reconciliation Commission of Canada) in 2008 regarding the residential schools. Previous thought was that these schools should keep the Indigenous children away from their parents and at the same time from their cultural influence. The use of their respective native language was strictly forbidden and instead they should learn English or French. Associated with this was a general civilization mission. An overview about this topic can be found in Andrew Woolford and Jeff Benvenuto, "Canada and Colonial Genocide," *Journal of Genocide Research* 17, no. 4 (2015): 373–90.

22 John W. Friesen, *The Cultural Maze: Complex Questions on Native Destiny in Western Canada* (Calgary: Detselig, 1991), 243–44.

23 Marianne Boelscher and Ronald E. Ignace, "The Old Wolf in Sheep's Clothing? Canadian Aboriginal Peoples and Multiculturalism," in *Multiculturalism in a World of Leaking Boundaries*, ed. Dieter Haselbach (Münster: LIT Verlag, 1998), 141.

24 Ian Angus, "Cultural Plurality and Democracy," *International Journal of Canadian Studies / Revue Internationale d'études canadiennes* 25 (2002): 69–85.

25 Boelscher and Ignace, "The Old Wolf," 151.

26 Taiaiake Alfred, *Peace, Power, Righteousness: An Indigenous Manifesto* (Don Mills: Oxford University Press, 1999), xvii.

27 Luis Villoro, *Estado plural, pluralidad de culturas* (Mexico City: Paidos-UNAM, 1998), 40.

28 Boelscher and Ignace, "The Old Wolf," 136.

29 Villoro, *Estado plural*, 41.

30 Pablo González Casanova, "Internal Colonialism and National Development," *Studies in Comparative International Development* 1, no. 2 (1965): 27.

31 Héctor Díaz Polanco, *La Rebelion Zapatista y la Autonomia* (Mexico City: Siglo XXI, 1997).

32 Pascal Lupien, "The Incorporation of Indigenous Concepts of Plurinationality into the New Constitutions of Ecuador and Bolivia," *Democratization* 18, no. 3 (2011): 774–96.

33 George Parkin Grant (1918–1988) was one of the most influential Canadian thinkers of his time. He was educated at the Canadian University of Queen's in history and in theology at Oxford. He taught philosophy at the University of Dalhousie from 1947 to 1960, then he was professor of religion at the University of McMaster. In his last years (since 1980) he worked again at the University of Dalhousie, teaching in the disciplines of political science, Greek-Latin studies, and religion.

Leopoldo Zea (1912–2004) was educated at the UNAM (National Autonomous University of Mexico) in philosophy and law. His doctoral thesis was a pioneering work on positivism in Mexico under the direction of José Gaos. In 1944 he received a chair at his alma mater and in 1947 he started a research project on the history of ideas that was carried out with the support of researchers from all over the Latin American continent. Zea gave a great boost to Latin American studies by organizing congresses and seminars around the world.

34 The quotes of John Wood Oman can be found in Michael A. Weinstein, "George Grant y Leopoldo Zea: Conciencia de marginalidad," in *Filosofar a la altura del hombre: Discrepar para comprender*, ed. Leopoldo Zea (Mexico City: UNAM, 1993), 332.

35 Weinstein, "George Grant y Leopoldo Zea," 332.

36 George Grant, *Technology and Empire: Perspectives on North America* (Toronto: House of Anansi, 1969); Leopoldo Zea, *La esencia de lo Americano* (Buenos Aires: Peamar, 1971).

37 Arthur Kroker, *Technology and the Canadian Mind: Innis/McLuhan/Grant* (Montréal: New World Perspectives, 1984), 7.

38 Angus, *A Border Within*, 77.

39 Zea, *La escencia*, 55.

40 Armour, *Idea of Canada*, xiv.

41 Harris Athanasiadis, "Review of the George Grant Reader," *The Presbyterian Record* 123, no. 7 (1999): 44–45.

42 Angus, *A Border Within*, 231.

43 José Ortega y Gasset, *The Revolt of the Masses* (New York: Norton, 1957), 28.

44 Ian Angus, *Identity and Justice* (Toronto: University of Toronto Press, 2008), 8.

Chapter 9

Traditional Knowledge and Humanities

*A Perspective by a Blackfoot**

Leroy Little Bear

The author has always understood humanities in academia as being about humans and their culture, including philosophy, world view, and arts, and excluding hard sciences. A definition of humanities that strikes a deep chord with this writer is one framed by the Ohio Humanities Council as follows:

> The humanities are the stories, the ideas, and the words that help us make sense of our lives and our world. The humanities introduce us to people we have never met, places we have never visited, and ideas that may have never crossed our minds. By showing how others have lived and thought about life, the humanities help us decide what is important in our own lives and what we can do to make them better. By connecting us with other people, they point the way to answers about what is right or wrong, or what is true to our

> heritage and our history. The humanities help us address the challenges we face together in our families, our communities, and as a nation.[1]

The above definition of "the humanities," it seems, captures very well the experience of Aboriginal people in academia. In other words, Aboriginal people are forever explaining themselves to non-Aboriginal people: telling their stories, explaining their beliefs and ceremonies, and introducing ideas that, in many cases, have never crossed the non-Aboriginal mind. The following overview of traditional knowledge serves as a good example of what I mean by this.

Rosamond B. Spicer and Edward H. Spicer refer to Daniel Corkery to make a point about North American Indians. Corkery, in 1925, had written a book called *The Hidden Ireland*.[2] In it he points out that there existed a rich culture in Ireland hidden from the English colonizers:

"Few, if any, of the English people were aware of the Irish language, and those who were aware during the eighteen and nineteenth centuries associated it only with illiterate and backward peasantry.... That it had continued into the nineteenth century as a medium of literary life in Ireland was simply beyond the pale of English consciousness."[3]

In other words, Irish culture was hidden from the English. Spicer and Spicer point out, for instance, "In the United States, the Iroquois and the 'Americans' had known each other for more than two hundred years, but the Americans who made policy for New York State in the 1960s knew nothing of the language, the cultural history or the religion of the Seneca."[4] Writing in 1973, Vine Deloria Jr. in *God Is Red* states, "Sincere but unknowing whites honestly asked us less than a decade ago if we still lived in tents, if we were allowed to leave the reservations, and other relevant questions, indicating that for a substantial number of Americans, Indians were still shooting at the Union Pacific on their days off."[5] One can, in a similar manner, apply the concept of "hiddenness" to traditional knowledge of Aboriginal people in North America. Generally speaking, Euro-Canadians and Euro-Americans know very little of the languages, religions, traditions, sciences, and so on of North American Aboriginal people. Traditional knowledge of Aboriginal people has never been taken seriously because it is usually categorized as superstition or folklore. If one were to ask the typical academic about the utility or importance of traditional knowledge in the academic world, he/she would most likely answer, "not much."

There are "tons" of studies of Aboriginal peoples by government, missionaries, and social scientists. However, the majority, if not all, of those studies are done from a Eurocentric perspective based on Western paradigms. Only recently has traditional knowledge of Aboriginal people been experiencing a "coming out" in Canada partially brought about by the intellectual property debate and recent Supreme Court of Canada decisions. As James (Sákéj) Youngblood Henderson and Marie Battiste say, "The rush on Indigenous knowledge systems, teachings, and heritage by outsiders is an effort to access, to know, and to assert control over these resources.... As Indigenous knowledge and heritage becomes more intensely attractive commercially, the cognitive heritage that gives Indigenous peoples their identity is under assault from those who would gather it up, strip away its honored meanings, convert it to a product, and sell it."[6] Deloria makes a similar observation: "When multitudes of young whites roam the West convinced they are Oglala Sioux Pipe Carriers and on a holy mission to protect 'Mother Earth' and when priests and ministers, scientists and drug companies, ecologists and environmentalists are crowding the reservations in search of new rituals, new medicines, or new ideas about the land, it would appear as if American Indians finally have it made."[7]

Aboriginal people have for a long time questioned the assumptions and methodologies superimposed on their knowledge systems. However, only within the recent past, with the reluctant acceptance of Native Studies in academia and the consequent increase in the number of Aboriginal scholars trained in the Eurocentric tradition, have the writings of Aboriginal scholars challenging Eurocentric assumptions and methodologies begun to make "inroads" into academia. However, the numbers of Aboriginal scholars and their works are very small in comparison with writings about North American Aboriginal people by non-Aboriginal scholars. The intent of this short article is not to pass on every piece of writing about Aboriginal traditional knowledge. (Aboriginal people have been explaining themselves to the colonizers ever since contact.) However, the intent is to look at a select number of Aboriginal scholars who have attempted to articulate the foundational bases of traditional knowledge.

I. Traditional Knowledge: Problems of Definition

As Henderson and Battiste point out, there is no easy answer to the question of the bases of traditional knowledge because it is a comparative question, and no satisfactory research methodology exists to answer the question.[8] It does not fit neatly into Eurocentric categories such as "culture" and its subcategories of religion, social culture, politics, economics, and so on. Using Eurocentric categories, one can divide knowledge into a whole number of specialized fields such as medicinal, environmental, geographic, cosmic, biological, psychological, scientific, and so forth. However, the categorizing processes in Aboriginal languages simply are not complementary to Eurocentric language-categorizing processes. Henderson and Battiste point out that "Indigenous scholars choose to view every way of life from two different but complementary perspectives: first as a manifestation of human knowledge, heritage, and consciousness, and second, as a mode of ecological order."[9] In other words, traditional knowledge is not a product or object that can be defined and studied in isolation. It is participatory and experiential. Gregory Cajete states, "Native science is not quantum physics or environmental science, but it has come to similar understandings about the workings of the natural laws through experience and participation with the natural world."[10] Traditional knowledge is about the spiritual and livingness of the natural world and the role of humans in it.

Knowledge of all creation by any one person is impossible. Consequently, as Henderson and Battiste say, "traditional knowledge is not a uniform concept across different Aboriginal cultures ... it is a diverse knowledge that is spread throughout different peoples in many layers."[11] It is, in many cases, "part of the clan, band, and the community, and even the individual, ... it cannot be separated from the bearer to be codified into a definition."[12] In other words, there is knowledge that the Aboriginal public knows or is expected to know. However, there is knowledge that is unique to clans, bands, societies, and individuals. Some of this knowledge is considered as belonging to the clan, band, society, or tribe but is given to individuals or groups to keep for the benefit of the tribe. The Aboriginal public is not privy to this knowledge but it is kept for their benefit by knowledge keepers.

II. Aboriginal Paradigms and Traditional Knowledge

It is an impossibility to explicate and articulate traditional knowledge in all its aspects in a short article. However, in the view of this writer, the most important aspect of traditional knowledge is its philosophical and/or paradigmatic base. The philosophy/paradigm is the lens through which all sense data are interpreted to define reality. The actual application of knowledge is the manifestations of the interpretation of the sense datum based on the philosophy/paradigm.

What are the tenets of native philosophy as articulated by Aboriginal scholars? Leroy Little Bear and Amethyst First Rider have articulated native philosophy in both published and unpublished works. Both scholars state that native philosophy consists of and includes ideas of constant motion/flux, all creation consisting of energy waves, everything being animate, all creation being interrelated, reality requiring renewal, and space as a major referent.[13] Gary Witherspoon, a non-Aboriginal, studying the Navajo, observes, "The assumption that underlies this dualistic aspect of all being and existence is that the world is in motion, that things are constantly undergoing processes of transformation, deformation, and restoration, and that the essence of life and being is movement."[14]

With regard to interrelations, the Task Force on the Criminal Justice System and Its Impact on the Indian and Métis Peoples of Alberta states: "The holistic view leads to an implicit assumption that everything is interrelated. Interrelatedness leads to an implicit idea of equality among all creation. Equality is brought about [by] the implicit belief that everything—humans, animals, plants, and inorganic matter—has a spirit. Anthropomorphic factors are not important because metamorphosis readily occurs. The common denominator is the spirit."[15]

Little Bear states that Aboriginal philosophy incorporates the idea of renewal. "There is a tacit assumption that, in the cosmic flux, there exist particular combinations of energy waves that allow for our continuing existence. If those particular combinations of energy waves dissolve, this particular reality we are in will disappear in the flux."[16]

Cajete, writing about native science, observes, "Chaos is both movement and evolution. It is the process through which everything in the universe becomes manifest and then returns to the chaos field. The flux, or ebb and flow, of chaos appears in everything and envelops us at all times and in all places. From the evolving universe to the mountain to the human brain, chaos is the field from which all things come into being. No wonder Native Science envisions the spirit of the natural world alive with disorder becoming order and all the mystery of mirrored relationships."[17]

Consequently, Aboriginal people have a large number of ceremonies revolving around renewal. These ceremonies manifest as sweatlodge, sundance, medicine bundle ceremonies, and the like.

First Rider contends that space is a very important referent in the minds of Aboriginal people. Certain events, patterns, cycles, and happenings are readily observable on and from the land: for example, animal migrations, cycles of plant life, seasonal rounds, and so on. The cosmos is also observable and its patterns detected from particular special locations.[18] Vine Deloria Jr. in *God Is Red* states:

> In shifting from temporal concepts to spatial terms, we find that a revelation is not so much the period of time in which it occurs as the place it may occur. Revelation becomes a particular experience at a particular place, no universal truth emerging but an awareness arising that certain places have a qualitative holiness over and above other places. The universality of truth then becomes the relevance of the experience for a community of people, not its continual adjustment to evolving scientific and philosophical conceptions of the universe. Holy places are well known in what have been classified as primitive religions. The vast majority of Indian tribal religions have a center at a particular place, be it river, mountain, plateau, valley, or other natural feature.[19]

Little Bear compares and contrasts Western thought with Aboriginal thought.

> Space is a major referent in the mind of Aboriginal peoples as opposed to time, which is a major referent in the minds of Westerners. The constant flux notion results in a holistic and repetitive view. If everything is forever moving and changing, one has to look at the whole of being to discern developing patterns. It is a way of thinking that looks at the forest and not the trees. The holistic view, in turn, gives rise to values that regard the group as more important than the individual. It values a 'generalist' more than the 'specialist.'[20]

For Westerners, according to Little Bear, time is a major referent. Time is a good example of the Western way of thinking.

> Time is conceptualized as a straight line. If a Nacirema (American spelled backwards) attempted to picture 'time' in his mind, he would see something like a river flowing toward and on past him. What is behind would be the past. What is immediately around him would be the present. The future would be upstream, but he would not be able to see very far upstream because of a waterfall, the waterfall symbolizing the barrier to knowing the future. This line of time is conceptualized as quantity especially as lengths made of units. A length of time is envisioned as a row of similar units.

"A logical and inherent characteristic of the concept of time is that once a unit of the river of time flows past a Nacirema it never returns—it is gone forever." This characteristic lends itself to other concepts as "wasting time," "making up time," "buying time," and "being on time," which are unique to the Nacirema. "Another characteristic is that each unit of time is totally different and independent of similar units. Consequently, for the Nacirema, each day is considered a different unit, and thus a different day; every year is a new year. From this the reader can readily understand why there is a need among the Nacirema to have names for days and months and numbers for years."[21]

For Aboriginal people, time just is. Benjamin Whorf, writing about the Hopi concept of time, states:

"[Time] is a realm of expectancy, of desire and purpose, of vitalizing life, of efficient causes, of thought thinking itself out from inner realm [the Hopian heart] into manifestation. It is in a dynamic state, yet not a state of motion. It is not advancing toward us out of a future, but already with us in vital form, and its dynamism is at work in the field of eventuating or manifesting, i.e. evolving without motion from the subjective by degrees to a result which is the objective."[22]

Plains Indians, Little Bear says, have similar time concepts. "Blackfoot thinks of time on a two-day operational." There is "now," "tomorrow," and "day-after tomorrow." And backwards, "now," "yesterday," and "day-before yesterday." Beyond the two-day limit, forward or backward, past and present amalgamate and become one and the same. Plains Indians are not incapable of talking or thinking of the distant future or past, but it is always done with the "constant flux" in mind. One of the implications arising out of this notion of time is that the ancestors are always only two days away. The stories, the songs, the ceremonies, the teachings are never more than two days old in the memory of the people. This is quite different from Pierre Elliott Trudeau's statement, typifying the Euro-Canadian world view, to the effect that "these treaties are not worth the paper they are written on." As Little Bear states, "In other words, what is past is past … it is gone forever. The only thing that matters is the future."[23]

Cajete lists the following as the guiding thoughts pervading native science:

- Native science integrates a spiritual orientation.
- Dynamic multidimensional harmony is a perpetual state of the universe.
- All human knowledge is related to the creation of the world and the emergence of humans; therefore, human knowledge is based on human cosmology.
- Humanity has an important role in the perpetuation of the natural processes of the world.
- Every "thing" is animate and has spirit.
- There is significance to each natural place because each place reflects the whole order of nature.
- The history of relationship must be respected with regard to places, plants, animals, and natural phenomena.

- Technology should be appropriate and reflect balanced relationships to the natural world.
- There are basic relationships, patterns, and cycles in the world that need to be understood; this is the proper role of mathematics.
- There are stages of initiation to knowledge.
- Elders are relied upon as the keepers of essential knowledge.
- Acting in the world must be sanctioned through ritual and ceremony.
- Properly fashioned artifacts contain the energy of the thoughts, materials, and contexts in which they are fashioned and therefore become symbols of those thoughts, entities, or processes.
- Dreams are considered gateways to creative possibilities if used wisely and practically.[24]

III. Language and Traditional Knowledge

Language plays a very important role in philosophy. For Battiste, native philosophy operates according to cognitive and linguistic maps: "In short, under tribal knowledge, language is cognitive power."[25] She says, "Aboriginal languages are sacred to Aboriginal people. They speak in the voice and lessons of a sacred place, an Aboriginal homeland. They are a central source of survival for the diverse people, as well as a critical link to a knowledge base given to them by their Creator."[26]

According to Little Bear, "It can be generally said that Euro-languages like English are very noun-oriented. English is a good language for dichotomies, categorizations, and reductionist-specificity. In its dichotomy mode, it manifests polarized, binary thinking: good and bad; saint and sinner; black and white; old and new; and so on. Aboriginal languages, generally, can be said to be action oriented.

Everything is about process, actions, and happenings. It can be said that constant flux manifests itself in the language."[27]

For Henderson and Battiste, "Where Indigenous knowledge survived, it is transmitted through symbolic and oral traditions."[28] Aboriginal languages are viewed as forms of spirituality: "Indigenous peoples view their languages as forms of spiritual identity. Indigenous languages are thus sacred to Indigenous peoples. They provide the deep cognitive bonds that affect all aspects of Indigenous life."[29] In other words, Aboriginal languages, because of their action and process orientations, are complementary to the participatory role of Aboriginal people in and with the natural world.

IV. Some Conclusionary Thoughts

From this brief review, it can be readily seen that Aboriginal traditional knowledge has a very different paradigmatic base from that of Western knowledge. Whereas Western knowledge operates from a linear, singular view, whereas Western knowledge views the world from order beneath chaos, whereas Western languages are very noun-oriented, knowledge is about you (first person) in relation to everything else in a relativistic sense. Aboriginal knowledge has a very different "coming to know." It is holistic and cyclical; it views the world from chaos underneath order; its languages are process- and action-oriented. Knowledge is about participation in and with the natural world. Policy and research implications arising out of Aboriginal paradigms cannot be underestimated. In the *Van der Peet* case, the Supreme Court of Canada stated, "The Courts must not undervalue the evidence presented by Aboriginal claimants simply because that evidence does not conform precisely with evidentiary standards that would be applied in, for example, a private law case."[30] In a similar manner, one can say that Aboriginal traditional knowledge should not be discounted simply because it does not fit neatly into academic standards and categories. If Aboriginal paradigms are not taken into consideration, policy, research, and the "humanities" will simply miss the mark.

The above overview is a good representation of what the humanities are about. It is the storytelling of what traditional knowledge is about; it is the ideas about reality from a Blackfoot perspective; it is about ideas that normally do not cross the Western mind; it is an attempt to connect with the Western mind so it will understand the world view, the customs, and lifeways of people like the Blackfoot. It resonates with the definition of the "humanities" in academia.

Notes to Chapter 9:

* This article was originally presented at the symposium "Is There, Can There Be, Such an Activity as World Humanities?" held at Simon Fraser University, January 27–28, 2012, and then published in *Journal of Chinese Philosophy* 39, no. 4 (December 2012): 518–27. It is reproduced here with the kind permission of the journal.

1 Ohio Humanities Council, "What Are the Humanities?" available at http://www.units.muohio.edu/technologyandhumanities/humanitiesdefinition.htm.

2 Daniel Corkery, *The Hidden Ireland: A Study of Gaelic Munster in the Eighteenth Century* (Dublin: M.H. Gill and Son, 1925).

3 Rosamond B. Spicer and Edward H. Spicer, "The Nations of a State," in *American Indian Persistence and Resurgence*, ed. Karl Kroeber (Durham: Duke University Press, 1994), 31,

4 Ibid.

5 Vine Deloria Jr., *God Is Red* (New York: Dell, 1973), 41.

6 James (Sákéj) Youngblood Henderson and Marie Battiste, *Protecting Indigenous Knowledge and Heritage: A Global Challenge* (Saskatoon: Purich Publishing, 2000), 12.

7 Vine Deloria Jr., *Red Earth White Lies: Native Americans and the Myth of Scientific Fact* (New York: Scribner, 1995), 13.

8 Henderson and Battiste, *Protecting Indigenous Knowledge*, 35 (paraphrase).

9 Ibid.

10 Gregory Cajete, *Native Science: Natural Laws of Interdependence* (Santa Fe: Clear Light Publishers, 2000), 14.

11 Henderson and Battiste, *Protecting Indigenous Knowledge*, 35.

12 Ibid., 36.

13 Amethyst First Rider, "Sweet Grass Visions: The Combination of Trickster and Theatre for the Transmission of Culture," MA thesis, University of Calgary, 1994 (paraphrase).

14 Gary Witherspoon, *Language and Art in the Navajo Universe* (Ann Arbor: University of Michigan Press, 1977), 48.

15 Task Force on the Criminal Justice System and Its Impact on the Indian and Métis Peoples of Alberta, *Justice on Trial*, Report of the Task Force on the Criminal Justice System and Its Impact on the Indian and Métis Peoples of Alberta, vol. 1 (Edmonton: Queen's Printer, 1991), 9–13.

16 Leroy Little Bear, *Aboriginal Paradigms: Implications for Relationships to Land and Treaty Making*, Expert Report for the Plaintiffs in *Buffalo vs. the Queen*, 2001, 3.

17 Cajete, *Native Science*, 16.

18 Rider, "Sweet Grass Visions," 14.

19 Deloria, *God Is Red*, 80–81.

20 Little Bear, *Aboriginal Paradigms*, 4.

21 Leroy Little Bear, "Dispute Settlement among the Nacirema," *Journal of Contemporary Law* 1, nos. 1–2 (1974): 337–38.

22 Benjamin Lee Whorf, "An American Indian Model of the Universe," in *Language, Thought and Reality*, ed. John B. Carroll (Cambridge: MIT Press, 1956), 60.

23 Little Bear, *Aboriginal Paradigms*, 5.

24 Cajete, *Native Science*, 64–65.

25 Marie Battiste, "A Reflective Analysis of the Theory and Implications of Tribal Epistemology to Modern Thought and Education," Qualifying Paper, School of Education, Stanford University, 1978, 17.

26 Marie Battiste, "You Can't Be the Doctor if You're the Disease: Tenets of Systematic Colonialism in Canadian Educational Research and Policy," paper presented to the Learned Society, University of Calgary, 1994, 3.

27 Little Bear, *Aboriginal Paradigms*, 5.

28 Henderson and Battiste, *Protecting Indigenous Knowledge*, 48.

29 Ibid., 49.

30 Supreme Court of Canada, *R.v.Van der Peet* [1996] 4 C.N.L.R. 177, para., 68.

Chapter 10

Limits to Social Representation of Value

*Response to Leroy Little Bear**

Ian Angus

The humanities today are in a beleaguered state. The richest countries in the world, especially the English-speaking world, cannot seem to find sufficient funding for study of the humanities. The humanities articulate a culture; they are its spiritual disciplines. As Leroy Little Bear has written,

> Culture … is what structures how a person determines ontological, epistemological, methodological, and axiological aspects of his/her very life and being. Ontology, generally, speaks to the nature of reality.… Epistemology speaks to theories of knowledge: how we come to know. How we come to know, in essence, is a methodology or a validation process. For Aboriginal peoples knowledge is validated through

> actual experience, stories, songs, ceremonies, dreams, and observation. Axiology speaks to what knowledge is important and worthy of pursuit. As stated above by differing authorities, spirituality, relationships, language, songs, stories, ceremonies, and teachings learned through dreams form the axiology of Aboriginal knowledge.[1]

There is no doubt that the commitments evident in the humanities can divide cultures when one insists upon the absoluteness of one's own tradition to the detriment of another. But, one may hope and one must argue, there is a way of holding to one's own commitments in a spirit of openness that allows the other to speak and a dialogue to emerge. Intercultural dialogue in the humanities is a necessity for a world being both brought into close relation and simultaneously endangered by economic and technological forces.

The meaning of a statement in a dialogue cannot be known just by looking at the statement itself.

A statement gains its meaning from a cultural context, which is operative in the meanings and connotations of the words, the mode of articulation—such as playfulness or seriousness, claims to knowledge, artistic creativity, and so on—as well as their relation to historical memory, forms of order, and the interplay of speech and silence. Every statement in a dialogue is thus not only an invitation to another statement, but that invitation to response is made possible by its embeddedness in a cultural context that establishes meaning. Contact between cultural contexts through individual statements requires translation where there are no exactly equivalent terms. It neither terminates in nor aims at a synthesis of cultural contexts, but rather to clear a transversal space of meaning that has a place in both. This space of meaning created by intercultural dialogue allows both a reflection back upon one's own cultural heritage that brings into focus its strengths and limitations and a reflection on the cultural heritage of the other as a source of inspiration.

The source of inspiration that I specifically have in mind is Leroy Little Bear's quotation of the Blackfoot Elder who stated that "I am the environment."[2]

I would like to begin my reflections by briefly recalling a recent series of events. In the late 1990s in Bolivia, due to neo-liberal pressures from the World Bank, there were two waves of privatization of water resources that led to a rise in water prices of 35 per cent. Mass demonstrations and a general strike in 2000 led to the termination of the private concessions and, in 2005, the election of Evo Morales—trade unionist, leader of the Movement for Socialism party, and member of the Aymara Aboriginal people.

The world is now in the midst of a catastrophic struggle over access to water. Within the United Nations (UN), there has been a concerted attempt to establish a right to water as a basic human right. At the same time, privatization of water systems and resources proceeds apace alongside the contamination of the existing water supply. Canada has opposed recognition of the right to clean water at the UN, while Canadian-based mining companies—one of which has made a donation to Simon Fraser University—contaminate water resources in Latin America and elsewhere. Water as a commodity is, like any other commodity, available only to those who pay for it, and those who pay can do anything they like with it. It is no exaggeration to say that the struggle over access to clean water will determine the form of world civilization in the future. Moreover, water is only one example. As for a long time, clean atmospheric air has had a shadow price in the cost of addressing asthma and other breathing problems, and also in the selling of residences on land distanced from industrial and city pollution, one can already glimpse on the horizon the selling of all basic needs for access to nature as commodities. Commodification of the basic necessities of life, and the natural world upon which human labour depends to produce those necessities, leading to the restriction of access to those with enough money, is already in a catastrophic phase in its struggle against those who would recognize a human right to dwell on our native earth.

In the wake of the failure of international conferences and treaties to uphold even the basic minimum of the Kyoto Protocol, let alone take any substantive action concerning climate change, Bolivia convened the 2010 World Peoples' Conference on Climate Change and the Rights of Mother Earth in Cochabamba, where, according to the Indigenous People's Working Group, "the recovery, revalidation and strengthening of our civilizations, identities, cultures and cosmovisions based on ancient and ancestral Indigenous knowledge and wisdom for the construction of alternative ways of life to the current 'development model', [was proposed] as a way to confront climate change."[3] In this and other documents from Cochabamba, as well as a UN speech by Evo Morales, the terminology of Mother Earth, or Pachamama, and that of ecological and environmental science are deployed alongside each other to argue for a radically new approach to ecological disturbance.[4] This debate is, I believe, extremely significant for our time.[5] It provides a compelling reason for dialogue between Aboriginal and European conceptions of the value of the Whole upon which human life depends. As Leroy Little Bear has said, "land is important because the earth is considered our Mother. The earth is the giver of life. Because of the inter-relational aspect of the Blackfoot paradigm, the Mother Earth cannot be separated from the actual being of Indians."[6]

This series of events speaks to the situation that prompts our symposium on the possibility of a world humanities. First, the provision of human needs through a commodity system to which one has access exclusively through money necessarily produces a hierarchical differentiation of access to the satisfaction of human needs and, at its extreme, denies access to the necessary goods of the earth, like water, to those too poor to buy them. So we need to analyze critically a system that registers value only through price. Second, the relationship of human civilization to nature is at a crisis point such that we have to think deeply about our conceptions of spirit and their relationship to nature. Third, our common situation must be addressed from within different systems of knowledge and value—so there must be translation between these systems—which requires an intercultural dialogue on the humanities. I will make a few remarks about each of these issues.

If we leave aside value for now, in the personal sense—what I might value in distinction from you—and focus on its social and institutional dimension, then value is registered in our era overwhelmingly by price. Because wealth appears to the capitalist society in the form of commodities, and because commodities are useful goods with an exchange value most immediately expressed as a price, the value of a commodity is socially represented by its price. This means that the value of one given commodity, registered as a price, is expressed as a quantity of other commodities also expressed by their price. In other words, the price of a commodity registers its value as a quantitative fraction of the commodity market as a whole. It follows that value registered as price is not related to the intrinsic nature of the commodity, per se—its concrete characteristics—but solely through its relationship to the totality of commodities considered as, in principle, equivalent. Of course, commodities also have a concrete use based on their specific characteristics, but for this value to be more than a private preference, it must enter the field of the social representation of value in which its specific value is determined in relation to the totality of relative prices. We may thus speak of two forms of value: the *restricted value* of a given commodity represented by its price, and the *general value* of the whole system of representation of value by price—which amounts to the sum of all restricted values but includes also the relations of quantity established between them such that they form an ordered system of value pertinent to current society. But the point here is not only the *distinction* between restricted and general concepts of value but that a commodity price system *reduces* general value to restricted value. Its only system of general value is available through the sum of restricted values of specific commodities. The total system of value is present as a simple aggregate of restricted values so that it is never addressed as such by any actor, neither pursued nor actualized directly, and is rarely focused upon as such. In contrast, both Mother Earth and ecology thematize the totality of relations—though not as relative values but as the sum of relations of intrinsic values.

Values not registered as prices have little purchase on social institutions and their priorities. It is a well-known problem in environmental economics that pollution, for example, is an *externality* to the production process of a pulp mill. This means that the cost—both monetary and non-monetary—of pollution is borne by others downstream. Thus, an ecological and/or environmental concept of value often defends the *intrinsic value* of a tree or river—which means its value *as* a tree or river in all of its relations with other beings. It is a major tendency in ecological thought to doubt the social representation of value as price and to argue for a conception of value rooted in the specific, concrete characteristics of beings, including those likewise specific and concrete relations in which that being is embedded.

This tendency has been countered by claiming that the only way in which a value can be registered socially and compellingly is for it to have a price and thus that the problem of externalities is precisely that they do not have a price. If the price of pollution, for example, could be *internalized* into the production process, then the motive to pollute would disappear. From this point of view, the solution would be to create new markets to internalize externalities. If every ecological being had a price, it is argued, then it would be registered within the social representation of value and treated accordingly.

Thus, one study for the Trilateral Commission has argued for the creation of markets in pollution credits in a manner that has become typical for attempts to register environmental value within the capitalist economy.

> This global commons has been exploited as a free and infinite resource, without regard to its ultimate capacity. With some ingenuity, markets can be created where none presently exist. The new market can then be left to operate largely unconstrained. Examples include systems of tradable emission permits, as is now proposed for sulfur emissions from power plants in the United States and for CO_2 emissions by nation states. Other examples include water rights, wildlife ranching, and systems of deposits and refunds on hazardous or recyclable wastes. By such an approach, the efficiency of markets can be harnessed to achieve efficient implementation of environmental goals articulated through political choice.[7]

The approach to ecological issues by dominant institutions is to push for a greater commodification of ecological goods so that, it is argued, they will not be degraded because they have value. The value they would have, however, is no longer their intrinsic value as the concrete beings that they are but their relative price. So clean water, for example, would have a market price and could not be degraded as a free good—but it could be bought and degraded at will, thus affecting the general system of value. For this strategy of internalization of externalities through the creation of new markets to be a viable long-term solution, it would have to be the case that the system of relative prices could register each and every ecological good such that relative price would mirror without distortion or remainder the ecosystem itself. For as long as a single ecological aspect was outside the price system, or not properly registered within it, its lack of value would reproduce the problem of externality.

I do not want to spend a lot of time at this point arguing that a system of sufficient complexity to register relative prices of all commodities cannot be consistent and complete in this sense. Consistency would refer to the demand that every price could be determined in relation to every other price—which is unproblematic for a quantitative price system but more difficult for an ecosystem because its qualitative relations have to be determined in every case and are not generalizable. Completeness would refer to the demand that each and every commodity had a value registered as a price. This can be shown to be impossible because the qualitative differences of an ecosystem's parts, produced by the totality of qualitative relations of the ecosystem as a whole, cannot be mirrored within a system in which there is only one quantitative measure. This quantitative measure would illegitimately measure different qualities by summing quantities over different qualities in a way that would render invisible the different qualities that are essential to the notion of ecosystem as such.

The point here is twofold. First, not all elements of an ecosystem can be registered within a price system—externalities always remain; and, second, the notion of totality, or system, is different in each case. The totality of a price system is an aggregate, a sum, and therefore can legitimately be called a "system" because it aims at being self-enclosed and self-regulating—even though it cannot achieve this ideal in practice. The totality of an ecosystem—to use the prevailing term—cannot be a system in this sense, because while it is self-regulating, it cannot be, in principle, self-enclosed. Its boundary is always a pragmatic, and never absolute, limit. It is a Whole given in the form of a horizon that stands behind each part but is not thematically present as such. Once the boundary is defined, it is surpassed by another unthematic boundary. An ecosystem preserves qualitative relations at the price of its boundaries, limits, and purpose becoming indeterminate.

The paradigm of modern biological science was empirical and began from the classification of individual organisms into species genus hierarchies. A new departure began with the science of evolution insofar as it implied that, in Gregory Bateson's words, the unit of evolution is "organism-*plus*- environment."[8] Nevertheless, this recognition took a long time to prevail and it was not until the formulation of the science of ecology that the focus shifted from the makeup of individual organisms to the relationships between organisms, including also non-organic features of the environment.

In a classic paper published in 1935, the British ecologist Arthur C. Tansley discussed the ecological realities of the world: "Though the organisms may claim our primary interest, when we are trying to think fundamentally we cannot separate them from their spatial environment with which they form one physical system. It is the systems so formed which from the point of view of the ecologist are the basic units of nature on the face of the earth."[9]

Ecology is the science of relationships, the dependence of individuals on relationships, and the contribution of the individual to sustaining relationships.

As Arne Naess has explained,

> The expression "ecology" is infused with many meanings. Here, it will mean the interdisciplinary scientific study of the living conditions of organisms in interaction with each other and with the surroundings, organic as well as inorganic.... [T]he aspect of the science of ecology that is most important is the fact that it is concerned first of all with the relationships between entities as an essential component of what these entities are in themselves. These include both internal and external relations. Example: when a bird eats a mosquito it gets in an external relation to that mosquito, but eating is an internal relation to its environment.... This approach can have application in many fields of inquiry—hence the growing influence of the subject of ecology outside its original biological domain.[10]

While ecology began with a strictly scientific meaning, it has come to take on also a popular meaning with the emergence of ecological problems such as environmental diseases, pollution, habitat degradation, and climate change that stem from the paradigm of techno-scientific application to individual problems while ignoring wider contexts and relationships. Through this interplay between scientific meaning and relevance to socio-cultural issues, ecology might well be considered the leading science of our time.

Ecology studies "wholes" made from and sustained by the interaction between their parts. A "whole," or local ecosystem, is distinguished from its outside by a boundary such that the interactions inside can be considered its defining features. The eminent Canadian ecologist J. Stan Rowe calls such a local ecosystem a *community*, a term that has the advantage, I think, of emphasizing that it cannot be a "system" in the rigorous sense: "The community is an aggregate of objects whose primary bond is common occupancy of area. This area basis confers a degree of apparent substantiality on the community, for once the area is bounded a spatial unit appears."[11] Place is thus a basic concept that specifies the *where* of the set of relationships that define a whole. The boundary that circumscribes a place-based community is therefore a plastic concept. A given bay, or the Burrard Inlet, can be considered an ecosystem because it has a boundary that intensifies interactions between the community resident in that place while de-emphasizing interactions between that community and the outside beyond its boundary. But the inlet, or bay, or even city, considered as an ecosystem for some purposes, nevertheless is itself embedded within larger contexts, for example, the Lower Mainland, or the Pacific Coast. One may say that the largest ecosystem is the earth ecosphere because it contains within itself all of the relationships that sustain life on earth.[12] Even so, the earth ecosystem requires incoming energy from the sun across its atmospheric boundary. In the end, "ecosystem" is a way of conceptualizing the Whole that is the universe of all that is through relationships of dependence and maintenance by the community of all beings. Humans, as one species of these beings, depend upon this Whole. A particular grouping of humans—humans within a larger community of beings in a given place circumscribed by an elastic boundary—develops the specifics of their culture in relation to the specifics of the local ecology. It is from this point of view that I understand Leroy Little Bear when he says that "the place acts as a repository of the stories and experiences of both individual and the tribe. In Blackfoot the word for the English word 'story' literally translates as 'involvement' in an event."

The development of ecology as a science and as a leading idea for contemporary world issues thus brings European-derived science into dialogue with Aboriginal conceptions of Mother Earth. Some Aboriginal thinkers use the term "ecology" as a translation of Aboriginal knowledge of dwelling in a place. For example, James (Sákéj) Youngblood Henderson says that "aboriginal knowledge is not a description of reality but an understanding of the processes of ecological change and ever changing insights about diverse patterns or styles of flux."[13] He and coauthor Marie Battiste say that "most Indigenous spiritual teachings and practices flow from ecological understandings rather than from cosmology.... In Indigenous thought, ecologies are considered sacred realms, and they contain the keepers that taught Indigenous ancestors the core of Indigenous spiritual practices... . Such beliefs deny the distinction between the sacred and the profane, since all life processes are sacred."[14]

Here, then, is one problematic aspect of this translation between Mother Earth and ecology: Can the relationships that constitute an ecosystem be considered a sacred, spiritual system that provides ethical direction for human life? Is this a further step that those drawn to ecology might be inclined to make?

Stan Rowe also posed this question:

> Ecology is the science of context, a counterbalance to explanations of phenomena that look inward to their parts. A useful ecological viewpoint places every system of interest in the context of an enveloping system, in the relationship

> of part to whole. From this, a different kind of explanation than provided by reduction emerges, perhaps better called "comprehension." In the relating of phenomena to the supportive systems of which they are components, it goes by various names: "roles," "niches," "significance," "meaning," and the disgraceful "P" word: "purpose."[15]

Rowe's ironic reference to the "disgracefulness" of the idea of purpose refers back to the scientific origins of ecology and, as I read it, contains his hope that ecology can indeed come to reintegrate purpose into science and thereby reverse the expelling of ethic and spirit accomplished by the mathematical science of nature. As Leroy Little Bear has explained, "for the Blackfoot the ensoulment of the land results in a web of relationships with the earth, animals, plants, inorganic matter, and the cosmos. The ensoulment is captured in the stories, songs, and ceremonies." Ecology, understood in the widest sense, perhaps contains the hope of an integration of knowledge and value that would justify an intercultural dialogue with the guardians of Mother Earth or Pachamama.

But let us not forget the fact that Stan Rowe had to express himself with irony. In arguing that placing phenomena into the supportive context of the Whole might be called "purpose," he advocates an immanent conception of spirit very much like Leroy Little Bear's statement that "everything is animate, that everything is imbued with spirit." But is it really the case that ecology can reverse the dualism of nature and spirit that dominates European culture and expels spirit from scientific discourse? The separation between nature and spirit stems from the Biblical creation story in which God is understood as the prior cause of nature. The resemblance of human spirit to God is understood as an addition to something that is lacking in nature. This question takes us back to the relationship between Athens and Jerusalem in European culture. It seems to me that only if it were possible to subtract the concept of transcendent creation could an immanence of spirit be accepted.[16] There have been, of course, several prominent thinkers who have elected for this pantheistic option—but it has been understood by the dominant tradition as a pagan heresy. It seems to me that ecology, understood as both a scientific paradigm and a cultural project, wavers between the hope for incorporation of spirit into nature and resignation to its impossibility. I would, for this reason, caution against using the term "creation" in place of "Being" or "the Whole."

It is from the spirit of the Whole that humans could find their place and from the lack of this Whole that contemporary problems of identity may stem. As Leroy Little Bear has explained, "the trouble may come in the form of a loss of identity brought about by the loss of stories, songs, and ceremonies that arise out of Mother Earth.... It may be a loss of the songs, the stories, and ceremonies that happen at certain places. In other words, the trouble referred to may manifest as the Mother Earth not recognizing you." It seems to me that an ecological conception places value on the Whole and on each part insofar as it sustains the Whole. But it would not seem to imply that any single part is essential to the Whole or, to come to the point, that humans are a necessary part of Being. To that extent, it could not ground human action and value within nature.

But what if one begins from the other side of the issue? If one's own life is perceived, or taken, to be of value, and if something like the ecological account of relationships is true, then it is rational to act to preserve the ecosystem upon which one depends. This thought does not *prove* its premise. It is always a logical possibility to deny that human life has meaning. But if one does suppose that human life has meaning, then so does the Whole that it needs to live. Something like this is being slowly perceived to be true, it seems to me, and it is this perception that grounds the contemporary dialogue between ecology and Mother Earth. But to the extent that this perception cannot be proven, there remains still an inherent tendency to despair that the ecosystem, and one's own life, are of value at all.

I think that I have shown that it is not too much to say that an ecological ethic grounded in European philosophy and culture contains a hope for the integration of knowledge and value that can find meaning in the Whole of Being, but it would be too much to say that it is more than a hope because this hope corresponds to the indeterminacy of the Whole understood as a horizon that applies to ecology. A philosophy that would be ecological—in the sense that it would focus on the concrete relations that construct a Whole; and that would be Marxist, in the sense that it would critique a social representation of value that relies on commodity price—is a possibility that would enact this hope. I must admit that I feel this tension in myself. Sometimes when I am out of the city among the trees, mountains, and water, I feel that my intelligence might touch and merge with the intelligence of the greater order of the Whole—a greater order that I can sense at the horizon. But in my teaching and my philosophy, I can speak of this only in admiration as the belief of others. It cannot find a place in the public representation of value insofar as I have the resources to speak of it.

Notes to Chapter 10:

* This article was originally presented at the symposium "Is There, Can There Be, Such an Activity as World Humanities?" held at Simon Fraser University, January 27–28, 2012, and then published in *Journal of Chinese Philosophy* 39, no. 4 (December 2012): 518–27. It is reproduced here with the kind permission of the journal.

1 Leroy Little Bear, *Naturalizing Indigenous Knowledge: Synthesis Paper* (Saskatoon: Canadian Council on Learning/Conseil canadien sur l'apprentissage, University of Saskatchewan, 2009), 10.

2 This and all subsequent quotations from Leroy Little Bear are from Leroy Little Bear, "Land: The Blackfoot Source of Identity," paper prepared for the conference of "Beyond Race and Citizenship: Indigeneity in the 21st Century," University of California, Berkeley, California, October 28–30, 2004.

3 From the statement "Mother Earth Can Live without Us, but We Can't Live without Her," by the Indigenous People's Working Group at the World Peoples' Conference on Climate Change and the Rights of Mother Earth, held April 19–22, 2010, in Tiquipaya, Cochabamba, Bolivia.

4 "Let's Respect Our Mother Earth," address from President Evo Morales to the member representatives of the UN on the issue of the environment, September 24, 2007; "Conferencia Mundial de los Pueblos sobre el Cambio Climático y los Derechos de la Madre Tierra," 22 de Abril, Cochabamba, Bolivia; "Mother Earth Can Live without Us, but We Can't Live without Her," created in unity in Tiquipaya, Cochabamba, Bolivia, April 21, 2010. Trans. by Ben Powless, cochair of the Indigenous People's Working Group.

5 See, for a thoughtful account that delineates this debate in Latin America: Arturo Escobar, "Pachamámicos versus Modérnicos," in *Política y Economía: Miradas Latinoamericanas Heterodoxas* (2010), http://www.politicayeconomia.com/2010/05/%C2%BFpachamamicos-versus-modernicos/#more-227.

6 Little Bear, "Land: The Blackfoot Source of Identity."

7 Jim MacNeill, Pieter Winsemius, and Taizo Yakushiji, *Beyond Independence: The Meshing of the World's Economy and the Earth's Ecology: A Trilateral Commission Book* (Oxford: Oxford University Press, 1991), 39. See also: "Even undistorted markets are limited in several ways, the most important being that they cannot take into account the external environmental costs associated with producing, consuming, and disposing of goods and services. The market treats the resources of the atmosphere, the oceans, and the other commons as 'free goods', with a zero price. It 'externalizes', or transfers to the broader community, the costs of resource depletion and of air, water, land, and noise pollution. The broader community shoulders the costs in the form of damages to health, property, and ecosystems," ibid., 37–38. Cf. Bill McKibben, *Deep Economy: The Wealth of Communities and the Durable Future* (New York: Holt, 2007), 27–28.

8 Gregory Bateson, *Steps to an Ecology of Mind* (Toronto: Ballantine, 1972), 499, cf. 451. Development of this insight actually seems to entail the development of ecology out of biology. As Stan Rowe has said, "Ecology tells us that what we call organisms and environment are inseparable, except as words," in "Arks Can't Save Aardvarks," in *Home Place: Essays on Ecology* (Edmonton: NeWest Publishers, 1990), 104.

9 Stan Rowe, "Ecology and Popular Science," in *Home Place: Essays on Ecology* (Edmonton: NeWest Publishers, 1990), 45.

10 Arne Naess, *Ecology, Community and Lifestyle*, trans. David Rothenberg (Cambridge: Cambridge University Press, 1990), 36.

11 J. S. Rowe, "The Level-of-Integration Concept and Ecology," *Ecology* 42, no. 2 (1961): 426.

12 Stan Rowe, "Crimes against the Ecosphere," in *Home Place: Essays on Ecology* (Edmonton: NeWest Publishers, 1990), 118. "[Here is] the essential insight of the ecosystem concept: that all life participates in a complex and interactive system where boundaries between living and non-living are vague or non-existent. The largest ecological system, the Earth Ecosphere, is the reality of which

people are one part; they are embedded in it and totally dependent on it. Here is the scientific source of the environment's intrinsic value."

13 James (Sákéj) Youngblood Henderson, "*Ayukpachi*: Empowering Aboriginal Thought," in *Reclaiming Indigenous Voice and Vision*, ed. Marie Battiste (Vancouver: University of British Columbia Press, 2009), 265.

14 Marie Battiste and James (Sákéj) Youngblood Henderson, *Protecting Indigenous Knowledge and Heritage: A Global Challenge* (Saskatoon: Purich Publishing, 2000), 99–100.

15 J. Stan Rowe, "'Earth' as the Metaphor for 'Life', A Letter to *BioScience*," *Bioscience* 48, no. 6. (1998): 428–29. 16 The well-known argument by Lynn White Jr. in his influential and often republished article "The Historic Origins of the Ecological Crisis" is the classic statement of the argument within ecological literature that the Christian concept of creation underlies the domination of nature in European modernity. A more thorough and philosophically convincing account is given in William Leiss, *The Domination of Nature* (New York: George Brazillier, 1972).

Part III
Communications and Cultural Studies

Chapter 11

The Primacy of Communication

Lenore Langsdorf

> I argue that any ensemble of social relations and material objects can be viewed either from the viewpoint of its *results,* in which case it is a *technology,* or from the viewpoint of its internal *organization,* in which case it is a form of *communication* in the constitutive sense of social relations. Thus, technology and communication are not different *objects* but different ways of viewing a social-material ensemble.... Andy Feenberg has suggested that *Primal Scenes* is a philosophy of technology disguised as a theory of communication which I think is a perceptive comment, though I would add that this "disguise" is a necessary one depending on the specialized perspective that one adopts.
>
> IAN ANGUS, "INTERVIEW WITH IAN ANGUS" (2010)

Human beings are temporal and communicative entities. Before birth—that is, as zygote, embryo, and fetus—there are stages of development via input to the womb provided by the pregnant body's nutrition and activities. This input is primordial communication that can support—but also limit/disturb—development (examples: a nutritious diet, rather than malnutrition; beneficial or harmful drug usage; tranquil in contrast to injurious activities). At diverse developmental stages, access to sensory information broadens to include touch, hearing, taste, and sight. At some time in the development from zygote to fetus to newborn person, the mind begins to function.[1]

At birth, fetuses who have been materially embodied and culturally embedded through practices of their maternal bodies that have been communicated to them begin to expand upon that inheritance by using their developing communication skills as instruments—techniques—that enable organizing their needs and thereby accomplishing satisfaction of those needs.

John Dewey's definition of technology assists in understanding this communication as our initial experience of using technology: "'Technology' signifies all the intelligent techniques by which the energies of nature and man are directed and used in satisfaction of human needs; it cannot be limited to a few outer and comparatively mechanical forms. In the face of its possibilities, the traditional conception of experience is obsolete."[2]

Larry Hickman expands on this definition in describing Dewey as a philosopher of technology:

> The key to understanding Dewey's work as a contribution to the philosophy of technology is, I suggest, an appreciation of his contention that all inquiry or deliberation that involves tools and artifacts, whether those tools and artifacts be abstract or concrete, tangible or intangible, should be viewed as instrumental: in other words, as a form of technology. In short, he understood that technology involves more than just tangible tools, machines, and factories. It also involves the abstract thought and cultural practices that provide the contexts for such things and make them possible.[3]

In his new introduction to the revised edition of *Experience and Nature,* Dewey noted regret concerning his use of the term "experience" because of "insurmountable" misunderstanding of that term. It "had become effectively identified with experiencing in the sense of the psychological, and the psychological had become established as that which is intrinsically psychical, mental, private."[4] In retrospect, he noted, he wished he had used "culture" in order to emphasize the socio-cultural (rather than "psychical, mental, private") character of experience: "Social organization cannot be really understood except as a part of culture."[5]

The moment of birth is one of delivery into increased primordial communication via multiple sensory engagements. Sensory information that newborns received as fetuses in the womb from beyond the flesh of their own bodies may remain operative. Culture, already permeated with socio-political "intelligent techniques," has already been communicated to them. These techniques certainly are increased by their independent embodied engagements and augmented by healthy newborns' immediate use of voice as an instrument for communication. Children's ability to accomplish their purposes vastly expands as they develop additional means of communication, including and especially speech. Haptic, kinetic, kinaesthetic, and speech communication surround and influence children's well-being (for better or worse). These culturally provided and physically developed instruments become embedded in the larger and more diverse "ensemble of social relations and material objects"[6] that comprises their material and socio-cultural environments. Long before we might engage in study of the particular abstract system (language) that we employ in verbal and written communicative events, we have become accomplished users of diverse sensory (embodied) means of communication—including speech—to organize our needs and as instruments to inform ourselves and others.

The doings and undergoings of embodied communal relationships, enacted continually in the surrounding culture, communicate a dynamic structure of possibilities for daily life. New parents communicate to all, including their infants, approval of extended periods of sleep during the night, of desired facial gestures that can be interpreted as reciprocal, and of audible events that resemble words—especially their own families' names. The cultural practices that parents and a widening social circle communicate include negative assessments of conduct that is not acceptable in their social environment—perhaps beginning with infants' handling of their excretions, and continuing in a list of unacceptable behaviours that grows as infants and toddlers become more mobile and so can access more of the possibilities they encounter. Each expansion of possibilities for mobility—from womb to birth canal; to swaddling clothes, cradle, or crib; to a dwelling in which others also live and move; to still wider material and social environments—brings an inexhaustible supply of as-yet un-enacted possibilities into the dynamic structure of experience. As we develop an expanding variety of needs and purposes, we bring technologies—"intelligent techniques"—to bear upon the tacit structure of possibilities instituted within the forms of life that comprise a culture.

As Dewey noted in the quotation given earlier, the "traditional conception of experience" as "intrinsically psychical, mental, [and] private" events within an already enacted environment of things and relations becomes "obsolete" as we engage, whether tacitly or through choice, these possibilities that are afforded by the "intelligent techniques" we inherit from a culture into which we are born and which continues to inform us. We can recognize the dynamic structure of a culture as a context that enables participants to organize their experience in ways that it promotes. Even a cursory glance at the history of human beings shows that needs and purposes are not static, and that we have persistently both created and responded to those needs and purposes via technologies—the "intelligent techniques" that exceed "mechanical forms"—to which Dewey pointed. What is not as readily recognized are the "possibilities" implicated by those techniques. Those possibilities are actualized, ignored, or thwarted in and by the "ensemble of social relations and material objects" that, as Angus notes in the epigraph that opens this chapter, "can be viewed either from the point of view of its results, in which case it is a technology, or from the viewpoint of its internal organization, in which case it is a form of communication in the constitutive sense of social relations."[7]

Husserlian Phenomenology

The reflection on the function of communication in organizing socio-cultural experience that I develop here is motivated by current political commentary on the diversity of cultural orientations that are operative, and often conflict, in contemporary society. Although this is a phenomenological exploration of the role of communication in that organization, I agree with Ian Angus's "rejection of Husserl's views concerning communication."[8] Angus identifies those views as operative early in the *Logical Investigations*, when Edmund Husserl restricts his attention to the constitutive, rather than indicative, function of communication. This restriction, Angus proposes, was prompted by Husserl's interest in developing phenomenology as a rigorous science. Thus, phenomenology was to use "scientific discourse" reliant upon "a logical edifice" that furthers knowledge formulated in constitutive, rather than indicative, communication.[8] Indications, in contrast to assertions (expressions, statements, utterances), convey "an association of ideas"—an empirical "motivational unity" that "is operative throughout ordinary life and culture," and conveys "emotional and volitional phenomena" within "practical reasoning embedded in everyday life."[9]

Angus notes that his interest in "primal scenes of communication" (which I share) is "precisely in the practical reasoning that includes emotion and volition and particularly, in the instituting moments that shape and legitimate a specific form of practical reasoning as valid throughout a given space and time, that is to say, which is constitutive of the way of life of a culture."[10] The following consideration of the primacy of communication in practical reasoning that informs a diversity of cultural orientations—as can be witnessed within contemporary life—focuses on the indicative function of "instituting moments" that begin, quite literally, pre-personally, as sensory information is accessed in the womb. Insofar as these moments remain operative throughout the "way of life of a culture," we can identify their presence in interrelational communication—which is not constrained to use scientific discourse.[11] They provide an emotional and volitional dimension to the practical reasoning that, I find, dominates interrelational communication in the everyday world.

Husserlian phenomenology expanded in the course of Husserl's voluminous writing, perhaps influenced by the socio-political events that surrounded him from 1900 (the original publication of *Logical Investigations*) and enforced his retirement in 1929. Although, as Husserl wrote in a letter to Paul Natorp, 1922, "the greatest part of my work is stuck in my manuscripts," that work brought about a "recrystallization" of Husserl's thinking.[12] The expansion—even reorientation—that is evident in those manuscripts, which became accessible in the Husserl Archives, was consulted by other scholars. Only gradually, and relatively recently, they were published in English translation. They document an increasing awareness of the intrinsic limitations of judgments constituted in abstraction from the experiences of everyday life, and led others to investigate the "practical reasoning embedded in everyday life" that remains as the background context of scientific discourse's "logical edifice."[13]

As Donn Welton explains,

> Phenomenology takes its starting point in our everyday experience, what Husserl calls appearances. Appearances, however, are complex. An *object* of experience is always present through multiple modes of givenness, each of which

> forms a *profile* of the object. The interplay of object and profile transpires according to the sense (*Sinn*) of the whole, both determining and being determined by the sense of the profiles. Without senses the object would lack its experiental qualities. But senses exist not in the object or its profiles but in the *relationship* between them and the one to whom they appear… . Profiles … point to or indicate other profiles in such a way that we find things situated in a field of possible appearances, i.e., in a determinate horizon [that] … is always pregiven.[14]

The objects that appear to us in experience are meaningful; they provide sense that may be taken up in the constitution of empirical science's "logical edifice." Yet, they also "point to or indicate" a more expansive "profile" of sense; a pre-given horizon of "possible appearances" in the everyday reasoning that surrounds and informs that edifice. Thus, Welton's subtitle for the book in which that quotation appears: *The Horizons of Transcendental Phenomenology*.

In what follows, I focus on communication as the context for the relationship to which Welton draws our attention, as well as on the practical reasoning and indicative communication to which Angus points. This more complex understanding of communication requires expanding upon Husserl's limitation to the phenomena that appear in the reductive view of scientific discourse and his correlative reliance upon intentionality and constitution. Without minimizing the value of traditional phenomenology's focus on "the things themselves," what's needed to fulfill the trajectory of Husserl's later work is attention to the communicative process in which those things become objects of interest, as well as to the profiles that may be indicated—pointed to—as individuals' intentions constitute those objects. A phenomenology that is mindful of Dewey's rejection of "experience" as "intrinsically psychical, mental, private" (as in the quotation at the start of this chapter) benefits from understanding how "intelligent techniques" may develop in the practical reasoning of everyday conversation. In what follows, I turn first to a sociologist's analysis of communication and then to postphenomenology for insight on that process.

Niklas Luhmann: Communication as Selective Materialization

Granting that both expressions (utterances; assertions—as in scientific discourse) and indications (which point to a horizon of possibilities) are operative in constituting "any ensemble of social relations and material objects,"[15] as Angus says, suggests asking how organization of these disparate elements that inform everyday communication happens. Despite an established tradition that understood action as the basis for social organization, Niklas Luhmann placed communication in that role. His early work, following that of Talcott Parsons (with whom he studied in the early 1960s), understood that ensemble as accomplished by actions. However, he increasingly focused on the sociality that enables human development in general, and communication in particular. By the time of his *Social Systems*, Luhmann questioned whether Parsons's position—that "social systems are based on either a type of action or on an aspect of action"—was one that "accurately grasped the relationship between action and sociality, above all, whether it grasps this relationship in a sufficiently productive way."[16] He proposed that it does not: "There is much to suggest simply reversing the relationship ... action is constituted in social systems by means of communication and attribution as a reduction of complexity ... the basal process of social systems ... can only be communications."[17]

Given the need to distinguish the operational effects of communication and action, although they cannot be separated, Luhmann notes that "a clarification of the concept of communication" is needed.[18] He rejects "the metaphor of transmission" as "unusable.... It suggests that the sender gives up something that the receiver then acquires."[19] Although that metaphor "locates what is essential about communication ... in the utterance,"[20] he cautions that "the utterance is nothing more than a selection proposal, a suggestion. Communication emerges only to the extent that this suggestion is picked up, that its stimulation is processed."[21]

Luhmann's extensive consideration and condemnation of the transmission metaphor emphasizes the selectivity of utterances within any process of communication:

> Communication grasps *something* out of the actual referential horizon that it itself constitutes and leaves *other things* aside. Communication is the process of selection. Of course, it does not select in the same way in which one grabs one thing or another off the rack. That would bring us back to the substance theory and the transmission metaphor. The selection that is actualized in communication constitutes its own horizon.... Therefore communication must be viewed not as a two-part, but as a three-part selection process.... Selectivity as such attracts further communication; it recruits communications that direct themselves to aspects that selectivity has excluded.[22]

Senders select both information—what of that "referential horizon" is to be communicated—and utterance—a behaviour that expresses that information. Luhmann notes, in "a small digression," that "the difference between information and utterance, to which understanding relates ... appears in Husserl's *Logical Investigations* as the difference between indication and expression.... Translated into our conceptual language, 'expression' means nothing more than the autopoiesis of consciousness, and 'sense' or 'meaning' means the need to acquire structure for this in the form of an intentional relation."[23]

Receivers gain both information and access to its "horizon" of meaning, which contribute an "understanding [that] normally includes more or less extensive misunderstandings ... that can be controlled and corrected."[24] Senders expect that receivers will understand their meaning. But the event is not communicative without a third selection, in which receivers can include aspects of the horizon of possible meaning that stimulates misunderstanding—but also proposes alternatives that do not conform to senders' intentions, and thus contribute to further communication. "Communication is made possible, so to speak, from behind, contrary to the temporal course of the process. To develop the chances for complexity that this provides, one must attend to anticipation.... The fact that understanding is an indispensable feature in how communication comes about has far-reaching significance for comprehending communication."[25]

In sum, Luhmann understands a communication event as a tripartite unity consisting of information, utterance, and understanding within a persistent, ongoing selection process: "Society produces and reproduces itself as a social system. Once communication is set into and kept in motion, the formation of a bounded social system cannot be avoided, nor can the development of further bounded systems produced by the transformation of expectations about what is improbable into what is sufficiently probable [be avoided]. On the level of social systems, this is an exclusively autopoietic process, which produces what enables it Itself."[26]

This may be translated, I suggest, into a phenomenological understanding that is proposed in the quotation that provides the epigraph for this chapter. Communication can be investigated as focusing on *results*: as a process that produces technology, in Dewey's sense of "intelligent techniques." Or, it can focus on *organization*, a process in and by which selections produce a "bounded social system"; a unity that produces itself in the process of creating those techniques, and continues to do so in a process that "recruits communications that direct themselves to aspects that selectivity has excluded."[27] This information remains accessible in the horizon of meanings that inform what has been selected, as well as what has been left aside by previous selections.

Luhmann's analysis of the process of meaningful communication within social systems enables an understanding of how diverse, and often conflicting, cultural subsystems emerge within social systems. "The phenomenon of meaning," he notes, "can best be presented in the form of phenomenological description ... as a surplus of references to other possibilities of experience and action ... indicated marginally as the horizon of an 'and so forth' of experience and meaning."[28] That surplus indicates alternative meaningful contexts that emerge in ongoing processes of communication, each of which provides a history and tradition for the distinct subsystems—cultures—that unify communicators whose association is bounded culturally, geographically, historically, linguistically, religiously, or temporally.

That the phenomenon of communication is an ongoing process in which participants' understanding may accept or reject a particular utterance sheds light on the creation of social systems, their distinction (but not separation) from action, and the indispensability of indication as well as constitution in practical reasoning. Rejection of a message may be stimulated by the appeal of alternative information that is indicated within a horizon of possibilities suggested by the sender's message.

Luhmann emphasizes that "the *possibility* of rejection is *necessarily* built into the communication process."[29] Thus, rejection of proffered meaning terminates a particular unity of sense that the sender has selected as a communicative event, but if the participants continue their relation, the sender or receiver can offer another possibility. If they select to dissolve that unity, or their process is dissolved in a transition to action, the "surplus of references to other possibilities of experience and action" that has been "indicated marginally" affords renewal of the process.[30] As noted earlier: "Communication grasps *something* out of the actual referential horizon that it itself constitutes and leaves *other things* aside."[31]

What is left aside remains in the horizon of possibilities as that "surplus of reference to other possibilities of experience and action ...

indicated marginally as the horizon of an 'and so forth' of experience and meaning."[32] Given the temporal nature of humans, what has been rejected at any point in the selectivity of communication is not lost; rather, it remains in that horizon of possibilities. Insofar as these participants enact the selections that they do accept, those selections are embodied in their communication (through hearing, sight, smell, taste, and touch), embedded in their cultural history, and extended as we use those selected senses to constitute material engagements in the environment that is the context for their communication.

Postphenomenology

Don Ihde reports that his interest in technologies began when, early in his teaching career, he was assigned to participate in a team-taught course on work and leisure. The theme of the readings was "leisure in a work society," and readings posed the likelihood that "leisure would grow" with the introduction of new technologies.[33] In the context of developing a "phenomenology of work," he "asked students to keep a sort of action technology diary and count up and itemize [their] encounters with technologies."[34]

The "overwhelming" result was lists that began with alarm clocks, plumbing systems, and kitchen equipment, went on to classroom paraphernalia, and continued with "literally hundreds of human-technology encounters" with "tools and instruments" that "were means by which one could interact with an environment."[35] This interest "matured into *the phenomenology of techniques*, or experiental-actional relations to, through, and with technologies," each of which "has its own distinctive set of affordances and constraints."[36]

As with Husserlian phenomenology, which evolved from the *Philosophy of Arithmetic* and *Logical Investigations* at the turn of the last century to *Analyses Concerning Passive and Active Synthesis* in the final decades of Husserl's life, postphenomenology has evolved. Ihde's early work in the philosophy of technology was on "encounters" with the use of "tools and instruments" in "experiental-actional relations" that would make a transient "machinic call" upon users' attention.[37] The context for that interest evolved from reflection on those classroom examples that engaged their users' attention and enabled specific actions, to interest in technologies such as prostheses, which could not (so to speak) easily go missing, as happened with Galileo's telescope and Husserl's eyeglasses.[38]

Ihde's recognition of the compatibility of themes in Husserl's later work with Deweyean pragmatism stimulated a "postphenomenological pragmatism" or "pragmatic postphenomenology" (he uses both titles) and development of an "interrelational ontology," as well as attention to our material engagement with the tools and instruments that came to mind when his students were asked to itemize their encounters with technology. This development was encouraged by Ihde's focus on technoscience, in contrast to Husserl, who "remained throughout his life a believer in the primacy of science."[39] Ihde's "response to Edmund Husserl's phenomenology and his notion of science" is a "Deweyean-inspired form of pragmatism."[40]

Further developments occurred in conversations between Don Ihde and Lambros Malafouris, an archaeologist who studied the interrelational shaping of mind and things throughout human history.

Malafouris characterized his Material Engagement Theory as one that "refers to a process of becoming with and through the world, leaning towards Alfred North Whitehead's notion of prehension … and John Dewey's 'transactional' sense of 'situation'… [and] embodies a distinctive anthropological interest in the comparative study of materiality, materials and techniques … which it blends with perspectives from postphenomenology."[41] In their coauthored work, Ihde and Malafouris propose that "we become constituted through making and using technologies that shape our minds and extend our bodies" and note "the human predisposition for technological embodiment and creativity," which enables us to "make things" and be "made by them."[42]

Luhmann's analysis of communication suggests that this recursive making begins in the interrelational accepting or rejecting of what is selected from a horizon of possibilities. Reconsidering that engagement in the context of Dewey's and Hickman's broader understanding of technology as inclusive of "all the intelligent techniques by which the energies of nature and man are directed and used in satisfaction of human needs"[43] suggests that communication, understood as the process of selectivity analyzed by Niklas Luhmann—and thus, as inclusive of horizonal possibilities—is another of Husserl's missing technologies.

Notes to Chapter 11:

1 In awareness of contemporary cultural and political controversies, I note that this tracing of pre-birth development does not imply that a status of personhood is compatible with, or should be inferred at, any stage prior to birth.

Rather, I propose that both cultural and physical factors are effective during the stages of development from zygote to embryo to fetus. See, for example, "Fetal Development: Stages of Growth," Cleveland Clinic, accessed 1 December 2018, https://my.clevelandclinic.org/health/acticles/7247-fetal-development-stages-of-growth.

2 John Dewey, "What I Believe," in *The Later Works, 1925–1953*, ed. Jo Ann Boydston (Carbondale: Southern Illinois University Press, 1984), 270. Also see: Emmanuel G. Mesthene: "we define technology as the organization of knowledge for the achievement of practical purposes." (Mesthene, Emmanuel G. 1970. *Technological Change: Its Impact on Man and Society*. Cambridge: Harvard University Press. p. 25.); and Thomas P. Hughes: "Technology is the *effort* to organize the world for problem solving so that goods and services can be invented, developed, produced, and used." (Hughes, Thomas P. 1989. *American Genesis: A Century of Invention and Technological Enthusiasm 1870-1970*. Chicago: The University of Chicago Press, 2004, 6; emphasis in original). I follow current postphenomenological practice in using the term "technology," although it diverges from the stricter sense as is summarized by Kåre Stokholm Poulsgaard, "Enactive Individuation: Technics, Temporality, and Affect in Digital Design and Fabrication," *Phenomenology and the Cognitive Sciences* 18 (2019): 281: "The word technology fuses the Greek root *tekhne* (art or craft) with *logos* (discourse, branch of learning), a dual meaning that is often downplayed (Stiegler 1998:1 cf. Marx 2010). In this sense, 'technology is to technics what linguistics is to language, what every science is or would be to its objects', writes French anthropologist François Sigaut (Sigaut 1994:422). Technique

and technics are material engagements with the world that we can know by the change they effect in people and their surroundings. They emerge as social goals, take the form of material needs and crystallize in infrastructure, expertise and practices; by enquiring into the *tekhne* and *logos* of this nexus, we can begin to understand the deep entanglement of human mind with our material and technical milieus."

Adopting this strict usage would suggest characterizing communication as analyzed by Luhmann (in what follows) as "techniques"—"material engagements with the world that we can know by the change they effect in people and their surroundings" rather than as "technology;" that is, the "science" of those "engagements." I defer to the prevalent contemporary usage of the phrase "philosophy of technology," although my focus is on the phenomena themselves, techniques of "material engagement" accomplished in communicative relations that indicate, and result in, action, rather than a "science" of those effective engagements.

3 Larry A. Hickman, personal email communication, Larry Hickman to Lenore Langsdorf, March 4, 2019.

4 John Dewey, *The Later Works 1: Experience and Nature*, ed. Jo Ann Boydston (Carbondale: Southern Illinois University Press, 1988), 363. In a footnote, Dewey notes that the quotation is from "Malinowski's article 'Culture' in the *Encyclopedia of the Social Sciences*."

5 Ibid.

6 Laureano Ralòn, "Interview with Ian Angus," *Figure/Ground*, 25 August 2010, http://figureground.org/fg/interview-with-ian-angus/; (my emphasis in epigraph).

7 Ibid.

8 Ian Angus, *Primal Scenes of Communication* (Albany: State University of New York Press, 2000), 67.

9 Ibid., 69.

10 Ibid., 68–69.

11 Ibid., 69.

12 Ibid.

13 Ibid., 68–69.

14 Donn Welton, *The Essential Husserl: Basic Writings in Transcendental Phenomenology* (Bloomington: Indiana University Press, 1999), xi.

15 Donn Welton, *The Other Husserl: The Horizons of Transcendental Phenomenology* (Bloomington: Indiana University Press, 2000), 331; my emphasis.

16 Ralòn, "Interview with Ian Angus."

17 Niklas Luhmann, *Social Systems*, trans. John Bednarz Jr. and Dirk Baecker (Stanford, CA: Stanford University Press, 1995), 137 (German publication in

1984; all quotations are from the English translation). Luhmann develops a complex—and lengthy—analysis of the distinct, although not separate, processes of communication and action in social systems. I can offer only a sketch of a theme in that analysis, in support of the importance of including indication as well as constitution—indicated horizons of meaningfulness as well as constituted selections of sense—for understanding communication as a process of selection from among multiple horizons of meaning.

18 Ibid., 137–38.

19 Ibid., 139.

20 Ibid.

21 Luhmann, *Social Systems*, 139.

22 Ibid.

23 Ibid., 140; author's emphasis.

24 Ibid., 145–46. In a footnote, Luhmann adds: "we will avoid detailed proofs so as to not lengthen the text needlessly" (p. 530 n14). I concur with this avoidance.

25 Ibid., 141.

26 Ibid., 143.

27 Ibid., 162.

28 Ibid., 140.

29 Ibid., 60.

30 Ibid., 154; author's emphasis.

31 Ibid., 140.

32 Although Luhmann does not use the term "cybernetic" in *Social Systems*, later cybernetic theory distinguishes between "first" and "second" order cybernetics. The concept of homeostasis was central for the former; observation was not. The latter, attuned to living rather than mechanical systems, included the participation of an actor/observer. Luhmann's analysis of communication as a process that is distinct from action—but utilizes a plurality of observations as the basis for selection from a horizon of possible meaning—would fit within the "second" category. The difference is important in considering commentary on Luhmann's theory; for example, John Mingers, "Can Social Systems be Autopoietic? Assessing Luhmann's Social Theory." *The Sociological Review* (2002): 278-299.

33 Luhmann, *Social Systems*, 60.

34 Don Ihde, *Husserl's Missing Technologies* (New York: Fordham University Press, 2016), xiv.

35 Ibid., xiv–xv.

36 Ibid., xv.

37 Ibid., xiv.

38 Ibid., xiv–xvi.

39 Ibid., 2–3, 13–14. Ihde returns to the topic of Galileo's and Husserl's missing (forgotten) technologies with extensive analyses in chs. 1 and 2 (pp. 13–58).

40 Ibid., 1.

41 Ibid., 1, 4.

42 Lambros Malafouris, "Mind and Material Engagement," *Philosophy and the Cognitive Sciences* 17, no. 1 (2019): 1–17.

43 Their engagement is accessible in "*Homo Faber* Revisited: Postphenomenology and Material Engagement Theory," coauthored by Don Ihde and Lambros Malafouris, *Philosophy and Technology* (forthcoming). The following quoted phrases are from the (unpaged) July 2018 online publication. Don Ihde noted the cross-disciplinary (archaeology and philosophy) nature of that engagement in personal communication (Don Ihde to Lenore Langsdorf, Feb.17, 2016).

Chapter 12

Conduits of the Faculties

Rhetoric, Ecology, Media (and the Wends of Pedagogy)

Daniel Adleman

> The effect of speech upon the condition of the soul is comparable to the power of drugs over the nature of bodies. For just as different drugs dispel different secretions from the body, and some bring an end to disease and others to life, so in the case of speeches, some distress, others delight, some cause fear, others make the hearers bold, and some drug and bewitch the soul with a kind of evil persuasion.
>
> GORGIAS, *ENCOMIUM OF HELEN* (1982)

> With an argument that can never be heeded enough, Quintilian reverses the relation tendentiously misrepresented by Plato between true thinkers and the sophists who give mere speeches, insofar as he points out that one can of course easily simulate being a philosopher, but could not possibly pretend to be a good speaker.
>
> PETER SLOTERDIJK, *NOT SAVED: ESSAYS AFTER HEIDEGGER* (2017)

Selecting *Rhecomedial Theoroi*

It is more than a little ironic that the Celtic name *Angus* means "one choice." After all, what is so significant about Ian Angus's critical interventions is their singular interdisciplinary character. As a scholar and activist who refuses to choose one discursive channel and operate at its conventional frequency, he articulates an approach to long-standing disciplinary squabbles from which scholars of many stripes can learn a great deal. The question of his idiosyncratic approach takes on recursive trappings in that interdisciplinarity is not merely something that his work performs; it is a matter that he takes up explicitly and trenchantly theorizes in the context of the history of disciplinary struggles, osmoses, and conjunctures. This essay will explore some of the implications of Angus's incremental subversions of Platonic philosophy's dominion with a view to reconfiguring what all too often manifests itself as a battlefield of the disciplines.

When the putative theatre of disciplinary conflict is reinterpreted as a rhetorical plane of resonance—one marked by mutual collaboration and negotiation, coalition building, shared sympathy and investment, ecological sensitivity, and partial identifications, rather than tribalistic conflict—obtuse assumptions of disciplinary supremacy and attendant territorial squabbles begin to dissolve. This reboot opens onto an emerging post-humanistic constellation that metabolizes and mobilizes the historical theoretical nexus without succumbing to its internecine preoccupations, rivalries, and zones of exclusion. Angus's observations about this state of affairs gesture towards a nascent critical frontier oriented by three important material-semiotic registers: rhetoric, ecology, and media. In the spirit of his approach to this configuration, I will toss a number of different nets in the service of exploring the philosophical and political implications of this unfolding *rhecomedial* matrix.

The entangled theoretical triad of rhetoric, ecology, and media that emerges out of Angus's work is grounded in the interpenetration and shared substance of symbolic, natural, and techno-infrastructural environments. Even though this is a somewhat new interdisciplinary cluster, it also seems to exhume the nearly forgotten ancient genesis of the ancient Greek term *theoros*, whose resonances subtend and suffuse the humanistic theoretical tradition to this day. The *theoroi* were Greek city-state emissaries who were sent out on missions to attend ceremonial events in neighbouring regions, consult oracles, and make offerings to the gods at shrines and festivals.[1] As such, their *theoretical* task was profoundly *rhetorical* in that they engaged in diplomatic relations with the officials and civilians of other city states; it was *ecological* in that it involved fostering and suturing together relations among the diverse archipelago of the Delian League; and it was *medial* in that these envoys were literally the *middle men* between city states who also engaged with the oracular *mediums* at temples and shrines constellated around the region. This chapter will therefore begin by tracking Angus's historically sensitive orientation towards this simultaneously ancient and new *rhecomedial* configuration. Drawing on these reverberations, I will stage a number of encounters between Ian's work and the ideas of Kenneth Burke and Marshall McLuhan (two rhetoricians whose work Angus refers to periodically), as well as a number of contemporary thinkers, with a view to launching *rhecomedial theoroi* into the digital twenty-first century.

Twilight of the *Eidos*

Casting a number of sidelong glances at the intertwined histories of philosophy, rhetoric, and media ecology, Angus makes the case that that the gatekeepers of philosophy, in particular, have long deluded themselves (and others) that a normative version of philosophical theory should assume the position of rightful sovereign of the humanities. In their introduction to *The Critical Turn*, he and Lenore Langsdorf put this dynamic under the microscope as they conduct a brief survey of the lengthy coevolution of philosophy and rhetoric. Drawing on the continually resurfacing classical trope of ratiocinative philosophy as the "queen of the sciences" (a position that mathematicians and theologians have often also staked claims to for their respective disciplines), they unpack the biopolitical implications of the erosion of philosophy's self-evident sovereignty over time:

> Philosophy needs rhetoric to reach those who must be persuaded to be patient and yet to embark upon one or another of the specialized domains of sciences. But, as is often the way with servants and rulers, the servant may come to be so capable, and the ruler may come to be so distant, that the queen of the sciences seems unnecessary. Furthermore, the field appears to be broad enough to allow everyone the right to speak and persuade. Thus emerges the vision of a new queenless regime populated by liberated servants.[2]

This quasi-Hegelian allegorical account of the dissolution and dispersion of philosophy's exclusive purview to hierarchize and coordinate the disciplinary field is brimming with significance. Plato's imagined republic was founded on a range of disciplinary and technological exclusions. Not only rhetoric but writing, democracy, theatre, poetry, narrative, and music all threatened the fragile integrity of its umbilical cord to eidetic Truth. Although much of contemporary critical theory has dispatched the trappings of Platonism, the art of wisdom has been remarkably slow to open itself up to meaningful new kinship relations with its erstwhile rivals and doppelgängers.

As Angus points out, the classical borders delimiting the dominion of philosophy have been rendered more or less inoperative by the increasingly rapid metamorphoses of all of the disciplines, along with the rest of the world, beyond the imaginings of their gatekeeping erectors. The swirling pandemonium of digital-anthropocenic modernity is so far removed from Plato's quaint fictional *polis* that the immunizing fantasy of building a higher wall between philosophy and rhetoric quickly gives way to a hybrid "philosophy/rhetoric that is dialogically, rather than diametrically, delimited. [Instead of] limiting and devaluing the other, both extend into and require the other. The very means for conceptualizing dualities of reason and speech, knowledge and persuasion, truth and opinion—in short, mind and body—are annulled."[3]

This call for a cooperative coagulation of "philosophy/rhetoric" is not altogether unprecedented. Angus's assertion evokes a tumultuous history of divergent attitudes towards "the Greek division of [disciplinary] territory."[4] For instance, the Roman rhetorician Cicero called for a revised intellectual cartography and ridiculed Plato for "depict[ing] in his pages an unknown sort of republic, so completely in contrast with everyday life and the customs of human communities."[5] Against Plato's insular, hallucinated model of wisdom, Cicero articulated an environmentally cognizant rhetorical-philosophical "man of sharpness" who "ought to feel the pulses of every class, time of life, and degree, and to taste the thoughts and feelings of those before whom he is pleading or intending to plead any cause; but his philosophical books he should keep back for a restful holiday."[6] Cicero's rhetorical *theoros* supplants (we might even say *sublates*) the rigid, monastic Platonic philosopher by moving around in time and space in a manner that is attuned to the warp and weft of the social tapestry and the vicissitudes of opportunity (a subtle rhetorical principle known as *kairos*).

Equally hostile to the influence of a moribund Platonic theology, Friedrich Nietzsche, in his important lectures on rhetoric, blames Plato for the long history of superficial treatments of rhetoric and the media technology of writing: "The [Platonic] truth can be articulated neither in a written nor in a rhetorical form. The mythical and the rhetorical are employed [only] when the brevity of time allows for no scientific instruction."[7] As Jacques Derrida later suggests in "Plato's Pharmacy," Socratic philosophy's purifying purge all too readily contorts itself into a phobic deadlock marked by the indistinguishability of theory and narrative, Truth and persuasion, *logos* and *pathos*, medicine and poison, friends and enemies, the faithful and the faithless, et cetera. No philosophical gated community can sufficiently securitize itself against the perfidious influx of rhetoric, media, narrative, and affect. The eidetic wall could not hold. "After Socrates," writes Peter Sloterdijk, "all philosophers were ... involved in the media revolution of written culture and urban rhetoric."[8]

The Burkean Watershed

Kenneth Burke's mid-twentieth-century body of work inaugurated the New Rhetoric, which ceaselessly returned to the well of classical rhetorical and philosophical theory but (in a manner echoic of Jacques Lacan's return to Sigmund Freud) insisted on making diplomatic detours through the ideas of Nietzsche, Freud, John Dewey, Thorstein Veblen, William Carlos Williams, Shakespeare, and a range of others. The cumulative result was an approach to communication studies that realigned itself with purportedly rival disciplines and technologies under the banner of a collaborative praxis that treats ambiguity as a vital resource. This new configuration decoupled rhetoric from the Aristotelian paradigm of the soapbox orator endeavouring to persuade others of a certain course of interpretation or action. Since Burke, rhetorical influence has been deemed to be thoroughly in effect anywhere in the socio-symbolic ether where we can speak of identifications, identities, orientations, attitudes, ideologies, and the unconscious.

Rhetoric, through this lens, figures as a mad, decentred function of the symbolic order's dispersed, alien propensity for influencing humanity and fractalizing discourse, regardless of any individual's authorial intentions or any other discipline's ideological fantasy systems about the immutable Truth. "Madness," writes Angus, "which is the unfixity of meaning, invades each utterance within a discourse from its outside. General rhetoric is thus haunted by madness. Rhetorical criticism re-establishes plurality of discourses and therefore unfixity of meaning within discourse."[9] Apropos of Nietzsche and Michel Foucault, Angus identifies the rhetorical madness lurking within all discourse; and he does so not to pathologize rhetoricity but to underscore its role as a Dionysian principle underlying even the most Apollonian philosophical concepts.

Poking fun at Platonism's all-too-Apollonian circumscription of rhetoric, Burke writes:

> Perhaps, as a first rough approximate, we might think of the matter thus: Bring several rhetoricians together, let their speeches contribute to the maturing of one another by the give and take of question and answer, and you have the dialectic of a Platonic dialogue. But ideally the dialogue seeks to attain a higher order of truth, as the speakers, in competing with one another, cooperate towards an end transcending their individual positions. Here is the paradigm of the dialectical process for "reconciling opposites" in a "higher synthesis."[10]

Socrates would surely bristle at Burke's facetious idea of a more primordial rhetoricity, of which philosophizing is merely one of many possible species. But, as Angus explains, the provocative notion of a cooperative philosophical-rhetorical tension—one that unfolds into new theoretical positions and cohabitations—harbours a mainspring of potential for the cultivation of vital conduits between estranged disciplines. Such disciplinary osmoses are a far cry from the amoral "sophism" that Plato figured as the antithesis of proper philosophizing.[11] When thinkers treat ambiguity and generalized unhinging not as enemies but as boons to further interrogation of orientations (including their own), new pathways have a way of opening up in a fashion that actually augments philosophical and political inquiry.

In a world that is constantly bombarding us with images, opinions, identifications, attitudes, seductions, invitations, and other mesmeric shrapnel, a philosophy organized around ahistorical Truths seems, to many, quaint at best. Counterpoised against the Platonic pretense of a stable perspective on reality, Burke insists that we are always already awash in simulacral "interpretations of interpretations" of the world. Underscoring the mediality of new-rhetorical optics, David Wellbery and John Bender call this "post-Truth" environmental mechanism "rhetoricality," which they define as "the groundless, infinitely ramifying character of discourse in the modern world ... rhetoric is no longer the title of a doctrine and a practice, nor a form of cultural memory; it becomes instead something like the condition of our existence."[12]

Rhemedia Ecology

Refreshingly, Angus characterizes the "newly unsettled relation between rhetoric and philosophy" as a significant development for the cross-pollination and coevolution of the disciplines. Looking to the work of Kenneth Burke, Marshall McLuhan, Chaim Perelman, and Harold Innis, he advocates for an expansively rhetorical approach to theory, one sensitive to the pulses of the contemporary media environment. This means that recent developments in media studies must be thoughtfully incorporated into the theoretical milieu. Only such a configuration can aspire to rise to the occasions that press down upon it. "The literature comprising comparative media theory," he writes, "poses radical issues for the relation between philosophy and the human sciences. Comparative media theory is, from this point of view, a concern with rhetoric expanded to deal with media forms, rather than their contents."[13]

Angus makes it clear that once philosophy and rhetoric have sufficiently reconciled, the prevailing condition of turbulent rhetoricality (which he characterizes as a necessary corollary of the Lyotardian "postmodern condition") dictates that media ecology emerges as a necessary "third side" of the theoretical coin. The assertion that developments in media studies must be funnelled into the emerging metamorphoses of critical theory would perhaps sound self-evident to anyone who knew that McLuhan was a Cambridge-trained rhetorician who read Aristotle, Cicero, Marcus Quintilian, Burke, and Wayne Booth as voraciously as he did Innis and James Joyce.[14] It is undeniably no coincidence that his seminal *The Medium Is the Massage* is subtitled *An Inventory of Effects*, as it is precisely media's rhetorical effects (that is, its influence, rather than its inherent meaning) that he takes up and renders available for theoretical scrutiny.

In an effort to properly appreciate the multivalent "lifeworld[s] of ... social groups," Angus proposes that rhetoric and media theory are best understood as chiastically consubstantial:

> McLuhan's famous phrase 'the medium is the message' condenses this thought rather nicely, though I would really prefer it to be 'the message is the medium,' which also emphasizes that the rhetoric of media forms is only itself expressable as/through a content.... The thesis proper to communication in this expanded sense is that media of communication constitute human experience in its perceptual, institutional and cognitive aspects.[15]

This suggests that any cogent approach to the lifeworlds of digital modernity must strive to patch together pathways between critical understandings of media environments (that is, "the medium is the message") and those of the radical rhetoricality of the symbolic order (that is, "the message is the medium"). Although such a Möbius-strip-like theoretical architecture should immediately resonate as a necessary corrective, rhetoricians (even digital rhetoricians) and media theorists have been just as guilty of subordinating their labours to retrograde disciplinary boundaries as the atavistic philosophical approaches with which Angus takes issue. In spite of the "rhetorical" currency of "interdisciplinarity" as a buzzword, scholars working in the humanities and social sciences have often been sluggish to relinquish their conventional moorings and truly embrace the kind of disciplinary contamination required to attune themselves to the vibrations of the current historical moment.

Placing this recalcitrance in the crosshairs, he goes a step further to advocate for the cultivation of a media-rhetorical post-humanistic sensibility; such an approach would remediate the aforementioned disciplines into a theoretical prism that benefits from their respective paradigmatic optics without recognizing any one sovereign disciplinary authority over particular content. The necessary by-product of such an orientation is an appreciation of culture as a domain whose complexity surpasses the prerogative of any one disciplinary lens:

> 'Culture'… is not … distinct from society, economics, politics and so forth, but in a more anthropological sense as the specific pervasive style that pervades these areas and unifies them into a 'whole way of life.' Any communication, besides taking place within the horizon of this cultural form, contributes to the definition of the cultural form through its medium. If the thesis proper to rhetoric in its historical form concerns the persuasive power of language, comparative media theory is a 'media rhetorics.'[16]

If there is no culture without communication, no communication without media, and no media communication without persuasion, then theoretical approaches to culture and society are obligated to attune themselves to emerging optics on the mediatic circulation of influence. In order to aspire to conduct and process the environmental pulses of media modernity, post-humanistic theory must reflexively fan out and become more permeable to different disciplinary inflections of what Angus refers to alternately as "comparative media theory" and "media rhetorics." Only in so doing can it endeavour to appreciate the contours of the world's ceaselessly ramifying cultural environments.

But what shape do these environments take? Half a century ago, Innis's and McLuhan's insistence that media technology constitutes an overriding infrastructural environment might have seemed naïve to many people. In 2019, planetary-scale computation so permeates every domain of cultural experience that McLuhan's once-mystical aphorisms about media ecology register as merely commonsensical. In recent history, the suffusion of "the cloud" has led to what we might call an atmospheric turn in digital media studies. Media theorist Mark Hansen argues that digital-computational media contours our cultural environments in a fashion that is decentred and utterly atmospheric: "Human experience is currently undergoing a fundamental transformation caused by the complex entanglement of humans within networks of media technologies that operate predominantly, if not almost entirely, outside the scope of human modes of awareness (consciousness, attention, sense perception, etc.)."[17] This paradigm shift migrates media's ontological status from that of window, extension, substrate, vehicle, or infrastructure to an ambient elementality that permeates everything, constituting an undetected enabling background. Of course, McLuhan was perhaps the first to anticipate this atmospheric tonality, which he seemed to gesture towards in one of Angus's favourite McLuhan adages: "One thing about which fish know exactly nothing is water, since they have no anti-environment which would enable them to perceive the element they live in."[18]

For Angus, like McLuhan, artful theorizing is one of many modalities of "anti-environment" (that is, reflexive perspectival shifters) that affords denizens of modernity a measure of critical distance from our immersion in cultural ecosystems. Here, it is important that culture be understood as the vibratory spheres of social activity through which we extract and create meaning within a socio-symbolic milieu increasingly saturated with noisy data vortices. Any meaningful inquiry into the moorings of contemporary culture must emerge out of such a *rhecomedial* understanding. "Our problem," Angus avers, "is how individual pieces of information within this indefinite horizon can become sufficiently organized to express cultural meaning and not fall back into the persistent background buzz of accumulating information. Out of this organization, through the process of emergent meaning—if there can indeed be such a process—would be constructed a subject of discourse."[19] The flickering oscillations and high-bandwidth thoroughfares between data and meaning, like those between media and messages, call for more nuanced and expansive theoretical infrastructure than the classical categories can afford.

In the digital twenty-first century, it would be absurdly pedantic to wonder whether social media addiction, algorithmic smart cities, Chinese troll farms, and the new metastases of cyber warfare are rhetorical situations or mediatic situations. In an unfurling informatic landscape marked by the entanglement of humans with planetary-scale computational networks that seem to dissolve into the very air we breathe, attuned theories must become protean *theoroi*, undertaking *rhecomedial* pilgrimages that imaginatively, but diplomatically, trespass arbitrary disciplinary jurisdictions. Only then could they aspire to incisively explore the crackling interplay of attention, cognition, memory, imagination, embodiment, influence, orientation, ideology, narrative, identity, environments, ethics, culture, and politics.

Rhecomedial Lifeworlds and Other *Anthropo Scenes*

Angus's "queenless" approach to the coagulation of rhetoric and media (not to mention cultural studies) merits closer scrutiny. An integral *sub-stance* that all of the nodes of this constellation have in common is a concern with material-semiotic environments. If "the message is the medium" for Kenneth Burke, it is because the symbolic order constitutes a lifeworld, one whose circuits are replete with ecological influx and import. As Burke observes, "All living things are critics":

> Though all organisms are critics in the sense that they all interpret the signs about them, the experimental speculative techniques made available by speech would seem to

> single out the human species as the only one possessing an equipment for living beyond the criticism of experience to a criticism of criticism. We not only interpret the character of events ... we may also interpret our interpretations."[20]

Burke views humanity's symbolic ecosystems as both its crowning achievement and its most onerous stumbling block. The semiotic gravity fields are vertiginous. Not only is it impossible to cultivate a god's-eye view on the socio-symbolic ether, but our immediate milieus also condition us—as "symbol-using (symbol-making, symbol-misusing) animal[s]"[21]—to universalize and operationalize our protocols. This often leads to ossified worldviews and practices that are ill-adapted to the environmental vicissitudes of a rapidly changing world.

Burke refers to such orientational lifeworlds as "occupational psychoses," by which he means states of mind that emerge out of overhabituation to a particular station in the world. When the coordinates of that world or one's position within it changes, such a prosthetic semiotic bubble tends to become a disorienting form of "trained incapacity." A stockbroker's risk-taking behaviour that is rewarded in 2006 may bankrupt her in 2007. By the same token, a college student's racist quip that garners laughter in the fraternity house may render him unemployable when it is broadcast over social media. Context, it turns out, is almost everything in such matters. So much of significance resides not in the signifier-signified relationship, but in the abyssal vascular system of the world within which it circulates.[22]

Ecology figures prominently in this state of affairs in that humanity also suffers from an overriding meta-level trained incapacity, which Burke refers to as the "technological psychosis." This entails what we might view as the "psychotic" tendency of technoscientific culture to ceaselessly improve technology, even when its effects are potentially apocalyptic in their import. Once, for example, the notions of nuclear weapons and industrial agriculture were "in the air," networks of scientists, entrepreneurs, and politicians all began to work feverishly to pursue their "perfection." When the profit motive is paramount and ecology is systematically treated as an "externality," society readily turns a blind eye to the evisceration of its natural enabling environments.

It should come as no surprise, then, that Burke was one of the first humanistic thinkers to employ the term "ecology" in its present colloquial sense. He wrote presciently in the 1930s:

> Among the sciences, there is one little fellow named Ecology, and in time we shall pay him more attention. He teaches us that the total economy of this planet cannot be guided by an efficient rationale of exploitation alone, but that the exploiting part must itself eventually suffer if it too greatly disturbs the balance of the whole (as big beasts would starve if they succeeded in catching all the little beasts that are their prey, their very lack of efficiency in the exploitation of their ability as hunters thus acting as efficiency on a higher level, where considerations of balance count for more than consideration of one-tracked purposiveness).[23]

A Burkean account of humanity's technopsychotic tendency towards ever-greater levels of exploitation for economic profit registers the dire stakes of different approaches to civilizational progress under conditions of *anthropo-scenic* crisis. This conjuncture of rhetorical environments and technological environments thus necessarily leads to the consideration of an even more primordial environment, that of nature itself, the irrefutable material backbone of even the most ethereal atmospheric mediations.

Multiply-Mediated Ecologies

Since the mid-twentieth century, both media theory and the New Rhetoric have migrated increasingly towards environmental perspectives. This convergence on environmental paradigms necessitates the recognition of a third interpenetrating register, that of so-called natural ecology. In this vein, a great deal of contemporary media-ecological thought attempts to traverse a similar chiasmus to that between the medium and the message: whereas Innis, McLuhan, and Friedrich Kittler inaugurated seminal waves of thinking about media networks as environmental (or even atmospheric) phenomena, contemporary media-ecological thinkers have been recursively reversing the tide in the direction of considering the medial qualities of life-affording environments. Communication theorist John Durham Peters observes that this association is nothing new. "The concept of media," he writes, "was connected to nature long before it was connected to technology. It has roots in ancient Greece and Rome, but many of its key twists and turns are medieval and modern. *Medium* has always meant an element, environment, or vehicle in the middle of things."[24]

In the wake of Burke's initial refulgence, rhetorical thought has been a little slower to accommodate the "little fellow named Ecology." But recently, pioneering environmental rhetorician Andrew McMurry has advocated for a more robust *ecorhetorical* stance that breaks out of the deadlock of the discipline's long-standing fixation on symbolic environments. On this matter, he writes, "we must insist that our all-penetrating rhetoricality is itself conditioned by an even more pervasive *environmentality*. The nonsymbolic, the environmental Real, the thing-world—all that we have hitherto understood as nonparticipating and nonpersuasive—must come to be part and parcel of rhetorical culture."[25] Such an overhaul would go significantly further than even Burke by recognizing the fields of agency and sentience outside of the human experiential universe. The whole Burkean dramaturgy would have to be updated and refashioned to take into account the dynamic fluxes of organisms and ecosystems that live within, alongside, and against the symbol-using, symbol-misusing animal.

As though in response to Burke and McMurry, Angus levels his gaze on the genealogy of ecological thought. In his brief survey of the discipline, he carves a path through biology, cybernetics, and Indigenous epistemologies. Cybernetician Gregory Bateson's phenomenological insistence on the inextricability of organisms from their environments, asserts Angus, reverberates through the Blackfoot maxim "I am the environment." These are two profound gestures, in two different vernaculars, of identification with the environment meant to disabuse us of our investments in technological psychoses. Reflecting on the recent individuation of ecology as a dire matter of concern, he observes, "While ecology began with a strictly scientific meaning, it has come to take on also a popular meaning with the emergence of ecological problems such as environmental diseases, pollution, habitat degradation and climate change."[26] By and large, these ecological problems stem from a technoscientific world view that "ignore[s] wider contexts and relationships." He concludes that ecology must be understood as "the science of relationships, the dependence of individuals on relationships, and the contribution of the individual to sustaining relationships." As such, he concurs with Burke and McMurry that it "might well be considered the leading science of our time."[27]

Deconstricting the Enlightened University

These entangled lines of inquiry lead Angus to two timely but atypical interrogations of the Enlightenment legacy. They are anomalous because they jolt theory out of the hermetic field of contemplation into the theatre of action. The first concern pertains to the rhetorical media ecology of the modern public university. In *Love the Questions: University Education and Enlightenment,* he probes how we ought to understand the mission of the public university in the twenty-first century. If the public university is routinely troped as some kind of knowledge-transmitting machine or mediatic computation device (as it often is), how should we think about what it actually produces or does? If it is a community or polity, what sort of relationships does it foster? Since such institutions are becoming increasingly dependent on donations from mining, petrochemical, and military-industrial corporations, can they still aspire to contribute to the open exchange of ideas in the pursuit of greater public freedom, maturity, and intelligence?

Cycling through and entertaining these various provisional positions, he suggests that the public university, as a potential locus of Kantian public reason (that is, freedom of thought and expression), is clearly undergoing a kind of identity crisis, one that can't be resolved through formulaic branding strategies of the sort proffered by ballooning university marketing offices. The constitution of the public university is arguably in a volatile state of transformation. Major Canadian universities, in particular, are beholden to conflicting agendas and ideologies. These include the Enlightenment Imaginary's still-influential lionization of knowledge and reason, poorly thought-through federal and provincial governmental regulations, internal corporate best-practices regimes, and external stakeholder demands. As such, they house a veritable crash test derby between different visions of the public good and increasingly powerful hybrid corporate-governmental agendas.

The perils confronting the most integral democratic potentials of the public university behoove thinkers to raise, as Angus says, uncomfortable "questions about the meaning and function of the university in a corporate environment and press for the greatest possible collaborative autonomy that will sustain criticism of that environment."[28] Public intellectuals of all creeds can play a significant role in sparking public conversations about the roles, duties, and orientations of public universities. This suggests they must also be willing to periodically go out on a limb and pressure the public university to change (or avoid changing) in accordance with educational and societal ideals in which administrators may not be especially invested.

Nevertheless, *pace* Kant, scholars must also recognize the limits of conversations within the university and move beyond the academy's confines in response to developments in the enveloping world that houses and affords it. For Angus, this includes engaging in a range of educational activities (like teaching in experimental educational projects and writing journalistic editorials)[29] that penetrate into the life of the *polis* beyond the purview of the university. But above and beyond what we might call predominantly *symbolic* pedagogical interventions, Angus's post-Kantian approach to the public use of reason entails the call to more contentious forms of activism and civil disobedience when the *rhecomedial* situation calls for a rupture out of the impasses of docile instrumental rationality.

On this score, he has arguably made his most significant contribution. Concerned about the ramifications of Kinder Morgan's diluted bitumen pipeline expansion along the First Nations territories and fragile ecosystems of western Canada, he recently decided to join a coalition of Indigenous sovereignty and environmental activists determined to impede the company's work at Burnaby Mountain (also the site of Simon Fraser University). After his arrest, Ian was asked to explain his unlawful behaviour to the court. He did so in terms that impressively summon and reconstitute the Enlightenment mission of the public intellectual:

> I do not deny that I was physically present at the place in question at the time in question. My understanding of civil disobedience is that one commits a certain act for definite and considered reasons, one admits to the act, explains one's reasons, and accepts the penalty. The purpose of the act is to bring a state of affairs to the attention of the public and the authorities with the intention and hope that it may serve to correct an error in justice.[30]

At such times, concerned scholar-citizens cannot merely conform to the Kantian injunction to think and say what one wants but *obey* nonetheless. Just as *rhecomedial* intellects must be able to recognize the embeddedness of rhetoricality within a more primordial environmentality (that is, the symbolic order is nested in living material ecologies, even though it is not merely reducible to them), they also need to be able to distinguish situations that call for further Habermasian dialogue and analysis from those that call for direct action. This *kairotic* calibration of adjudication, communication, and intervention to the vicissitudes of the times might, in fact, be the subtlest extradisciplinary art form of them all. When executed artfully, activist strategies such as Angus's funnel back into the still laudable Enlightenment project to educate the public and potentially "correct error[s] in justice."

Aufklärung: Theoroi and Praxis

An important take-away lesson to draw from Angus's activity inside and outside the academy is that the metamorphoses of disciplines and institutions necessarily lag behind those of the world. As scholars encounter the inertia-bound obstacles of some of the humanities' most ossified "trained incapacities," we should consider following Angus's example in revisiting the historical reservoirs of ideas and values—with a view to not just imagining a better world but actually contributing meaningfully towards creating one.

Intellectually conservative accounts of this fraught terrain articulate a simple dichotomy between doe-eyed optimism and misanthropic pessimism. "The difference here, to a cynic," writes McMurry, is between two irreconcilable rhetorical postures, uncritical optimism and fatalistic pessimism: "the one group seeking scope for future actions, buoyed by a vision of the virtuous life and the 'good [person] speaking well' (*vir bonus, dicendi peritus*), the other determining the cold facts of a murderous deed already done by a murderous ape."[31] Angus's work and life gesture hopefully in the direction of an alternative trajectory from the one route impeded by the Scylla of rose-coloured liberal optimism and the other leading up to the conservative Charybdis of sardonic pessimism.

Such a hope-driven politics should not be confused with facile optimism. It is, to the contrary, necessarily predicated on the acknowledgement of a crisis. The *Evental* rupture out of lassitude begins with an appropriately urgent recognition of the shared stakes. Angus says, "The convergence of issues of reconciliation with Indigenous nations, environmental and ecological danger, and social inequality due to the rapacious pursuit of private profit has made this not only a difficult time but one of crisis. The forces who wish to maintain the current system have come together to oppose those who seek a new future."[32]

Once moribund monopolies on the legitimate use of critique have been neutralized and dismantled, engaged communities will uncover more and more political horizons of solidarity in the clearing. Angus's approach to this new configuration transcends petty disciplinary fiefdoms. Guided by a hopeful orientation towards the possibility of a better world, his thinking reinvests in a heuristic principle provisionally resembling the classical philosophical idea of the Good: "The hope for justice may well appear to us hedged and tentative," he cautions, "its implementation unclear and even impossible, its demand too high for redemption. But thought without hope for justice would retreat from its public responsibility."[33] There is a bewildering surfeit of positions at our disposal. Ian's work and life evince the fact that apathy simply isn't one of them.

Notes to Chapter 12:

1 Andrew Samuels, *The Political Psyche* (Abingdon: Routledge, 1993), 42.

2 Ian Angus, *The Critical Turn: Rhetoric and Philosophy in Postmodern Discourse* (Carbondale and Edwardsville: Southern Illinois University Press, 1993), 6.

3 Ibid., 14.

4 Ian Angus, *(Dis)figurations: Discourse/Critique/Ethics* (London: Verso, 2000), 121.

5 Cicero, *De Oratore*, trans. H. Rackha (Boston: Harvard University Press, 1959), 159.

6 Ibid.

7 Friedrich Nietzsche, "Lecture Notes on Rhetoric," trans. Carole Blair, *Philosophy & Rhetoric* 16, no. 2 (1983): 99.

8 Peter Sloterdijk, *Philosophical Temperaments: From Plato to Foucault* (New York: Columbia University Press, 2013), 10.

9 Angus, *(Dis)figurations*, 243.

10 Kenneth Burke, *A Rhetoric of Motives* (Berkeley: University of California Press, 1950), 53.

11 Not that Gorgiastic mendacity—especially the sophisticated forms of dissimulation circulating through the interpenetrating worlds of politics, new media, and the advertising industry—and the analysis thereof should be precluded from proper rhetorical standing.

12 John B. Bender and David E. Wellbery, *The Ends of Rhetoric: History, Theory, Practice* (Stanford, CA: Stanford University Press, 1997), 25.

13 Ian Angus, "A Blank Sheet of Paper: The Phenomenological Foundations of Comparative Media Theory," *Human Studies* 17, no. 1 (1994): 19.

14 In my capacity as an assistant professor of Writing and Rhetoric at the University of Toronto, I was enlisted by the McLuhan Centre of Culture and Technology to give a presentation on McLuhan's rhetorical influences at the celebration of UNESCO's designation of his personal library as a world treasure in 2018. As a part of my research program, I was fortunate enough to have the opportunity to sift through a number of McLuhan's most beloved books. His dazzling annotations to Aristotle, Cicero, and Burke merit their own essay-level treatment.

15 Angus, "A Blank Sheet of Paper, 17–18.

16 Ibid., 18.

17 Mark B. N. Hansen, *Feed-forward: On the Future of Twenty-first-century Media* (Chicago: University of Chicago Press, 2015), 5.

18 Marshall McLuhan and Quentin Fiore, *War and Peace in the Global Village* (New York: Bantam, 1968), 175.

19 Ian Angus, "Emergent Meaning in the Information Age," in *The Digital Nexus*, ed. Rafael Foshay (Edmonton: Athabasca University Press, 2016), 59.

20 Kenneth Burke, *Permanence and Change: An Anatomy of Purpose* (Los Altos: Hermes Publications, 1964), 6.

21 Kenneth Burke, *Language as Symbolic Action* (Berkeley: University of California Press, 1966), 16.

22 In language studies, this context-dependency principle is often characterized as "pragmatic enrichment."

23 Kenneth Burke, *Attitudes Towards History* (Boston: Beacon Press, 1961), 150.

24 John Durham Peters, *The Marvelous Clouds: Toward a Philosophy of Elemental Media* (Chicago: University of Chicago Press, 2016), 46.

25 Andrew McMurry, "Rhetoric and Environment," in *Oxford Handbooks Online* (Oxford: Oxford University Press, 2015), 11.

26 Ian Angus, "On the Limits of the Social Representation of Value: A Response to Leroy Little Bear," SFUblogs, http://www.sfu.ca/sfublogs-archive/departments/humanities-institute/1107_response-to-leroy-little-bear-by-ian- angus.html. This article is presented in chapter 10 of this book.

27 Ibid.

28 Ian Angus, *Love the Questions: University Education and Enlightenment* (Winnipeg: Arbeiter Ring, 2010), 101.

29 Ian Angus has participated in a range of public lecture series and para-academic free school projects (including Samir Gandesha's "Spectres of Fascism" free school and the Vancouver Institute for Social Research) across Vancouver.

30 Ian Angus, "Civil Disobedience against Kinder Morgan Is a Civic Responsibility," *Ricochet*, 14 May 2018, https://ricochet.media/en/2203/civil-disobedience-against-kinder-morgan-is-a-civic-responsibility. The statement is presented in chapter 20 of this book.

31 McMurry, "Rhetoric and Environment," 10.

32 Angus, "Civil Disobedience."

33 Ian Angus, "Continuing Dispossession: Clearances as a Philosophical and Literary Theme," *Modern Horizons* 3 (2012): 1.

Chapter 13

Exterritoriality

An "Open Letter" to Siegfried Kracauer, or, the Last Letter Not Lost in the Dead Letter Office in the Game of History

Jerry Zaslove

In "Louis Riel and English-Canadian Political Thought," Ian Angus tells a story:

> The persisting *disorder* of Canadian history was perhaps most apparent during the Riel Rebellions, which show "the difficulties of the dominant legal regime's acceptance of pluralistic legal subjectivities, which its very logic paradoxically keeps bringing to the fore."... The Métis differentiated themselves from both Indians and whites. The Manitoba Act (1870) recognized a new civil status of "half-breeds" and their land title—though in the form of alienable private property that extinguished the French river-lot system while at the same time affirming federal sovereignty. The close of

> the later 1885 Rebellion and the hanging of Riel confirmed this result.[1]

And Siegfried Kracauer writes:

> Lately I came across my piece on "Photography" and was completely amazed at noticing that I had compared historicism with photography already in this article of the twenties. Had I been struck with blindness up to this moment? ... This discovery made me feel happy for two reasons: It unexpectedly confirmed the legitimacy and inner necessity of my historical pursuits; and by the same token it justified, in my own eyes and after the event, the years I had spent on *Theory of Film*. This book of which I had always conceived as an aesthetics of the photographic media, not less and not more ... appears to me in its true light: as another attempt of mine to bring out the significance of areas whose claim to be acknowledged in their own right has not yet been recognized.[2]

The Following should be read as Letters, or even Postcards, written from the land of exterritoriality.

I. Breeding Grounds: Epochal Shadows Boxing with Time[3]

Ian Angus writes warm philosophy in a cold climate. I write to, for, and about Ian Angus through my writing on Siegfried Kracauer. My "Open Letter to Siegfried Kracauer" is a dialectical essay that discovers complementarities, a middle path where one throws off moorings. Jean Paul Sartre asks in *What Is Literature?* "For Whom Does One Write?" and replies about his own crisis in the postwar of 1948: "I shall say that a writer is engaged when he tries to achieve the most lucid and the most complete consciousness of being embarked, that is, when he causes the engagement of immediate spontaneity to advance, for himself and others, to the reflective. The writer is ...

a mediator and his engagement is mediation ... no one is obliged to choose himself as a writer. Hence, freedom is at the origin."[4]

So here in the spirit of a *Festschrift* for Ian Angus's life-project, I frame an "open letter" for Siegfried Kracauer about *exilic writing* as a "Zone of Experience." *The open letter should stand on its own.* However, in contiguity with my abiding interest in Siegfried Kracauer, Weimar exile and radical phenomenologist of the exterritorial, I write of the borders within and the "inalienable subjectivities" at the borders of the exterritorial where the sovereign force of the state meets the strangers at the gates.[5] An "open letter" is a lens, like the camera that fascinated Kracauer in his search for the *unstaged arrangements* that come to the surface in the *epochal* condition of exile that he names "exterritoriality."

The camera documents the unstaged, showing what is missing in the staged real. Letters written in exile testify about borders. An Open Letter is a Borderland of Friendships that *protected and maintained an inner life* in the countless letters Kracauer wrote during exile. The letter is the *tertium datur* that plays the role of the missing persona, the one who does not intend to return to Germany to be a *Mitmacher*, one-who-goes-along. Kracauer's letters are exchanges that go over the terrain of the non-synchronicity of no-return by Remaining where you are: you stay on the border of the pure negation of the possibility of thinking about return. You often hid your name, using different names in your novels and essays. You refused to say how old you were when you went into exile. The posthumously published *History: The Last Things before the Last* was a last will and testament not unlike Walter Benjamin's "Theses on a Philosophy of History."

I think of an "open letter" like a "*Skaz*," the Russian "tale."[6] Kracauer decoded the institutions of everyday life in story-like essays in the border regions that the film and the photograph expose to day-light. So in writing about my abiding interest in Kracauer's writing, the borders are the perishable and imperishable times that threaten collective existence with ruin. This is writing that *creates the reader through narratives that recount time*. For Kracauer, the border was a stage where those who were living in *Obdachlosigkeit*, those who were "without a shelter" in their collective existence as employees, did not see the State-produced violence, *Herrschaft*, in the shadows. They are half-breeds who surface on the streets at dusk.[7]

II. Darkening Times Situate: The Subjects We Write about Choose Us

Ian Angus writes essays at the borders of forms of time: *epochal considerations*. Our writings have followed different paths. I have felt an affinity to his phenomenological thinking. The open letter looks for solidarity with friends when we might fear that our studies of productive understanding have no beginning or end.[8] Kracauer's writing focuses on the signs. He was the man with the movie camera.[9]

Those who know Ian Angus's studies will know his writing on rhetoric. An open letter creates contiguities with the voice of the author simultaneously of and in the work. An open letter opens to the figure to whom it is addressed: open like a postcard.

Even then, letters written in the darkening times of exile are like dream works. Siegfried Kracauer passed through several stages of his exile from Nazi Germany. He wrote countless letters that expressed his own reality of exile, his acute fear of return, and the reality of no return. So the open letter is also a *dialogue as a configuration*: we unlock the "non-identical" within the concrete universal of the individual-in-the-making. The letter constitutes the incommensurable present moment.[10] A letter is a reverie. In Angus's "Phenomenology as Critique of Institutions: Movements, Authentic Sociality and Nothingness," I see fragmented experiences through the tangle of natural and man-made rights. Naming epochs is crucial to looking into the radical humanistic and socialist humanism as a form of restitution. I see also a natural anarchism or Marxist Humanism; but labels are a risk; they will always mislabel.[11]

For the phenomenologist, writing is *as an enactment of thought*; writing is dialogue and Angus "situates [it] ... in a particular place, in order to talk about this place."[12] In *A Border Within: National Identity, Cultural Plurality, and Wilderness*, we have a study of what is missing while we rush to frame "identity." Here is the actuality of the lived experience of "exilic thinking." Identity? Does it thaw frozen time and explain us through thinking about deep relationships?[13] So we are at a borderland where exile and the missing come together at the edge of utopic thinking.[14]

An open letter is "another kind of order. It is a place of "emergence" of the in-between times when the political forms of society seem deaf and dumb. We stumble over *the borders within* at the gates of exile and loss. *Here is the feeling of homeland and no return and the continuous preoccupation with lost time.*[15] Waiting is hovering in the in-between time at the border.

While in exile Kracauer learned that his mother and aunt were murdered in concentration camps.[16] Friendships anchored exile-time. Kracauer, like Angus, comingles nationalism as an epochal transition zone and refigures time lost. *The letter is a testimony about transience* and allows me to think about the felicitous title of Angus's book *A Border Within*, to juxtapose Kracauer and Angus.[17] Kracauer's Weimar film essays and his study *The Salaried Masses, Duty and Distraction in Weimar Germany* follow from his studies of Georg Simmel's phenomenology. Born in 1889, Kracauer was 62 when he arrived in the United States. Consciousness of exile is about the missing years and missing voices, not only one's own voice. He avoided mentioning his own age.

In the United States, at 62, he discovered that his history contained a *prophecy of his own exterritoriality*. In *The Last Things before the Last*, his posthumously published final work, he characterized history as Proustian memory work. I call this reparative or "posthumous memory." For Kracauer, unrecounted memory is held on the surfaces of memory and sharpened by the fragments that we hold in transient time, learning about the unpast.

III. Exterritoriality and Exile: Posthumous Memory

Kracauer named this epoch *Exterritoriality*. He explored their surfaces. Weimar portraits of the "hired office workers" framed the tragic epoch of post-WWI labour. The photograph and film rescued a lived experience while repudiating any hope for an image of historical continuity.[18] An emerging fascist "public" sphere was anchored by bureaucracy. Each chapter is rendered as if it could be background for a film: uprisings, riots, strikes, workers' councils that opposed the war; exterritoriality is in the epoch. The majority had wanted the war. Regret and denial pervade the postwar and fear of the return of the bloody November revolutions: the "Caligiari Nightmare" revealed longing for security and safety.

The middle-class fears: submission to wage labour or alliance with proletarian solidarity.

Kracauer says, "Ideational homelessness is fear of being unable to find refuge in the liberal system so shaken by economic crisis … unwilling to take shelter within Marxism … they are standing in a void."[19] *The present is a particularity and immanent critique* that comingles politics, philosophy, and the situational. The writer commits to the here and now—the destiny of thought enacts what is missing. So I think about Angus's *Love the Questions, A Border Within*, and the "Phenomenology of Social Institutions," which are "immanent critiques" that pose my question: For whom does one write? The question hovers.

IV. Memory and Reparation: Letters as Digressive Memory Work Casting off Moorings

Kracauer continually wrote letters to addressees living in exile. Letters are emergency writing, are also "Scenes of the Exterritorial" at the border of the inside and outside. For this reason, *Theory of Film* carries the subtitle *The Redemption of Physical Reality*. Letters *carry out* the piecemeal present of the lived experience of now-time. Here the contemporaneity of the non-contemporary lives in reverie where Time hovers.[20] One writes *through* the pathos of one's *situational existence*. Time is omnipresent in Ian Angus' writing. *Love the Questions*, *A Border Within*, and the "Phenomenology of Social Institutions," relate to my open letter and the presence of exile *as a form of life* in Siegfried Kracauer.[21]

V. Now to Hazard a Beginning ...

Here I leave direct reference to Ian Angus and compose a brief open letter to Siegfried Kracauer that opens to the phenomenological digression.

Dear Siegfried Kracauer, ...

This "Open Letter" comes many years after your own "last letter before the last," the letter to your mother and aunt appended at the end, entitled, "*Vanque-Spiel der Geschichte*, the Gambling with History," where you put a Proustian stamp and seal to writings formed in exile. Letters in exile are written at the time you place your film aesthetic into your own Exterritorial existence. Your home language is frozen time. Georg Simmel expressed this pathos of "frozen time" of wandering as the "stranger" ... the wanderer who comes today and goes tomorrow, but rather as the person who comes today and stays tomorrow ... so to speak, the *potential* wanderer: although he has not moved on, he has not quite overcome the freedom of coming and going.[22]

Like Simmel's writing, your writing is about *potentiality*; we are working out "things" for ourselves, inside of the phenomenal borders of "Exterritoriality." After the war you write to your friend Leo Lowenthal that you cannot return to Europe because you want to be a *transplanted* European in America. You are unapologetically in the middle paths of the montage of time. You construct phenomenal experience of the times of the exterritorial: film and you are an assemblage. Your last book is an "as if" letter to yourself; however, your writing has always been an *operative literature* in now-time.[23] This is also reparative memory.

VI. A Post-Mortem? The "Operative Use of Exile": The Inside and Outside

Your poignant letters at the war's end are to Friedrich Gubler, who had been a senior editor at the *Frankfurter Zeitung*. He was, like you, hounded into exile. To him you reveal the deaths of friends and in a letter the murder of your mother and aunt in Auschwitz.[24]

Your fear: you would be unable to reclaim your life of writing as an analyst of the film and effects of the precarious situations of city life—life lived on the surfaces. The fascists saw you as a Marxist cultural agitator-insider, one of those Jewish newspaper writers who were dangerous because you addressed the anxieties of the liberal bourgeoisie and the fearful rumblings of violence below the surfaces. You *founded a style of writing* as a radical sociologist experimenting in the "new sociology" about the traumas of change *visualized* in film. Collective watching of films moors a new epoch. The new photography *situates*. Film scenes are stills frozen in time. You had no peer in how you write about collectives. The emerging Fascist Public Sphere is fair game. It was, and you knew it, the coming of the Film Century. Enigmatic scenes of streets of the city spoke to you and now the film is a tableau of the times.[25]

In Paris virtual poverty makes you dependent on others. Your letters search for sponsors and emigration affidavits. Here you write one of the first studies of Nazi propaganda, fiercely edited by Theodor Adorno.[26] Not a biographer, you choose to write a cultural biography of Jacques Offenbach's nineteenth-century operettas *as an epoch* in which the German composer in exile makes it big on the boulevards of Paris where journalists, Baudelaireans, and the homeless rub shoulders. Offenbach's operettas express the phantasmagoria of the boulevard's consumer culture. You need to make money. Exchange value is entertainment value. Adorno and Walter Benjamin ignored how your *own situation of the use of exile* became the biography of Offenbach's musical theatre. Homelessness should be on the marquee. The emerging middle classes find in transitory entertainment escape and precariousness; the distraction industries are an insurance policy against the future. The unsheltered masses are waiting in the *anterooms of history.*

In Germany *over the border, the passivity of the Weimar citizens and migration of peoples and fugitives* from the Nazi State bear witness to the everyday life of the now-time of the defeated State and the collapse of the socialist discourse. *From Caligiari to Hitler* will be an anatomy of an age. No one reads the ruins and fears of the Fascist "public" sphere better than you.

VII. An Art History of the Film and History Clinging to the Last Thing ...

Your Kantian-Simmel project examined film *at the borders within* Weimar's culture. Here is the undying wish—the *Unsterblichkeit*—of the idea of universal peace. Here, in Weimar Berlin, where you named streets *"anderswo"*—Elsewhere and Somewhere—witnessing a new type of individual, which in Georg Simmel is a new type of person: the Metropolitan Person hides inside the shelters of worn-out ideologies. The wanderers are reflected in Athena's polished shield, which you refer to in *The Last Things before the Last.* The shield exposes the alienated *homelessness* of the exile: *Posthumous time is exposed.*

There is no sanctuary for the survivors of WWI.[27] *Caligiari* looks back but is prophetic. The new elites in the film industry reach out to mass culture where biological racism, insecurity and scapegoating, the discrediting of intellectuals, demonizing of women, and the nervous male psyche reinforced images of defeat and hope. The film industry does not challenge the ruling classes but creates artistic forms of endlessness. The illusions are projected onto Athena's Shield.

Exile is marked by "endlessness" and discontinuity. This becomes the primary theme in your "American" *Theory of Film* (1960) on the threshold of remaining in America: "Like photography, film shows material phenomena virtually within reach of the camera." The camera animates "the continuum of physical existence"; your subtitle is "the redemption of physical reality."[28] Letters are a script for "the redemption of physical reality" and they, like film images, "cling to the surface of life."[29]

VIII. Open Letters Are Jump Cuts into the Future[30]

You narrate stories in your letters.[31] In *Theory of Film you trace the past through its aftermath-ness.* Your Exiles are not the recollections like Adorno's shattered subjectivity in *Minima Moralia*; instead you reflect on Marcel Proust and the phantasmagoria of lost time. Childhood is woven into *Theory of Film* and clings to you as a second skin: "the flow [of time] ... [is] an equal partner in the game ... worlds which are spontaneous creations arise... from nowhere in the flow of time."[32] Time appears as "things"; even friendship becomes a thing-representation reduced to letter writing. For Adorno, "things" are "annulled" into words on the forms that document the life of émigrés as word-objects.[33] *Theory of Film* mirrors hope in film: Athena's Shield.

Your letters written in fear from Paris to Frankfurt to your mother and aunt is an *Exile as a yet-incomplete film,* bearing out your essay "Photography" (1927), where you wrote about memory "assembl[ing] in effigy the last elements of a nature alienated from meaning."[34] "Exterritoriality" is exile that repudiates yet retains the historical. There is no autobiographical "I" or narrative of the self. Marcel Proust is your guide. Proust's chronologically successive worlds: worlds are "spontaneous creations arising from nowhere in the flow of time ... involves a detour ... [that] establishes temporal continuity in retrospect ... [where] the discontinuous worlds of his past as a continuity of time, vicariously ... redeem his past from the curse of time.... *He sets out to write the novel he has written.*"[35] Time is a riddle.

In letters to friends you risk mentioning the murder of your mother and aunt in Auschwitz, or Benjamin's suicide in Spain. Your letters are chilling figures of the transitional strangers who have performed History in the spirit of "the most imperishable, and most tenuous, connecting links between successive worlds in what you name *Niemansland, Nomansland*."[36]

IX. Exile Opens the Twilight Zone of "Enemy Aliens," "Half-Breeds," and Memory

At the Museum of Modern Art, you view hundreds of films and look at the present through the lens of the film that "discovers the marvels of everyday life" transfigured by the ephemera of reality and the collectivization in which we are immersed.[37] Teaching is closed to you. Return to Europe is not a question. In *Theory of Film*, the neighbourhoods, shops, civil law, police, streets, and buildings serve the winners and losers alike.

Emigration to South Africa or Palestine is out. Returning to Germany is return to the Caligiari world.[38] At the very time when you are coming to terms with the suicide of Benjamin and the murder of your mother and aunt, suddenly, your trunk-loads of former writings and letters are returned in New York. *You always made copies of your letters.* Thinking about suicide was never far away; Theodor Adorno labels you an "intellectual Schweik."[39]

You wrote in *History: The Last Things before the Last*: "The gulf is unbridgeable; time, far from being the All-Father, does not father anything."[40] You straddle time with and in the epistolary where the flow of natural time allows no intervention or miraculous coming to terms with the past. Proust is the guide in a mosaic of "close-ups" that reveal stations of life where shaping time is the narrative. Writing in English is a stepmother tongue.[41] Letter writing is a redemptive act shadowed by the loss of the mother tongue.

You need the addressee. The addressee assists the writer in believing that the new language will lift the weight of exile. You trust the addressee with present time, not only the unpast. There is no apocalyptic break in time that you criticize in Walter Benjamin, whose last works plot the catastrophic. You want ontological concreteness and *complementary life* that surfaces in your *redemption of physical reality and the place of the border within.*

X. Scenes in a Letter: The Murder of Your Mother and Aunt that You Barely Speak of in Your Letters Emerge in the Letter to Heinrich Gubler

I read your letter from your aunt sent to you via the Red Cross. Reading the two documents is a side-by- side montage.[42] You did not know of this report in which the *writer* describes being in the same transport with Frau Hedwig Kracauer, widow of Professor Isidor Kracauer, the writer of the history of Jews of Frankfurt, and her sister, Kracauer's mother. The letter reports that they were in the same room in Theresienstadt. The letter: these two women were then deported to the extermination camp in Auschwitz. Others disappeared as well.[43]

The destructive forces of memory are written at the borderlands of disavowal. Just how do we know this? *The letters in your Paris exile to your mother and aunt: you saved copies!* These letters documented the incommensurable. Letters grasp at the experience of time but also frozen and dead time.

The letters live as snapshots in an album of the beholder-reader's knowledge of what *then* happened to you and them.

XI. First Letters Are the Last Letters before the Next in Exile Where Age Is a Borderland of Forces

Why Write Letters? One must. I end this *Open Letter* with reference to Georg Simmel. In a passage about old age in Simmel's extraordinary *Rembrandt, An Essay in the Philosophy of Art* (1916), Simmel writes about the entwinement of age with the subjective elements in our life of borders. Rembrandt floods his own portraits with time. In 1945, entwined with age and history, and when returning to Germany would freeze time and space. There is no leave-taking or return at this time of your life.[44] Simmel had written of "*suffused reality*" in the philosophical image of the individual. *Old age is a borderland* where the turn in the depiction of individuality "is the step-by-step withdrawal from appearance."[45]

XII. Postscriptum—Under the Surfaces Time Stands Still

"It is only in this state of self-effacement, or homelessness, that the historian can commune with the material of his concern. I assume that he really wants to get the feel of it and not only aims at verifying his initial hypotheses and hunches with its aid. A stranger to the world evoked by the sources, he is faced with the task—the exile's task—of penetrating its outward appearances, so that he may learn to understand that world from within."[46]

Siegfried Kracauer's letter to close friends, Friedrich Gubler and his wife, uses the same title that Kracauer used in a Feulliton essay (Sunday, 12 July 1931), "under the surfaces." I have created here one letter out of the only exchanges between Siegfried Kracauer and his mother, Rosette Kracauer, and her sister, Hedwig Kracauer, written to them from America at the very time when they were being transported from Frankfurt to Theresienstadt and then to Auschwitz. These communications to his mother and aunt are delivered by the Red Cross. Did they receive the letter? *No one knows.*

Your staccato letter is a coded communication in telegraphic icy form to show the censors that nothing of extraordinary concern is happening "under the surfaces" of the letters. For this open letter on borders and exile, they are "unstaged-unstaged reality"[47] (58 West 75th Street, New York 23, NY, September 10, 1945). The letter via the American Red Cross, New York Chapter, reads:

> Both we are in good health. Hope same of you. Job goes on. Think of you with most cordial wishes. Yearn for seeing you again [in English] SIGNED: Dr. Siegfried Kracauer Sep 15, 1942. The Answer to the message is via the German Red Cross, 10 March 1942 #272162 From Rosette Sara Krakauer, Frankfurt a.M., Sandweg 7 Are healthy Thanks, Since 11. November in home on Sandweg 7. Letter of November received. Write how you are, what you are doing. Relatives are in Berlin, Dresden 6.3.42/ Stamp: 27 March 1942 (SIGNED) Rosette Sara Krakauer. [Trans. JZ][48]

The staccato letter says all we need to know.

Notes to Chapter 13:

1 Ian Angus, "Louis Riel and English-Canadian Political Thought," *University of Toronto Quarterly* 74, no. 4 (Fall 2005): 885. Characters in the "Open Letter: The Exile, Siegfried Kracauer the addressee of the 'Open Letter'." Ian Angus, Writer of warm books in a cold climate; The Author of the "Open Letter," friend of Ian Angus, Researcher over the years on Siegfried Kracauer's life and works. Walk on Authors see Endnotes.

2 Siegfried Kracauer, *History: The Last Things Before the Last* (New York: Oxford University Press, 1969), 4.

3 See: Reinhart Koselleck, *Futures Past on the Semantics of Historical Time*, trans. Keith Tribe (New York: Columbia University Press, 2004), 183. Koselleck writes of memory and history as an asymmetrical concept of time: "The accumulation of temporalities finally makes it possible for the structure of all these counter concepts to appear together...." See below, note 8.

4 Jean Paul Sartre, "For Whom Does One Write?" in *What Is Literature and Other Essays* (Cambridge, MA: Harvard University Press, 1988), 77. In *(Dis) figurations, Discourse/Critique/Ethics* (London and New York: Verso, 2000),

Angus discusses empathic consciousness through Sartre and Husserl, 167–83. In the letter to Adorno in Note #3, Kracauer emphasizes that Husserl expressed praise for Kracauer' *Sociology as Knowledge*, 1922, which, along with Kracauer's *The Detective Novel*, 1925, remain untranslated. Both expand on Georg Lukács's epochal homelessness.

5 On "inalienable subjectivities," see on George Simmel below.

6 Bakhtin's understanding of the *Skaz the tale* relates to how I see letter writing. See Walter Benjamin's "The Storyteller," *Illuminations* (pp. 83-110). Letter writing recounts now-time as productive understanding in memory and history.

7 See: "Those Who Wait" in Siegfried Kracauer, *The Ornament of the Mass* (Berlin: Suhrkamp Verlag, 1963) 129.

8 For fuller interpretations of Kracauer, see my "The Reparation of Dead Souls—Siegfried Kracauer's Archimedean Exile—The Prophetic Journey from Death to Bildung," in *Exile, Science and Bildung, The Contested Legacy of German Émigré Intellectuals*, ed. David Kettler and Gerhard Lauer (London: Palgrave, 2005); and "Siegfried Kracauer's Cosmopolitan Homelessness—The Lost Cause of an Idea," in *Cosmopolitans in the Modern World*, ed. Suzanne Kirkbright (Munich: Judicum, 2000). These essays will appear in: Jerry Zaslove, *From the Other Shore, Untimely Meditations* (Vancouver: Talonbooks, forthcoming). Also: Jerry Zaslove, "The Return of Kracauer," in *Seminar, A Journal of German Studies* XXX (November 1997): 419–24; see n26.

9 Dziga Vertov's Kino-eye in *Man with the Movie Camera* inspired Kracauer to contemplate staged reality, what is left out and falls by the wayside. Chaplin's films release the gestures of resistance and capture this salience of the seen/unseen.

10 Ian Angus, *Love the Questions: University Education and Enlightenment* (Winnipeg: Arbeiter Ring Press, 2009), shows more faith in the university as a social movement than I do. For Kracauer and me, the university is a white-collar institution.

11 Ian Angus, "Movements, Authentic Sociality and Nothingness," *PhaenEx* 1, no.1 (spring/summer 2006): 175–96.

12 Graeme Nicholson, "Review of Identity and Justice by Ian Angus," Modern Horizons June 20, (2012), http://modernhorizonsjournal.ca/wp-content/uploads/Issues/201206/Issue-201206-Nicholson.pdf

13 See: Peyman Vahabzadeh, *Exilic Meditations, Essays on a Displaced Life* (London: H&S Media, 2012). Angus does not discuss exile directly; however, his *(Dis)figurations Discourse, Critique, Ethics* (London: Verso, 2000) suggests an epochal outside as inside, the time bound and yet out of time. Thinking about nationalism reflects the influence of Jan Patočka's historical phenomenology and existential struggle with emergent nationalism.

14 See Ernst Bloch's Utopian formulation about rights: *Natural Law and Human Dignity*, trans. Dennis J. Schmidt (Cambridge, MA: MIT Press: 1986), xxix–xxx.

15 See Ian Angus's insightful commentary about my *Kafka in the Penal Colony* (Vancouver: West Coast Line Books, 2008), 87–88.

16 On Kracauer, see note 18 below. Theodor W. Adorno was one anchor in Kracauer's perilous exile. Their complicated friendship in exile was not always what Kracauer wanted it to be. See below, Kracauer on Proustian time.

17 The epistolary discourse of inner life can be found in Goethe, Dostoevsky, Kafka, Smollett, Rousseau, Laclos, Virginia Woolf. On Winfried G. Sebald's inwardness: see my essay "W. G. Sebald and Exilic Memory—His Photographic Images of the Cosmogony of Exile and Restitution," David Kettler and Zvi Ben-Dor, eds., *The Limits of Exile*, *Journal of the Interdisciplinary Crossroads* 3, no. 1 (April 2006).

18 Translated as *The Salaried Masses: Duty and Distraction in Weimar Germany*, trans. Quintin Hoare, introd. Inka Mülder-Bach (London: Verso Press, 1998). Each chapter is rendered as if it were a scene for a film. Background: uprisings, riots, strikes against WWI, workers' councils that opposed the war. The majority wanted the war. Regret and denial pervade the postwar and fear of the return of the bloody November revolutions: the Caligiari Nightmare.

19 Siegfried Kracauer, "Revolt of the Middle Classes," in *Ornament of the Mass*, 123.

20 See Benjamin's "The Storyteller," *Illuminations* (pp. 83-110): *Eindenken* is memory as a "language entering into one's past like dead cities lie interred": Walter Benjamin, "A Berlin Chronicle," in *Reflections*, trans. Edmund Jephcott, ed. Peter Demetz (New York and London: Harcourt Brace Jovanovich, 1978), 26.

21 Siegfried Kracauer, "Photography," in *Ornament of the Mass*, 61: "instead of preserving the 'history' that consciousness reads out of the temporal succession of events," the letter-writer plays with the "go-for-broke-game" of history. The letter like a film, "combines parts and segments to create strange constructs" by the consciousness related to imagining the addressee (62).

22 Georg Simmel, "The Stranger," in *The Sociology of Georg Simmel*, trans. Kurt Wolff (New York: Free Press, 1950), 402.

23 See David Frisby on Sergei Tretjakov's "operative literature," in *Fragments of Modernity: Theories of Modernity in the Work of Simmel, Kracauer and Benjamin* (Cambridge, MA: MIT Press, 1986), 163. Frisby's study is one of the best on Kracauer and does not discuss the exilic as the *operative condition of your writing*.

24 Friedrich Gubler was the editor of the *Frankfurter Zeitung* in Berlin. He was forced to leave Germany and return to Switzerland by Joseph Goebbels's threat of being sent to a concentration camp.

25 I became aware of *From Caligiari to Hitler: A Psychological History of the German Film* (Princeton: Princeton University Press, 1947) in the early 1950s, and *Theory of Film* in the early 1960s. Kracauer informed my study of Jeff Wall's photographs: *Jeff Wall 1990* (Vancouver Art Gallery, 1990).

26 Adorno's edits of Kracauer's two Paris-exile studies, Propaganda and Offenbach, was fierce. Kracauer rejected the edits because they weakened Kracauer's critique of fascism. The study became *Propaganda and the Nazi War Film* (New York: Museum of Modern Art Film Library, 1942) and a supplement in *From Caligiari to Hitler* (Princeton: Princeton University Press, 1946).

27 Kracauer held no academic positions. He produced some studies of migrants fleeing the Iron Curtain countries. His wife, Lily Ehrenreich, worked for Jewish immigration services. Other émigré-exiles established cold-war credentials. See: Udi Greenberg, *The Weimar Century, German Émigrés and the Ideological Foundations of the Cold War* (Princeton: Princeton University Press, 2014).

28 Siegfried Kracauer, *Theory of Film: The Redemption of Physical Reality* (London: Oxford University Press, 1960), 63. The first edition in England was *Nature of Film*, "reading" film as images that flow and exhibit "raw material" of life virtually intact ... film clings to the surface of things.

29 Kracauer never stopped writing letters to former newspaper colleagues. *The typewriter is a way of life*. I describe his letters in his Paris exile, 1934 to 1941, to his mother and aunt in Jerry Zaslove, "Zeitgenossen without Genossen: The Contemporary without Friendship or History," *Contested Legacies, Essays from the No Happy End Workshop*, Bard College, August 2002, accessed March 31, 2019, www.bard.edu/contestedlegacies.

30 The City Berlin, a *mise en scène* of streets and architecture, is the stage of more than 100 film reviews. Kracauer- Panofsky's exchange is in the Warburg tradition of art and ethnography. German film "was nursed in a period of revolutionary crises and social insecurity ... the homeless soul not only drove straightway toward the fantastic region of horrors ... of normal reality, embracing conventional forms that forced them into weird, abnormal figures in ... the city street where the 'Man of the Crowd' experiences kaleidoscopic configurations of everyday life... ." "Notes on the Planned History of Film" to Erwin Panofsky, October 16, 1942, in Volker Breidecker, *Siegfried Kracauer—Erwin Panofsky, Briefwechsel, 1941–1956*, ed. Tom Levin (Berlin, Academic Verlag,1996), 17.

31 In 1940 Alfred Schutz, schooled in phenomenology, wrote to Aron Gurwitsch that he is "receiving despairing letters from Kracauer with threats of suicide"—Kracauer "pleads" for help in speeding up the naturalization process. Aron

Gurwitsch, *Briefwechsel, 1939–1959* (Munich: Wilhelm Fink Verlag, n.d.), 19. Gurwitsch and Kracauer were held in the same French Internment Camp in Gurs. This remarkable exchange of letters by two phenomenological social thinkers shows the importance of letter writing as form-giving experience for truth-value in the making.

32 Kracauer, *History*, 178.

33 Theodor Adorno, *Minima Moralia, Reflections on a Damaged Life*, #13, trans. E. F. N. Jephcott (London: New Left Books, 1951), 33.

34 Kracauer, "Photography," in *Ornament of the Mass*, 62,

35 Kracauer, *History*, 162–63; emphasis added.

36 Ibid., 161.

37 Kracauer's *Theory of Film* refers to more than 100 films. Camera reality fuses the image with the eye just when the life of the image may be dissolving. What is left over is the husk of an image lost in time.

38 See: Jerry Zaslove, "Siegfried Kracauer's Cosmopolitan Homelessness—The Lost Cause of an Idea in the Film Age," in *Cosmopolitans in the Modern World*, ed. Suzanne Kirkbright (München: Judicum, 2000).

39 Theodor W. Adorno, "The Curious Realist," in *Notes to Literature*, vol. two, trans. Shierry Nicholsen Weber (New York: Columbia University, 1994), 69.

40 See: Walter Benjamin, *Briefe an Siegfried Kracauer* (hrsg. Theodor W. Adorno: Archive, Marbach am Neckar, 1987). The German translation elides the comical moment by eliminating the father: "The Gulf is unbridgeable: time far from being the All-Father, does not father anything." Kracauer was a "ragpicker at daylight ... in the dawn of the day of revolution," 112. Benjamin is thinking about Atget's photograph of the "Lumpensammler."

41 See: Georg Simmel, "Bridge and Door," *Theory, Culture and Society* 11, no. 1 (February 1994): 5–10.

42 *Documents of the History of the Frankfurt Jews*. Kracauer's uncle wrote a history of the Jews of Frankfurt, 1914. 43 Lisa Katz, *Deportationen 1941 und 1942, Geschrieben 1961* (Frankfurt am Main: Verlag Waldemar Kramer, n.d.), 508. This document is the only evidence of the fate of Kracauer's mother and aunt that to my knowledge exists.

44 Simmel's remarkable essay on Rembrandt and old age, 1916: Georg Simmel, *Rembrandt: An Essay on the Philosophy of Art*, trans. Alan Scott and Helmut Staubmann (New York: Routledge, 2005), 96. Rembrandt painted portraits of himself at different stages of his life. I bring Kracauer back to Simmel, his first influence on the inner life. Simmel dies in 1918. Simmel's reference to withdrawal from appearance is to Goethe.

45 Simmel, *Rembrandt*, 96. Rembrandt painted portraits of himself at different stages of his life. The "Open Letter" expresses inner life on growing older. I bring Kracauer back to Simmel, his first major influence.

46 Siegfried Kracauer, "The Historian's Journey," in *History*, 84.

47 Siegfried Kracauer, Archive, German National Library, Marbach. That testimony about exile is catastrophic goes without saying; however, consciousness of exile also searches for lost and missing voices within the traumatic event. Exile is an immanent reality that entwines the *inner borders with external time*; the author not only shows a border but opens leaking boundaries and finds new borders. See note 31.

48 On this letter, see note 45.

Chapter 14

Media and Translations of Nature

The Feeling of Skiing Jackson Hole

Kevin Michael DeLuca

> The specific prevailing configuration of this cultural environment is defined by a continuous translation between a plurality of media.
>
> IAN ANGUS, *THE PRIMAL SCENES OF COMMUNICATION* (2000)

The social sciences and the humanities are facing something of a media crisis, a digital delirium. A long time ago, Gregory Bateson noted a grievous error in such scholarship, which "tried to build the bridge to the wrong half of the ancient dichotomy between form and substance. Mental process, ideas, communication, organization, differentiation, pattern, and so on, are matters of form rather than substance."[1] That error, the focus on content to the near-total neglect of form, persists, even in an age of social media and digital humanities. We live in a time of digital addendum, an easy linguistic fix for a scholarly blind spot. In the discipline of Communication, for example, such a move is epidemic, so that we get calls for academics who study health communication *and* social media, organizational communication *and* digital media, and rhetoric *and* digital humanities. Fortunately, for many scholars, what follows the "and" is an addendum, that which may be added but is not particularly essential. For example, one may study messages that appear on Facebook or via email with a focus on their content and paying little attention to media forms. Although the intensification of social media in every aspect of our lives has forced a nod to media, scholarship can proceed largely as it has always done, highlighting content and neglecting form. With such a habitual move, much is lost. Fortunately, on the margins persists an interest about media *qua* media and media studies retains its quirky niche.

In Communication, Ian Angus's work on media theory (and social movements) has been provocative. In Communication, as noted, content consistently trumps form, so the impact of media is neglected. Drawing and extending the Canadian tradition of media studies and highlighting the work of Harold Innis and Marshall McLuhan, Angus has foregrounded questions of technology (media). In his focus on media, Angus has explored the processes and impacts of mediation/translation, a move with vital implications for studying a world saturated in media. This essay will concentrate on Angus's attention to media forms, with a link to his study of environmental social movements.

Drawing from the Frankfurt School's critical theory, especially Max Horkheimer's and Theodor Adorno's thinking of the dialectic of enlightenment and William Leiss's take on the domination of nature, Angus has long engaged key concerns for environmentalism. In contemplating how the world is changed, these two foci of Angus's work supplement each other when exploring how media mediate and translate our relations with nature. I use these key contributions by Angus to explore how technological translations mediate, enable, and transform relations with the natural world. Perhaps more than most, I emphasize the concepts of mediation and translation as absolutely critical for a shift to environmental pragmatism. As a case study, I analyze how skis, maps, ski literature, ski resort architecture, and ski towns translate snow and mountains into an ecstatic feeling of the world that both inspires environmental actions whilst inevitably inflicting ecological damages on an earth beyond purity.

Making Media Matter

Angus's charge is blunt and challenging: "The thesis proper to communication studies, in the context of the philosophy of the human sciences, is the constitution of perception, social relations, institutions, and thought by media of communication."[2] Outside of the niche of media studies, Angus's challenge is usually elided in Communication despite the present moment being one of vast and fundamental transformations enabled by the Internet and social media. Most communication scholarship ignores the medium in favour of focusing on content, thus treating media as transparent. Even when an area such as cultural studies purportedly pays attention to media, there is a tendency to offer obtuse takes of media subordinated to ineffectual critiques of caricatures of capitalism. In this respect, Robert Gehl's predictable and stultifying neo-Marxist critique of Web 2.0 social media as subservient to an omnipotent Capitalism is exemplary.[3] The refusal to engage media *qua* media as events that disrupt the world as it is severely truncates communication studies.

Angus seeks to answer his own challenge, primarily in two books, *Primal Scenes of Communication* and *A Border Within*. Especially in *Primal Scenes of Communication*, Angus constructs a comparative theory of media that understands "the media of communication that have been developed throughout human culture are expressions of the socio-historical Being of human life. They are the embodied rhetorical form that institutes, or establishes, a world."[4] In developing his comparative media theory, Angus relies heavily on the thought of Harold Innis and Marshall McLuhan.

Angus works from Innis's radical claim that media are central to the history of institutions and civilizations—"the grand scope of the later studies of communication as a theory of civilization."[5] Innis argues that a medium has a time or space bias, that is, that it effectively communicates over time, such as stone tablets, or that it successfully communicates over distances, such as writing on paper. The bias of the dominant medium in a society leads to dramatically different organizations of society. An oral culture dependent on the spoken word is often stable over time but travels poorly; witness the many languages and dialects across the relatively small space of Europe or the many languages that developed in oral cultures across North America. In contrast, papyrus enabled the Roman Empire to communicate effectively across vast distances. Similarly, paper, the railroad, and the telegraph enabled the United States and English to expand across the continent. As Angus summarizes, "the most important component of Innis's communication theory of society—[is] that a medium is not a neutral channel, but an active formation of perceptual, institutional, and cognitive dimensions of human experience. As such, it necessarily contains a 'bias' that identifies the specific socio-cultural orientations built upon the dominant medium."[6] Notably, for Innis, "A 'medium of communication' is understood in a very wide sense as any kind of a formative and integrating social mechanism."[7] This catholic notion of medium is extended by McLuhan and adopted in this essay.

While Innis focused on the effects of a dominant medium at the level of institutions and civilizations, McLuhan, writing in the decades after Innis, added consideration of the impacts of media on the subject as well as a focus on the interplay of media. Innis took an historical perspective on past civilizations, and although McLuhan did that in *The Gutenberg Galaxy*, in *Understanding Media* and his later work he attempted to make sense of the contemporary 1960s and 1970s media matrix, performing the work of the artist: "The serious artist is the only person able to encounter technology with impunity, just because he is an expert aware of the changes in sense perception."[8] McLuhan continues, "The ability of the artist to sidestep the bully blow of new technology of any age, and to parry such violence with full awareness, is age-old."[9] For McLuhan, the impacts of media are both civilizational and individual: "The personal and social consequences of any medium—that is, of any extension of ourselves—result from the new scale that is introduced into our affairs by each extension of ourselves, or by any new technology."[10] This is what McLuhan means by his famous aphorism, "the medium is the message."[11] As McLuhan elaborates, "For the message of any medium or technology is the change of scale or pace or pattern that it introduces into human affairs."[12] Like Innis, McLuhan has a very broad understanding of media, and in *Understanding Media: The Extensions of Man* has chapters dedicated to speech, writing, roads, clothing, housing, money, clocks, print, bicycles, photographs, cars, radio, television, weapons, and so on.

As with Innis, Angus finds himself largely in agreement with McLuhan, but places emphasis on the translation among a plurality of media suggested by the list of chapters in *Understanding Media*. This point will be particularly important for this essay. Unlike the tendency in media studies to analyze a dominant medium in isolation—for example, describing the essential characteristics of film photography or the telegraph[13]—McLuhan insists on media always in interaction with each other: "What I am saying is that media as extensions of our senses institute new ratios, not only among our private senses, but among themselves, when they interact among themselves."[14] This crucial move by McLuhan moves him beyond charges of technological determinism since the effects of any medium are relational, dependent not only on the social context but also the media matrix within which any particular medium is acting and interacting. While orality dominated for many thousands of years and writing was a co-dominant medium (with orality) for millennia and print dominated for centuries, we now experience a cacophonous plurality of media creating ceaseless translations of our social and natural environments. In our world of ever-proliferating and -intensifying media—think computers, television, film, Netflix, the Internet, emails, Facebook, Twitter, WeChat, Instagram, Apple iTunes, Alexa, and on and on, with so much of this panmediation being concentrated in smart phones—the task becomes not simply to think through a medium but to think the ceaseless process of panmediation; with the emergence of smart phones we live in multiple spaces of multiple media, immersed in clouds of Wi-Fi with space and time no longer barriers to living in a mediated world at all moments.

Angus develops and extends this point: "Media continuously translate each other; thus, they constitute an *environment*, rather than a simple plurality" (see also the epigraph).[15] This media environment becomes the world we live in: "It is a rhetoric of media forms in which one is persuaded not primarily to a given content, but to see the world with a certain perceptual, social, and cognitive emphasis."[16] To put it in an aphorism: our media, ourselves, our world. In our current media environment, what happens next? As social media are accelerating affective intensities in ways that produce unpredictable and often unexpected social changes, what are the implications for social change, especially environmentalism? Our moment suggests ever-accelerating velocities of mediations and translations.

Amidst this mediation maelstrom, we risk technological trauma as media truncate our reciprocal relations with the earth, stunting our senses and threatening to incarcerate us in a techno-soliloquy.

Engaging the Earth in the Media World

As our techno-industrial juggernaut rampages across the planet, wreaking havoc on an ecocidal scale impossible to imagine, how are we to respond? One important response has been environmentalism, a movement literally birthed by the rise of industrialism and technology such as the camera.[17] One of the most beautiful and important pillars of environmentalism has been wilderness environmentalism, a ferocious defense of wild worlds outside the control of humans. At the fount of wilderness environmentalism is Henry Thoreau proclaiming in "Walking" that "in Wildness is the preservation of the World."[18] John Muir, the prophet of Yosemite and the Sierras, advocated that "the clearest way into the Universe is through a forest wilderness."[19] Aldo Leopold, the quietly radical professor of wilderness, suggests "a shift of values can be achieved by reappraising things unnatural, tame, and confined in terms of things natural, wild, and free."[20] Writing in the 1940s, Leopold is already thoroughly alarmed by technology and mediation tainting our relationship with wilderness: "A gadget industry pads the bumps against nature-in-the-raw; woodcraft becomes the art of using gadgets.... By and large, our present problem is one of attitudes and implements."[21]

These germinal figures, along with many others, advocate for wilderness both as something beyond the human that has a right to exist and as something that may provoke ecological social change. Evental experiences have for many environmentalists shifted their feeling of the world, from John Muir's revelation in the Sierra Nevadas to Ansel Adams first visiting Yosemite to Aldo Leopold watching a wolf die to Julia Butterfly Hill being overwhelmed by redwoods. Such transformative and seemingly unmediated events call many people to environmentalism. An event disrupts the world as it is: "The possible does not pre-exist, it is created by the event."[22] Gilles Deleuze continues, "They appear for a moment, and it's that moment that matters, it's the chance we must seize."[23]

These activists, and so many more, have seized the event and been worthy of it and their work has transformed the world. Wilderness environmentalism has inspired the US national park system (America's "best idea" and the first example of setting aside wilderness for its own sake, starting in 1864 when President Lincoln preserved Yosemite), the 1964 Wilderness Act, and environmental groups, including the Sierra Club, the Wilderness Society, Greenpeace, and Earth First!.

Wilderness environmentalism remains a vibrant and vital strategy in the face of industrial ravages, but if we live in a mediated world it behooves us to consider other tactics and strategies that build upon mediation. As Angus recommends, "I want to suggest that the key question facing social change at the present time is rather 'mediation.'"[24] This is not to suggest an either/or with respect to environmentalism but a proliferation. If our experience is almost always already one of mediation and media translations, how might mediated experiences of nature and wilderness promote love for the more than human world? What sort of mediations enable affinity for nature? Which mediations provoke affective encounters with wilderness? How might mediations enable us to feel the world differently?

In a world saturated in mediations, the chances for unmediated or even lightly mediated wilderness experiences are quite limited. Given the number of people and the shrinking of wilderness around the planet, bringing billions of people to wilderness places will ensure only the destruction of such places. This has been a problem for wilderness advocates for over a century. John Muir fretted over the choice of connecting people to wilderness through personal experiences and bringing too many people to the Sierras. One of his solutions was the mediation of writing with his popular books and magazine articles. Ansel Adams struggled with this dilemma his whole life as his photography and his photography studio in Yosemite Valley popularized wilderness for the masses, drawing millions of people to places like Yosemite and other sublime spots. Of course, the danger is that the mediation draws in more people seeking the embodied experience, something approaching the unmediated, even if such a dream always recedes. Angus laments that this results in *staged authenticity* as subjects are "confirmed in his or her cultural being by touristic pilgrimage to view originals."[25] Although Angus advocates forms of resistance that seek to jam mediation,[26] I adopt a different tack. Cognizant of the risks, I will proceed to explore the possibilities of mediations upon mediations.

The Feel of Skis, Snow, and Mountains

The mediations are endless. From the Dodge Durango and the roads that carry me from Salt Lake City to Jackson Hole Mountain Resort, the multiplying mediations form the atmosphere through which I move. Inevitably, I will begin in the middle and with certain choices in the hopes of exploring how the mediations not only impinge upon affective and sublime experiences but enable affective and sublime experiences leading to new feelings of wild places. Skis, snow, maps, mountain contours, trail design, trees, elk, rocks, and moose are all media that shape my experience.

The Jackson Hole ski area is a heterotopia, as Michel Foucault says, "capable of juxtaposing in a single real place several spaces, several sites that are in themselves incompatible,"[27] a fantastical place where high-tech skis, moose, billionaires, wolves, ski bums, remnants of the Old West, high fashion, elk, a range of restaurants, private jets, eco-conscious virtue signalling, cattle ranchers, imported workers, trashy trinket tourist shops, elitist art galleries, fur coats, locals, a banal supermarket of excess, gateways of elk antlers, snow, and more collide and conspire to create a globally resonant iconic place.

As I pull into the Teton Village parking lot at 8:00 a.m., Jackson Hole looks welcoming, the more treacherous terrain and the towering Rendezvous Mountain (3,187 metres) hidden by the front of the mountain. The weather, the elemental medium as John Peters reminds us,[28] provides the next welcome, with the temperature at -20°C but the promise of a blue sky day to compensate for the lack of warmth. Once dressed in my winter warmth battle gear—layers of merino wool and face mask and ski helmet and ski boots, I assume a ludicrous gait to Sweetwater Gondola, while noting the already hour-long line for the nearby famous tram. The gondola squeezes six of us into awkward intimacy as we scan the slopes for potential lines or watch the Jackson Hole Valley unfurl below us. We top a ridge and the grand ski landscape and our day unfold before us.

Sweetwater deposits us only mid-mountain and a short drop connects me to the Casper Quad Chair. This lift takes us to over 2,438.4 metres and starts putting me in my element. Skiing is certainly about snow, it is a wintertime water sport, but it is also about wind. Often we seek shelter from the wind, but skiing is different. In skiing we seek and hope for the wind, the portent of storms and more snow. The lift raises us above the shelter of the trees, exposing us to the wind, and we go higher still on the mountain and into even more wind. Too often forgetting the wind in our sheltered techno-boxes, skiing makes us remember the wind. And treasure the wind. Luce Irigaray starkly reminded us of the fundamental role of the wind/air. Correlating with our discussion of mediation, Irigaray writes, "Air would be the arch-mediation: of the *logos*, of thinking, of the world."[29] Air is the elemental element that makes possible possibility. Humans become a mere manifestation of the air, connected with all the other myriad things made possible by air.

The wind is the original medium, the medium that makes possible all other media, starting with speech. As David Abram observes, "*Words, here, are nothing other than shaped breath*. Hence the fluid air is the implicit intermediary in all communication, the very medium of meaning."[30] Abram tracks winds/air around the earth, finding revealing traces in etymology.[31] The Greek term *psyche* signifies breath and a gust of wind as well as soul or mind. The English words "spirit" and "respiration" derive from the Latin word *spiritus*, meaning both breath and wind. The Latin *anima* signifies air, breath, and soul. In Sanskrit *atman* means air, breath, and soul. The Hebrew word *ruach* denotes both wind and spirit. Across cultures, air, wind, become the ineffable and yet omnipresent groundless ground that makes possible worlds. Already, without having started to ski, the media of this ski resort, specifically the ski lifts, have connected me to nature, to wind, to vantage points impossible without mediation.

Now I am on the snow and flying. Although riding the lift might look like a slow-motion form of flying, skiing wide-open groomers at up to 80 kilometres per hour feels like flying. The texture of the groomers is firm yet fresh and yielding, so carving down Sundog is effortless and exhilarating, the wind cold against my smile. After a few warm-up runs, I take Moran Traverse over to the black Moran Woods run, named after Thomas Moran, the 1800s landscape painter whose watercolours of Yellowstone for the 1871 US Geological Survey Expedition were instrumental in getting Congress to pass legislation designating Yellowstone a national park. It is nice to see that Moran is remembered, and, of course, he is also remembered in Grand Teton National Park with Mount Moran, at 3,843.5 metres an impressive peak with a massive summit adorned with glaciers and providing a dramatic contrast to the Snake River.

Moran Woods feels steep but is nowhere near the steepest or most difficult run at Jackson Hole.

Whether flying down open groomers, assiduously turning down steeper black runs, or navigating through trees, my experiences are mediated by my skis, Blizzard Bonafides circa 2018, a popular all-mountain ski. Although a couple of decades ago the Bonafides would have been considered a massive powder ski with measurements of 135.5–98–119.5 mm, now it is a normal sized all-mountain ski. Ski technology has undergone dizzying changes in the past two decades, and skis as media have become paradoxically both ever-more versatile and specialized. Blizzard is a renowned ski company in the Austrian Alps, the mecca of skiing. The Bonafide is their flagship ski and it exhibits the characteristics of current ski technology, including tip and tail rocker and reverse camber underfoot. It also has Blizzard's patented carbon flipcore technology. As Blizzard describes this ski,

> The legendary Bonafide continues to set the bar in the all-mountain freeride world. A versatile all-mountain side-cut and reduced rocker profile makes this ski nimble and easy handling, while the proven Carbon Flipcore™ with two sheets of Titinal makes them calm, confident and powerful. Attack the mountain in powder, crud, groomers or rock hard snow and feel the precision and exhilaration that athletes and testers rave about. Try for yourself to see what the hype is all about.[32]

A slightly more independent review raves,

> Whether there's powder, wind-buffed chalk, a thin layer of corn, or bulletproof hardpack, the Blizzard Bonafide Ski will easily rip the mountain from top to bottom. This favorite of ski testers everywhere has an even more accessible feel thanks to its Carbon Flipcore technology with double Titanal. Directional carbon fiber in the tip and tail helps to stabilize the rocker when you're rallying groomers, eliminates tip chatter, and helps to reduce the swing weight of the ski, while two full sheets of Titanal further add dampening properties and even pressure distribution for a smooth, quick feel. Its mid-fat 98 millimeter waist and rockered tip and tail offer excellent flotation in the steep and deep and provides easy turn initiation wherever you are on the mountain. This daily driver tears up groomers, open bowls, crud, bumps, boilerplate ice, and blower pow with flying colors. Sandwich sidewall construction makes it a precise and powerful turning machine, and a poplar-beech wood core provides smooth and fluid turning. Utilizing its revolutionary Flipcore technology, Blizzard put the Bonafide's core into the mold upside-down, giving the tip and tail a naturally rockered shape rather than weakening the ski's integrity by pressing it into shape as is the case with most rockered skis.[33]

How does the hype translate into the *feel* of the skis? And *feel* is the key. As Alfred Whitehead argues, "the primitive experience is an emotional feeling, felt in its relevance to a world beyond."[34] The primary activity is feeling the world. Our primary encounter with the things of the world is through feeling. Steven Shaviro concludes that, for Whitehead, "the questions of how we feel, and what we feel, are more fundamental than the epistemological and hermeneutical questions that are the focus of most philosophy and criticism."[35] Shaviro elaborates, "Feeling, as such, is the primordial form of all relation and all communication.... An act of feeling is an encounter—a contingent event, an opening to the outside."[36]

Crucially, feeling is how we engage things in the world in myriad ways. In buying skis, we try them out first "to get a feel" for them. For many items, Internet shopping is difficult because we cannot get a feel for the thing. As we get on the skis on snow, we can immediately get a feel for them in moments. I have skied multiple skis, and my feel for the Bonafide was forceful, compelling, and difficult to translate into words. "Feel" also depends on a complex network of relations. It depends on how the components of the skis (shape, titanium, poplar, and wax), bindings, and boots feel in relation to the things that compose me. How does the shape and flex interact with my feet and legs and skill? How do the skis move me? How does my feeling of the ski and the skis's feeling of me produce fun or discomfort or joy? Of course, all of these things are not quantitative measures but feelings. In this, feel for the ski is crucial because the ski provides my feel for the mountain as I ski the trails. In practice, the ski translates the trail for me, my encounter with snow, wind, and light. Through the skis I feel the mountain. The ski is a medium. The skis translate the snow to me and via this mediation a world becomes.

We must be careful here to not reduce the assemblage to a person, a ski, and the mountain. As Whitehead emphasizes, the feelings or prehensions that become the world are endless. There are infinite becomings and perpetual perishings. Deleuze elaborates, "Everything prehends its antecedents and its concomitants and, by degrees, prehends a world. The eye is a prehension of light. Living beings prehend water, soil, carbon, and salts."[37] And these things doing these feelings are similarly infinite. As Deleuze puts it, an assemblage, "a body, however small it may be, is composed of an infinite number of particles; it is the relations of motion and rest, of speed and slownesses between particles, that define a body."[38] The composite ski and composite I mutually feel each other and feel the composite ski run. These mutual becomings are always perishing and becoming again. The ski, an infinite composition, changes as it feels soft snow, ice, chop, and further variations. The ski flexes in relation to me and the trail, and is in constant transition and translation. The composition that becomes me is also always transforming. Depending on the decline of the trail, my heart rate accelerates or decelerates. My glucose levels fluctuate. Lactic acid accumulates in my thighs as different muscles are recruited for power, balance, turning. My body absorbs and secretes water. My eyes process light fluctuations so I can see what is happening with the aid of my extraordinarily sensitive goggles. My nervous system transmits stimulations and information so that I am constantly acting and reacting before thinking. Feeling before cognition. Endorphins ebb and flow as parts of the trail provoke fear and ecstasy. My skin responds to temperature changes and the lashings of tree branches along the trail. I am in a dance with all the other skiers on the mountain. Deleuze says, "So an animal, a thing, is never separable from its relations with the world.... The speed or slowness of metabolisms, perceptions, actions, and reactions link together to constitute a particular individual in the world."[39] This infinite body is both a cacophonous composition and subtle symphony. As Deleuze and Felix Guattari argue, "Flows of intensity, their fluids, their fibers, their continuums and conjunctions of affects, the wind, fine segmentation, microperceptions, have replaced the world of the subject."[40]

This feeling of the world and this feel for technology and feeling of the world via technology is common in sports but also in many other areas of life. In the larger sense, this feeling of different things in the world is how we experience the world. With the Bonafide the result is a ski that mediates and enhances my experience of the mountain and snow in astonishing ways, adept and quick to carve, stable at dangerous speeds, agile among trees, and fun and comforting in almost any situation. As the medium, the Bonafide extends my skills, reassures me, and connects me to the mountain across a variety of terrain. As I ski down a run, the Bonafide both mediates and communicates the terrain to me as they grip into the icy patches, smooth out chop, and absorb the variety of vibrations the slope presents to me.

After a couple of blue-sky days, two days of snow provide over a foot of powder. The Bonafides would handle that, but I choose another medium, another feel. I decide to go bigger with the DPS Wailer112RP2—141–112–128 mm and 190 cm long. The extra width provides greater float, making the 30+ centimetres feel deeper. Powder emphasizes the three-dimensional nature of skiing and the Wailer is an adept medium.

DPS is a local Salt Lake City ski company and the Wailer is a famous resort powder ski, the brainchild of Stephen Drake (and his team), who started making skis to match his obsession with powder. While the Bonafide is understated and nuanced, the DPS Wailer is loud both in form and colour, with an exaggerated tip rocker announced by bright yellow. DPS promotes the Wailer as an ideal medium and it has put this niche Salt Lake City company on the global ski map:

> The Wailer 112 is a legendary ski, virtually unchanged over the years. New for the 2015 however, the DPS Wailer 112 RP.2 Ski has seen some re-design and improvement. The tip and tail rocker profile has been lowered, reducing deflection and increasing power in mixed snow.
>
> Re-shaped sidecut delivers a bigger sweet spot at a greater range of speeds thanks to Paddle Tech. The DPS

> Wailer 112 RP.2 Ski still lives up to the name and maintains its all-mountain chops; the Hybrid core still crushes variable conditions both inbounds and in the backcountry from Aspen to Mount Baker. We think there's a reason the Wailer 112 RP.2 is so loved, and we want you to see what the hype is about.[41]

I embrace the heterotopia, the infinite cacophonous symphony of mediations. As Michel Foucault says, "We are in the epoch of simultaneity: we are in the epoch of juxtaposition, the epoch of the near and far, of the side-by-side, of the dispersed. We are at a moment, I believe, when our experience of the world is less that of a long life developing through time than that of a network that connects points and intersects with its own skein."[42] I surf the powder, the Wailers floating in and out, sometimes disappearing under a foot of ephemeral essence, other times planing, all depending on the shape of the turn, the angle of the mountain, the speed of the I-ski assemblage. It is snowing and the wind is whipping the snow into a beautiful maelstrom. With my vision obscured, feeling is even more intensified. Deleuze gets at this: "Lived experience is 'intensive': *I feel* … I feel means that something is happening in me, I am experiencing an intensity, and intensity is not the same thing as sensible qualities; in fact, it's totally different."[43] The skis mediate the mountain for me, mediate the world, making possible feeling and experiencing the world in a way impossible for an unmediated human. Like a pelican surfing the air currents, a porpoise surfing waves, the I-ski assemblage surfs through the powder and down the mountain, dissipating into the ecstasy of the storm.

Notes to Chapter 14

1 Gregory Bateson, *Steps to an Ecology of Mind* (New York: Ballantine, 1972), xxv.

2 Angus, *Primal Scenes of Communication*, 55.

3 For examples, see: Robert Gehl, "Youtube as Archive," *International Journal of Cultural Studies* 12, no. 1 (2009): 43–60; and "Ladders, Samurai, and Blue Collars: Personal Branding in Web 2.0," *First Monday* 16, no. 9 (2011), https://firstmonday.org/ojs/index.php/fm/article/view/3579/3041.

4 Gehl, "Youtube as Archive," 53.

5 Ian Angus, *A Border Within: National Identity, Cultural Plurality, and Wilderness* (Montreal and Kingston: McGill- Queen's University Press, 1997).

6 Ibid., 62–63.

7 Ibid., 58.

8 Marshall McLuhan, *Understanding Media: The Extensions of Man* (Signet Books, 1964), 33.

9 Ibid., 71.

10 Ibid., 23.

11 Ibid.

12 Ibid., 24.

13 James Carey, *Communication as Culture* (New York and London: Routledge, 1989).

14 Marshall McLuhan, *Understanding Media: The Extensions of Man: Critical Edition* (Berkeley: Gingko Press, 2002), 61.

15 Angus, *Primal Scenes of Communication*, 110.

16 Ibid., 55.

17 Kevin Michael Deluca and Anne Teresa Demo, "Imaging Nature: Watkins, Yosemite, and the Birth of Environmentalism," *Critical Studies in Media Communication* 17, no. 3 (2000): 241–60.

18 Henry David Thoreau, *The Portable Thoreau* (New York: Viking, 1964), 609.

19 John Muir, *John of the Mountains: The Unpublished Journals of John Muir*, ed. Linnie Marsh Wolfe (1938; Madison: University of Wisconsin Press, 1979), 313.

20 Aldo Leopold, *A Sand County Almanac: And Sketches Here and There* (Oxford: Oxford University Press, 1989), ix.

21 Ibid., 225–26.

22 Gilles Deleuze, *Two Regimes of Madness: Texts and Interviews, 1975–1995*, ed. David Lapoujade, trans. Ames Hodges and Mike Taormina (Los Angeles: Semiotext(e), 2007), 234.

23 Gilles Deleuze, *Negotiations 1972–1990*, trans. Martin Joughin (New York: Columbia University Press, 1997), 176.

24 Angus, *Primal Scenes of Communication*, 163.

25 Ian Angus, "Circumscribing Postmodern Culture," in *Cultural Politics in Contemporary America*, ed. Ian Angus and Sut Jhally (New York: Routledge, 1989), 100.

26 Angus, *Primal Scenes of Communication*.

27 Michel Foucault, "Of Other Spaces," *Diacritics*, 16, no. 1 (1986), 22-27, http://www.jstor.org/stable/464648.

28 John Durham Peters, *The Marvelous Clouds* (Chicago: University of Chicago Press, 2015).

29 Luce Irigaray, *The Forgetting of Air in Martin Heidegger* (Austin: University of Texas Press, 1999), 12.

30 David Abram, "Afterword: The Commonwealth of Breath," in *Material Ecocriticism*, ed. Serenella Iovino and Serpil Oppermann (Bloomington: Indiana University press, 2014), 301–14.

31 David Abram, *The Spell of the Sensuous* (New York: Vintage, 1996), 237–39.

32 "Bonafide," Blizzard Sports USA, accessed 22 February 2019, https://www.blizzardsports.com/usa/ski- detail/?product_uid=357559&color_number=RED.

33 Ibid.

34 Alfred North Whitehead, *Process and Reality* (1929; New York: The Free Press, 1978), 163.

35 Steven Shaviro, *Without Criteria: Kant, Whitehead, Deleuze, and Aesthetics* (Cambridge, MA: MIT Press, 2009), 47.

36 Ibid., 63.

37 Gilles Deleuze, *The Fold: Leibniz and the Baroque* (Minneapolis: University of Minnesota Press, 1988), 78.

38 Gilles Deleuze, *Spinoza: Practical Philosophy* (San Francisco: City Lights Books, 1988), 173.

39 Ibid., 125.

40 Gilles Deleuze and Felix Guattari, *A Thousand Plateaus: Capitalism and Schizophrenia*, trans. Brian Massumi (Minneapolis: University of Minnesota Press), 162.

41 "DPS Wailer 112RP.2 Hybrid Skis 2016," evo, accessed 22 February 2019, https://www.evo.com/outlet/skis/dps- wailer-112rp2-hybrid.

42 Foucault, "Of Other Spaces," (1986), 22.

43 Giles Deleuze, *Desert Islands and Other Texts 1953–1974*, ed. David Lapoujade, trans. Mike Taormina (New York: Semiotext(e), 2004), 238.

Chapter 15

Psychoanalysis

*Critiques and Possibilities, Then and Now**

Hilda Fernandez-Alvarez

Focusing on a moment in time, 1968, when the revolutionary spirit seized the public will around the world, this chapter explores the differences in the reception of psychotherapy in the mental health system, contrasting two discourses 50 years apart: then and now. I compare La Borde Clinic, a psychiatric institution in Cour-Cheverny, France, which incorporated a Marxist-Lacanian approach in the treatment of those suffering from mental illnesses, with current globalized, evidence-based psychotherapies, whose main approach consists in the implementation of cognitive-behavioural techniques that deploy what Jacques Lacan calls the "university discourse." This discourse claims to be able to explain, systematize, and measure the disarrangements caused by mental illnesses. I aim to provide some insight on the limits and possibilities of these two radically opposed responses to human suffering.

1968: Anti-Institutional Agitation

During the month of May in 1968, France saw the unfolding of a series of intensifying political events that had started as a student protest and escalated to a general strike, halting the public life of the country for several months. This movement officially ignited on March 22 when students protested the University of Nanterre for its outdated curricula and for authoritarian practices in the dorms and classrooms; this movement soon received the solidarity of students of the University of Sorbonne, culminating in a strike, which was joined later by workers from factories and administrative positions and professionals who protested the government and called for new elections in a massive general strike of about six to seven million people by the end of May.[1]

This political agitation rejected the laws and norms of educational, judicial, and labour institutions and coincided with similar manifestations all around the globe in what Rudi Dutschke, the German student leader, called the "long march through the institutions."[2] This revolutionary spirit ran parallel to similar manifestations in diverse parts of the world. For example, in the United States the civil rights movement took aim against institutionalized racism and the Vietnam War; in West Germany demonstrations were organized demanding the recognition of East Germany and the need of "working through" the Nazi past; in Spain, Italy, Czechoslovakia, Brazil, Scandinavia, the United Kingdom, and Mexico, among others, a militant call for a radical critique against government institutions emerged.[3]

In France the bustling theoretical activity emerging from existentialism (Jean-Paul Sartre), phenomenology (Maurice Merleau-Ponty), Freudo-Marxism (influenced by Wilhelm Reich and Herbert Marcuse from the Frankfurt School), and the structuralist turn commanded by Ferdinand Saussure, Claude Levi-Strauss, Michel Foucault, Roland Barthes, and Jacques Lacan created a fecund milieu that generated several initiatives targeting dominant paradigms in diverse fields within philosophy, social sciences, and the arts. This antinomian agitation notably reached the sphere of the mental institution and its practices, as Julian Bourg indicates, and "the immediate post-1968 period rejected both straitjackets and palliatives."[4] In contrast with their British counterparts such as David Cooper and Ronald D. Laing, who took psychiatric concerns as primarily socially construed and rejected the notion of diagnosis, French anti-psychiatry, significantly influenced by the psychoanalysis developed by Jacques Lacan, believed that mentally illness was linked, as François Dousse says, to "intellectual development, to language and to poetry,"[5] but also that, in fact, the mentally ill were in need of treatment.[6] Attuned to the world anti-psychiatric movement (Franco Basiagla in Italy, Thomas Szasz in the United States), French anti-psychiatry was also influenced by radical left politics and sought to emancipate the mentally ill.

Then: La Borde

One amazing experiment emerging from this socio-political and cultural environment was Institutional Psychotherapy, a project still alive today that began in the early 1950s in the Saint Alban clinic where influential anti-colonial psychiatrist Frantz Fanon and well-known psychoanalyst Jean Oury received their training. This postwar clinic incorporated a Marxist spirit with the intention of approaching the unconscious exchanges within the institution. An extension of Saint Alban, where the Catalan psychiatrist Francois Tosquelles ran a psychiatric clinic that supported the resistance during the war, La Borde was led by Jean Oury and Felix Guattari, both analyzed by Lacan and influenced by his thought. Guattari was a philosopher whose experience at La Borde turned him into a clinician; he attended Lacan's seminars and conducted an analysis with Lacan for a few years. His relationship to Lacan was so close and his passion for transmitting this line of psychoanalysis so profound that Guattari appeared as the natural heir of his thought, even nicknamed "Lacan" by his friends.[7] However, alongside Gilles Deleuze, Guattari later launched an important critique contra the institution of psychoanalysis in *Anti-Oedipus*.[8]

La Borde envisions the psychiatric institution as a centre of emancipation and liberation.

Committed to equality among all the participants as well as anti-segregation and de-alienation of the mentally ill, this astonishing project, however, lacked material means, which, as it is often the case, was compensated by a determined desire. The La Bordian project incorporated ethnography, Marxism, structuralism, Freudian psychoanalysis, and key Lacanian concepts to guide the management of logics, logistics, and the consequent embodied relationships involved in the service provision for the mentally ill, guided by, Dousse says, "spatial permeability, freedom of movement, a critique of professional roles and qualifications, institutional flexibility, and the need for a patients' therapy club."[9]

It was in La Borde where Institutional Psychotherapy was born, whose major tenets consisted of a self-reflection of its own operation as a condition of the mental health institution, and the imperative of supporting mechanisms of social bonding in the treatment of the mentally ill, which required moving away from exclusive interactions between doctor and patient towards interventions in the collective as a whole.[10]

Bourg mentions four periods in the life of the La Borde clinic, according to the publications by CERFI (the Centre d'etude, de recherche et de formation institutionelle). The first period (1953 to 1959) entailed "a work structure known as the grille, based on a rotation of tasks and a blurring of work identities.... Félix [Guattari] cleans the kitchen on Monday, Jean-François [Oury] gives the electro-shocks on Wednesday, Liane [Mozere] organizes the art group on Friday."[11] There were assemblies and committees where people could express their thoughts, fantasies, and desires. This egalitarian radicality did not last because efforts to reshape social relationships, roles, and tasks to de- alienate people create other forms of dissatisfaction and alienation.

The second period (1959 to 1964) shifted the focus from the distribution of work to the unconscious relationships within the institution, which utilizes the Lacanian concept of "empty speech" (*parole vide*). "Empty speech" refers to the quotidian chatter of the speaking being, which, beyond the emptiness of the subject's words, always signals, Lacan argues, "an appeal to truth at its very core."[12] Rather than having a focused agenda, group discussions invited participants to speak freely—resembling both the "free association" of the analysand and the "even hovering attention" of the analyst—to address issues of the work within the clinic, the ethical articulation of emancipatory desires of the group, and the conflicting desires. To be able to deal with the limits of the sayable, not only the impossibility of what cannot be signified but also the limits of what can be discussed in public when you involved the unconscious of a group—Eros and Thanatos—they brought about the creation of the "local law," which consisted of articulating the ethics or principles guiding the law of the manifested desire, followed by an exploration of what was excluded in those laws. Bourg refers to this process as an attempt to reach "the 'non-totalized totality' of the institutional field."[13] These "golden years" of La Borde clinic gave way to the third period (1965 to 1969), characterized by its emphasis on group modalities and the separation of analytic and functional groups; and the fourth period (1969 to 1972) when CERFI emerged, prioritizing self-management and declining interest in Institutional Psychotherapy, which was to resurface in the 1980s.[14]

One important aspect of the La Bordian practice consisted of the implementation of transversality, Guattari's theory containing already several concepts that would shape his later collaboration with Deleuze, which consisted of an analysis of the transferencial phenomena beyond the dyad of the doctor-patient and towards the relations connecting the individual to the social, institutional, and political aspects of the psychiatric practice. The analysis of transversal relations expanded the focus of intervention from the individual to the social and was partially inspired by Sartre's differentiation of "group-subjects" and "subjected groups"; transversality also was seen as the site of the group's unconscious desire.[15]

La Borde clinic instantiates a quasi-utopian project in constant search of democratic emancipation for workers and patients, while scrutinizing their unconscious interactions as a collectivity. This clinic is also an example of vivacious creativity nourished by collaborations with non-clinicians, such as Guattari himself or those known as "Barbarians," who were mostly students of the humanities and political militants and who worked with La Borde's patients in artistic, social, or educational activities, allowing the practice of psychiatry to be nourished with fresh ideas from outside the field and thus producing lively and fun exchanges. For example, the spatiality of the clinic was thought of in relation to phonemes and signifying units—the proximity between the laundry and the insulin room—revitalizing boring spaces with new metaphoric textures.[16] La Borde constitutes an immanent critique, firmly grounded in theory, pragmatic and radical, that intervenes critically from *within* the institution, maintaining flexibility and singularity and reinventing its laws to create ethical practices that test the possibilities and limits of both Marxian and Lacanian theory. It is for this reason that La Borde represents a more relevant critique than that outlined in *Anti-Oedipus*.

Anti-Oedipus: Schizo-Desire against Capitalism

A thorough critique of *Anti-Oedipus* is not possible in this chapter, yet I want to substantiate why I suggest that La Borde constitutes a more relevant critique than the one provided by this text. Let's start by saying that *Anti-Oedipus* is a boisterously sharp text, humorous and poetic, caustic, yet heartwarming; it sets its gaze on the modes of gaining power and aims to answer the Spinozan question:

"Why do men fight *for* their servitude as stubbornly as if it were their salvation?"[17]

The publication of *Anti-Oedipus* constituted a radical critique of psychoanalysis. It is tempting to say that it constitutes an "anti-psychoanalysis" movement, parallel to anti-psychiatry; yet, the solid grounding of many concepts in Lacanian psychoanalysis—such as desire, non-totality, and production—obviate such a possibility.

The point of departure of the text is the power of desire production from which the Freudian triangulation of the Oedipus complex, as the text says, "subjected to the requirements of *representation,*"[18] is seen as both normalizing and repressive. *Anti-Oedipus* sees human subjects as "handymen: each with his little machines," proliferating all sorts of productions "of actions and of passions; *production of recording processes ... production of consumptions.*"[19] These desiring machines embody "the force of the unconscious itself, the investment by desire of the social field, the disinvestment of repressive structures,"[20] and its multiplying potential is drawn upon the model of the schizophrenic, exemplified by the German judge Daniel Schreber, whose "*solar anus,*" or organ machine, allows his desire to remain "fluid and slippery."[21] *Anti-Oedipus* sees the schizo form of desire production, compared with the neurotic, as successfully rejecting Oedipalization and, thus, able to resist the territorialization of bodies by capitalism.[22] Furthermore, the text claims that Oedipus is "the great agent of antiproduction in desire. The same history as that of the Capital."[23] Such anti-production of desire manifests itself in the notion of "the body without organs."[24]

Anti-Oedipus rejects the concept of "lack": "Desire does not lack anything; it does not lack its object. It is, rather, the *subject* that is missing on desire, or desire that lacks a fixed subject."[25] *Anti-Oedipus* also refuses castration and the death drive, which it locates, rather, in the very structures of Oedipalization and the phallus; Deleuze and Guattari rebel against the Lacanian ternary of the real, symbolic, and imaginary. "The real is not impossible,"[26] they suggest and argue that the differentiation between the Lacanian imaginary and symbolic Oedipus leads to crushing and repressing desiring-production.[27]

Alain Badiou and Slavoj Žižek have both done thorough, not very favourable, critiques *of Anti-Oedipus*'s treatment of Lacan,[28] although their focus has been on Deleuze primarily. Badiou articulates a number of theses against Deleuze's vitalism and ontology of the "multiple," which Daniel Smith sees as caused by rivalry.[29] Žižek, for his part, argues that *Anti-Oedipus* fails to understand the Lacanian Real and that Deleuze and Guattari does to Lacan what Carl Jung did to Sigmund Freud.[30]

Although *les désirants* Deleuze and Guattari are radically critical of psychoanalysis, there is evidence that a mutual influence existed between them and Lacan, who read *Anti-Oedipus,*[31] discussed it with Guattari, and had considered Deleuze as a "desired" pupil.[32] On their part, Deleuze and Guattari followed Lacan's seminar, and the ontology they proposed in *Anti-Oedipus* is marked by several critical notions already well established in Lacanian psychoanalysis: the concept of "desiring machine" is consistent with a critique of ego-psychology, and the notion of "*schizo*" challenges the idea of totality or wholes, which Lacan tried to formalize throughout his whole intellectual journey. *Anti-Oedipus* is akin to Lacan's view of the Oedipus complex, which sees it as Freud's mythopoetic complex: the subject must produce their own mythical truth, written in the social, in order to surpass it and *produce* a Master signifier of their own.[33] *Anti-Oedipus* is also concerned with Lacan's contemporary preoccupation regarding surplus *jouissance,*[34] which concerns the problematic of the production of the body that Deleuze and Guattari characterized as the human's "body without organs," territorialized by the Capital as a producer of surplus value.[35]

Would revolutionary schizoanalysis suffice to sustain a critique that speaks to our times? *Anti-Oedipus* exudes the romantic power of an undetermined, unleashed, positive force, but it fails to trace the way the death drive can seize such a force. Deleuze and Guattari ignore or repress the fact that the same libido that unleashes desire is precisely that which turns the erotic into an entropic energy commandeered by the death drive. Their rebellion against the pretended "familialism" of psychoanalysis was a denial of the fact, which clinical practice does not stop demonstrating, that oppression starts in the family and that an analytic intervention is needed to approach the core of these early formations of the social bond to theoretically formalize them to dismantle them in the collectivity. The aim of psychoanalysis has always, since Freud, been an emancipatory project regarding the subject's oppression transmitted through tradition, which is inscribed in each of us.

Both kinds of interventions, *Anti-Oedipus* and La Borde, are needed at any political conjuncture. The embodied praxis, the *mise en scène* of La Borde, is the first step of an immanent critique that *Anti-Oedipus* would theoretically unleash a few years later, whereas the intellectual labour behind the cultural production of the book, its literary practice in all its beauty and freedom of thought, aims at disrupting political economy through inscription. Yet, La Borde constitutes, in my opinion, a more relevant critique because it probes theory, thanks to Guattari's left militancy and his commitment to a movement from practice to theory and back to practice.[36] La Borde demonstrates criticism in action that confronts idealism directly: for example, it was possibly very difficult to ignore manifestations of the death drive—conflicts, dissatisfactions, jealousies—while interacting among humans in such a practice, as it required that the actors figured out a way to surpass the conflicts—a heuristic approach. These pragmatic difficulties contrast with the way theory works; when *Anti-Oedipus* interprets situations and its potential solution—a hermeneutic approach—the theory smooths out human disarrangement by the absence of embodied practice. In other words, La Borde engages effectively in praxis with the limits and potentials of the Marxist and Lacanian theories, because the embodiment among others calls out conflict and a poetic solution. I believe that the symbolic saturation of cultural productions—the book, the article, the journal, the artifact—should be balanced with a viable praxis grounded in intellectual and ethical thought. La Borde provided, precisely, such intellectual pragmatism.

Now: Institutional Psychotherapies

Now, fast-forward 50 years to contemporary Canada, or any country of the globe. We not only lack 1968's audacity of hope,[37] but we are also deeply entrenched in a system that excludes desire and enjoins obedience. No matter how well-intentioned psychotherapists are, no matter how diversely trained and passionate about their jobs, the system relies on the replication of a model that serves neo-liberal capitalist interests by privileging pharmacologic treatments, manualization of hegemonic psychotherapies, and a measurement of well-being according to narrow definitions.

The radical critique constituted by the psychotherapeutic modalities of the *soixante-huit*, as we saw with La Borde, was concerned with the treatment of the mentally ill within a collective model; it protested against the asylum and the mere focus of individual therapy, moving the discussion to the larger conglomerate of the institution in which treatments dwell. This situation, as Ian Angus has suggested, resulted in a recovering of "individual therapy but not necessarily a re-justifying of institutions."[38] The managerial model of business enterprise has been reshaping all institutions for the past 50 years: university, schools, judicial systems. Pertaining to the mental health institution, in particular, not only are the mentally ill often deprived of psychotherapy, there is an emphasis on metric evaluation of effectivity through quantitative scales, the delivery of services through manualized therapies, rigidity of protocols, and the hegemony of the so-called evidence-based treatments. These treatments possess "scientific" status and are the dominant form of therapy deployed in the public mental health systems all around the world. Based on research that uses randomized clinical trials as the "highest standard," these therapies are granted superiority over other types of interventions as supposedly the most effective. Two of those dominant therapies are the Cognitive-Behavioral Therapy or CBT, prescribed for depression and anxiety, among many other conditions,[39] and the Dialectical Behavioral Therapy or DBT, which focuses on personality disorders.[40]

These therapies no doubt have helped some people, but is the "scientific" status of all these therapies a successful response to the problems of depression, anxiety, psychosis, et cetera? Do these therapies answer sufficiently the question of the suffering subject whom we encounter in the clinical situation of the post-capitalist, digitally driven, social milieu of present time? These "evidence-based treatments" intervene by targeting the ego and presuppose that: (a) mental health issues equate to maladaptive learning; (b) the issues are consciously transparent to both the suffering individual and the therapist; (c) the solution consists of the implementation of formulaic approaches that target cognition, emotion, and behaviour; and, (d) the interventions are a matter of "skills training." These assumptions are problematic as there is a poverty of conceptualization and, thus, they cannot respond to the complexity of the human subject, specifically regarding the relational aspect of the mind's constitution, always in co-production with others and accessible only through the analysis of transference. Neither can they approach emancipatory change for the person who struggles with mental health issues, as they do not articulate procedures to approach historical agency and its symptom, whose elucidation becomes available only if we partially suspend predetermined outcomes such as regulating emotions, managing stress, cognitive counterargument to destructive thoughts, and so on.

Most psychiatric services of the global mental health systems are medicine-based and psychosocial case management; therapies are very short term, addressing mainly pragmatic strategies to cope with the affect rather than processing histories, identities, or meaning. The traditional idea of therapy as a form of inquiring subjectivity appears to be disappearing in the mental health institutions to accommodate neo-liberal techno-pharmaceutical reason: overmedication as preferred and foremost treatment, which Bonnie Burstow calls "Pharmageddon"[41] and China Mills refers to as "the "McDonaldization of people's health."[42] The point is not to exclude psychiatric practices or psychotropic medications but rather to prevent the reductive fetishization of the "brain" and its disorders or the dominance of certain treatments that produce alienated subjectivities.

The dominant therapeutic modalities of mental health treatments are based on what Lacan called the "university discourse," formalized within his theory of discourses, which was Lacan's response to the movements of 1968. The university discourse needs to be differentiated from the common connotation of the term "discourse," as it is used, for example, in "discourse of philosophy" or "discourse of history," because Lacan means very specific structural arrangements that account for particular forms of social links. This theory consists of four structural relations of social bonding (along with "University," there are "Master," "Hysteric," and "Psychoanalytic" discourses) that aim to understand overdetermined embodied practices. These discursive modes of representation and production map the spaces that people and objects occupy in language to advance the problematization of what Freud named as the impossible professions "governing, educating and analyzing."[43] By discourse, Lacan understands "fundamental ... stable relations ... of one signifier to another" that subsist in the deep structure of language (*langue*) without the need of speech (*parole*).[44] The Lacanian discourse of the university—also called "Science discourse"—consists of a social link whose agent occupies an "all-knowing" (*tout savoir*) position.[45] Such an agent (the therapist) is motivated by the Master signifier (a normative idea of mental health) to address the traumatic element of the subject's suffering. The agent-therapist injects into the gap ready-made knowledge, producing consequently a subject who is not permitted to find their bearings in their own truth. Lacan, in "Science and Truth," spells it out ironically: "science-does-not-want-to-know-anything about the truth as cause."[46] Jeanne Schroeder points out that "the university's discourse that scientizes and explains the subject's desire has no room for the individual subject and her suffering."[47]

The scientific discourse of all-knowledge, as a privileged mode of institutionalized mental health service, exerts domination—it has a negative impact on people's well-being—and prevents the incorporation of the case-by-case golden rule of "singularity"—that is, the irreducibility of the subject—that any self-respecting psychotherapeutic treatment needs to observe as an ethical imperative to honour the complexity of the human subject.

Psychoanalysis gave birth to concepts such as transference, repression, resistance, et cetera; without these concepts psychotherapy in general could not be thought about nowadays. Psychoanalysis is by far the most elaborated theoretical framework to think about the clinical practice, offering us the possibility of guiding the clinician with a compass different from those provided by techniques based on suggestion. But there is always a spirit of hope in the interstices of the mental health institution. In health authorities and other settings all around the world, psychoanalysis has nurtured and informed many different therapeutic approaches. It is practised in communities with a wide range of population (the developmentally challenged, inmates, addictions, mentally ill, et cetera).

Thus, psychoanalytic discourse opens space to truth as cause and provides the possibility to think of the institution as a site of critique: for example, the critique of the oppressive nature of anti-oppression movements or the critique of the university as institution with its adamant defense of phallic knowledge—a paranoid, competitive knowledge based on self-indulgent imposture or masquerade—that works in detriment to truthful community building, which prevents the inclusion of the student/researcher's own subjectivity. What kind of world would come into being if we would attempt the radical egalitarian practices of La Borde? Would it be possible to exist, work, produce, and create ethically on the truth of our own unconscious with others?

Conclusions

By comparing these two models of praxis, La Borde, on the one hand, and the hegemonic models of cognitive behavioural models, on the other, I conclude that institutional critique is a practice whose ethical endeavour is the promotion of political agency and democratic values. Such a practice is needed more urgently today than ever before—times in which we witness the rise of far-right populism, impending climate catastrophe, and the worst displacement of peoples since World War II. We are symbolically saturated with academic and cultural productions in the form of the written text or the artifact. I propose to think of *Realpolitik* endeavours through the institutions we inhabit to join thought with action in a way that reaches the collectivity beyond *only* ideas, which are, however, an absolute necessity and whose absence leads action astray. We need to infuse actions with intellectual discussion, and, equally, we need to write as much as we act to impact our communities.

As Angus has advocated, the institution should be a site of critique in which more flexible and democratic changes can be implemented as a way of sustaining practices that do not dehumanize workers and the people they interact with. The critique of the subject in its immediate social cell requires, however, a certain disposition to include oneself in the critique, to admit the subjective division (division between what I say and the truth that inhabits me) that can be navigated truthfully only when one includes the unconscious.

Are we able to rely on the ethical inquiry of the unconscious to link thought and action? This is the ongoing (im)possible challenge we all face.

Notes to Chapter 15:

* This paper is part of my current research as a PhD candidate in the Department of Geography at Simon Fraser University, which looks at the way in which institutional discourses struggle for hegemony over certain forms of mental health treatments. A version of this paper was presented on November 3, 2019, at the conference "Then and Now: 1968–2018," organized by Ian Angus and co-sponsored by Simon Fraser University's Institute for the Humanities, Department of Humanities,.J.S. Woodsworth Chair in the Humanities, Faculty of Arts and Social Sciences, Department of History, School of Communication, SFU Public Square, and the Lacan Salon. A modified chapter of this article will be published in *Canadian Review of American Studies* (Forthcoming).

1 Julian Bourg, *From Revolution to Ethics: May 1968 and Contemporary French Thought*, 2nd ed. (Montreal and Kingston: McGill-Queen's University Press, 2017), 23.

2 Gerard J. DeGroot, *Student Protest: The Sixties and After* (London: Routledge, 1998), 10.

3 In the global agitation of 1968, Mexico is a tragic example. Students were joined by the civil society at large to express their discontent at the sheer authoritarianism of the government in power, who with impunity retaliated with torture, persecution, and massacre of 200 to 1,500 people on the long night of Tlatelolco, October 2, 1968. "Los Muertos de Tlatelolco," *The National Security Archive*, accessed 29 April 2019, https://nsarchive2.gwu.edu//NSAEBB/NSAEBB201/index2.htm.

4 Bourg, *From Revolution to Ethics*, 105.

5 François Dousse, *Gilles Deleuze and Félix Guattari: Intersecting Lives*, trans. D. Glassman (New York: Columbia Press, 2007), 49.

6 Bourg, *From Revolution to Ethics*, 136.

7 Dousse, *Intersecting Lives*, 37.

8 Gilles Deleuze and Felix Guattari, *Anti-Oedipus: Capitalism and Schizophrenia*, trans. R. Hurley, M. Seem, and H. Lane (1972; New York: Penguin, 2009).

9 Dousse, *Intersecting Lives*, 44.

10 Ibid., 60.

11 Bourg, *From Revolution to Ethics*, 130.

12 Jacques Lacan, *Ecrits*, trans. B. Fink (New York: Norton, 2006), 206.

13 Bourg, *From Revolution to Ethics*, 133.

14 Ibid., 131.

15 Dousse, *Intersecting Lives*, 62; Bourg, *From Revolution to Ethics*, 141.

16 Dousse, *Intersecting Lives*, 61.

17 Deleuze and Guattari, *Anti-Oedipus*, 29.

18 Ibid., 54.

19 Ibid., 4.

20 Ibid., 61.

21 Ibid., 14–15.

22 Ibid., 52.

23 Ibid., 56.

24 Ibid., 8.

25 Ibid., 26.

26 Ibid., 27.

27 Ibid., 52.

28 For a thorough account of *Anti-Oedipus*'s reception, see: Dousse, *Intersecting Lives*, 206.

29 Daniel W. Smith, "The Inverse Side of the Structure: Žižek on Deleuze on Lacan," *Criticism* 46, no. 4 (Fall 2004): 637.

30 Slavoj Žižek, "Notes on a Debate: 'From within the People,'" *Criticism* 46, no. 4 (Fall 2004): 662.

31 Elisabeth Roudinesco, *Lacan: Esbozo de una vida, historia de un sistema de pensamiento* (Buenos Aires: FCE de Argentina, 1994), 506.

32 Smith, "Inverse Side of the Structure," 636.

33 Jacques Lacan, *The Seminars of Jacques Lacan*, ed. J. Miller, trans. R. Grigg (New York: Norton, 2007), 17:128.

34 Ibid., 17:50.

35 Deleuze and Guattari, *Anti-Oedipus*, 10.

36 Bourg, *From Revolution to Ethics*, 164.

37 Paraphrasing the title by Palmer, "The Audacity of Hope: Reflecting on the Meaning of 1968 in 2018," which was presented in the aforementioned conference.

38 Ian Angus, e-mail communication, June 29, 2018.

39 Aaron Beck, *Cognitive Therapy and The Emotional Disorders* (Madison, CT: International Universities Press, 1975).

40 Marsha Linehan, *Cognitive-Behavioral Treatment of Borderline Personality Disorder* (New York: Guilford Press, 1993).

41 Bonnie Burstow, *Psychiatry and the Business of Madness* (New York: Palgrave, 2015), 167.

42 China Mills, *Decolonizing Global Mental Health* (London: Routledge, 2014), 42.

43 Lacan, *Seminars*, 166.

44 Ibid., 13.

45 Ibid., 17:31.

46 Lacan, *Ecrits*, 742.

47 Jeanne Lorraine Schroeder, *The Four Lacanian Discourses: Or Turning Law Inside-Out*. (New York: Birkbeck Law Press, 2008), 54.

Part IV
Philosophy

Chapter 16

Necessary Allusions

On the Necessity of an Alliance of Abilities and Needs

Jaden Adams

What kind of a world are we living in now, as the dawn of the 2020s begins to illuminate the emerging political landscape? What can be learned from the new century's first decades of composition, decomposition, and recomposition that might help to sharpen our perceptions as we proceed? What notions and concepts might help us to discern the emerging relationships between belonging and becoming, and between alliance and assemblage, as we enter a period requiring their assertion like never before—and all of this, while the majority of extra-parliamentary and parliamentary political currents seem incapable of responding to the urgency of this need? This chapter explores these questions through a consideration of one central component that seems to be missing in the present period: "necessary allusions," or the imminent necessity, in a period of intensive negative solidarity, of affirming the resonances and plasticities between multiple positionalities (and the particularities and singularities immanent to each of them), in order to compose generalizable political assemblages as a basis for a new approach to what Asad Haider calls insurgent universality."[1] While establishment thinkers of the last century famously used the term "necessary illusions" to refer to elites' belief in the necessity of propaganda to keep the public passive in the face of the existing order,[2] we depart from the post-Chomskyian left response in which the alternative remains that of occupying the position of the "cool observer," who ostensibly does not produce, distribute, and consume "propaganda" that circumvents reason but instead deploys an array of alarming and supposedly awakening facts and figures. To the contrary, we presuppose that not only *are* illusions necessary (in the sense that all experience is mediated)[3] but so, too, are *allusions*, in that, if an alternative hegemony to the prevailing one is to be successfully composed, the melancholic logic of pity must give way to a joyous one of "allusive solidarity." Whereas today's identity politics tend to reject allusion, resonance, and universality, and today's populist politics tend to reject divergence, dissonance, and particularity, the emerging politics will need to be founded not on the basis of the direct articulation of relations of equivalence, as in the past, but on an indirect, yet resolutely materialist aesthetics of sympathy and solidarity.

But first, let's consider what we're up against as we enter the new century. Like a globalized intensification of the more dystopian sequences in Alfonso Cuarón's *Children of Men* (2006), right-wing populism has seized state power in government after government across the planet, including in Brazil, India, Italy, Russia, the US, and the UK,[4] amongst other countries, seemingly without any social mobilization preceding the events. And in the wake of their successes, right-wing politicians like Jair Bolsanaro, Narenda Modi, Matteo Salvini, Vladimir Putin, Donald Trump, and Boris Johnson are now increasingly bolstered by an outpouring of even more extreme street movements like the Proud Boys and propagandistic media outlets like Breitbart. On the left, the process has unfolded via nearly the exact opposite trajectory. Rather than moving from seizing the state to reorienting society, it has moved from reorienting society to seizing the state. While the period from 1999 to 2011 was punctuated by the "change the world without taking power" ethos of the anti-globalization movement and Occupy Wall Street, from the mid-2010s forward, left populists have moved on from attachments to social mobilization to focus upon winning seats in regional and national governments in Greece, Spain, the US, and the UK. Propelled forward by organizations like SYRIZA, Podemos, DSA (Democratic Socialists of America), and Momentum, contextualized by left populist media like *Avgi/Left.gr, Público, Jacobin,* and *Tribune,* and helmed by figures like Alexis Tsipras, Pablo Iglesias, Bernie Sanders, and Jeremy Corbyn, at the end of the 2010s this coalescence is capturing the affects of significant portions of the mainstream public.

Clearly, then, the primary political conflict today is that between populisms: right versus left.

However, because left populism began from reorienting society to seizing the state rather than the reverse, the assemblage upon which it is based is not a particularly cohesive one. Its currents include many who align their arguments with the liberal metaphysics that Crawford B. Macpherson once called "possessive individualism."[5] In short, a free-floating individualism in which one's sense of self, with all of its intersecting identities, is conceptualized as a kind of "pure form," a Platonist property or self-possession. Perhaps we might call that "turfism," referencing the slang meaning of the term "turf": a "territory considered by a gang to be under its control."[6] The reason TERF (Trans-Exclusionary Radical Feminism) resonates in contemporary culture is that it sonically references this definition, which suggests that TERFs are asserting a model of identity based upon possessive individualism, zero-sum games, and the exclusive control or ownership of territory. But the issue is not "cis women"—another zero-sum game, in reverse. The issue is the proprietary model of identity upon which TERFist/turfist claims are made, not to mention that it is a model in which one particular combination of identity attributes hierarchizes, downgrades, and sometimes even excludes the concurrent claims of others, as if capitalist metaphysics is rendering the politics of alliance in the form of a zero-sum game. Allusion, resonance, and universality are all off the table as polite topics of conversation. However ironically, in practice, the more liberal elements of the left populist assemblage invite this, too, not only by refusing collective reconceptualization but also by engaging in its own turfism of class, in which class is framed as identity—or even, property—rather than politics.[7]

Rather than proceeding in either mode, then, we begin from the materiality of need common to all of them, presupposing that the identities involved are multiple, that they are themselves internally complex, conjoined, and changing. Proceeding by defining bodies according to their capacities for being affected and their capacities for affecting, rather than according to more abstract attributes, we presuppose, for instance, that there are greater differences between, say, a "working-class cisgendered woman of colour" and a "billionaire white cisgendered man" than there are between a "working-class cisgendered woman of colour" and a "middle-class white transwoman."[8] With this model of allusive solidarity in mind, we proceed immanently from one of the primary categories of identity politics itself—the politics of ability—in order to make the case for how, rather than articulating chains of equivalence between supposedly entirely distinct communities, a left populism capable of taking on today's right populism might focus instead on the material basis of the divergent commonality of need—of need itself—as framed in Karl Marx's famous rallying cry, "from each according to their ability, to each according to their need."[9] While he privileged the proletariat as the agent of historical change, we emphasize that he did not see proletarians as the only relevant social assemblage, and, given changes in economic composition since his time, we circumvent, for the moment, the question of who the revolutionary subject might or might not be, focusing instead upon a diversity of abilities, conjoined by the commonality of need as such.

All of which alludes to a diversity of "identities" conjoined to a diversity of "economies" (they are not distinct in the first place),[10] and therefore also to the generality of need in all of its forms, including basic needs, but also to "new needs."[11] To do so, we centre the legacy of political philosopher, media theorist, and humanities scholar Ian Angus's engagements with both the Proudhonian principle of association and Canadian theories of federalism, in dialogue with two protopopulist movements in our century that, from 1999 to 2011 at least, formed a resonant assemblage on the basis of what Angus calls the "post-national person," providing a material basis for contemporary left populism as a non-identitarian mode of collectivity that can be both reactivated and reoriented in a form more appropriate to our time, such that allusive solidarity might displace negative solidarity, possessive individualism, and turfism.[12] Noting that Angus articulates a mode of alliance as one in which there is no single centre, thereby allowing all to be recognized through the "treaty-form" without forming a single identity, we assert that an assemblage of needs can accomplish this via the communist ethos in which, although situated abilities remain multiple and distinct due to the divergent social positionalities of particular individuals and groups, need as such remains universal. In other words, for Angus, the "post-national person" is a singularity that accesses the universal neither via intersectional identities that then result in a particular individual nor via a class identity that then captures multiplicity in the image of "the worker" but, as we parse it, via the multiplicity of abilities and needs that they share in common, abstractly and materially, pre- and post-communist.

The Draft Horse and the Ox: Reflections on the Principle of Association

Angus's *ouevre* diverges from both conventional left populism and identity politics alike, while weaving together important elements of each that cannot simply be discarded, which is what makes it such an excellent starting point for developing a concept of allusive solidarity, in a period of elusive solidarity. It is because it proceeds in this manner that it also provides a basis upon which the multiple and divergent needs of both could be collectively asserted and satisfied, without being reduced to the kinds of zero-sum games when different groups are pitted against one another, as though, due to the logic of scarcity, only one group can benefit at a time. Angus's metaphysics of a "living materiality," as he articulates in his media theory, is not entirely unlike Karl Marx's historical materialism, but it is not reducible to it either. For Angus, bodies and communication media, for example, are not separate phenomena but are instead threads that form a knot of always-already mediated, embodied relations.[13] The same metaphysics holds true for his principle of association, the concept derived from Pierre-Joseph Proudhon, which is the basis for his federalist model of alliance: unlike negative solidarity, possessive individualist, or turfist frames, Angus's immanent approach to bodies and their media extensions—including race, class, gender, sexuality, or ability—affords neither proprietary nor free-floating, possessive, individualist models of selfhood but instead a model closer to what might be thought of as a trans-individual communalism in which horizontal multiplicities, and not only intersectional identities on a vertical axis, also become bases for multiple levels and forms of becoming and belonging, out of which the post-national person emerges.

Whereas intersectionality theory, if imagined in contradistinction to or in the absence of a trans-individual communalism, might position a particular body as exclusively a white, heterosexual, middle-class, first-world male, an approach like Angus's assumes the contemporaneity of pre-individual particularities and singularities prior to any legitimate claims to universality, such that one who is accurately describable in that manner might also be so as part-Indigenous, of mixed-class background, as semi-peripheral rather core-originating (for example, Canadian, rather than a citizen of the US), or as, say, non-binary or transgender rather than cisgender.

The complex of mediations, then, constitutes a culture within which both singularity and universality are located at once, even while a potentially limitless variety of particularities do, as well. What we add to this is the assertion that the most important modality through which this can be achieved is the constitution of a resonant assemblage of abilities and needs, rather than *only* the intersectional alliance of particularities and identities, which often resort to propertarianism when not more wholly contextualized. In order for a truly decentred, federalist model of alliance to be actualized along the lines proposed by Angus, it is necessary to begin, as he asserts, from the presupposition that cross-membership and multiple identity are the rule rather than the exception, and, at the same time, that empathy, sympathy, and solidarity are possible regardless of one's positionality, not only because of a specific person's greater emotional cultivation vis-à-vis others but primarily because selfhood is always multiply differential and rhizomatic. The reason the French philosopher Gilles Deleuze emphasizes that there are greater differences, for instance, between a draft horse and a racehorse than between a draft horse and an ox is the same reason one might assert there are greater differences between Scottish small beef cattle and Brahman cattle than there are between Scottish small beef cattle and bison. Oxen and bison are neither horses nor cattle, but they share a non-identity-based affective orientation to external elements with the draft horse and Scottish small beef cattle nevertheless, which is not the case for officially adjacent categories within their "own" scientific genus—which is composed via some attributes that are officially associated, while other attributes that are of equal relevance are officially dissociated. Thus, the greater commonality of the working-class ciswoman of colour and the middle-class white transwoman mentioned above, compared with that of the working-class ciswoman of colour and the billionaire white cisman.[14]

As Angus asserts:

> The individual, or person, can be a member of more than one group. It is the cross-membership, or multiple identity, that constitutes the "person" who is involved in the politics of the new alliance proposed by social movements. The international, or post-national, "person" is a member of a plurality of communities, not a liberal "individual" constituted outside community and only subsequently, and instrumentally, entering into it. This plurality of intersecting communities overcomes the closed character of traditional communities and insists de facto that communities adapt themselves to the possibility that their members may leave, which functions to strengthen the rights of participation within communities. The post-national person thus can postulate the importance of "community" as such to human life, independent of a specific community, which raises the question of the recovery of "belonging" in a new form.[15]

At first glance, particularly at the outset of this passage, Angus's approach might seem to bolster the more liberal forms of intersectionality that lead to negative solidarity, possessive individualism, and turfism treated earlier, in which the multiple groups and identities that constitute a person intersectionally are the be-all and end-all for the formation of an alliance or "popular front." However, for Angus, the question of instrumentality has been central from his first published writings: instrumental rationality, which frames the logic of possessive individualism, is based not upon the living materiality of the body-in-relation but instead upon the transcendental, proprietary possession of oneself, first and foremost, and the economic gain one might expect by carrying out one's purported rational self-interest, specifically as a property owner (including the self-as-property).[16] To some degree, the circumvention of this way of engaging the political could be said to already be happening in the US case with the allusive aesthetic evident in the recently formed Justice Democrats, who promise "a new generation of diverse working class leaders … [and] a unified campaign to replace every corporate-backed member of Congress and rebuild the Democratic Party from scratch,"[17] as their website originally stated. The organization, which seeks to win elections entirely via microdonations, includes seven current US Congressional representatives, most of whom are women and people of colour, and several of whom are also members of DSA. However, in the US, Justice Democrats emerged not only as a response to the failure of the 1999 to 2011 extra-parliamentary social movement context but also from the failure of the 2012 to 2016 parliamentary reorientation to elect Bernie Sanders on the basis of economics (redistribution) alone, just as liberal forms of identity politics failed to elect Hillary Clinton on the basis of identity (recognition) alone.

For Angus, the anti-globalization movement and the Occupy movement that created the foundation for today's post-2016 parliamentary left populism in the US, the UK, Greece, and Spain (amongst other places) was based upon a neo-Proudhonian principle of association oriented primarily towards the external conditions for alliance between divergent and multiple groups, rather than primarily towards the internal conditions constitutive of groups, in mutually exclusive fashion. Justice Democrats, DSA, and *Jacobin Magazine*, for example, are not organized around intersectional identities per se, yet their leading, most prominent figures are primarily members of gender, racial, or religious minorities of one variety or another, in addition to hailing, for the most part, from working-class and middle-class backgrounds.[18] Arguably, this "matter of fact" emerges neither from the proprietary logic of intersectionality politics nor from liberal variations on class politics as identity politics (found in campaigns such as Joe Biden's) but, instead, from an extension of the logic of treaty that prevailed in the anti-globalization and Occupy movements, 1999 to 2011: that which, in Proudhon, enables divergent groups to "bind themselves by mutual and equal agreements for one or several determinate aims, for which the responsibility falls specifically and exclusively on the members of the federation."[19] Crucially, all parties to the neo-Proudhonian association assure themselves more freedom and equality than they give up in the process of associating, and in this case, the "determinate aims" are the divergent and multiple needs of the constituents on behalf of whom they act. Ironically, despite their distance from contemporary intersectionality, the slate of candidates and media figures is much more reflective of its constituent populations than those who ran in the 2016 Democratic Primary Campaign, mobilized largely upon the basis of non-class identity to the exclusion of class, or those who mobilized on the basis of class to the exclusion of non-class identity.[20]

There is a reason the emerging left populism has proceeded from the extra-parliamentary to the parliamentary, rather than the reverse: as the 2016 Primary Campaign showed, the Democratic Party establishment could not be successfully dislodged without the translation of extra-parliamentary social recomposition into insurgent processes that would exceed publics' desires to be represented by a diversity of identities, to embody the more allusive affirmation of a diversity of abilities and needs, directly.

Intersectionalism is insufficient as a tool for the circumvention of the prevailing collective narcissism, however well intentioned: thus, moving beyond, while acknowledging the kyriarchical insight that people can be *both* privileged *and* not-privileged, thinkers such as Jasbir Puar and Jennifer C. Nash have asserted that "defensiveness" and "policing" are the primary affects and behaviours to have resulted from the indirect, intersectional approach, as its employment and diffusion have generalized away from its original, more radical articulations.[21] Rather than a renewed form of proprietary politics, then, something closer to Angus's model of the post-national person who can have an array of multiple identities that do not necessarily reduce to intersectionality is increasingly on the ascendant. Nash's "critique of proprietary impulses," for instance, asserts that what is needed is an ethos of vulnerability and generosity.[22] Puar's proposal to augment intersectionality theory with "queer assemblage," in a non-oppositional, "frictional" manner, does much the same: rather than "an ironic reification of sexual difference as the foundational one," in which women of colour "must invariably be shown to be resistant, subversive, or articulating a grievance," Nash and Puar, amongst others, assert a politics that refuses to simplify women of colour, or even singular, individual people, either.[23]

Rather than continuing to reify difference for the white woman as the only valid model, then, for Nash and Puar, a morphological model of difference is affirmed such that gender, even, no longer serves as the foundational category undergirding all the others. Similarly, and in league with Angus's "post-national" person, intersectionality's nationalist presuppositions are circumvented, such that even if women of colour are centred, this centring can no longer be reduced to US women of colour, alone (or even to women of colour at all). What Nash and Puar emphasize is the destabilizing element of becoming and the critique of the reification of being that liberal metaphysics reinforces. Just as "LGBTQIA" (particularly without the "+" sign) arguably essentializes sexual or gendered otherness, intersectionality ignores the post- or non-liberal metaphysics of becoming, reifying idealist and representational models while ignoring materialist, anti-representational alternatives. Recognizing that "bodies are unstable assemblages," the model of queer assemblage, like that of the post-national person, allows for complex forms of alliance that construct new, non-binary assemblages that assume mutual constitution through immanent connections and hybridizations.[24]

Un Pour Tous, Tous Pour Un: Towards a Higher Communism

Karl Marx retained this type of openness to new, unexpected possibilities: in his famous definition of communism as one asserting a politics of "from each according to their ability, to each according to their need," he arguably produced an auto-critique of the revolutionary proletarian subject. As Marx's most thorough statement of revolutionary strategy, in his "higher stage" of communism, unitarity recedes and opens itself to difference, the difference of identities, and of singularities within particularities, implied in differential abilities and differential needs.[25] Rather than each person only getting back from society what each puts into it, the higher stage of communism assumes abundance and embodies an ethos of generosity to difference. As in Nash, Puar, and Angus, this "higher communism" (or, as Mark Fisher once put it, "acid communism") implies a Spinozan affirmation rather than rejection of power, in which power is understood as the increase in one's capacity to be affected in order to increase one's capacity to affect.[26] Only that political body that has sufficiently increased its power in both respects by abolishing the law of value could satisfy all abilities and all needs. In this way, then, conventional left populism's assertion of a simple universality of the majority interest ignores one thing: *the interest of the future*, of the higher communism to come. Beyond identities and even the concept of "the subject" as such (including the proletarian subject), higher communism asserts the all-round individual as its sole inhabitant type, one for whom the body is invaded by and invasive of its habitus, and categories like race, gender, or sexuality are not subjects but events that are composed not of attributes but of abilities and needs.

Another example of Marx's openness to multiplicity lies in his dialectical approach to intellectual engagement: for example, he was both a celebrant and a critic of one of his foremost, ostensible opponents, the French anarchist Pierre Joseph Proudhon. Proudhon's *What Is Property?* was one basis upon which Marx first advocated the abolition of private property, and it was thus crucial to his intellectual development, but Proudhon's book *The Philosophy of Poverty* led to Marx's famous critique, *The Poverty of Philosophy*.[27] Their primary divergence in the latter text centred upon the question of dialectics, which was concerned with his perception that Proudhon simply wanted to keep "the good side" of capitalism without noticing how "the bad side," despite seeming morally "bad," provided a material basis for class conflict and political struggle, enabling the arrival of communism, both lower and higher.[28]

Unlike Proudhon's, Marx's non-teleological materialism began from the material conditions of possibility as they presented themselves, affording opportunities that could be brought to a higher stage through the revolutionization of society. Thus, rather than returning to old models of craft labour as a way of keeping the "good side" of capitalism or its predecessors, Marx emphasized the manner in which automated production breaks down specialization and "craft-idiocy" such that the need for universality and individuality could be felt palpably by the worker.

Not everyone has the ability to work, and not everyone, therefore, can rely solely upon the fruits of belonging to neo-Proudhonian workers' collectives. Instead, those whose abilities are differently arranged, including young people, elderly people, and differently abled people, would benefit much more from Marx's privileging of the assertion and satisfaction of differential abilities and needs. Just as the emancipation of the proletariat is also the emancipation of humanity as whole, so, too, would the emancipation of young people, elderly people, and differently abled people be the emancipation of humanity as a whole. The same goes for those who have been historically excluded or discriminated against: if one cannot count on being hired into a position that pays a living wage with sufficient security and continuity to plan out a life, one's needs are certainly greater than they are for one who can count on all of those things. If we take for granted, then, that both conventional left populism and identity politics are conceptually and strategically lacking when it comes to this question,[29] then it is useful to engage those instances in which it has been articulated otherwise. For example, in Theodor Adorno's letter of recommendation for Angela Davis after she had studied with Herbert Marcuse, he mentions her dissertation on Immanuel

Kant and Friedrich Schiller, and Davis's particular emphasis upon freedom as an aesthetic category. In her later material/example-focused work, she refers to a variety of ways in which "the universal resides within the particular," a statement other students of Marcuse besides Davis have also made, such as George Katsiaficas.[30]

As Davis recalls in her autobiography:

> I began to see the problems of Black people within the context of a large working-class movement. My ideas about Black liberation were imprecise, and I could not find the right concepts to articulate them; still, I was acquiring some understanding about how capitalism could be abolished. I was particularly impressed by a passage in the Manifesto which portrayed the proletariat as the savior of all oppressed people: "All previous historical movements were movements of minorities, or in the interests of minorities. The proletarian movement is the self- conscious, independent movement of the immense majority, in the interest of the immense majority. The proletariat, the lowest stratum of our present society, cannot stir, cannot raise itself up, without the whole super-incumbent strata of official society being sprung into the air."[31]

The tension here, of course, is that between the "movements of minorities" and "movements of the immense majority." For Davis, this was initially reconcilable because, "once the emancipation of the proletariat became a reality, the foundation was laid for the emancipation of all oppressed groups in the society."[32] At the same time, in more recent years, she has formulated the reverse: once the emancipation of particular oppressed identities has become a reality, it not only lays a foundation for the emancipation of all other oppressed groups but is at the same time part of the process of the liberation of humanity as such.[33] In a letter to Davis, Marcuse writes, attempting to be something of a mute witness to the encounter between her direct engagement with the Frankfurt School and the Black Panther Party alike, "What does your life for the liberation of the black people, what does your present plight have to do with the philosophy of German Idealism?"[34] Upon rereading her prospectus, however, he recounts her statement that "the notion (in Kant) that force provides the link between the theory and practice of freedom leads back to Rousseau."[35] Marcuse credits Davis as the source of his later realization that force, or the practice of freedom that is not only the goal of liberation but its origin, is the basis for new modes of concrete universality that exceed that of proletarian universality. Prior to this encounter with Davis, Marcuse states, he had rejected Jean-Paul Sartre's notion of a "freedom which is truly inalienable," and thereby ignored the categorical imperative to link thought and action, ironically due to privileging physically embodied, sensuous human beings who are, objectively speaking, not free when they are not free.[36] Only by opening up to this link via Davis's greater comfort with abstraction would he later write "An Essay on Liberation," in which he argued that "the solidarity of the species" could be realized only by grounding it in a particularity capable of coinciding with concrete universality, of a subjectivity capable of coinciding with material objectivity. Historically, this had been the domain of the proletariat, but by the time of "An Essay," Marcuse had become convinced that "the majority of organized labor shares the stabilizing, counterrevolutionary needs of the middle classes," whereas revolutionary needs that could not be satisfied within the existing order continued to be asserted amongst African Americans and other populations.[37]

One example of the difference of where the satisfaction of revolutionary needs might lead in a manner that could not be satisfied in a counterrevolutionary manner can be seen in Marcuse's articulation of feminism and socialism, in which he argued that in a socialist society, the particularity of the feminine would be universalized and thereby "the masculine-feminine antithesis would then have been transformed into a synthesis—the legendary idea of androgynism."[38]

For Marcuse, revolutionary androgynism would mean the fusion of the mental and the somatic in a manner that would universalize the dynamic capacities that patriarchal capitalism had partitioned between genders and sexes on the levels of the economic, the cultural, and the political. For example, revolutionary androgynism would involve the satisfaction of the need not only for reduction of time spent working but also for developing a richer lifeworld, including pacifying aggression, emancipating sensory-aesthetic capacities, and liberating the intellect for both receptive and creative modes of rationality, such that the Performance Principle would be overcome by the Pleasure Principle. Katsiaficas formalizes this in his essay "The Latent Universality of Identity Politics," arguing that, while the new social movements resulted in the fragmentation of proletarian universality, "a totality of such quests can eventually become a radically new concrete universal."[39] While economic politics require a long-coming revolutionary overthrow to form a concrete universal, gender, racial, sexual, and other forms of identity-based equality can begin to be pursued immediately, benefiting not only minority groups as embodied particularities but also all humans: "No matter how much they respond to intrusive outsiders, each form of identity politics contains a latent universality. Gender equality is a universal aim, benefitting all of us. The celebration of racial diversity and mutual recognition of our humanity is in all our interests. Unlocking sexual repression and an end to the compulsory channeling of libido into exclusive heterosexuality benefits all. Cleaning up the environment and disarming the world's nation-states is in the interest of all humanity."[40]

Much like Nash's and Puar's critiques of Kimberlé Crenshaw and other intersectionalists (or perhaps, Marx's critique of Pierre-Joseph Proudhon), Angus's critique of the post-Marcusean ethos is not exactly that a greater compound universality is unachievable, but that the humanist subject upon which it was based "was taken to subtend all of the different forms of oppression and exploitation."[41] For this reason, he often reminds his reader that one always experiences and researches from a specific locus of enunciation, in his case that of an anglophone Canadian—a reminder that Angus leans more closely to Edmund Husserl than to Sartre. Marcuse, too, once did, in 1948, but by 1972 he shifted towards Sartre: that shift occurred through his interactions with Davis, and was the origin of Marcuse's realization that, as Angus put it, "a subject fully immersed in the world but nevertheless with the freedom to choose to revolt could enter into the historical analysis and revolutionary transformation proposed by Marxism with sacrifice of neither individual value nor responsibility."[42] Angus begins phenomenologically, not only in terms of space but also in terms of time: from the standpoint of 2018, a half-century after 1968, he asserts that the primary difference between then and now is that then, the welfare state compromise following WWII was fully in play and the extension of consumer capitalism through national liberation and comparably modelled identity liberation movements was still possible. Today, however, we are faced with "a rapacious extractivist resource economy" coupled with "an emerging digital economy whose form sometimes threatens to escape a capitalist model."[43] As a result, a thorough rethinking of how to recompose an alliance is in order, along with a rethinking of how to relate to the current order of abilities and needs.

Angus draws attention to Michel Foucault, whose distance from Marcuse on the repressive hypothesis, for example, could not be starker: where Marcuse sought to replace the Performance Principle with the Pleasure Principle, Foucault sought to question the "Use of Pleasure." The presupposed stability of received subjectivities, then, is faced by a much more complex account of power, one in which disalienation alone would surely prove insufficient. Angus's legacy in relation to these two threads—Marxist Humanism, on one side, and contemporary Continental philosophy, on the other—has been to synthesize the two. Rather than seeing Marcusean humanism or Althusserian structuralism as opposites, Angus opts for both the early and late Marx, seeing in the late Marx's addition of technology as a mediation between humanity and nature a more robust account of alienation, as "self-other-expanded selfhood."[44] But since the subject is structurally generated, we cannot simply return to the disalienation path: instead, for Angus, our task is "to understand the plural constitution of subjectivities alongside an ethical universality."[45] Doing this would mean engaging external forces constituting subjectivities from a perspective that recognizes the non-transparent nature of the process while we remain within it, such that compound universality would be based upon an intersubjectivity-in-flux, a trans-subjective belonging-to-becoming, rather than belonging-to-Being. Marcuse's revolutionary androgynism, after all, involved the self-assured statement that, although the goal was the fusion of mental and somatic characteristics in a manner that would no longer privilege masculinity, "no degree of androgynous fusion could ever abolish the natural differences between male and female as individuals."[46] Given how such a statement fails to resonate today, it is clear why a more careful rethinking is necessary.

Conclusion: Left Populism: A 2020s Vision

Which brings us back to need: as Angus would likely agree, Marcuse's entire approach to the philosophy of need suffers from this very problem, insofar as it is rooted in an account of biology that is, at present, not only being questioned philosophically but circumvented aesthetically and remade technologically.

Marcuse envisioned a new compound universality emerging not only from the tutelage of immiseration, which would unconceal the truth of need and necessity, or alternately, from later Marxist insights that "a highly developed consciousness and imagination may generate a vital need for radical change in advanced material conditions."[47] He also saw it arising from a compound alignment of interests, conjoining not an increasingly comfortable organized labour with the pampered middle and upper-middle classes but, instead, the nonconformist intelligentsia, the exploited African-American population, the unemployed generally, and radicalized sectors of organized labour and the middle classes, expanded through education and organization. Marcuse argued that this could not be done through an appeal to needs in general but only through the development and satisfaction of destabilizing rather than restabilizing needs. However, as with the radicalization of androgyny in his project, so, too, here did Marcuse resort to biological reductionism.[48]

Rather than proceeding in this manner, Angus's post-Marxist non-humanism[49] could allow for a more fluid, process-centred approach, one not rooted in the essentialist logic of repressed "instinctual needs" but rather in the productive cultivation of new needs, as well as, potentially, new biologies. This would surely look something like Marcuse's affirmation of a post-Kantian "imagination mediating between the rational faculties and sensuous needs,"[50] but it would also be decidedly post-Marxist and post-Freudian, in that it would not move from the repressive to the productive, as Marcuse had it, but from one form of "desiring production" to another. Whereas Marcuse presupposes knowledge of what basic needs versus imposed needs are, a post-Marxist non-humanist approach refuses moralizing ontologies, extending the production of needs to their multiplication, including previously unimaginable ones. And, where Marcuse sneers at traditional Marxism's inability to conceptualize his self-proclaimed iconoclastic emphasis on "biological and aesthetic needs," this approach would instead be a politics of aesthetics, and nothing other than that. Where Marcuse imagines a new biological solidarity of needs, we might instead imagine a techno-aesthetic solidarity of needs, asserted as new formations converge with prior formations.

For Angus, the defining feature of twenty-first-century social movements thus far has been that rather than accepting the subjectivities that are bequeathed to them from above, they are instead continually constructing new transindividual subjectivities, such as "antigobalization" or "Occupy." Moving beyond the classical Marxist conceptions of social struggle, Angus asserts that the question of radical subjectivity is the central issue in socialist thinking, "the relationship between particularity and universality ... [and] the claim that equality does not mean sameness, or identity."[51] As he sees it, there are three possible approaches to the relationship between particularity and universality. First is an explicitly imperial model in which the relation is directly framed according to the preferences of one of the parties over and against the preferences of the other, subsuming their particularity beneath the universalization of another particularity, such that the subjugated particularity is both inside and outside the universal, and is explicitly recognized as "other." Second is a quasi-imperial model in which the universal becomes a kind of common sense that subsumes all particularities due to its imperceptibility.

Model three, which Angus prefers, is one in which imperial rule is directly addressed, and the universal is only and exclusively that which emerges from this recognition and ensuing transformation of the particular-universal relation. For Angus, the language that should be used to describe this is that of "friendship" and "treaty"—which recognizes difference, does not demand full agreement, and seeks mutual prosperity and ongoing connection. In other words, one that would "open the possibility of a future of peace and treaty where it is not our sameness but rather our difference that grounds association."[52] But, for Angus, importantly, independence and self-determination do not mean isolation, zero-sum games, and mutual exclusivity but "independence among others, a plurality of independences, a new federation."[53] As in Marx's post-scarcity economics between particularities, Angus articulates a non- state relationship between particularities, in which those included enable mutually reinforcing modes of universalization, such that "each included particularity can become the context for assessment of universalizing claims." Because there is no overarching hierarchy to mediate relations (and to impose a false universality), "the degree of inclusion of a cultural particularity" remains undefined, so it, too, can be a source of universalization.[54]

What this shows is that there is no "right populism" in reality, because right-wing politics are not about the attendance to the abilities and satisfaction of the needs of the people as such but, instead, the attendance to the abilities and satisfaction of the needs of the most powerful subset of it, which is necessarily numerically the minority. Just as Marx spoke of false universalism, right populism is a false majoritarianism, while left populism, after it has parted ways with liberal, propertarian, turfist forms, is the only populism that can properly be called "populist," while also satisfying and exceeding the highest aims of intersectionality. Rather than attempting to articulate how one group is more versus less oppressed than another (and should therefore be prioritized or deprioritized), higher communism begins from the assumption that all communities have needs, despite their different manifestations, and that the central chain of equivalence that needs to be articulated is not that of the common enemy, as in the anti- globalization or Occupy movements, but rather that of the *universality of the particularity of need*. "Need," as frame, allows for the assertion of both particular needs appropriate to specific groups and also universal needs, such as material needs, but also more broadly still, of the right to express needs, including those that can be fully satisfied only beyond the purview of the capitalist horizon. Where Marx argues that needs are both central to the functioning of capitalism and the basis for its overcoming, Angus emphasizes that nationalized individuals are both central to the functioning of the state and, in the form of post-national persons, the basis for its overcoming.

Notes to Chapter 16:

1 Samir Gandesha, "Insurgent Universality," *Radical Philosophy* (Spring 2019), https://www.radicalphilosophy.com/reviews/individual-reviews/insurgent-universality. Gandesha reads Asad Haider's work as a politics committed to "the original spirit of the earliest statement of identity politics by articulating a case for an 'insurgent universality,' based not on an abstract concept of rights-bearers but, rather, on 'particular and concrete individuals—women, the poor, and

slaves—and their political and social agency'.... Haider engages in a genuinely immanent critique of identity; that is, he criticises its contemporary practice on the basis of its own strongest theoretical self-understanding" (ibid.).

2 Reinhold Neibuhr, *Moral Man and Immoral Society* (Westminster: John Knox Press, 2001), 221. Also see the early work of Leo Strauss and other neo-conservatives on the thematic of the exoteric and the esoteric (Leo Strauss, *Persecution and the Art of Writing* [Chicago: University of Chicago Press, 1988]).

3 While recognizing the equal necessity of critical rationality.

4 Although Teresa May's government is questionably "right populist" (her rhetoric is often selective and mechanical), she was selected by *The Guardian* as the second-most rhetorically populist female leader of the past two decades, invoking, for instance, a "'quiet revolution' by 'the people' to 'defy the establishment.'" Paul Lewis, Seán Clarke, and Caelainn Barr, "Theresa May's Rhetoric Can Be as Populist as Trump's," *The Guardian*, March 6, 2019, https://www.theguardian.com/world/2019/mar/06/theresa-may-british-prime-minister-populism-rhetoric-is-as- rife-as-in-donald-trump-speeches.

5 "The difficulties of modern liberal-democratic theory lie ... in its conception of the individual as essentially the proprietor of his own person or capacities, owing nothing to society for them. The individual was seen neither as a moral whole, nor as part of a larger social whole, but as an owner of himself... . The human essence is freedom from dependence on the wills of others, and freedom is a function of possession... . Society consists of relations of exchange between proprietors. Political society becomes a calculated device for the protection of this property." Crawford B. Macpherson, *The Political Theory of Possessive Individualism: Hobbes to Locke* (Oxford: Oxford University Press, 1962), 3.

6 I am using the second definition from the Merriam-Webster Dictionary since it includes US English more readily than the Oxford English Dictionary. "turf," Merriam-Webster, accessed May 16, 2019, https://www.merriam-webster.com/dictionary/turf?fbclid=IwAR28v9smlz1xG_dDULyndfaT_JKpK66jop6XdVf85dj7ULYc6hXul8uAzWs.

7 I am not arguing that this is the case, for example, in Ernesto Laclau and Chantal Mouffe (who are consistently more nuanced) but rather that it recurs in the everyday discursive practice of left populist discussion. This has been changing recently, however, and this chapter is intended as a contribution towards that end.

8 As Deleuze once put it, "there are greater differences between a plow horse or draft horse and a racehorse than between an ox and a plow horse." Gilles Deleuze, *Spinoza: Practical Philosophy* (San Francisco, CA: City Lights Books, 1988), 46. Thank you to Samson K. Opondo for pointing out this passage to me, following the "Deleuze and Race" panel at the 2010 Cultural Studies Association conference in Chicago. See: Sam Okoth Opondo and Michael

J. Shapiro, *The New Violent Cartography: Geo-Analysis After the Aesthetic Turn* (London: Routledge, 2012); and Sam Okoth Opondo, "Cinema-Body-Thought: Race-Habits and the Ethics of Encounter," in *Deleuze and Race*, ed. A. Saldanha and J. Adams (Edinburgh: Edinburgh University Press, 2012).

9 Karl Marx, "Critique of the Gotha Program," in *Karl Marx: Selected Writings*, ed. D. McLellan (Oxford: Oxford University Press, 2000), 615.

10 Wendy Brown articulates this relation better than most, in her chapter "Freedom and the Plastic Cage" in Wendy Brown, *States of Injury* (Princeton: Princeton University Press, 1995). Thank you to Alex Gebhardt for pointing this out to me.

11 Though, not in the manner that this concept was usually used by the thinkers of the New Left. Herbert Marcuse articulated this concept at the height of the New Left, but did so primarily in order to dismiss it. See, for example: Herbert Marcuse, *An Essay on Liberation* (Boston: Beacon Press: 2000), 50. However, he did occasionally refer to "the needs of a new type of man," which, he argued, would develop once technology was developed in accordance with socialist values (19). Our argument is that many of the "counterrevolutionary needs" Marcuse identifies are not nearly as counterrevolutionary as he presumed.

12 Ian Angus, *Identity and Justice* (Toronto: University of Toronto Press, 2008), 85.

13 Ian Angus, *Primal Scenes of Communication* (Albany: State University of New York Press, 2000), 190. 14 The greater commonality here being gender and class in the former example, and the lack thereof in the latter example. As I conceive it, even in managerial and "petit bourgeois" form (and forced entrepreneurialism due to career market collapse is increasingly common), the middle class is not typically distinct from the working class in terms of its relation to the production of surplus value. One could, of course, reference reactionary upper middle-class white transwomen such as Caitlyn Jenner; however, I would argue that Jenner is not actually middle class (and thus, also not working class), but owning class.

15 Ian Angus, "Globalization Versus Social Movements: Towards a New Alliance?" accessed 16 May 2019, http://www.sfu.ca/personal/iangus/global.pdf.

16 Ian Angus, *Technique and Enlightenment: Limits of Instrumental Reason* (Memphis: Centre for Advanced Research in Phenomenology and University Press of America, 1984).

17 Originally stated on the Justice Democrats website, though now removed, following right-wing media criticism. The original wording is quoted in: Eric Pfeiffer, "Kyle Kulinski of the Young Turks Says Democrats Need to Change before They Can Defeat Trump," *Good*, July 11, 2017, https://www.good.is/features/kyle-kulinski-sanders-trump.

18 However, what I have called "turfism" has sometimes manifested in the denial of differences within groups as part of the reification of differences between

groups: for instance, when Uday Jain implied in *New Socialist* that people such as Bhaskar Sunkara and Adolph Reed Jr. are "White Marxists." Uday Jain, "White Marxism: A Critique of Jacobin Magazine," *New Socialist*, August 11, 2017, https://newsocialist.org.uk/white-marxism-critique/.

19 Quoted in Angus, *Identity and Justice*, 74.

20 To be clear, I am not suggesting in saying that class and non-class identities are the same categorically: the goal of Marxism is the abolition of class identity, while the goal of liberal identity politics is typically recognition.

21 Jasbir Puar, "I Would Rather Be a Cyborg Than a Goddess: Intersectionality, Assemblage, and Affective Politics," *EIPCP: European Institute for Progressive Cultural Policies*, January 2011, accessed May 16, 2019, http://eipcp.net/transversal/0811/puar/en. See also: Jennifer Nash, *Black Feminism Reimagined: After Intersectionality* (Durham: Duke University Press, 2019), 3.

22 Nash, *Black Feminism Reimagined*.

23 Puar, "I Would Rather Be a Cyborg." Puar argues that the language that intersectionalists use ends up naturalizing a "white feminist" perspective, even though the whole point initially was to decentre it. Asad Haider makes the same argument in his recent work.

24 Ibid. The "third worldism" of the Non-Aligned Movement and related currents was a kind of "abilities and needs"-oriented perspective of its own and involved the nation-state, but that particular form also suggested an alternative internationalism being connected to it.

25 "In a higher phase of communist society, after the enslaving subordination of the individual to the division of labour, and therewith also the antithesis between mental and physical labour, has vanished; after labour has become not only a means of life but life's prime want; after the productive forces have also increased with the all-round development of the individual, and all the springs of cooperative wealth flow more abundantly—only then can the narrow horizon of bourgeois right be crossed in its entirety and society inscribe on its banners: from each according to his ability, to each according to his needs!" Marx, "Critique of the Gotha Program,"

26 Referenced in Matt Colquhoun, "Acid Communism," *Krisis: Journal for Contemporary Philosophy* 2, no. 1 (2018), https://krisis.eu/acid-communism/.

27 "Proudhon's treatise *Qu'est-ce que la propriété?* is the criticism of political economy from the standpoint of political economy.... Proudhon's treatise will therefore be scientifically superseded by a criticism of political economy, including Proudhon's conception of political economy. This work became possible only owing to the work of Proudhon himself." Karl Marx, "The Poverty of Philosophy," in *Karl Marx: Selected Writings*, ed. D. McLellan (Oxford: Oxford University Press, 2000), 147.

28 Ibid.

29 Here, I mean the kind of left populism that offers no guaranteed, livable income for those without access to sufficient work opportunities or who are unable to work and the kind of liberal identity politics that focuses primarily on the needs of minority groups who already have sufficient economic resources to survive.

30 This is also found in Walter Benjamin's approach to allegory and in his concept of "profane illumination."

31 Angela Davis, *Angela Davis—An Autobiography* (New York: International Publishers, 1988), 110.

32 Ibid.

33 "Oftentimes the slogan 'Black Lives Matter' is interpreted as only Black lives matter. So why is it that so many people counter by saying all lives matter. You say Black lives matter, they say no, all lives matter. But the whole point is that if ever Black lives were to truly matter, then all lives would really matter" (quoted in S. Rimer, "Controversial Civil Rights Activist Angela Davis Draws Big Crowd to BU Talk." *BU Today*, February 11, 2019).

34 Herbert Marcuse, "Dear Angela," in *The New Left and the 1960s: Herbert Marcuse*, ed. D. Kellner (London: Routledge, 2005), 49.

35 Ibid.

36 Ibid.

37 Herbert Marcuse, *An Essay on Liberation* (Boston: Beacon Press, 2000), 15.

38 Herbert Marcuse, "Marxism and Feminism," in *The New Left and the 1960s*, ed. D. Kellner (London/New York: Routledge, 2004), 171.

39 George Katsiaficas, "The Latent Universality Within Identity Politics," *New Political Science* 19, no. 1 (1997): 82.

40 "A failure to comprehend the contradictory character of identity politics unites both their advocates and opponents.... By themselves, identity politics are not sufficient to transform qualitatively problematic political- economic structures. Indeed, not only are they insufficient for the formulation of a revolutionary transcendence of the class-structured multinational corporate world system, they sometimes conceal that very system by seeking to treat as identical a variety of people who occupy very different positions within the system." Ibid., 87.

41 Ian Angus, "The Dissolution of Marxist Humanism," lecture at "Then and Now: 1968–2018," November 2–3, 2018, Simon Fraser University, Vancouver, BC. Printed in *Pensamiento Critico* (November 2018): 5, accessed August 8, 2019, http://www.pensamientocritico.org/wp-content/uploads/2018/11/The_Dissolution_of_Marxist_Humanism.pdf.

42 Ibid.

43 Ibid.

44 Ibid., 11.

45 Ibid.

46 Marcuse, *An Essay on Liberation* 171. 47 Ibid., 15.

48 Ibid., 17.

49 As mentioned above, Angus's work does not adhere strictly to Marxist precepts, although it is indebted to them; similarly, while Angus is critical of humanism, to describe his work as anti-humanist seems excessively absolutist. 50 Marcuse, *An Essay on Liberation*, 30.

51 Ian Angus, "Globalization Versus Social Movements: Towards a New Alliance?," accessed May 16, 2019, http://www.sfu.ca/personal/iangus/global.pdf

52 Ian Angus, *Identity and Justice* (Toronto: University of Toronto Press, 2008), 85.

53 Ibid., 86.

54 Ibid., 88.

Chapter 17

The Truth and Untruth of the Enlightenment

Graeme Nicholson

Histories of culture and philosophy regularly describe the eighteenth-century epoch of western Europe as the Age of Enlightenment. We are told of the salons and coffee houses in which *philosophes* interacted with aristocratic ladies and gentlemen, and we have a prodigious wealth of documentation—literary, musical, painterly—for sampling their ideas and their tastes. And, without a doubt, there was one predominant style in this epoch: the work of John Locke on human understanding had an affinity with the medical information conveyed by the French *Encyclopedia;* Adam Smith's economics have much in common with the legal thought of Baron de Montesquieu; and so on. But we cannot treat the culture of eighteenth-century Europe as if it were a self-contained object of our contemplation. The Enlightenment is not merely one epoch of the past—it reaches out beyond that period and continues to guide us. We shall understand this better if we realize that it was not only one kind of thinking but a *movement*, conscious of itself, with an intent to make history (its partisans gave it the name *lumières*). That gave it the energy to bring forth great results over the centuries. It was a philosophy, but it was not only that. It was the seedbed for what we call the social sciences.

Locke intended his *Essay Concerning Human Understanding* as a contribution to philosophy, but now we can see it as the prototype for modern empirical psychology. Montesquieu certainly intended *The Spirit of the Laws* as a program for legal reform—and it was that—but it was also a foundational document for modern anthropology and sociology. Adam Smith understood himself as a moral philosopher, but *The Wealth of Nations* has proved to be the basic text for modern economics. A bit later on, Wilhelm von Humboldt's work became the inaugural text of the science of linguistics. All these scientific fields are today enshrined in universities. If the natural sciences of the seventeenth century accomplished the application of reason, understanding, and empirical observation to the world of nature, the Enlightenment undertook an equivalent achievement for society and history. And we cannot believe that its work has been completed. Every one of these sciences is a field of continuing research. Since they have brought us much truth and understanding, these sciences are the first bit of evidence I shall mention for what I call "the truth of the Enlightenment."

And it could be that Enlightenment *philosophy* as such still has an authority and a further mission for us. That last point is the agenda of two different books that have appeared recently: *Enlightenment Now* by Steven Pinker,[1] and *Enlightenment 2.0 by* Joseph Heath.[2]

The first is the work of a psychologist who has taken on the mantle of a social critic and finds the climate of modern life (especially in the USA) poisoned by currents of irrationality that must be corrected by a renewal of "Enlightenment now." The long middle section of the book shows how greatly modern life has benefited from the thought, science, and technology bequeathed us by the eighteenth-century Enlightenment—measured by many criteria such as longevity, health, safety, education, and prosperity—an argument that I do not dispute and shall not discuss here. These practical benefits, stemming from the eighteenth, nineteenth, and twentieth centuries, count to me as further evidence for "the truth of the Enlightenment." My interest in this paper will be the grounding that Pinker discerns for all these practical benefits: he attributes them to the guiding philosophy of the Enlightenment, which he summarizes under three headings, "reason, science and humanism." And it is this triad, too, that he is promoting as the cure for the irrationality that he sees pervading modern life. But the questions of this paper will be: When he comes to outline this triad in the concluding pages of his book, how convincing is his account of reason, how accurate is his anatomizing of science, and does he make a good case for humanism?

Heath is a philosopher who draws on a lot of psychology, evolutionary biology, and computer science to buttress his arguments. Like Pinker, he sees foolishness and irrationality penetrating almost every sector of life in our times, particularly in the USA, but also in Canada. He, too, is calling for a new Enlightenment to correct our course. His philosophical discipline enables him to anatomize *reason* more effectively than Pinker has done. Moreover, he differs from Pinker further in making a critical appraisal of the eighteenth-century Enlightenment. Acknowledging the criticisms made by Edmund Burke and others, Heath faults the *philosophes* for having a purely individualist account of reason rather than a social one, and, even more seriously, he criticizes the revolutionaries for destroying traditions while having nothing to put in their place—a neglect that showed up when the French Revolution moved on into violence and eventual failure, leading to Napoleon's dictatorship. The title *Enlightenment 2.0* is to signify a different kind of Enlightenment. I appropriate Heath's criticism of the historical Enlightenment in this paper, taking it as a first bit of evidence for what I call the "untruth of the Enlightenment."

Martin Heidegger and other phenomenologists have taught us to understand truth more broadly than was common in the past, when logicians would generally assign truth to singular statements like "The cat is on the mat." We have come to see that a science (whether natural science or social science) incorporates truths that cannot be accessed outside that science—economic truths or chemical truths, for instance. For that reason, we are able to say that the science itself is true. What that means, according to Heidegger, is that the science reveals or discloses a whole range of phenomena that can then become subjects of investigation, where a particular kind of discourse (the science itself) highlights many different items. It is because the science itself is true that it can bring forth many observations and statements that are true.

We noted above that the Enlightenment was a movement that generated many new sciences: it allowed us to see things that had not been seen before. It is because the Enlightenment is true that its sciences are true.

> Nature and Nature's laws lay hid in night;
> God said, "Let *Newton* be," and all was light. (Alexander Pope)

When a great movement first brings a manifold of phenomena into the light of day, we are witnessing the most fundamental experience of truth. The many particular phenomena that then become newly revealed (laws of gases; laws of economic exchange) have the status of truths, but they became possible only because of a universal disclosure of reality, the truth of the movement as a whole.[3]

But just as such movements engage in disclosure quite universally, they are also capable of promoting obfuscation and error. We have already seen some evidence of the untruth of the historical Enlightenment in the observations of Heath about both reason and tradition. And even as we probe the work of the present-day soldiers of the Enlightenment, Pinker and Heath themselves, we shall be led to see layers of untruth that lie within their thinking. It opens out the broader possibility that, in all cases, truth has an intimate involvement with untruth, whether in particular observations and statements or in a science as a whole or in the kind of movement (like the Enlightenment) that brings sciences forth. We come here to see the tragedy of human finitude, manifested in the intimate conjunction of disclosure and obfuscation, truth and untruth. My guide in this argument is Heidegger's account of truth and untruth in his essay "On the Essence of Truth."[4] He shows, first, that the essence of truth is disclosure or unconcealedness. Then he undertakes to show that untruth belongs, essentially, to truth, but that untruth arises in two main forms. The first of these is concealment, or obfuscation, which is the privation of unconcealedness. The second form of untruth is what he calls "erring."

I look at Heath's account of reason to see in what way it is true, and then to probe into its foundations, where I believe we shall discern an important element of concealment or obfuscation. In Pinker's account of reason and science, I discover a concealment that it promotes. My scrutiny of Pinker's humanism and atheism shows not only what is concealed there but also how it promotes deceptions that spring from erroneous thinking. In all three of these, I trace the concealment and erring to sources in the historical Enlightenment of the eighteenth century.

Heath on Reason

Heath rightly sees it as the office of the philosopher to characterize reason. His chapter 1 draws a distinct profile of our rational mind, which sets it over against our intuitive mind, the two of them coexisting in us as the outcome of our distinctive biology, our evolution, and our cultural history. The intuitive mind is swift, imagistic, self-certain, focused on the single phenomenon rather than universal structures. The rational mind developed later, as the product of language. It practises abstraction; it works by serial processing rather than parallel, implements working memory (which intuition does not), perfectly instantiated by our mathematical competence. Heath gives clear descriptions of the two forms of mentality.[5]

Heath has embedded his account in an evolutionary framework—how we got from the brain stem to the cortex—and also adds many elaborations drawn from computer science. Analytic philosophers of his persuasion will always attempt to ground their theories with biological or cybernetic findings, considering it unsporting to rely on *a priori* investigation in the manner of Gottfried Leibniz or Immanuel Kant. But I believe that his descriptions of the rational and intuitive powers of the mind can stand independently of those other sciences and can be confirmed by a purely philosophical phenomenology. His dichotomy of the rational and intuitive powers seems to be exactly what René Descartes established in the *Rules for the Direction of the Mind*, notably Rule 3.[6] And if we left the evolutionary and cybernetic evidence to one side, nothing would be lost of Heath's efforts to correct the follies of irrational politics and culture that take up most of his book. The reforms he proposes are guided by the inherent character of the "two minds" he has separated.

Still, I would add that philosophy would certainly need to ask about the cooperation and integration of the "two minds."

The typical bias of Enlightenment thought, whether in the eighteenth century or today, is to favour the rational mind over the intuitive, and this bias shows up everywhere in Heath's book, especially in chapter 1 where he first introduces them. Where intuition leaps to false conclusions, reason comes to the rescue. I do not see that he ever presented the opposite case, of reason going astray and needing to be corrected by intuition. But this does occur, and it manifests the higher reaches of the intuitive mind, where it operates as imagination. A poor actor may enunciate his lines clearly enough and might even be able to explain the motivations of the character he portrays but may still be rightly reproached by the play's director for lack of inspiration in capturing the spirit of the lines when he utters them.

Even in everyday settings, the limits of the rational mind are clear to all: you might labour to copy a recipe for soup and study the foreign cuisine of which it is a part, but it is the taste that will be the test. Post-Enlightenment philosophers, notably Friedrich von Schelling, devoted great effort to establish the possibility of intellectual intuition, whereby our rational mind would make immediate, intuitive contact with the highest objects of knowledge, what they called the "Idea" or the "Absolute." This was an initiative taken against the epistemology of Kant, who had confined intuition purely to the domain of sensation. Yet, even the sober Kant was eventually obliged to make room in his *Critique of Judgment* for the creative faculty of artistic imagination, virtually withdrawing his earlier strictures against intellectual intuition. In the *Critique of Judgment,* he is especially interested in how the critic appraises works of art, and he does not have as much to say about the process of composing them. What he does say is that works of art do not spring from the intellect or reason but from the extraordinary gifts of genius that express the faculty of spirit: "Spirit [*Geist*] in an aesthetic sense is the animating principle in the mind.... This principle is nothing but the ability to exhibit *aesthetic ideas* ... presentation[s] of the imagination which prompt much thought."[7] Thus, it is a highly developed spirit that finds expression in the genius.[8] Spirit is a kind of thinking that does not eliminate the influence of feeling or emotion but rather unites thoughts, feelings, and intuitions into one. In a work of poetry or art, their union is encoded in the words or the work, in which the spirit has outed itself.

I recognize that Heath's territory did not include judgments of taste, whether of art or cookery—his domain is that of "public deliberation," the law and the state, where the more prosaic works of reason are found. Nevertheless, a theory of the mind that excludes, in principle, all the higher reaches of intuition and imagination has *concealed* something important from us, and must be reckoned as an untruth belonging to the Enlightenment. It should not be thought that the higher reaches of intuition are found only in exceptional cases such as artistic creation and aesthetic judgment. There is reason to believe that our everyday perception and the everyday competence we exhibit in interacting with the environment depend on our intuitive familiarity with the forms and shapes of things, as Plato proved once and for all.

Moreover, the typical situations that we anticipate every day have a certain shape that is known to us intuitively, forms and shapes that guide us, as Plato also knew: the *polis*, its institutions, justice, and injustice.

The favouring of reason over intuition is not characteristic just of Heath—it is to be found all over the eighteenth-century Enlightenment texts that inspired him. Many of these authors offered a diminished intuition overpowered by what they called "reason" (though, in many cases, "intellect" or "understanding" would be a more appropriate term). One example, of many, can be found in the philosophy of George Berkeley. His ingenious arguments seek to undermine the perceiver's conviction that it is a material object that he is perceiving—the intuitive life of perception is deceptive. Berkeley's improbable metaphysics of immaterialism is certainly a triumph of the reasoning intellect over intuition.

Pinker on Reason and Science

Pinker's book is an odd combination of celebration and angry polemic: celebration of the achievements of modern society for which we should all be grateful and denunciation of a variety of critics who are deficient in gratitude. I do not intend to treat the celebratory chapters of Part II: Progress, though I would call attention to chapter 10, "The Environment," and chapter 19, "Existential Threats," for both these chapters come to grips with contentious issues such as climate change and nuclear war, and express a confidence in our post-Enlightenment science and politics that rebukes well-known doomsayers such as Jonathan Schell and Naomi Klein. Pinker argues that there can be a technological fix for many a problem that haunts us, and I found his review of these proposals most informative, adding up in my view to a further argument for the truth of the Enlightenment. He sustains the cheerful note until we come to the three chapters of Part III: Reason, Science, and Humanism. It was this triad that gave birth to the historical Enlightenment and all its benefits—but now it is this same triad that is under attack on a variety of fronts, provoking Pinker's anger.

Yet, the oppositions that concern him can be understood only within the larger history of the USA itself. The Enlightenment rationalism that he espouses was never more than a minority tendency in the USA. Thomas Jefferson's Declaration of Independence was not only the first American text to express an Enlightenment viewpoint—it may have been the last. American literature from the beginning has been indelibly Romantic, from Nathaniel Hawthorne and Herman Melville, through Walt Whitman, to Jack Kerouac and Allen Ginsberg. The American historiography of the frontier and the Civil War was focused on the subjective aspirations and passions of the people, not with sovereign overviews in the style of Edward Gibbon. American theatre had nothing in common with eighteenth-century comedy. Thus, Pinker has a formidable list of cultural figures arrayed against him when he tries to make his Enlightenment case. Just as important is the hold that religion has had upon the American people. Although its grip may have weakened these days among the coastal "elites," it remains central to the people of the "fly-over" states who labour in the economies of agriculture, ranching, and manufacture. And, to look at more recent history, it was the upheavals of the 1960s (totally Romantic in inspiration) that prompted Pinker to write his book—they brought structural changes to higher education, to popular music, and eventually to gender relations and the family; and then arrived the resistance of the right, with all its many faces, finally yielding the implacable standoff we see today in American politics. Pinker hopes that a balm of reason, science, and humanism will dissolve the Romanticism of the left and the religion of the right. What are his chances?

Chapter 22 recounts glumly how intellectuals and politicians collaborate in running the sciences down, though it is not very detailed in outlining what science actually *is*. Basically, he says that science is committed (a) to the view that the world is intelligible, and (b) to "allowing the world to tell us whether our ideas about it are correct,"[9] his variant on the inductive model. His real point is that you cannot combine science with religion, for the main source texts of religion are full of factual errors.[10] But Pinker is obviously unacquainted with the modern preaching that reaches through the details of archaic cosmologies to proclaim a religious message; he is insistent on looking at modern religious practice only from the outside, concealing the inner dynamics of the life of faith. His other enemy is the kind of Romanticism that he attributes to imported un-American philosophy: the Nietzschean Superman, Michel Foucault's power and discourse, hermeneutics and Heideggerian gloom, and deconstruction. Such movements locate modern science as just one discourse among many, showing its "social construction."

Science, for Pinker, is the application to nature of our power of reason, and chapter 21, devoted to Reason, offered many examples in which he assumes that reason and science are the same, though, in contrast to Heath, it is very sketchy in outlining what reason *is*. He emphasizes the role of reason in dialogue: "It's in the very nature of arguing that people stake a claim to being right. As soon as they do so, they have committed themselves to reason."[11] Indeed they have, but this commitment takes us into much deeper territory that Pinker does not explore at all. The commitment is not merely to a contest in arguing; above all, it is a commitment to finding a good reason, one that will withstand fuller investigation. This is the only appropriate guide to study and research, whether conducted with others or in solitude; reason is fulfilled when we discover truth. The topic of reason is just as fundamental as the topics of truth and justice. But Pinker takes up most of his chapter in reporting on deficiencies of reasoning that people have exhibited in taking psychological tests. Just how this is to cast light on reason itself is left unexplained.

Later in the chapter, he turns to the media and the well-known pundits who comment on economic and political trends. He is scornful of the best-known pundits, who are wrong more often than they are right. Here we are given what could have been an account of reason itself, for the mark of a good pundit is the power to make accurate predictions; could we not take that as a genuine criterion of "reason" itself? But that would require a much deeper account of what the good pundits know and what factors they adduce in achieving their true predictions. They do not read the future out of the entrails of birds.

Pinker would have been led into a study of the deepest structures of society and the deepest currents of history, currents that actually account for the superficial phenomena that are evident to all. But that would involve a doctrine of reason that goes much further than Pinker was able to do: we would have discovered the *objective reasons* that determine the world, which the *subjective reason* of the informed commentator had discerned. The structure of reason, as *subjective-and-objective*, is the subject matter of Leibniz's philosophy, summarized in the principle of sufficient reason: "Nothing is without a grounding," *nihil est sine ratione*. But since Pinker contents himself with a purely subjective account of reason (and science), we have to see here an occlusion, the concealment of objective reason.

Even though Leibniz's philosophy was not unknown in the eighteenth century, its force of argument was often missed. Voltaire's comedy *Candide*, supposedly one of the triumphs of the Enlightenment, was thought to have refuted Leibniz's philosophy, with the absurd figure of Doctor Pangloss, who brushed aside all the sufferings and evils of life with his slogan of complacency: "All is for the best in the best of all possible worlds." That was a popular but trivializing concealment of the depths of reason into which Leibniz had probed.

Pinker on Humanism

We soon learn that he understands humanism to include atheism. And here Pinker shows himself to be the heir of the radical current of the eighteenth-century Enlightenment, figures such as Denis Diderot and the Baron d'Holbach. I shall include a few references here to the work of Holbach.[12] His work and that of others such as Julien Offray de La Mettrie are enough to convince anyone that the "new atheism" of the twenty-first century has nothing new about it;[13] every significant point made by Pinker on behalf of atheism was already advanced by Holbach in his *System*, and I believe that that holds for the other "new" atheists as well (Richard Dawkins, Sam Harris, Daniel Dennett, and Christopher Hitchens), though I cannot undertake all that documentation here. It is worth noting, however, that Heath, being critical of the eighteenth-century Enlightenment, does not include atheism as a part of his program of "Enlightenment 2.0."

Pinker opens his argument by securing the naturalistic conditions for our existence and morality—the two ultimate determinants of everything: the law of physics, that entropy always increases in a closed system; and the law of biology, that life forms emerge through evolution.[14] These two factors are the twenty-first-century equivalents of the laws of "Nature" that Holbach started from, as we shall see below. Like all Enlightenment authors, Pinker stresses that the intellectual and moral attributes of human beings are to be explained naturalistically: "Evolution thus selects for the moral sentiments: sympathy, trust, gratitude."[15]

This line of thought leads Pinker to propose utilitarian morality, which he defends against the alternative: deontological morality; one part of his case is that utilitarianism is persuasive to almost everyone's common sense.[16]

Having given his humanistic grounding for morality, Pinker makes the point that God and divine commandments are by no means necessary for morality,[17] and he appropriates Plato's argument in the *Euthyphro* as a buttress for this: something is not right just *because* the gods decree it, but rather they decree it *because* it is right.

This "*Euthyphro-*" argument was one of Pinker's points in defence of atheism: God is not necessary for ethics. But, of course, there is the further question whether God even exists. On this point, Pinker's text is astonishing. He disposes of God's existence in a single paragraph[18] with the claim that the question has been finally settled by a novel written by Rebecca Newberger Goldstein called *Thirty-Six Arguments for the Existence of God: A Work of Fiction*. (Perhaps there is an in-joke here, since the novelist in question is Pinker's wife.)

Turning now directly to the topic of religion, we see that, for Pinker, it offers a spurious response to "the deepest yearnings of the human heart."[19] But I cannot see that Pinker shows the slightest sign of understanding for the believers: his text becomes jokey and contemptuous whenever religion comes up for discussion. He is ready to summarize Christianity in the words of the children's Christmas jingle "Santa Claus is coming to town."[20] He introduces the topic of divine providence and is content to treat it by way of a comedy sketch from the TV performer Amy Schumer, who does a young woman saying: "So I was texting while I was driving? And I ended up taking a wrong turn that took me directly past a vitamin shop? And I was just like, this is totally the universe telling me I should be taking calcium."[21] The full text of the TV sketch that Pinker quotes on this page is so crude that it would have appalled the Baron d'Holbach, and no doubt the Marquis de Sade as well.

Although Pinker laughs at the religious beliefs of Christians and Jews, when he comes to Islam the tone is not so merry.[22] Perhaps the reason is that he sees Islam as an utterly foreign system, the "Islamic world," lying entirely in the eastern hemisphere. Although the USA has between three and four million Muslims in its population, Pinker never refers to them or to their beliefs and practices. Focused on the Islam-majority states, he denounces Islam for blighting the lives of those who profess it and endangering the world outside.

Parenthetically, we may now review Holbach's argument for atheism as the prototype for Pinker's. First, there is the naturalistic account of the universe, and human existence and morality:

> Everybody in the universe is in motion.... Motion is inherent in nature, which is the great whole, out of which nothing can exist. Matter moves by its own energy.[23]
>
> ...
>
> Man, like everything else, is a production of nature. What is his origin? ... It is probable that he was produced at a particular period of our globe ... and will exist so long as the globe remains in its present state. When that is changed, the human species must give way to new beings, capable of incorporating themselves with the new qualities which the globe will then possess.... To talk of God and of creation is but confessing our ignorance of the energy of nature.[24]
>
> ...
>
> Man has no right to believe himself a privileged being in nature. He is subject to the same vicissitudes as its other productions. The idea of human excellence is merely founded on the partiality which man feels for himself.[25]

Like Pinker, Holbach argues on behalf of utilitarianism, though without the name: "Politics should be the art of directing the passions of men to the good of society. Laws ought to have no other object than the direction of their actions also to the same object. Happiness is the uniform object of all the passions."[26] Holbach separates ethics from God, just as Pinker does, although without reference to Plato:

"The idea of a God is both useless and contrary to sound morality … abstract and unintelligible speculations can never serve as a foundation to morality, which must rest upon clear and evident principles."[27] But Holbach himself was not nearly as casual and brief as Pinker on the question of God's existence and the arguments for it. He devotes several chapters of his main work (well summarized in the supplement) to reviewing and rebutting such arguments, especially Dr. Samuel Clarke's version of the cosmological argument. Clarke thought that contingent entities stood in need of a supernatural Being that existed eternally and necessarily; but Holbach argues that *matter* was what existed eternally and necessarily.[28] And, on the question of religion, there is a solemnity and dignity of his work that compares favourably with Pinker's. Certainly, Holbach denounces the mysteries and absurdities of Christianity on page after page;[29] he traces them all to our human desire to transcend our proper sphere, Nature. But it does seem that, with all his hardness, Holbach speaks with some compassion and sympathy for those whom he sees as victimized by the Church that he hates so much. The atheists of the eighteenth century were anti-clerical first and foremost, and, in Continental Europe, confronted a Catholic Church that possessed great wealth and exercised a power that had great impact on lesser mortals. But in Pinker's world there is no established church, so one is rather at a loss to understand his anger.

Conclusion

I have tried to review some of the concealments brought about by the Enlightenment even as it has also accomplished important works of truth. But now, following Heidegger, I want to call attention to a further form of untruth, over and above concealment, which he has called *die Irre*, "erring," understood as an active distortion in our reasoning that promotes deceptions. And I think that this does appear in Pinker's text.

As a crucial component of Pinker's style of argument, there is a further element besides the jokiness, which shows up prominently in his brief paragraph on God's existence. Here, he employs a rhetorical style that I call the "blunt assertion": the dogmatic assertion of a claim essential to his case without even the pretence of argumentation: "The Cosmological and Ontological arguments for the existence of God are logically invalid."[30] That's it! Case closed! I have found the technique of the blunt assertion to be common among atheist authors, often including Holbach himself. One can sample this in Pinker's chapter on science, where he offers a sketch of what the world's religions teach: their "belief systems are factually mistaken."[31] That settles it! Richard Dawkins is also fond of the blunt assertion: "God's existence or non-existence is a scientific fact about the universe."[32] I think that the jokiness of Pinker's text works together with the blunt assertions in the overall rhetorical effect. A reader might not swallow the blunt assertions as they stand, but some readers will find that the jokes make Pinker seem more credible than those whom he ridicules.

Notes to Chapter 17:

1 Steven Pinker, *Enlightenment Now: The Case for Reason, Science, Humanism and Progress* (New York: Viking, 2018).

2 Joseph Heath, *Enlightenment 2.0: Restoring Sanity to Our Politics, Our Economy, and Our Lives* (Toronto: Harper Perennial, 2015).

3 I have defended this idea in a paper, "Truth as a Phenomenon," *Review of Metaphysics* 68 (June 2015): 830–32, and in the concluding chapter of *Heidegger on Truth: Its Essence and Its Fate* (Toronto: University of Toronto Press, 2019).

4 *Vom Wesen der Wahrheit* (Frankfurt: Klostermann, 1949), reprinted in Martin Heidegger, *Gesamtausgabe*, vol. 9 (Frankfurt: Klostermann, 1976); in Martin Heidegger, *Pathmarks*, ed. William McNeill, transl. John Sallis (Cambridge: Cambridge University Press, 1998).

5 Heath, *Enlightenment*, 31–37, summarized on p. 58.

6 René Descartes, *Philosophical Writings of Descartes*, ed. J. Cottingham et al. (Cambridge: Cambridge University Press, 1984), 1:9–75.

7 Immanuel Kant, *Critique of Judgment*, trans. Werner Pluhar (Indianapolis: Hackett, 1987), 313–14 (marginal German pagination).

8 Ibid., 311–12.

9 Pinker, *Enlightenment*, 392–93.

10 Errors listed in Pinker, *Enlightenment*, 394.

11 Pinker, *Enlightenment*, 352.

12 His best-known work is Baron d'Holbach, *Système de la nature* (1770), which, when it was republished in 1774, was accompanied by a short summary by C.-A. Helvétius. The work and the summary were translated by H. D. Robinson and published in New York by Burt Franklin in 1868, reprinted in 1970. I quote from the summary, "The True Meaning of the System of Nature," pp. 339–62 of the New York edition.

13 Pinker refers to it in *Enlightenment*, 430–33.

14 Pinker, *Enlightenment*, 413–15.

15 Ibid., 415.

16 Ibid., 415–19.

17 Ibid., 428–29.

18 Ibid., 421.

19 Ibid., 433.

20 Ibid., 421.

21 Ibid., 434.

22 See the excursus in Pinker, *Enlightenment*, 439–43.

23 Holbach, *Système*, 341.

24 Ibid., 343.

25 Ibid.

26 Ibid., 345.

27 Ibid., 357.

28 Ibid., 353–55.

29 Ibid., 347–53.

30 Pinker, *Enlightenment*, 421.

31 Ibid., 394–95.

32 Richard Dawkins, *The God Delusion* (Boston: Houghton Mifflin, 2006), 50.

Chapter 18

Identity and Injustice*

Samir Gandesha

Platonic "political philosophy" is a contradiction in terms insofar as in his dialogues Plato places "politics" and "philosophy" in an antagonistic relationship with one another. And, as dramatized in dialogues such as *Phaedo, Crito,* and *Apology,* such antagonism has roots in Athenian democracy's punishment of Plato's teacher, Socrates, offering him the choice of either exile or death for "corrupting the minds of the young, and of believing in deities of his own invention instead of the gods recognized by the state."[1] Socrates, of course, chose to drink the lethal hemlock. Philosophy, one could then say, is born less of *Thaumazein* (wonder)[2] than it is of *trauma,* about which the tragic poets like Aeschylus and Sophocles knew much. They intimated something of this hidden origin of philosophy, as in the exemplary case of Oedipus, whose own "philosophical" solution to the Sphinx's riddle saves the city.

The inauguration of Western philosophy as a response to this original trauma in Plato's writings is repeated (with important differences) throughout its long history: St. Augustine writes *City of God* in response to the sacking of Rome; Machiavelli composes the *Prince* after being physically tortured in the aftermath of losing his position with the Florentine Republic with the triumph of the Medici Family; Thomas Hobbes produces *Leviathan* as the hostilities in the English Civil War reach a fevered pitch; G.W.F. Hegel famously completes the *Phenomenology of Spirit* just as he glimpses Napoleon ("*Geist* on horseback") and his armies enter the city of Jena; and Theodor W. Adorno writes *Negative Dialectics* with the hope that Auschwitz will not repeat itself. Philosophy represents, contra Alain Badiou, a kind of *negative* fidelity to the event.

Propelled by its originary trauma, Platonism embodies the aspiration to, as it were, make the world safe for philosophy. It seeks to do so by mastering the manifestly dangerous unpredictability of political life. Platonism can never forget the perils confronting the philosopher who, acting as a gadfly, poses questions to his interlocutors they are unable to answer, leading to the maddening recognition that the opinions (*doxa*) they confidently set forth as truthful fail to stand up to reasoned scrutiny.

Plato's obsessive drive to master contingency is exemplified by the late-period dialogue, the *Laws*, in which he seeks to outline with detailed precision the good city as a kind of rule of forms or ideas or an "ideocracy." The precarious position of the philosopher is no more dramatically expressed, however, than in the *Republic*'s famous cave allegory.[3] After having returned from the arduous journey up beyond the cave and having glimpsed the Form of the Good, the philosopher heroically takes upon himself the task—at the risk of torture or worse—of returning to the cave to convince its inhabitants that what they take for reality is, in actual fact, appearance, mere shadow play, from which shackles they need to be freed by way of an arduous dialectic.

The characterization of Plato's mobilization of philosophy in a kind of "tyranny of truth" against politics is the interpretation that Hannah Arendt offers.[4] It is an interpretation of particular importance for her unique appreciation of the political as the realm of contingency, plurality, and, above all, appearances. Were Plato's account of politics as the shadowy realm of the cave correct, then political judgment would entail subsuming particulars beneath pre-given rules or *Eidos* (forms), accessible through an act of *anamnesis* or unforgetting.

Yet, politics cannot rightfully be understood in such terms but, rather, is rooted in particulars from which one then must, through an act of imagination, generate a general rule or a concept, which is to say: a *universal*. Politics, in other words, has to do not with the *unum verum* understood in opposition to *doxa* but rather, according to Arendt, starts with an understanding of doxa as the phenomenological articulation of the *dokei moi*, "what appears to me."[5] This is the assumption that the shared world opens up to me *differently* from the way it does to others. Not unlike the Church's treatment of the teachings of Jesus Christ, Plato's response to the trauma of Socrates's death, to remember and honour his mentor, is, in actuality, the opposite insofar as Plato replaces the latter's phenomenological *maiuetics* aiming at bringing forth the citizen's truth from doxa with an account, *dialegesthai*, that aimed at destroying such doxa.[6]

For Plato, construing the cave as an allegory for politics as the realm of a kind of shadow play showed clearly that the only way to properly address the realm of the political was by way of an exit strategy. In this sense, the allegory is to be taken with utmost seriousness. The philosopher, in leaving the cave, exits the political space and enters into the light cast by the eternal form of the Good. And such an exit from the political, at least on this non-ironic reading, entailed its constitution as a mirroring or mimesis of divine logos accessible only by virtue of the conceptual journey of dialectic that retraced the philosopher's haptic ascent upwards towards the sunlight. The highest good, in this account, was the *Vita Contemplativa*, the life spent in quiet contemplation. The highest good, therefore, lay somewhere beyond or outside of the space of the political.

Plato's anti-political bias provides the context necessary to fully grasp the key importance of the concepts "pariah" and "parvenu" to Arendt's political theory. If philosophy seeks to take its leave of the political, then, in Arendt's view, the pariah can find a home only within this space in which difference is permitted to appear as such. Pariah and parvenu denote social difference and identity, respectively.

These two categories represent the two options for members of a minority group in the midst of a majority with different culture, religion, or ethnic identity. Arendt's example, of course, was that of the unique position of Jews in Germany.[7] Before what Max Weber refers to as this original European "pariah people"[8] lay two options. The first was to remain separate and apart from the larger gentile society and maintain their own language, Yiddish, and religious and cultural practices, and face from time to time the occasional pogrom and restrictions on their political liberties. The second, in contrast, was to assimilate, often by conversion to Christianity and attendant change of name, into the norms, values, and ultimately identity of the dominant society.

As becomes clear in Arendt's vitally important biography of Rahel Varnhagen, the pariah was to be understood specifically in terms of European-Jewish experience in the eighteenth and nineteenth centuries. Out of experiences of social exclusion, marginalization, and anti-Semitism, the figure of the pariah constituted a "hidden tradition."[9] This hidden tradition emphasized "all vaunted Jewish qualities—the 'Jewish heart,' humanity, humour, disinterested intelligence—(as) pariah qualities."[10] Above all, the pariah was clear about the importance of thinking as a prelude to speech and action—central categories for understanding Arendt's political theory.

This tradition manifests what, for Arendt, constitutes a third option, adopted from Bernard Lazare, the idea of a "conscious pariah," one who is aware of and embraces as a matter of political decision their position as someone "never quite at home in this world."[11] Such an awareness made possible solidarity with other such outcasts.

For Arendt, thinking through the fraught and shifting relations between these two categories, again as initially applied to Jews, enabled her to clarify the relation that is so central to her mature political theory as set forth in her 1958 book, *The Human Condition*. This is the relation between the "social" and the "political": as she puts it in the *Origins of Totalitarianism*: "During the 150 years when Jews truly lived amidst, and not just in the neighborhood of, Western European peoples, they always had to pay with political misery for social glory and with social insult for political success."[12] The pariah in this sense, perched as he was on the boundary between the social and the political, being simultaneously insider *and* outsider, embodies a central political virtue as expressed by both Socrates and Immanuel Kant: the capacity to view things from an "enlarged mentality," which, interestingly, in Arendt's gloss on Kant, entails training "one's imagination to go visiting."[13]

For Arendt, Platonism establishes the dominance of identity over difference insofar as it establishes the real Idea over and against the particular, understood as Appearance. By formulating a third alternative, that of the "conscious pariah," the outsider capable of acting with other such outsiders, Arendt is able to articulate a nuanced relation between difference and identity. Such a relation becomes central to Arendt's notion of the political as the realm of appearances comprised by the being together of those who are different. If totalitarian space is constituted by the "squeezing of individuals together as if by a band of iron,"[14] then the space of the genuinely public realm is one that, far from being reduced or minimized, is opened up between subjects. Such an openness is precisely, then, the space of *appearances*. The conscious pariah was he whose pariahdom was, as it were, a free act, and in such a free act was grounded the capability of acting together with others who had also freely embraced their own pariah status. In such capacity for collective action, Arendt located an alternative source of power as an "acting together" to the conventional Hobbesian-Weberian definition understood as domination, as "power over."

Like Hannah Arendt, Ian Angus can be read as offering a profound challenge to Platonism throughout his myriad writings. Philosophically, Angus's work begins with the experience of "what appears to me" in his early engagement with Husserlian phenomenology. In his later work in the field of Communication Studies, in which he produces a fascinating communications theoretical approach to the social, quite different from that of Jürgen Habermas, Angus deconstructs the fundamental Platonic opposition between philosophy and rhetoric, concept and metaphor, so crucial to the *agon* between philosophy, on the one side, and rhetoric and poetry, on the other. In Canadian Studies, Angus emphasizes, again, the necessity of engaging in the activity of "locative thought," on reflecting on the situated and indeed peripheral nature of English Canada and of beginning there with what is "one's own" (*Eigenen*). All of these concerns, I think, are brought together in a robust, original, and enduring defence of democracy understood not simply as a constellation of institutions comprised of periodic elections and majoritarian rule tempered by constitutional limits, the rule of law, and procedural justice. Rather, for Angus, democracy can be seen as a set of *struggles* between precisely the realm of the social and that of the political, as Arendt has it.[15] Democracy is not identical with the state; rather, as Miguel Abansour suggests in his reading of Karl Marx's critique of G.W.F. Hegel: "A disorder that is not destined to be another order, democracy has an irreducible meaning as a refusal of synthesis, a refusal of order—an invention in time of the political relation that overflows and overtakes the State. For if democracy sets itself in opposition to the State, it is because politics comes up ceaselessly against it."[16]

That is, democratic forms are developed and extended through the struggles for inclusion by historically excluded groups—*pariahs*—such as workers and (white) suffragettes, and subsequently the civil rights movement and later Indigenous liberation movements such as AIM. Today, we could say that democracy is deepened and extended by social movements that bring plurality, struggle, and a principle of criticality into the public real. As Abansour notes,

> In order to understand properly this peculiarity of democracy, it is essential not only to reject the ideologies of consensus—notably that of a consensus between democracy and the State—but moreover to revitalize the idea of conflict, to be wary of making democracy tilt toward the banality of compromise, and to grant it instead a maximum of power. Which is to say that democracy is the always possible emergence of human struggle, the surge of the originary division that brings with it the menace of dissolution, of social explosion.[17]

For Angus, social movements such as queer and ecological movements, to take but two examples, struggling for the rights of sex and gender dissidents to express their love and identities freely and for better environmental protections if not the recognition of, as in Bolivia, the rights of "mother earth," respectively, are the lifeblood of democracy. Such social movements constitute what he felicitously calls "emergent publics," which, in his view, then seek inclusion within the broader public sphere, and such struggles for inclusion have an enlightening function of deepening democratic practice and broadening democratic self-understandings.[18] Queer and ecological movements critically challenge and transform given understandings of sex and gender relations of each to another as well as our relation to the non-human animal world and to the "land."

Excluded particulars perform the function of revealing the existing universal as failing to live up to its own *Eidos* or idea and, at the same time, contributing to an ongoing and, indeed, interminable process of *universalization*. Perhaps implicitly evoking Arendt's emphasis on natality or the "new beginning," Angus argues that "democracy isn't a finished set of institutions. It is just starting. What is important about democracy is always just starting." Or, as Jacques

Derrida says, democracy, properly understood, is always "to come" (*la démocratie à venir*).

What is somewhat questionable about Angus's account of democracy, however, is that it relies on the undefended assumption that the boundaries of particular groups constituting emergent publics will remain "fluid and difficult to define."[19] It doesn't fully recognize the possibility of a reification of the particular in identity politics: in other words, an all-too-sharp and exclusionary process of "identification" that subverts the possibility of solidarity among, to use Arendt's appropriation of Bernard Lazare's term, "conscious pariahs" (although he does acknowledge this in our conversation with him, see Chapter 1). That is to say, by no longer being understood as a *specific kind of relation* to other particulars and a given (partial) universal, the particular becomes substantialized, or "thingified" (reified). In contrast with the enlightening function of previous social movements understood as emergent and therefore also *critical* publics, with identity politics we witness the closing down of the possibility of criticism and therefore publicity.

Today, identity politics of the left reinforces the neo-liberal consensus[20] on the socio-economic order of society, while offering to include "marginalized" groups or at least their representatives. So here we witness the increasingly exclusionary appeals to categories of race, ethnicity, gender, sexual orientation, and expression, leading to not a deepening but an authoritarian foreshortening of publicity itself. On the right, we see the rise of various forms of ethno-nationalism and religious fundamentalisms. Asad Haider provides an exemplary critique of identity politics. Haider's account of identity politics must be regarded as a missed opportunity, however, insofar as it fails to make an immanent critique of some of the implicit premises upon which contemporary identity politics is elaborated.

In an editorial in the *New York Times* written 10 days after the 2016 presidential election, Professor of Humanities at Columbia University Mark Lilla argued that the reason for Trump's victory wasn't, as the leftist "Whitelash" thesis held, due to his ability to translate economic insecurity into racism but rather that the Democrats under Hillary Clinton were overly focused on identity questions. Identity politics, Lilla argued, were more "expressive" than "persuasive," and therefore never won elections but often lost them.[21] Clearly, Lilla was oblivious to the way in which Trump had actually won the election, in part, on the basis of a white identity politics. Leaving that to one side, Lilla's argument, subsequently elaborated in his 2017 book entitled *The Once and Future Liberal: After Identity Politics*,[22] was that US liberals within the Democratic Party needed to spend less time on emphasizing race, ethnicity, sexual orientation, et cetera—that is, what *divided* Americans—than on what held them together, what they shared *in common*, in particular the great liberal-democratic institutions as bequeathed by the Founding Fathers.

This former protégé of neo-conservative Irving Kristol was, as might have been anticipated, pilloried for his intervention, which was in typical *ad hominem* fashion attributed to his privileged white male status. The rancour produced by Lilla's first foray into public discourse indicated two things about identity politics. The first is how very American identity politics appears to be in its origins, though it has made significant headway in the larger English-speaking world, Canada, and the United Kingdom, in particular, probably in Germany and France as well. Running counter to the US's general trade deficit, American "theory" remains a major export. The second is how increasingly contentious, and frankly dysfunctional, US politics has become. Nonetheless, since Lilla's op-ed and book, two other notable books have appeared on identity politics in the wake of Trump's election: *Identity: The Demand for Dignity and the Politics of Resentment*[23] by Francis Fukuyama, the author of the once celebrated "end of history" thesis; and *The Lies That Bind: Rethinking Identity*[24] by the esteemed gay Ghanaian-English philosopher Kwame Anthony Appiah. The former argues that the rise of identity politics is the result of an excessive form of what the Greeks called *thymos* (θυμός), or "spiritedness," entailing the desire for recognition; the latter shows the fuzzy or imprecise nature of the identity categories that are often taken as immutable givens or essences.

While Lilla's liberalism emphasizes universality rather than particularity, for the left the key question has been the relative priority of class, on the one side, and race, on the other, within social movements since at least Herbert Marcuse's call for a "Great Refusal." This debate has been a feature of left politics since the late 1970s and has, in recent years, come in for increasing critical scrutiny. For example, Adolph Reed Jr. and Walter Benn Michaels have been especially indefatigable critics of identity politics, arguing that it is central to the neo-liberal transformation of the market-state relations. As Benn Michaels put it in a special issue of the left-liberal magazine *The Nation*, identity politics is "the politics of an upper class that has no problem with seeing people being left behind as long as they're not being left behind because of their race or sex. They're seeking to legitimate class structure, rather than abolish it."[25] So, in other words, from this perspective, identity politics represents the attempt on the part of historically oppressed and excluded groups to gain inclusion to a social order founded on exploitation and violence. It is not difficult to discern the perversity of this logic, for inasmuch as identity-based anti-racism is a strategy of what Keeanga-Yamahtta Taylor calls in her book, *From Black Lives Matter to Black Liberation*, "putting Black faces in high places,"[26] it deepens a key structural condition for the perpetuation of racism in the first place: socio-economic inequality.[27] What we witness, therefore, is the collision of skyrocketing inequality, on the one side, and an accelerated transformation of cultural values, on the other. This can be seen to contribute to the context in which authoritarian populism can flourish.

As Lilla's contribution shows, it wasn't, however, until the US presidential election of 2016 that identity politics went mainstream. The terms of debate, particularly within the Democratic

Party, paralleled certain debates within political theory on the relative priority between a "politics of recognition" and a "politics of redistribution," as in the debate between Axel Honneth and Nancy Fraser.[28] Hillary Clinton, the wife of a man who, long before Barack Obama, was referred to by Toni Morrison in the *New Yorker* as the "first Black President,"[29] used Kimblerlé Crenshaw's concept of "intersectionality"[30]—the idea that there exist several overlapping, which is to say, "intersecting," structures of oppression—to appeal to women, Latinos, African Americans, and other "marginalized" groups while dismissing what she insultingly called "a basket of deplorables," the "racists and the haters," in her bid to become a presidential nominee.[31] In contrast, the independent senator from Vermont, Bernie Sanders, riding the wave of Occupy and like left populism in the UK and Spain, emphasized the growing wealth gap between the 1 per cent and the 99 per cent and advocated breaking up large investment banks, free tuition, and so forth. Sanders was thought not to have properly "resonated' with Black voters, even after his critical dialogue with members of Black Lives Matter (BLM), sparked by the disruption by Marissa Johnson and others of one of Sanders's rallies in Seattle in August 2015, leading to the inclusion of BLM personnel in his staff.

The 2016 election was also the jumping-off point for Asad Haider's book, *Mistaken Identity: Race and Class in the Age of Trump*.[32] Haider first offers a genealogy of an identity politics initially theorized as central to a revolutionary transformation of a racist, patriarchal-capitalist order to its recent appropriation by the Democratic Party. Absent a structural critique of capitalism, Haider argues, identity politics ends up taking the bourgeois, heterosexual, white masculinist ideal as normative. He goes on to poignantly show how identity politics has not only become the ideology of the prevailing neo-liberal order, as critics such as Walter Benn Michaels and Adolph Reed Jr. have cogently argued, but also short-circuits genuine movements on the left seeking to transform it. He provides the example of the counter-productive and occasionally comical debates amongst people of colour on the campus of UC Santa Cruz, where Haider was a graduate student, over the use of the word "occupy" in reference to protests against the administration, which had recently raised tuition fees. He also shows the much more serious political conundrum of the "Afro-Pessimism" of Frank Wilderson that was to exercise growing influence on #BlackLivesMatter insofar as it refused to reciprocate the solidarity offered to the movement by Palestinian activists.[33] This, I think, is the most important aspect of Haider's argument but one that he fails to develop fully enough.

Haider addresses the deep paradox of a tenacious attachment among young activists to the idea of race, in spite of the fact that it has been thoroughly demystified as possessing little or no substance in biological terms. The following chapter is a fascinating reflection on the standoff between Philip Roth and Amiri Baraka, as well as a reflection on what is, for Haider, the exemplary case of Rachel Dolezal. A white woman who passed for several years as African American and, indeed, played a role in her local chapter of the National Association for the Advancement of Colored People (NAACP), Dolezal is exemplary, Haider argues, precisely because she engages in "a peculiar introjection of white guilt."[34] Haider then seeks to understand the rise of Trump through Stuart Hall's pioneering work on authoritarian populism as well as Wendy Brown's development of Walter Benjamin's notion of "Left-wing Melancholy"—the full-scale embrace by the left of its own marginality and failure. Drawing upon the work of Massimiliano Tomba, Haider develops an alternative that returns to the original spirit of the earliest statement of identity politics by articulating a case for an "insurgent universality," based not on an abstract concept of rights bearers but, rather, on "particular and concrete individuals—women, the poor, and slaves—and their political and social agency."[35]

Overall, Haider's is a bracing and valuable contribution *from the left* to the often vituperative debates swirling around identity politics. Rather than focusing, like Lilla, on the Democratic Party, however, Haider locates its origins in the earlier, pioneering work of the Black lesbian feminist Combahee River Collective. At the same time, Haider articulates a worry about the capacity of identity politics today to serve as the basis for a radical political agenda. In contrast, therefore, to Lilla's rather patronizing dismissal, Haider engages in a genuinely immanent critique of identity; that is, he criticizes its contemporary *practice* on the basis of its own strongest *theoretical self-understanding*. Accordingly, Haider defines contemporary identity politics as the "neutralisation of movements against racial oppression."[36] This relocates identity politics in a liberal agenda of seeking restitution for victimhood by way of a juridical discourse. Quoting Judith Butler, Haider maintains that "what we call identity politics is produced by a state which can only allocate recognition and rights to subjects totalised by the particularity that constitutes their plaintiff status."[37] Contemporary identity politics, in this view, remains fatally trapped within the liberal-bourgeois institutions of the state and its laws.

While Haider's impulse to try to understand the intertwined nature of race and class is correct, it is important to emphasize the way in which race cannot in any straightforward way be understood in terms of Stuart Hall's Althusserian formulation—which Haider himself draws upon—as "the modality in which class is lived."[38] In contemporary identity politics, race, gender, ethnicity, sexual orientation, and other identities demand recognition and affirmation, and in societies constituted, in part, by the mis-recognition or non-recognition of these identities, this is perfectly understandable and legitimate, to some extent at least. This is especially the case with trans and Indigenous identities that have asserted and reasserted themselves, respectively, in recent years with particular force. Yet, proletarian identity—not unlike the condition of homelessness—cannot be understood in quite the same way. Thought of in radical terms, such a form of identity is not simply an empirical sociological category but manifests a form of structural negativity that, as such, demands its own *negation*, just as people who are homeless, far from wanting their homeless condition to be recognized and affirmed, want it to be abolished through, amongst other things, the provision of adequate housing. Capital cannot properly "include" the proletariat on the basis of whose un-remunerated surplus labour its own expanded reproduction is premised. In other words, while other identity categories have an interest in recognition and affirmation that, arguably, can be met within capitalism, the proletariat simply cannot. The realization of proletarian identity is, ultimately, negative rather than affirmative; proletarian "identity," unlike most other identities, has an interest in *its own self-dissolution along with that of class society as a whole*.

I would suggest that rather than an individualistic, rights-based model, as Haider argues in invoking Butler, identity politics is based on a particularly reified account of identity. Identity politics entails a *proprietary* relation to a reified form of experience—unchanging, fixed, substantive—that can be understood as the possession or property of a given group that is, paradoxically, constituted by that very form of experience. In German the word for "authenticity" or *Eigentlichkeit* is closely associated with the word for "property" or *Eigentum*. Identity politics often makes a claim to authenticity, and such claims are closely linked to questions of ownership rights. This is why identity politics is often embroiled in questions of cultural appropriation. One suspects that, despite his telling anecdotes, it is far from clear that Haider fully appreciates precisely how deleterious and fractious identity politics can be for left politics, a glimpse of which we saw in the treatment of the Sanders campaign by Hillary Clinton and her backers at the Democratic National Committee.

I want to illustrate some of the profound dangers of identity politics for the left, broadly understood. Along with the case of the Hillary Clinton's presidential run, these can be seen in three additional important cases: those of Rebecca Tuvel, Sky Gilbert, and Dana Schutz.

The first is the case of Rebecca Tuvel, an assistant professor of philosophy in the US, who wrote an article entitled "In Defence of Transracialism,"[39] which was published in the feminist philosophy journal *Hypatia*. The article compared transgendered and transracial identities, comparing the celebrated cases of Caitlyn Jenner, who underwent a public transition from male to female, and Rachel Dolezal, the white woman who assumed an African-American identity and even played a role in her local NAACP—an historically important civil rights organization. Despite the fact that her article went through the formal process of peer review, upon its appearance, it drew the considerable anger of a large contingent of Tuvel's peers, some 800 in fact, who signed a petition demanding the article's retraction. The claims were that by "dead-naming" Caitlyn Jenner, she had committed "epistemic violence." She had also, apparently, failed to consult with particular Critical Race theorists, which, if she had done so, would not have made the grave, even dangerous, errors that she did. The larger, implicit argument—counter-intuitive as it sounds—was that it could in no way be possible for such an analogy to hold—gender was performative and malleable while race was apparently not. The larger claim that is of interest for our purpose is that this was one of the pitfalls of "ideal theory": having someone who was neither trans nor racialized addressing such matters. That is to say, only trans philosophers can address questions that pertain to the trans community. This, of course, means that only Germans can legitimately write about the *Science of Logic* or that only Hindus can legitimately comment on the *Upanishads*. Yet, one wonders: Would the inverse corollary hold? That is, the corollary that, say, neither African Americans nor Hispanics should be permitted to write about Greek philosophy or Roman poetry?

The second case is that of queer Canadian playwright and drag queen Sky Gilbert, who founded Toronto's Buddies in Bad Times Theatre in 1979—the "bad times" in the name would quickly come to signify the time of the AIDS crisis and the conservative homophobic backlash with which it would be met in the mid- to late 1980s. Gilbert himself personally faced routine attempts to have the theatre's funding pulled; he faced frequent abuse and attacks and even death threats. But he managed to maintain what would come to be a pillar of the progressive arts scene, particularly for the gay community in Canada. A reading of his 1984 play, *Drag Queens in Outer Space*, was planned for the 40th-anniversary celebrations of the theatre. But in the meantime, Gilbert had written an open letter criticizing a book entitled *I'm Afraid of Men* by transwoman of colour Vivek Sharya, followed by a poem, "I'm afraid of Woke People," documenting persecution that he experienced by some in the trans community. As a result of the controversy spawned by these two interventions, the artistic director of the theatre, Evalyn Parry, "pressed pause" (her words) on the reading of Gilbert's play and instead hosted a "longtable" to enable a discussion of how certain groups felt marginalized by Gilbert's interventions.

While the other two examples exemplify the way in which identity politics relies on a proprietary relation to a reified form of experience, an especially good case is that of Hannah Black's infamous open letter attacking white painter Dana Schutz's painting of Emmett Till, the African-American boy beaten to death by white supremacists for allegedly looking the "wrong way" at a white woman in 1955. The painting is entitled *Open Casket* (2016) and was exhibited during the Whitney Biennale in 2016. "The painting," the letter reiterates several times, "must go." Co-signed by some 47 other artists, curators, and critics, it demands not only that the painting be removed from the exhibition but also that it actually be *destroyed*. The key reason for this, according to Black, is that Schutz has *no right* to the experience of Black suffering. One immediately wonders whether West German students required a "right" to Jewish suffering to raise the question of the Holocaust and collective German guilt in the tumultuous years of 1967 to 1977? Why Dana Schutz should be any different is far from clear.

Black's letter is instructive because it makes a truth claim about a particular representation of suffering without carefully attending to the painting's own sensuous particularity (as Zadie Smith precisely does in her response to *Open Casket* in a 2017 article in *Harper's Magazine*). The very premise of the claim confuses ontology with epistemology: that the representation was bereft of truthfulness by virtue of fact that the race of the artist was simply wrong. The claim has the status of an a priori over an a posteriori; it is apodictic rather than based on attention to the details of the framing of its subject matter, its composition, use of colour, texture of its brush strokes, et cetera. It therefore rules out in advance the possibility of a critical judgment of the work's overall success or failure. The claim, surely, is not simply that the work cannot *succeed* but that it also cannot *fail*. It ought not even be permitted to fail. It rules out in advance Samuel Beckett's claim that artworks can fail and they can fail better and they can fail worse. Artworks, as Walter Benjamin and Theodor Adorno both suggested, are constituted by both truth and falsity, and the work of criticism is to draw out their "truth content" (*Wahrgehalt*). When they fail better, they fail in such a way that we can learn something from them, including, for example, the conditions of their own (im) possibility. Perhaps, at some level, *all* artworks seeking to express or represent suffering must fail insofar as such artworks remain deeply complicit with the world that produces such suffering in the first place. Surely, it is the role of art criticism to make such judgments about the nature of such failures? Yet, Hannah Black moralistically rules out such criticism in advance by advocating the painting's liquidation.

This demand for the work's destruction is the logical conclusion of the radical particularism of identity politics or the idea that identity-based groups are unified by certain experiences that other groups simply have no *right* to. The relationship is one suggestive of property ownership, yet a relationship also overdetermined by a sense that the loss of such property entails not just a monetary loss but an ontological one—a loss of being itself. From this perspective, claims or representations made by members of one group about another are not simply to be addressed by judgments, and, therefore, criticisms, because such claims and/or representations constitute hateful and harmful attacks on these very groups.

This is also, for example, what came into play in the much-discussed case of Rebecca Tuvel's March 2017 *Hypatia* article on transracial identities and the open letter signed by over 800 academics demanding its retraction as opposed to its critical discussion (as mentioned above).

If it is true that central to identity politics is a reified account of experience, then a much more promising approach to it, I would suggest, is be found in Frantz Fanon's dynamic understanding of experience. Given that Fanon's work, especially *Black Skin, White Masks,* is so central to identity politics in general, and to Afro-pessimism in particular—from which, in fact, the main tropes of Hannah Black's letter seem to be drawn—it is unfortunate that Haider's immanent critique of identity politics remains confined to the US Black radical tradition. Or, to put it another way, it is unfortunate that it doesn't seek to engage in an immanent critique of Afro-pessimism's own rather one-sided appropriation of Fanon's thought. In what is surely one of the best accounts of Fanon's thought, *Fanon's Dialectic of Experience* (1997), Ghanaian philosopher Ato Sekyi-Otu argues that it is within a "dramaturgical" structure that we must seek to understand Fanon's "narrative of liberation." "Thanks to this formal characteristic," he argues, "Fanon's narrative can give credence to the apprehension of a historical object in its immediate mode of appearance, and yet prepare us for a comprehension of this object—that is to say, a fuller knowledge of its appearance and its conditions of intelligibility."[40] Attention must be paid, therefore, to the various speech acts that constitute the often contradictory dramaturgical "stagings" of experience itself.

Through a reading of Fanon's *Wretched of the Earth* (rather than *Black Skin, White Masks*), Sekyi-Otu charts the movement of experience beyond the Manichean world constituted by the binary logic of colonialism itself, a logic sedimented in the very architecture and built environment of colonized space as brilliantly represented by Gillo Pontecorvo in *The Battle of Algiers* (1966). Once the armed struggle commences, the colonial world, characterized by an Aristotelian logic of mutual exclusivity, quickly gives way to a more properly dialectical and temporal logic of mediation in which difference between colonized and colonizer is transformed into an internal differentiation of the colonized themselves. The becoming-human of the colonized corresponds, paradoxically, with the dynamic disclosure of difference within the colonized rather than the static and reified difference constituting the Manichean world of the colony. The immediacy of *identity* based on the supposedly "natural" fact of race now is fundamentally altered through what Karl Marx called, in the first volume of *Capital*, a transformation in the dramatis personae into *non-identity*; that is, divisions based on social class between a nascent national bourgeoisie, on the one hand, and workers and peasants, on the other, come into view. Sekyi-Otu felicitously calls this the "dialectical enlightenment" of the post-colonial world, one in which "Reason's triumph, the faculty of dialectical disclosure, is in Fanon achieved experientially through a corrosive destruction of the rigidity and simplicity to which a racialised apprehension of the world had reduced everything. Thanks to this 'bitter discovery' of exploitative relations and distributive injustice as intraracial facts, as human, all-too-human possibilities, the nascent postcolonial subject is ready for a veritable political and epistemic reorientation."[41]

What is important to grasp is the centrality of a reified or static understanding of *experience* lying at the heart of identity politics. If contemporary identity politics can be understood as *neo-liberal*, it is because it internalizes the logic of the value form at a particularly deep level. This becomes especially clear in the example of Hannah Black where we find precisely what Sekyi-Otu calls the "rigidity and simplicity to which a racialised apprehension of the world reduced everything." It is such a "racialised apprehension" that grounds her demand for the destruction of an artwork. If the work opens up a world, in Martin Heidegger's sense, then, in demanding *work*-destruction, Black nihilistically demands *world*-destruction—the destruction of the structure of meaning and of sense that the work generates, but also the basis on which that very same work may itself be *criticized*, as exemplified by the oppositional response of Afro-American painter Parker Bright to *Open Casket*. Such world destruction, at the same time, then, profoundly forecloses the possibility of the "insurgent universality" that Haider champions. Indeed, it forecloses the very possibility of politics as such.

Notes to Chapter 18:

* This is a revised and extended version of Samir Gandesha, "Insurgent Universality," *Radical Philosophy* 2, no. 4 (Spring 2019), 89-93.

1 Plato, *Apology, The Collected Dialogues of Plato Including the Letters*, ed. Edith Hamilton and Huntington Cairns (Princeton: Princeton University Press, 1989), 24b.

2 Ibid., *Theaetetus*, 155c-d.

3 Plato, *Republic, Collected Dialogues*, ed. Edith Hamilton and Huntington Cairns (Princeton: Princeton University Press, 1945), 514A–521B.

4 Hannah Arendt, "Philosophy and Politics," *Social Research* 57, no. 1 (Spring, 1990): 78. See also Alan Ryan's interpretation in his *On Politics*, vol. I: *A History of Political Thought: Herodotus to Machiavelli* (New York: Liveright Publishing Corporation, 2012), 31–70.

5 Arendt, "Philosophy and Politics," 80.

6 Ibid., 90–91.

7 Of course, "pariah" also referred to refugees and stateless persons more generally.

8 Hannah Arendt, *The Jewish Writings*, ed. Jerome Kohn and Ron H. Feldman (New York: Schocken Books, 2007), 276.

9 Hannah Arendt, "The Jew as Pariah: A Hidden Tradition," in *The Jewish Writings*, 275–97.

10 Hannah Arendt, "We Refugee," in *The Jewish Writings*, 274.

11 Arendt, "The Jew as Pariah," 283.

12 Hannah Arendt, *The Origins of Totalitarianism* (New York: Harcourt Inc., 1976), 56.

13 Hannah Arendt, *Lectures on Kant's Political Philosophy*, ed. Ronald Beiner (Chicago: University of Chicago Press, 1992), 43.

14 Hannah Arendt, *Origins of Totalitarianism* (New York: Harcourt, Brace, & Co., 1973), 465.

15 Ian Angus, *Emergent Publics: An Essay on Social Movements and Democracy* (Winnipeg: Arbeiter Ring Publishing, 2002).

16 Miguel Abansour, *Democracy Against the State: Marx's Machiavellian Moment* (Cambridge: Polity, 2011), 101.

17 Ibid., 99.

18 Angus, *Emergent Publics*, 67.

19 Angus, *Emergent Publics*, 63.

20 Chantal Mouffe, *For a Left Populism* (London: Verso, 2018).

21 Mark Lilla, "The End of Identity Liberalism," *New York Times*, November 18, 2016, accessed April 12, 2019, https://www.nytimes.com/2016/11/20/opinion/sunday/the-end-of-identity-liberalism.html.

22 Mark Lilla, *The Once and Future Liberal* (San Francisco: Harper, 2017).

23 Francis Fukuyama, *Identity: The Demand for Dignity and the Politics of Resentment* (New York: Farrar, Straus and Giroux, 2018).

24 Kwame Anthony Appiah, *The Lies That Bind: Rethinking Identity* (New York: Liveright, 2018).

25 Walter Benn Michael, "What Is the Left without Identity Politics?" *The Nation*, December 16, 2016, https://www.thenation.com/article/what-is-the-left-without-identity-politics/.

26 Keeanga-Yamahtta Taylor, *From Black Lives Matter to Black Liberation* (Chicago: Haymarket Books, 2016), ch. 3.

27 Samir Gandesha, "Is Symbolic Politics an Impediment to Economic Equality?" *openDemocracy*, April 18, 2018, *https://www.opendemocracy.net/en/is-symbolic-politics-impediment-to-economic-equality/.*

28 Axel Honneth and Nancy Fraser, *Redistribution or Recognition: A Politico-Philosophical Exchange* (London: Verso, 2004).

29 Toni Morrison, "Comment," *New Yorker*, October 5th, 1998, https://www.newyorker.com/magazine/1998/10/05/comment-6543.

30 Kimberlé Crenshaw, "Demarginalizing the Intersection of Race and Sex: A Black Feminist Critique of Antidiscrimination Doctrine, Feminist Theory and Antiracist Politics," *University of Chicago Legal*

Forum 1(1989), https://chicagounbound.uchicago.edu/cgi/viewcontent.cgi?referer=&httpsredir=1&article=1052&context=uclf.

31 See BBC September 10, 2016, accessed April 5, 2019, https://www.bbc.com/news/av/election-us-2016-37329812/clinton-half-of-trump-supporters-basket-of-deplorables.

32 Asad Haider, *Mistaken Identity: Race and Class in the Age of Trump* (London: Verso, 2018).

33 See the interview with Wilderson that is cited by Haider. http://sfbay-anarchists.org/wp- content/uploads/2015/01/frank-b-wilderson-iii-were-trying-to-destroy-the-world-antiblackness-police-violence- after-ferguson.pdf.

34 Haider, 81.

35 Massimiliano Tomba as quoted in Haider, 108

36 Haider, 12.

37 Judith Butler as quoted in Haider, 10.

38 The original formulation is from Hall et al.'s pioneering 1978 *Policing the Crisis: Mugging, the State and Law and Order* (London: Red Globe Press, 2013), 394.

39 Rebecca Tuvel, "In Defence of Transracialism," *Hypatia: Journal of Feminist Philosophy* 32, no. 2 (Spring, 2017): 263–78.

40 Ato Sekyi-Otu, *Fanon's Dialectic of Experience* (Cambridge, MA: Harvard University Press, 1997), 52-53.

41 Sekyi-Otu, 115.

Chapter 19

Toward Critical Topology, or How to Act in the Playgrounds of Being*

Peyman Vahabzadeh

> In order to escape the trap the System has become one must divest oneself both of the optimistic notion that it can be reformed, or replaced, and accept the parasitism on, and inessentiality to, the System that this implies. I was struck by the compatibility of this notion of anarchism with a Heideggerian concept of modernity as the scientific-technological domination of the world and also with Reiner Schürmann's construction of an anarchistic self-constituting practical subject as a "protest against busyness" on its ruins.
>
> IAN ANGUS, "SHARING SECRETS, OR ON BURROWING IN PUBLIC" (2001)

> Hegemony works much more by domesticating and absorbing criticism than by repressing it.
>
> IAN ANGUS, *THE PRIMAL SCENES OF COMMUNICATION* (2000)

If we consider Reiner Schürmann's "hypothesis of epochal or metaphysical closure"—inspired by Martin Heidegger—as speaking to the very history that we are living right now in the West, instead of some esoteric, conceptual plaything for the armchair academic, then we can revisit the cultural, social, and political processes of our time in light of the possibility of the changing principles of intelligibility governing our age—the (changing) *principles that spectrally appear to us primarily through action.*

Schürmann's "hypothesis" dwells in Heidegger's proposition that the age of metaphysics has reached its point of withering away in the West. For Heidegger, this age began with the end of the pre-Socratics in the classical Greek period and it has reached us at this time of the atomic bomb and prevalence of technology in which all beings, humans included, are reduced to resource. Different epochs within the history of the West have shared the domination of seemingly unshakable foundations that hold phenomena as absolute representations under an "ultimate referent."[1] The Greek *physis,* Latin *natur,* Christian God, and modern *ego cogito,* as foundational gestures rising from humble beginnings (*arché*) and growing into universal holds, each moor phenomena to their conceptual-explanatory frames, thus allowing certain and distinct modes of phenomenalization in each epoch. As such, acting and thinking in each epoch are conditioned, to say the least, by the horizons of the possible allowed by these ultimate representations. If the age of metaphysical ultimacies is coming to an end—and that remains a "hypothesis"—then the question is how to act in this time that is ours, in this age in which we are able to break away from representations sanctioned by privileged explanatory paradigms. In Schürmann's words, "To the question, What is to be done? when raised together with the question, What is being? a radical phenomenologist can only respond: dislodge all vestiges of a teleocratic economy from their hideouts—in common sense as much as in ideology—and thereby liberate things from the 'ordinary concept' which 'captures' them under ultimate representations."[2] But how does this "liberation" translate into the question of acting in our age?

The irony is that while the works of Schürmann himself scarcely attend to concrete and living references to such changing principles, some post-Heideggerian philosophers such as Gianni Vattimo remain engaged with the present-day concrete issues with which the West is grappling. Confronted by the challenge of decolonization in our day, Western thinkers are now facing a crisis of universal legitimation of science and philosophy—a crisis already anticipated by Edmund Husserl in *The Crisis of the European Sciences and Transcendental Phenomenology* (1936), albeit in an immanent way. This crisis reveals itself primarily through human collective action. In my own phenomenological contributions in the past two decades, I have been trying to develop a radical phenomenology that in its descriptive vein could be put into action and therefore an aid to changing the current, repressive arrangements of our otherwise multiversal worlds that are, sadly, bound together by neo-liberal homogenization of the planet and reduction of diversity of lifeworlds to mere resources for the profit for the one per cent.

In other words, while Heidegger unwaveringly declared that his "deconstruction" of the history of metaphysics related only to the history of the West,[3] and he found the "Europeanization of man and of the earth" inauthentic and alarming,[4] the fact of the matter is that it is due to colonialism and the subsequent emergence of the capitalist world-system[5] that today we witness a (Westernized) global hegemony of isomorphic technology that has led to reducing the earth and its inhabitants (including humans) to "standing-reserve" (*Bestand*), as Heidegger would say, and the nation-state as a uniform political organization governing over hegemonized rights-bearing subjects.[6] That Heidegger's radical *Destruktion* of the history of Western philosophy, as the history of the oblivion of the question of Being, did not entail addressing colonialism's reshaping of the irreducible plurality of life on earth remains disturbing: an indication of his Eurocentrism naturally but also Heidegger's being trapped in another kind of oblivion, which, as Enrique Dussel shows, was endemic to post-sixteenth-century Western philosophy: that "European expansion ... [had] built a global system on the basis of the continuous exploitation of the periphery."[7]

That history is retrieved, albeit marginally, in Schürmann's work.[8] In fact, by applying his Heideggerian phenomenology of epochal presence to the Inca, Schürmann opened a new way of thinking about rise, reign, and ruins of epochal codes as captured by empires—an original dimension of his work that is yet to be fully acknowledged and appreciated. Heidegger suggests that because the fate of the West is tied to the decline of metaphysics, which takes a disproportionately long time,[9] the West's "presupposition of its planetary dominance"[10] will follow suit. Interestingly, this "Europeanization of man and of the earth," quoted above, "attacks at the source everything that is of essential nature."[11] In other words, as Europe becomes globalized, it scaphizes itself and becomes hollowed. It reaches the farthest corners of the planet, and with the West its history of metaphysics, only to fold back upon itself and meet its own decline and, with it, the civilizations of the world in an integrated savage-capitalist system that has granted us a seemingly irreversible climate change with catastrophic consequences. This is why I argue that the history (*Geschichte*) and destiny (*Geschick*, mittence or sending) of the West has become inseparable from our shared global destiny as epitomized by global climate change, unhindered neo-liberalism, and the ongoing sixth mass extinction.

Here, at this historic junction when metaphysical solidities are being shaken and truth claims are increasingly questioned, I want to focus on the *one* key challenge of the actors of our time, those who are situated in the *possible* epochal openings afforded to us: *the very acting that defines our diremptive age*. From my personal experience, I have arrived at the realization that, arguably, the greatest threat to the possibility of acting in our age is *exhaustion*, both mental and physical: a certain exhaustion that reveals itself in the increasingly *noticeable loss of imagining another world* and succumbing, with the increasing professionalization and NGO-ization of social movements, to *realpolitik*. This, I believe, is a by-product of the technological automation of political life and rationalization of activism as purposive activity consumed by short-term plans and goals that are justified, more or less, in terms of self-righteousness (being on the self-acclaimed right side of history), moralization of politics, and political correctness that has enlivened a post-1968 brand of the left. This is a left that has succumbed to the liberal state's hegemonic discourse of reconciliation and multiculturalism, a left that remains bereft of the faculty of imagining the impossible. At this time that is ours, therefore, we need to ponder the ways in which the transgressive actors of our violent age of global, neo-liberal capitalism and nation-states based on technological-institutional regimes of hegemonized subjects can point out and create possible civilizational openings without exhausting themselves!

To this end, metaphysics, grasped as *technological globalization*, represents a certain way of thinking about our common global issues. Metaphysics has become a philosophical code name from a specific reading of the history of the West, a hermeneutical tool, that, despite its particularity, allows for the conceptual convergence of the irreducibly diverse experiences of our common institutionalized life in this age of technicity: global, neo-liberal capitalism; commodity fetishism, reification, and abstract exchange value; Wall Street in Manhattan; staggering class inequalities; five men owning wealth equal to that of half of humanity; austerity plans; skyrocketing military expenditures; large-scale social and economic impoverishments; extract economies; various structural discriminations; CNN and Fox News; societies of surveillance; digitization and pixillation of presence; digital surveillance through Twitter, Facebook, and the like; totalitarian rights-based citizenship regimes; unilateralism and exceptionalism; meaningless democracies; child labour and sweatshops; privatization of public services; technological liberalism; maintaining meaningless borders; or guaranteed ecological degradation and possibly collapse—to name just a few.

These are manifestations of the institutionalization and universalization of the principles of intelligibility of our age—all linked to technicity's global reach. Irreducibly diverse experiences arise from the phenomena enumerated above, but they can converge, philosophically speaking, through the concept of metaphysics and its decline. The phenomenologist of this time can oppose the above list to another—a list that, contrary to the previous, contains transgression and singularization—that is, the signature mode of action proper to this diremptive age: creative resistances of the poor (especially in Latin America); worker-run factories; public reclaiming of privatized means of survival or the "commons" (water, rivers, forests, land); Indigenous resurgence, uprisings, and exposition of the politics of recognition; collective action of urban movements; participatory democracy; Indymedia and citizen journalism, mutual-aid and anarchist model communities; reclaiming public spaces; the Arab Spring; the Occupy Movement; municipal democracies; use value and objects for loving, cherishing, and keeping; organized labour; public education and universal health care; cities of refuge and new internationalisms; World Social Forum; autonomous rebel zone in Chiapas, democratic confederalism in Rojava, the communist village of Marinaleda, and the communist governance since the 1950s in the Indian states of West Bengal and Kerala.

These actions and experiments are never pure in their performance, but something of a "family resemblance" allows for their coarticulation. Despite liberal promises, conflicts abound. Action is, expectedly, permeated by strife. As such, the two phenomenal bundles offered in my description above should not be taken as Manichaean opposites—although stark contrasts are at times useful, if not reassuring. Instead, let us look at these sets as the aspects of the "double bind" that permeates phenomenal unconcealedness.

Therefore, the phenomenologist who attends to describing this situation will politically and socially align herself with the left, although this futuristic referent inevitably remains nebulous and defies a positivist's definitions. This position takes me to Schürmann's philosophical anarchism and, for that matter, Vattimo's hermeneutic communism[12]—their serious difference aside.[13] The stakes are high when we also attend to the fact that transgressive action is constantly denied not only by the institutional forces but also by purposive, goal-oriented activism. Yes, continued friction can potentially lead action to exhaustion. But my concern here is that *action can also be exhausted by its own normative terms,* when purposive activism prevents action as creative playfulness within the field of the serious to flourish.

Critical Topology

I have spoken of action in our *diremptive* age. In order to properly proceed and situate this experience of our age, we need a description of critical topology that sheds further light on my previous reflections.

Schürmann's tripartite topology begins by stating that Being—viewed in relation to the double bind of natality and mortality—reveals itself in a conflictual manner in every act in our age of technicity.

Working under the hypothesis of metaphysical closure, radical phenomenology attends to the "thrust of time" that sets epochs apart through the "reversals in the history of truth."[14] To this end, Schürmann proposes a tripartite topology—a phenomenological inquiry into the places (*topoi*) in which Being reveals itself at the possible caesura between the epochs. He calls the first a *recapitulatory topology,* dedicated to inquiring about the conflictual, institutive discourses that the philosopher "had both to see and to deny."[15] The last one, which Schürmann calls *anticipatory topology,* looks into the possible historical openings and their loci.[16] The middle term, informing my approach, is *critical topology* in which "one topos only asks to be situated and described."[17] Critical topology describes the place in which the "having-been" stands in conflict with that which is "to-come."[18] Critical topology is thus a "bifrontal phenomenological thinking"[19]—corresponding to the Janus face granted to the phenomenologist by the very epochal caesuras in which she is situated.[20] Through critical topology the archic-anarchic strife is preserved.[21] This is how the normative-institutionalized hold meets the transgressive-subversive pull in every act. In this conflictual *topos*, the existing foundations reveal their violence, but attending to that violence invites a whole different direction, which this chapter cannot accommodate. Thinking and acting from out of a *topos* requires the knowledge that they actually come from a place. To act in this age, therefore, requires "locative thinking," as Ian Angus conceptualizes it: "Thinking in the locative case is a thinking which is permeated by the awareness of its own place, that will not abandon itself to abstract space, but neither can be restrained within a given place and defines itself in its relation to other places of significance."[22] In light of locative thought, my argument here shows its Angusian streak. Acting always arises from a particular place and grows universal, but its "universality" does not have to be imposing, making transcendental gestures. In fact, calling it "universal" is already misunderstood, revealing contamination of thinking by the European Enlightenment tradition. If thought is locative, then its reach beyond its location must be *multiversal*—that is to say, must remain true to its location, regardless of its global reach. Angus says, "Locative thinking is a thinking that does not simply occur somewhere, but whose location is integral to the meaning of what is thought."[23]

The direction that I take here is this: the creative actors of our age—and I view them as the embodiments of the "phenomenological actor"—are involved so much in their daily struggles against various forms of universalizing, institutional, hubristic, and procedural forms of violence in concrete situations and often under dire conditions that they do not really care, let alone perceive, if their resistances may have implications for epochal transmutations. Their activities relate to the ontic and the concrete, as they engage with the issues "practically," so much so that they happily leave the ontological to the armchair philosopher's gaze. That is why a radical phenomenologist should concern herself with concrete history: as Schürmann says, "Epochal principles are always ontic givens. Each of them opens modalities of possible interaction and forecloses on others. An epoch, then, is 'reduced' to the way things, words, and actions are mutually present in it."[24] In other words, the ontic points at the ontological, and politics is where the epochal stamp is revealed. In the ontic lies the conflictual manifestation of our age—the double bind of universalization and singularization, natality and mortality. It is in the concrete that the *"da-"* of *Dasein* reveals both actualities and possibilities. And this *"da-"* is connected to not just my locative thinking but also always already locative acting. Concrete resistances, then, have great implications for an endangered species called the "sociological phenomenologist" such as myself, as these resistances also are the subject matters of various phenomenological inquiries.

Subject, Agent, Actor

In this strife, that which threatens action is its dissolution into activism. Heidegger found it to be a real danger when calculative thinking becomes the only way of thinking.[25] To be precise, in relation to releasement and letting-be, the modes of comportment at this age of metaphysical decline, Heidegger makes a distinction between "higher acting" (acting proper to letting phenomena be without imposing normative expectations of them) and activity.[26] So *genuine* action, when facing the institutional and structural mandates that have captured us under the law that defines and imposes the rules of the game in this age of persistent but perhaps declining normative-legislative-predicative holds, is arguably exhausted not so much in resisting power as by resisting being into institutionally sanctioned activity, the hallowed mode of conflict that is positively sanctioned by the rights-granting and reconciliatory liberal institutions.

In this context, the activists of our time inevitably are pulled into the technological-administrative-bureaucratic grids through which they encounter the object of their transformations. As such, "activism," deployed here provisionally, can lend itself to the subject, the agent, or the actor. I have offered the distinctions between these three terms in a previous work.[27] The subjects of current hegemonic order remain within the ambits of assigned activities. The card-carrying agents of normative change are trained to know how to maintain the current order or have apparently an enviable knowledge about the future society to the last detail. The subjects of current hegemonic orders, now called the "citizens," are expected to be mobilized and provide their "consent" to the hegemonic master discourse of our age, thus allowing their private lives and potentially genuine (non-hegemonic) experiences to be normatively aligned with the hegemonic master discourse.[28]

A genuine actor engaging with the existing metaphysical order will have to join a "non-teleocratic movement" (a movement not oriented to any given purpose or end) wherein there is no room for the subject or the agent, strictly speaking.[29] Non-teleocratic action, therefore, is clearly and expectedly linked to *transgressive* action, but, perhaps more importantly, it is linked to the actors' ability to *imagine* an entirely different world from out of their own places, *locatively*. Transgression denotes defying the imposed, technological, terms on our being and acting by the hegemonic regimes within which we are inserted and in response to which we act. These regimes constantly try to reduce the actor to subjects and agents and action to the performance of institutionally sanctioned activities—however critical these activities may be. By reducing potentially transgressive action to task- and agenda-oriented activity of hegemonized subjects and zealous agents, the existing regimes draw on the energy and visions of the actors in order to reform and advance their technological-institutional grip upon the present.[30]

But here is the subtlety of the situation: since any present-day actor is inevitably born into this hegemonic-technological regime of our age and must respond to this regime within already established domains and parameters of acting, an actor cannot have a permanent embodiment. The actor, rather, is a *moment* when genuine action leaps forth from out of the activities assigned to subjects and agents of the regime. This is the moment when the non-hegemonic, non-teleocratic act of transgression shines forth with the new. The creative acts of the Zapatistas and activists in Rojava—in self-governing, breaking away from capitalism, introducing sophisticated participatory democracies, ending patriarchy and violence, introducing women's and Indigenous rights and the rights of minorities—stand out as examples. Against the silhouette of normative-legislative-predicative being and acting that is constantly managed by the hegemonic regimes, this humble action may shine with disproportionate brightness. But this moment allows us—to be precise, those of us who have not been numbed by the normative requirements of activities and activism—to register how precarious the governing principles of the existing regimes in our age actually are. As such, a genuine transgressive act shows that all principles are in the end non-universal.[31]

Thus, the question remains: Given that this hegemonic-technological age and its normative-legislative-predicative holds are the workings of a metaphysical history—culminating in today's capitalist order and the reign of instrumental rationality—how can acting, being, and thinking escape the many tentacles that ground action in institutionally and rationally sanctioned activity that reduces (potentially transgressive) actors to subjects and agents (of these regimes)? The *provisional* answer, which this chapter invites the reader to consider, is by changing the terrain.

On the Playgrounds of Being

So it remains for the actor, strictly speaking, to participate in possible transgressive modes of action beyond the hegemonic-normative formations. Action is therefore marked by transgression, and the actor is an embodiment of transgressive action, lending his or her abilities to the terms of available transgressive acts. This approach renders the actor secondary to action, since it is our epoch that opens and closes on modes of action in each epoch. Insofar as it is understood as transgressive, action takes place outside of the law and the norms, but certainly in reaction to the dominant laws and norms. For transgressive action, legal and normative impositions are the conditions of possibility. As such, genuine action must by definition always remain "experimental," while it must also remain sensitive toward, and cautious with respect to, its own consequences, since action, as Hannah Arendt reminds us, will have unpredictable outcomes. Now we can see how transgressive action, as "experimental," acquires the characteristic of being an-archic—that is, without attempting to found a first principle (*arché*) that would dominate subsequent action. Thus, action most certainly unleashes unpredictability as it transgresses the limits of laws and norms.

But if acting takes place under the existing hegemonic-technological regimes that foreclose on unsanctioned activity, then how is an-archic action possible? If, following Schürmann, the epochal code reveals itself in politics, then the political in our age is the domain of technicized activities. This means that both governance—in the broad sense of the term—and dissent—also in its broad sense—become carriers of assigned roles, necessary functions, abstract proceduralisms, and tunnel-vision plans. This is a serious matter, not just because it is actually "serious" but because it invites a certain seriousness as the attitude of both the regime's functionary and the dissenter! Stated differently, both functionaries and dissenters develop, under the current regime, a certain attentive comportment that renders them both to largely, though often solely, focus on the task at hand, on the assigned or perceived activity, although from a detached observer's point of view, in opposite directions. This seriousness refers to a certain epochal attunement—a legacy of our metaphysical age and a stamp of Being's unconcealedness at this specific time. I contend here that such seriousness falls within what Heidegger, in referring to science and research, calls "ongoing activity" (*Betrieb*): that is, the "industrious activity of mere 'busy-ness' (*des blossen Betriebs*)."[32] This happens when we lose sight of our methodologies (Heidegger refers to research in his work on the World-Picture), when our activities are transformed—both institutionally and through sanctioned matter-of-factness of life, here political life—into mere procedures and implementations without much reflection. From the phenomenological point of view, I surmise that we encounter such lack of reflection when the dissenter is still caught in a web of activity assigned and sanctioned by rational-technological institutions while in fact trying to undermine them.

Heidegger still reflects, "This is a 'serious' matter occupying time and thus eating into our existential finitude."[33] I am deeply inspired by this line. It tells me that seriousness, or being busy in terms of being constantly engaged in "ongoing activity" without critical reflection, permeates both our technological-administrative powers as well as our doctrinal revolutionaries. Good! Just as it pertains to the process of objectification of the work of art,[34] it makes us carry out activities without a meaningful and creative world context. "Originally, busyness is that modern scheme of transformation through which 'things' lose their 'world' by becoming 'objects.'"[35] Anyways, the busyness in carrying out activities, as my continuing concrete interviews with flesh-and-bone activists have shown, eats into our finitude and it has been the source of exhaustion of potentially transgressive action. These activists, who have dedicated themselves, through various campaigns, often complain about how much energy they should dedicate to win a minor cause and how the changes they help bring about are almost immediately co-opted by the existing rational-technological institutions. As such, I infer, the activists spent too much time and energy and get too busy (in many cases, to the point of exhaustion) to bring about change. It seems to me, and this is my interpretation, that depriving activism of "time" is in fact the greatest ploy of the powers that be. This busyness is characterized by our "lacking time." For one thing, we end up becoming aging, romantic revolutionaries witnessing our lifelong dreams gradually withering away (no resemblance to the author intended!).

Here, I would like to return to and extend Angus's contribution regarding "locative thought," hoping he will agree with me: if in this age when metaphysical holds are radically questioned, and consequently acting and thinking have become one, then *locative thinking* must always already be *locative acting*—a mode of action bound to a place, and only thus arising, without the normative expectations imposed on it. This mode of acting and thinking does not impose normative parameters to which other thoughts and acts are expected to conform. In the playgrounds of Being, we may end up having to play with the already given and available epochal playthings, but each of us will play in a slightly different way, as each comes from a different location, converging on the field of clearing where Being reveals its diminishment. This reveals that we may not really need universal principles to hold us together: acting and thinking in *multiversal* ways has the "unifying" character without imposing on us or reducing our diversity. We are connected to one another through the very *act of thinking* and *thought of acting* from out of our particular places. We become able to create solidarity without higher, pre-given, and hegemonic-epistemic principles. In fact, I think, and I hope Angus agrees with my interjection, that we are able to conceive of acting and thinking without theoretical or practical expectations is a gift of phenomenology. This is where locative acting shows its transgressive potential, and locative thinking and acting are linked with critical topology.

Critical topology, in linking the "has been" to the "to come," allows us to see outside of the ambit of seriousness. Transgressive action—which situates acting between "has been" and "to come"—can hardly be "serious" in the manner explained above: the case with transgression, once properly understood, is that one not only transgresses the law through one's act, but one transgresses the terms of one's transgression as well. Action in this age lives the strife between two poles of "isomorphic contextualizing" and "dispersive decontextualization" that correspond to the double bind of natality- mortality. One pole, isomorphic contextualizing, makes us, as Schürmann says, "all equal (*iso*) in [our] forms (*morphé*), that is, uniform,"[36] which echoes the technological-administrative logic. The other pole, dispersive decontextualization, captures the idea that as with "every mode of phenomenalization, technicity also singularizes them without any agent of reconciliation."[37] This means that while we are rendered isomorphic and homogeneous, we have the possibility of forcing our imposed, rational-technological identity into a dispersal of heterogeneous identities that would be ungraspable by the technological order.

Acting and living between these poles is a gift of our age—a gift without which my *provisional* reflections here would not have been possible.

If seriousness has been enabled by Being's specific unconcealedness in our time, and if the double bind permeates every mode of revealing, then Being must have revealed, alongside busyness, its playgrounds as well, except our remiss gazes, being too serious, have probably overlooked it. Instead of dwelling in the "serious" and "busy" grounds enabled by Being's unconcealedness, we are gifted with the possibility of acting in the playgrounds of Being. This is how we get Occupy Wall Street right in the middle of Manhattan's financial forced labour camp. In the playground, we act and express ourselves, with a certain innocence, using the implements that have been made available to us without their specific material configurations. In acting, we find ourselves—we *become* our action by *embodying* our role; that is, we lend our bodies to an available act—for the moment in which our role accommodates us. In this process, we get to know our playmates, our allies, and the playground becomes the field of experimental and experiential acting and thinking, a gift of Being's own exhaustion. We also potentially get a fresh view of the world, experiencing the world in our "phenomenological 'kindergarten,'"[38] as Heidegger would say, understanding playthings not merely as mundane present-at-hand but let-be in being out of fun. We might get hurt while playing: we might get a cut on the knee while hitting the ground at the bottom of the slide or we might get sand in our eye while building a sand castle, but hey, a loving and reassuring embrace later, we recover from it all. We go back to playing. Time, this curious time that we lacked and thus chased infinitely when we were "busy," now appears to us in abundance. We go back to our innocence, which is gifted to us by the playground, as we experiment in life.

The seriousness of our epochal busyness does not necessarily invite "serious" responses. The isomorphic pull of technicity is opposed by the singularizing dispersal of anarchic acting and thinking. We have the whole playground of Being to come up with creative responses. From time to time, the playgrounds of Being come to the fore in different *topoi*, under different names: workers' soviets, Chiapas, Tahrir Square, Porto Alegre, Rojava, or Unist'ot'en Camp, to name but a few.

To act in this world will involve projecting a critical and anticipatory gaze upon the places (*topoi*) in which, through continued strife presented to the actors, acting can transgress the normative holds while simultaneously transgressing its own seriousness. So my response to the question of how to avoid "activist fatigue" (though certainly not satisfactory to serious activists) is this: we do what we do without hanging our hopes entirely on the existing models of resistance, and if in the process (in this playground) we get hurt, or even die, well at least we had fun! Seeing our act as possibly situated within an epochal fissure, we act with detachment (so that what we do would not "eat into our existential finitude") and with a certain disinterest in the future of humankind, to paraphrase Schürmann,[39] so we won't force others into our reality while caring for the future of all—human and non-human. We begin to think not about revolutions but what Claude Lefort called "creative disorder"[40]—and here I emphasize the double meaning of the word "disorder," most probably against the author's intention, since genuine, transgressive actors, those capable of imagining another world, cannot be fully rational or normal, just like true poets.

This disorder would impede hegemony from integrating and absorbing the critical acts and creative imagination of playful actors. Thinking and acting locatively, instead of writing manifestos, we write memoires, since anticipatory thinking is inevitably recollective. When we must issue a declaration, we make sure we also publish a children's storybook. When we need to establish an international, we put together a World Social Forum instead of a Comintern (What about a Situationist International?). And when we must liberate our people, instead of a protracted and bloody civil war, we contemplate the Zapatistas of Chiapas or democratic confederalism in Rojava. We create model, transgressive communities, hoping we do not turn them into normative, archic models for future society, which requires us not to get too serious about our experiments, either. Back to the playgrounds of Being!

Notes to Chapter 19:

* The original version of this chapter was presented, as part of a panel, to Canadian Society of Continental Philosophy Annual Conference, held at Simon Fraser University, Harbour Centre, in Vancouver, on October 4, 2014.
The other two panellists were Ian Angus and Samir Gandesha. It is uncanny how this paper returns, in an expanded form, in a volume in which my two friends and co-panellists are also actively present.

1 Reiner Schürmann, *Heidegger on Being and Acting: From Principles to Anarchy* (Bloomington: Indiana University Press, 1990), 41.

2 Ibid., 280.

3 Martin Heidegger, *The End of Philosophy* (Chicago: The University of Chicago Press, 2003), 90.

4 Martin Heidegger, *On the Way to Language* (New York: Harper Collins, 1971), 16.

5 Immanuel Wallerstein, "The Rise and Future Demise of the World Capitalist System: Concepts for Comparative Analysis," *Comparative Studies in Society and History* 16, no. 4 (1974): 387–415.

6 Peyman Vahabzadeh, *Articulated Experiences: Toward a Radical Phenomenology of Contemporary Social Movements* (Albany: State University of New York Press, 2003), 103–40. Interestingly, growing economies such as the BRIC nations (Brazil, Russia, India, China), aiming for dominating the global capitalist, technologically driven, and extract-based economy, make it no longer possible to think of this trend as primarily Western. This is where I think Heidegger's point about the West must be viewed as a global issue.

7 Enrique Dussel, "Anti-Cartesian Meditations: On the Origins of the Philosophical Anti-Discourse of Modernity," *Journal of Cultural and Religious Theory* 13, no. 1 (2014): 33.

8 Schürmann, *Heidegger on Being*, 26–29, 163–67.

9 Heidegger, *End of Philosophy*, 85.

10 Ibid., 90.

11 Heidegger, *On the Way to Language*, 16.

12 Gianni Vattimo and Santiago Zabala, *Hermeneutic Communism: From Heidegger to Marx* (New York: Columbia University Press, 2011).

13 In *Hermeneutic Communism*, Vattimo and Zabala offer a specific reading of Heidegger and Marx, arguing that the end of metaphysics does not necessarily materialize in the triumph of capitalist, pluralistic democracy but instead in a form of democratic, "weak" communism—a communism without planned economy and authoritarian rule but just like a hermeneutical community—communitarian and dialogical.

14 Reiner Schürmann, "Technicity, Topology, Tragedy: Heidegger on 'That Which Saves' in the Global Reach," in Arthur M. Melzer, Jerry Weinberger, and M. Richard Zinman, eds., *Technology in the Western Political Tradition* (Ithaca: Cornell University Press, 1993), 196.

15 Ibid.

16 Ibid., 200.

17 Ibid., 197.

18 Ibid.

19 Ibid., 199.

20 See: Schürmann, *Heidegger on Being*.

21 Schürmann, "Technicity, Topology, Tragedy," 197.

22 Ian Angus, *Identity and Justice* (Toronto: University of Toronto Press, 2008), 26.

23 Ibid.

24 Schürmann, *Heidegger on Being*, 81.

25 Martin Heidegger, *Discourse on Thinking* (New York: Harper and Row, 1966), 56.

26 Ibid., 61.

27 Vahabzadeh, *Articulated Experiences*, 93.

28 Ibid., 118.

29 Ibid., 93.

30 See: ibid., 132.

31 Ibid., 136.

32 Martin Heidegger, *The Question Concerning Technology and Other Essays* (New York: Harper Torchbooks, 1977), 138.

33 Ibid.

34 Schürmann, *Heidegger on Being*, 265.

35 Ibid., 266.

36 Schürmann, "Technicity, Topology, Tragedy," 210.

37 Ibid., 211.

38 Martin Heidegger, *Four Seminars*, trans. A. Mitchell and F. Raffoul (Indianapolis: Indiana University Press, 2003), 11.

39 Schürmann, *Heidegger on Being*, 273.

40 Claude Lefort, "1968 Revisited: A French View, Not Revolution, but Creative Disorder." *Dissent* 35 (1988): 341– 46.

Chapter 20

Statement to the Court before Sentencing (7 May 2018)

Ian Angus

I would like to begin by acknowledging that the City of Vancouver, where this court is situated, lies on the traditional and unceded territories of the Tsleil-Waututh, Musqueam, and Squamish First Nations.

Having heard the recommendation of the Crown regarding my guilty plea to the charge of Criminal Contempt for "physically obstructing, impeding or otherwise preventing access"[1] to the Burnaby Terminal of Trans Mountain (Kinder Morgan) on 24 March 2018, I would like to make the following clarification, explanation, and request for an altered penalty. I have been encouraged to do so in the first place by the Provincial Court information on sentencing[2] and in the second place by the response of Judge Affleck to my question to him in court on 23rd April when he said that I would be allowed to explain the "context" of my action.

I do not deny that I was physically present at the place in question at the time in question.

My understanding of civil disobedience is that one commits a certain act for definite and considered reasons, one admits to the act, explains one's reasons, and accepts the penalty. The purpose of the act is to bring a state of affairs to the attention of the public and the authorities with the intention and hope that it may serve to correct an error in justice. Through this procedure, even though one may break a given law, or in this case an injunction issued by a court of law, one does not express disrespect for law in general.

This understanding was clear to me prior to the event and very much on my mind on that day.

Positive law is always flawed as human beings are flawed. It is also flawed insofar as it serves interests which are not required by public safety but are nevertheless entrenched in the unequal power structure of the social order. A social order in which citizens follow the law simply because it is the law, in which they do not assess the practice of the law with their own critical faculties, could not be called a democracy. The critical intelligence of citizens is essential to a non-repressive social order. Indeed, it is only through acts which test the practice of law in specific cases that law can be revised more closely to approximate justice. Justice is above law. It is how we assess and revise law. It is what we are fitted for, what can make us most human, that for which we must continually strive.

The classic understanding of civil disobedience is complicated in our own time and place. Since we are living in unceded territories whose formal economic, social, and political structure is a consequence of a colonial past and present, the dominant law represents such a colonial structure. There is also another law that has been established by the traditions and institutions of the Indigenous people of this place. Why are we not subject to that law also? I have lived for the last 26 years with my wife and daughter beside the Burrard Inlet. It is of great concern to me that this beautiful and fecund place be preserved for our children and grandchildren. I felt proud to be able to join my near neighbours, the Tsleil-Waututh people, who have cared for this place for thousands of years, in order to oppose a project that puts our common inhabitation in grave danger. I respect their law.

Our country is in a difficult time. There is much talk, both official and popular, about reconciliation with Indigenous people. After all, they have suffered greatly from government policies, and collaboration in rendering that suffering by dominant institutions that have tried to extinguish their cultures and their peoples. Many citizens have come to feel, knowing more than we used to about their suffering and the role of our institutions in causing it, that it is time to put an end to this legacy and to start anew. But for reconciliation to be more than symbolic, it has to make a difference in our actions. The Kinder Morgan pipeline is one important case in which real actions can make a difference. The action in front of the Kinder Morgan gate is, in my opinion, a case of real reconciliation that goes beyond mere lip- service.

Not only our country but the whole planet is in a difficult time because of the ravishes of industrial production and consumption. The foreseeable, near future of the human species, and also species of many other kinds, is threatened by the effects of climate change in destabilizing the ecological balance upon which we depend. Radical and immediate action is necessary to realign priorities in order even to begin to address this problem. Yet we look to our elected leaders in vain for any real action. They continue to put in place mega-projects of industrial infrastructure that deepen the problem and make it more difficult to change direction. If we do not place economic activity within an ecological context soon, the future of the human species, and the other species with whom we share the earth, looks very bleak.

For about 40 years, I taught in various institutions of higher education—most recently, at Simon Fraser University, whose location near the proposed expanded tank farm would put its population at grave risk in case of an accident. My vocation as a teacher, scholar, and writer has been to think as widely and deeply about natural and human issues as I can, and to communicate with the younger generation about the lessons of the past and the challenges of the future. I have tried to discharge that responsibility to the best of my ability, stressing independent and critical thinking, social and ecological responsibility, and, perhaps most difficult of all in recent years, finding sources of hope that can orient our living-toward-the- future. This spring I felt that this responsibility had to be taken beyond the seminar room, lecture hall, and written word to a site where all of these concerns converge.

The convergence of issues of reconciliation with Indigenous nations, environmental and ecological danger, and social inequality due to the rapacious pursuit of private profit has made this not only a difficult time but one of crisis. The forces who wish to maintain the current system have come together to oppose those who seek a new future. When a new future appears on the horizon, the repression of this future, the fear of change, expresses itself in more and more desperate attempts to hang on to the errors of the past. The Kinder Morgan pipeline is an important example of a desperate coalition of government, industry, and finance attempting to retain and even expand the past industrial economy with increasingly dangerous consequences. But, as creatures of thought, creativity, and hope, human beings will always seek to address, in any form that they can muster, the gravity of the crisis and to push for something new and better. There is a future struggling to be born in which environmental and ecological responsibility, social justice and equality, and reconciliation with the ancient claims of Indigenous peoples each play their part. The old forces are arrayed against its emergence. Thus we are here today.

I was there. I did it. I meant to do it. The Crown has proposed a penalty of a fine of $500.00. I propose an alternative penalty of a fine of $1.00. The fact of a fine would be an acknowledgement that I broke the law in disobeying the injunction. Its amount would be an acknowledgement that my reasons for doing so mean that the act amounts to the exercise of a civic, human, and natural responsibility.

Notes to Chapter 20:

1 Court File No. S-183541: Agreed Statement of Facts #9.

2 See: "Types of sentence available in Canada" posted on the website of the Provincial Court of British Columbia, available at http://provincialcourt.bc.ca/enews/enews-08-06-2016 (downloaded on April 24, 2018). It is stated that: "If a person charged with a criminal offence pleads guilty or is found guilty after a trial, they will be sentenced. In determining a fit sentence, the judge must consider all the information presented in court about the offender and the crime, including: The offender's personal circumstances (e.g. age, work or school, family situation); The type of crime; The way the crime was committed; The offender's criminal record, if they have one; The impact on the victim; Any other relevant information."

Ian Angus Timeline

1949	Ian Henderson Angus was born in London, UK
1958	Immigrated to Canada
1967	Graduated Secondary School
1967–1971	BA in Philosophy, University of Waterloo
1971–1973	MA in Philosophy, University of Waterloo
1974–1980	PhD in Social and Political Thought, York University
1984	Visiting Scholar, International Summer Institute for Semiotic & Structural Studies, Victoria College, University of Toronto
1981–1983	Visiting Assistant Professor, Department of Communication, Simon Fraser University
1984	Publication of *Technique and Enlightenment: Limits of Instrumental Reason* (Centre for Advanced Research in Phenomenology and University Press of America)
1984–1985	Assistant Professor, Cultural Studies Programme, Trent University 1985–1986
	Assistant Professor, Department of Communication, University of New Hampshire
1986–1989	Assistant Professor, Department of Communication, University of Massachusetts Amherst
1988	Publication of edited volume, *Ethnicity in a Technological Age* (Canadian Institute of Ukrainian Studies)
1988	Publication of *George Grant's Platonic Rejoinder to Heidegger: Contemporary Political Philosophy and the Question of Technology* (Edwin Mellen Press)
1989	Publication of co-edited volume (with Sut Jhally), *Cultural Politics in Contemporary America* (Routledge)

1989–1992	Associate Professor, Department of Communication, University of Massachusetts Amherst
1992–1997	Associate Professor, Department of Sociology and Anthropology, Simon Fraser University
1993	Publication of co-edited volume (with Lenore Langsdorf), *The Critical Turn: Rhetoric and Philosophy in Postmodern Discourse* (Southern Illinois University Press)
1997	Publication of *A Border Within: National Identity, Cultural Plurality and Wilderness* (McGill-Queen's University Press)
1997–2000	Associate Professor, Department of Sociology and Anthropology and Department of Humanities (cross-appointment), Simon Fraser University
2000	Publication of *(Dis)figurations: Discourse/Critique/Ethics* (Verso)
2000	Publication of *Primal Scenes of Communication: Communication, Consumerism, Social Movements* (State University of New York Press)
2000–2001	Professor, Department of Sociology and Anthropology and Department of Humanities (cross-appointment), Simon Fraser University
2001	Publication of edited volume, *Anarcho-Modernism: Toward a New Critical Theory. In Honour of Jerry Zaslove* (Talonbooks)
2001	*Emergent Publics: An Essay on Social Movements and Democracy* (Arbeiter Ring Press)
2006	Publication of co-edited volume (with Ronald Dart and Randy Peg Peters), *Athens and Jerusalem: George Grant's Theology, Philosophy and Politics* (University of Toronto Press).
2008	Publication of *Identity and Justice* (University of Toronto Press)
2009	Publication of *Love the Questions: University Education and Enlightenment* (Arbeiter Ring Press)
2013	Publication of *The Undiscovered Country: Essays in Canadian Intellectual Culture* (Athabasca University Press)
2017	Retired Professor of Humanities, Simon Fraser University

Compiled by Peyman Vahabzadeh

Notes on Contributors

JADEN ADAMS (aka Jason Adams, They/Them) is co-founder and co-director of the New Centre for Research & Practice (2014 to present), and the former managing editor of the Johns Hopkins University Press journal, *Theory & Event* (2004 to 2010). They have been published in *Critical Inquiry*, *Los Angeles Review of Books*, *New Political Science*, and *Radical Philosophy*, amongst other journals and periodicals. Following the publication of Adams's book *Occupy Time: Technoculture, Immediacy, & Resistance* (Palgrave Macmillan, 2013), and the co-edited volume *Deleuze & Race* (Edinburgh University Press, 2013), they are presently revising the final manuscript for a second authored book, *Virtual Virilio: Speed, Politics, Potentiality.*

DANIEL ADLEMAN is an assistant professor of Writing and Rhetoric at the University of Toronto, where he teaches Digital Rhetoric, A Brief History of Persuasion, and Writing for Social Change. He received his PhD in English Language and Literature from the University of British Columbia, in Vancouver, Canada. While working on his doctoral dissertation (on representations of media modernity and masculinity in contemporary American fiction), he co-founded and directed the Vancouver Institute for Social Research, a graduate-level critical theory free school held at Vancouver's Or Gallery since 2012. He has published essays about the role of the concept of utopia in J. M. Coetzee's *Disgrace*; the status of tragedy in *Star Wars*; the operation of mimetic rivalry in Bret Easton Ellis's *American Psycho*; and emerging entanglements of rhetoric, ecological thought, and media philosophy (forthcoming). He is currently writing a book about the concept of media modernity.

STEPHEN COLLIS is the author of a dozen books of poetry and prose, including *The Commons* (Talonbooks, 2008), *Once in Blockadia* (Talonbooks, 2016), and *Almost Islands: Phyllis Webb and the Pursuit of the Unwritten* (Talonbooks, 2018). Current research on the climate emergency and human and other displacements is involved in two in-process projects: *Future Imperfect* (poetry) and *A Sestina for Max Sebald* (prose). He lives near Vancouver, on unceded Coast Salish Territory, and teaches poetry and poetics at Simon Fraser University.

CLAUDE COUTURE is a professor of Social Sciences and Canadian Studies, Campus Saint-Jean, University of Alberta, since 1988. He was director of the Canadian Studies Institute of the University of Alberta from 2000 to 2010. His research interests are in the area of intellectual and social history. He is the author or co-author of 15 books, including: *Britannicité. Présence française dans l'Empire britannique au long XIXe siècle* (Presses de l'Université Laval, 2019, with Prof. Srilata Ravi); *Sports, modernité, et réseaux impériaux. Nap Lajoie, Kumar Shri Ranjitsinhi, baseball et cricket au tournant du XXe siècle* (Presses de l'Université Laval, 2017, with Srilata Ravi); *Imaginaires collectifs, interculturalisme et histoire: autour de l'oeuvre de Gérard Bouchard* (Presses de l'Université Laval, 2014); *Vingt ans après Charlottetown. L'ordre libéral colonial au Canada* (Presses de l'Université Laval, 2013); *La nation et son double. Essais sur les discours postcoloniaux au Canada* (Presses de l'Université Laval, 2012). He has also published extensively in academic journals and chapters in edited books. He spent the 2004–05 academic year as Fulbright Professor at the Jackson School of the University of Washington in Seattle. He received the Rutherford Award for excellence in teaching from the University of Alberta in 2006, a Killam Professorship in 2007–08, and the CAFA Distinguished Academic Award in 2008. He was awarded the University Cup of the University of Alberta in 2009, and in 2014, he was awarded the Governor General's International Award for his contribution in Canadian Studies.

KEVIN MICHAEL DELUCA is a professor of Communication, an Environmental Humanities Research professor, an adjunct professor in the Asian Studies Program, and a Tanner Fellow at the University of Utah. His scholarship explores how humanity's relations to nature are mediated by technology. In addition to the book *Image Politics*, DeLuca has published dozens of essays on media, activism, social theory, images, events, and force. His most recent work engages environmental activism and social media in China, including the co-authored essay "Weibo, WeChat, and the Transformative Events of Environmental Activism in China" in the *International Journal of Communication*. He is currently engaged in writing a book titled *Activism on the Wild Public Screens of China: Environmentism, Social Media, and Civil Society*.

HILDA FERNANDEZ-ALVAREZ received an MA on Clinical Psychology from the National Autonomous University of Mexico and an MA in Spanish Literature from the University of British Columbia, and she is engaged in a PhD program in the Department of Geography at Simon Fraser University (SFU), where she is conducting research on discursive spaces of trauma and healing in the mental health institution, awarded with a VCHRI Team Grant. She practises Lacanian psychoanalysis in Vancouver and is a therapist at Vancouver Coastal Health. She is the clinical director of the Lacan Salon, which she co-founded in 2007, and an academic associate with the SFU Institute for the Humanities. She has led a Clinical Seminar in Vancouver since 2015 and has published a number of articles on psychotherapy and psychoanalysis.

LEONARD FINDLAY is a Distinguished University Professor, director of the Humanities Research Unit, and founding member of the Indigenous Humanities Group at the University of Saskatchewan, and past president of Academy One (Arts and Humanities) of the Royal Society of Canada. He is also a Senior Fellow at the Centre for Free Expression at Ryerson University and a member of the board of directors of the Harry Crowe Foundation. He is trained in nineteenth-century European elite and radical cultural theory and production, and his more recent Canadianist work engages with the Indigenous/settler interface, historically and currently; the distinctiveness and endangerment of the humanities in Canada; and with connections between academic freedom and Canadian politics. He served for almost a decade on the Academic Freedom and Tenure Committee of the Canadian Association of University Teachers, including two terms as chair, and he is past chair of the University of Saskatchewan Faculty Association.

SAMIR GANDESHA has been a post-doctoral fellow at the University of California at Berkeley (1995 to 1997) and an Alexander von Humboldt Research Fellow at the Universität Potsdam (2001–02). He is currently an associate professor in the Department of the Humanities and the director of the Institute for the Humanities at Simon Fraser University. He specializes in modern European thought and culture, with a particular emphasis on the nineteenth and twentieth centuries. His work has appeared in a wide range of journals including *Political Theory, New German Critique, Constellations, Logos, Kant Studien, Philosophy and Social Criticism*, the *European Legacy, European Journal of Social Theory, Discipline Filosofiche, Estudios Politicos, Zeitschrift für kritische Theorie, Radical Philosophy, American Journal of Psychoanalysis, International Forum of Psychoanalysis*, and *Constelaciones: Revista de Teoria Critica*. He is co-editor with Lars Rensmann of *Arendt and Adorno: Political and Philosophical Investigations* (Stanford, 2012). He is co-editor (with Johan F. Hartle) of *Spell of Capital: Reification and*

Spectacle (University of Amsterdam Press, 2017), and *Aesthetic Marx* (Bloomsbury Press, 2017). He regularly contributes to popular publications such as *openDemocracy, Canadian Dimension, Vancouver Sun,* and *Globe and Mail*. In the spring of 2017, he was the Liu Boming Visiting Scholar in Philosophy at the University of Nanjing and Visiting Lecturer at Suzhou University of Science and Technology in China. In January 2019, he was Visiting Fellow at the Hochschule für Gestaltung in Karlsruhe, and in February 2019, he was Visiting Lecturer at Faculdade de Filosofia, Letras e Ciências Humanas—FFLCH-USP (Universidade de São Paulò). He is currently editing a book entitled *Spectres of Fascism* (Pluto Press) and preparing a manuscript on the "Neoliberal Personality."

LENORE LANGSDORF is Professor Emerita, Southern Illinois University Carbondale, and Visiting Research Professor, the University of Texas at San Antonio. Her research draws on a process phenomenological (postphenomenological) orientation toward the social/human sciences, with particular interests in communication, embodied cognition, and moral reasoning.

LEROY LITTLE BEAR is a Blackfoot researcher; Professor Emeritus at Native American Studies Department, University of Lethbridge; and a founding member of the first Native American Studies program in Canada. He specializes in Aboriginal thought, rights, self-government, and education. He holds honorary doctorates from the University of Northern British Columbia and Lethbridge University.

JOHANNES MAERK is the director of the Viennese Ideaz Institute and lecturer at the University of Vienna; and professor of International Relations at the University of Quintana Roo, Mexico (leave of absence). He is also a regular Visiting Fellow at the Latin American Center at the State University of Rio de Janeiro. Among his publications are the edited volumes *Existe una epistemologia latinoamericana?*

and *Cómo democratizar la democracia?* as well as numerous articles about political thought in comparative perspective, epistemology of the social sciences in the Global South, and Red Vienna.

GRAEME NICHOLSON is Professor Emeritus of Philosophy at the University of Toronto. He taught there from 1966 to 2002, specializing in German philosophy, with a particular focus on Martin Heidegger. Two recent books deal with Heidegger, both published by the University of Toronto Press: *Justifying Our Existence: An Essay in Applied Phenomenology* (2009), and *Heidegger on Truth: Its Essence and Its Fate* (2019).

SUSAN PELL is an associate professor of Communications at Richmond American University in London, UK. Her work focuses on public discourse, activist archives, social movements, and urban politics. She is currently researching gentrification archives and the formation of urban publics in Vancouver (Canada) and London (UK), investigating the relationship between knowledge production and possibilities for democratic participation. She has published in international journals, and her research has been presented at conferences in the UK, Canada, and Europe.

GEORGE RAMMELL was born in 1952 in Cranbrook, BC. He studied at the Vancouver School of Art from 1971 to 1975 and has been active as a sculptor and art instructor since 1975. He taught Sculpture at the Emily Carr University over an eight-year period and worked as a studio sculptor for Haida artist Bill Reid and other prominent artists. For 24 years George taught Sculpture and Drawing in the Studio Art Faculty at Capilano University. In addition to three European sculpture symposia, Rammell has participated in 18 exhibitions including solo exhibitions at the Burnaby Art Gallery and the Charles H. Scott Gallery in Vancouver. Rammell has recently completed a large mixed-media work entitled *Ursus Arctos, The Persistence* *of Instinct.* For more information on this and other works go to: http://www3.telus.net/4/rammell.

ROBERT SCHWARTZWALD is a professor in the Département de littératures et de langues du monde at the Université de Montréal (U de M). Before coming to U de M, he was a professor of French and Francophone Studies and director of the Center for Crossroads in the Study of the Americas at University of Massachusetts Amherst. His research and publications focus on the interface between notions of national and cultural modernity, with particular attention to issues of sexual representation, the literature and cinema of Québec, and the interwar years in Europe. Recent publications include a book on Jean-Marc Vallée's *C.R.A.Z.Y.* for the Queer Film Classics series, an essay on two exhibitions on sex and sexuality in Berlin and Vienna, and an essay on responses to Indigenous trauma in the wake of the Truth and Reconciliation Commission on Indian residential schools and in the installations of the Canadian Museum for Human Rights. He is a member of the International Research Training Group "Diversity," of the Centre de recherche interuniversitaire en littérature et culture québécoises, and the Centre for Interdisciplinary Research on Montréal. He is also a recipient of the Governor General's International Award for Canadian Studies.

PEYMAN VAHABZADEH is a professor of Sociology at University of Victoria. He is the author of *Articulated Experiences: Toward a Radical Phenomenology of Contemporary Social Movements* (SUNY Press, 2003); *A Guerrilla Odyssey: Modernization, Secularism, Democracy and the Fadai Discourse of National Liberation in Iran, 1971–1979* (Syracuse University Press, 2010); *Exilic Meditations: Essays on A Displaced Life* (H&S Media, 2012); *Parviz Sadri: A Political Biography* (Shahrgon Book, 2015; in Persian); *Violence and Nonviolence: Conceptual Excursions into Phantom Opposites* (University of Toronto Press, 2019); and *A Rebel's Journey: Mostafa Sho'aiyan and Revolutionary Theory* *in Iran* (OneWorld, 2019). He is also the editor of *Iran's Struggles for Social Justice: Economics, Agency, Justice, Activism* (Palgrave, 2017). He has published eight books of poetry, fiction, literary criticism, and memoir in Persian. His works have appeared in English, Persian, German, Kurdish, and Spanish.

JERRY ZASLOVE defines his work by the medium he works in: teaching and writing in the arts and critical theory and social radicalism. His writing includes essays on Kafka, Siegfried Kracauer, Herbert Read, Wayne Burns and the novel, Russian literary theory, Arnold Hauser, Walter Benjamin's anarcho-modernism and the city, Lewis Mumford, and photography and memory, as well as essays against the university as it has come to be. He is a founding member of Simon Fraser University's English Department, and founding director, Institute for the Humanities. A collection of essays is forthcoming from Talonbooks: *Untimely Passages, Dossiers from the Other Shores Essays, 1965–2015*.

Index

J

N

O

Q

X

Y

Z

SAMIR GANDESHA is Associate Professor of Humanities and Director of Institute for the Humanities at Simon Fraser University.

PEYMAN VAHABZADEH is Professor of Sociology at University of Victoria.